D1192413

NAVAL SURGEON: *Blockading the South, 1862-1866*

NAVAL SURGEON

Blockading the South
1862-1866

THE DIARY OF
DR. SAMUEL PELLMAN BOYER

Edited by
Elinor Barnes and James A. Barnes

Introduction by Allan Nevins

INDIANA UNIVERSITY PRESS
Bloomington

Barry University Library
Miami, FL 33161

Copyright © 1963 by Indiana University Press
All Rights Reserved
Library of Congress catalog card number: 63-9723
Manufactured in the United States of America

E
182
.B7

214650

IN MEMORY

OF

Elinor Barnes

who did more than her share of work on this manuscript, but did not live to see the book. With thanks to those who lent her a gentle hand in a fight she could not win.

Acknowledgments

I must alone extend to the host of friends and to the staff members of many institutions the heartfelt thanks of the editors of this diary for their invaluable assistance.

A constant source of encouragement and of more help than they know have been Mr. and Mrs. Allan Nevins, as well as Mr. and Mrs. Joseph C. Carter, Mr. and Mrs. Herman Blum, Mr. Bell Wiley, Miss Gladys Starr, Mr. Karl Trevor, Mr. Manny Kean of the Kean Studios of Philadelphia, Mr. Zohrab Kazanjian, and many others.

The Historical Society of Pennsylvania, the Manuscript Division of the Library of Congress, and the Navy and Military Service Branch of the National Archives in particular opened their rich resources freely. The staffs of the library of Temple University and the library of the University of Pennsylvania were ready always to lend their assistance.

Especially helpful in providing information concerning the islands along the coast of Georgia and the Carolinas, where the ships of the blockading fleet were often stationed, were Mrs. Burnette Vanstory of St. Simons Island, Mrs. Lilla M. Hawes of the Georgia Historical Society, the late Mrs. Margaret Davis Cate of Sea Island, and their friends and associates.

Photographs difficult to obtain elsewhere were generously offered by Mrs. Vanstory, Dr. Orrin Sage Wightman, the National Archives, the Navy Photographic Center, and Mr. Hamilton Cochran.

Editorial research on the diary was greatly encouraged by grants from the Research Committee of Temple University and extra time was made available through reductions in the teaching load by the administrative personnel of the University. The good will and good wishes of the History Department were always pleasantly obvious.

Patient and understanding were Miss Miriam S. Farley and Miss Jane Rodman of the editorial staff of Indiana University Press. To all these—and to those whose names are not here recorded—go deep thanks.

JAMES A. BARNES

Elkins Park, Pennsylvania

Contents

Illustrations

Introduction

THE PENNSYLVANIA medical graduate who participated in the American civil war 1862-65 and the naval surgeon who observed at close range the Japanese civil war of 1868-69 bore the same name; but it was by no means the same man who had these interesting experiences. Dr. Boyer was twenty-three when he went into the blockading service off the Carolina and Georgia coasts, and young for his years: fresh, ingenuous, eagerly sociable, uncritical. He was old for his still junior years when he reported for duty on the U. S. S. *Iroquois* off Yokohama: a man of the world by this time, his naïve exuberance of temper replaced by mature self-possession, his opinions on many subjects strongly formed, and his powers of observation deepened. It is well that we have a boyish record of the blockade years; for natural ebullience was needed to make the most of the often dull routine. It is also well that we have an adult view of Japan in turmoil as the Mikado and the Tycoon battled for supremacy; for an onlooker in this crisis needed the fullest perception.

Fortunate we are in the dichotomy of this fascinating record. The Civil War story will specially interest one large body of readers, while the Japanese story will particularly allure another audience. Yet certain elements in the personality of the narrator bind them together. He always kept his eyes open; he was as friendly (except to a few who earned his dislike) as a puppy; he had a candid, matter-of-fact outlook, never tinged by enthusiasm or prejudice; and though he grew in insight and in talent for graphic expression, he was always honest and trustworthy, whether he was relating the burning of Darien on the Southern coast, or describing the license of Japanese dancing girls.

Four squadrons of the Union Navy were maintaining what Secretary Gideon Welles called "a strict blockade of gigantic proportions" when Dr. Boyer, who had first clutched his medical diploma some three months earlier, went aboard the U.S.S. *Fernandina* in July, 1862. Excitement of the first order attended the adventures of the blockade runners; but the duty of blockade keepers was for the most part characterized by the words which Boyer set down in his diary on November 29, 1863—"Dull! Dull!! Dull!!!" Especially if the warships kept well out to sea, with no shore pursuits, one boring week followed another. "Oh! how I long to see a Northern port," Boyer exclaims one June day, no doubt thinking of an eastern Pennsylvania spring. "The idea of blockading is rather pleasing, but when you are compelled to come down to reality in the form of doing duty in one place for the term of one year without seeing either friend or foe of any account, you'll find the prospects are not so pleasing."

Yet it is a remarkably interesting and informative picture of the blockade that Boyer paints for us. He presents an account of his professional work that would have delighted Smollett. It was practically all medical, not surgical, though he lanced boils and pulled teeth; it ran the whole gamut of disease—phthisis, hemorrhoids, anthrax, cholera, erysipelas, scrofula, bronchitis, and what not; and it was heroically severe—he was never so happy as when purging a patient drastically or applying a caustic poultice. But he was not overworked and spent whole days simply reading, or keeping up his medical studies with books from the North and pamphlets plucked from plantation libraries. Venereal disease was the chief medical curse. When his ship had a week's holiday in Portsmouth, N. H., in August, 1863, he returned to find that the crew, averaging 110, had made active use of their time; they offered 28 venereal cases. A grog ration was issued to the men until September 1, 1862, when a cash payment supplanted it; but the officers kept their sherry, Madeira, and rum. Jollity often reigned among the crew. Though they worked hard drilling, polishing the brass, holystoning the deck, and manning the sails, they had long hours of singing, dancing, yarning, and sparring. "Truly they are a jolly set of tars," writes Boyer.

Boyer's ship hugged the Southern shores, and at times his record seems one of picnics and moonlight excursions rather than war. On St. Simons Island he visited plundered estates and mansions, caught glimpses of the corruption dogging the cotton trade, and watched the black regiments. In the various sounds—Doboy, St. Catherine's, Sapelo—he landed with parties of men to kill beeves, deer, and pigs, to buy or gather melons, blackberries, peaches, and figs, and to bring back boatloads of oysters, clams, and fish. For weeks the fleet would find its staple in salt horse, that is, salt beef. Then Boyer's ship would enjoy a bill of fare that surpassed Delmonico's. At one casual meal in the fall of 1863 the officers sat down to beef soup, roast turkey, boiled ham, mince pie, and fresh fruit, and at Thanksgiving each of the five courses would have been a repast in itself. Iron-billed mosquitoes and sand flies were constant pests, but sharp squalls would often blow them far away. And if shore landing palled, the sea lanes offered a steady procession of troopships, dispatch cruisers, army transports, water-conversion boats, schooners, and (not least welcome) vessels bearing sutlers and their wares. Altogether, the lot of sailors on blockade duty seems far preferable, if measured in safety and comfort, to that of the soldiers fighting at Chickamauga and Cold Harbor.

The naval forces of course longed for action, peril, and battle, and acquitted themselves herocially when opportunity offered. Through Boyer's taciturn diary pulses a hope for some encounter, some stormy hour of danger, some opportunity for shining achievement. How much better this than reading Dumas for excitement, or capturing a 300-pound loggerhead turtle, or measuring the pathetic squalor and ignorance of the freedmen! When luckier warships bring in the captured rebel ram *Fingal* or *Atlanta,* "one mass of filth and dirt," Boyer burns with envy. He has an hour of real pleasure when early in 1864 his ship at last seizes a prize. It takes a little sloop outward bound with cotton, turpentine, and tobacco, so that the ship's company can look forward to dividing prize money of $13,000. The great joyous moment of his naval experience, however, comes in May, when his new warship the *Mattabesett* encounters the Confederate ram *Albemarle,* with two gunboats, and drives her back to shelter. It is "quite a stormy naval fight," eight men on the Union side are killed or wounded, and Boyer has the satisfaction of finding himself smeared with blood. This furnishes the diary its most dramatic page, though Boyer's record is characteristically concise and unassuming. His very real ardor never expressed itself in flamboyant words.

Some passages in Boyer's diary of his Japanese experiences are unforgettable. His record of his medical attendance on the Great Prince—that is, Prince Hizen—is especially vivid. The naval surgeon found him suffering from the grossest malpractice; "with a dry brown-coated tongue, gums and inside of mouth one mass of ulcers, teeth all blackened, pains in chest, shoulders, bowels, and limbs, no appetite, very feeble, pulse 38." Yet a few simple specifics

disposed of all evil symptoms so completely that an attending noble-
man broke spontaneously into a "Congratulatory Song" reserved
for births, weddings, and recoveries from seemingly fatal disease;
Prince Hizen had come to life again. The diarist's description of
such places as the town of Kobe and the region around it, Osaka,
and Kyoto is executed with warm feeling, and is an important con-
tribution to a picture of Japan a century ago. What he has to say
about Japanese housing, dress, food, and a wide array of customs is
both entertaining and historically valuable.

In the latter part of this diary the material on the persecution of
Christians at Nagasaki, and on the activities of the "Foreign Ex-
pellers," illuminates the friction between the courtesy-loving Japanese, fearful that their land would be overrun by barbarians, and
Westerners anxious to bring the country into the full current of
modernization. Little more than a decade earlier (1864) British,
French, and Dutch warships had bombarded Shimonoseki in a dis-
play of European unity which convinced the imperial government
that it must bow to foreign intercourse, not repel it; but various
nobles and their clans, resenting new ways, hung back. Boyer hardly
does justice to the chief agent in applying Western pressure, the
British minister Sir Harry Parkes, an able and farsighted man (he
supported the Mikado in the years of turmoil) of offensively stiff
temper. He hardly foresees the imminent collapse of feudalism in
Japan, and is curiously silent about the abuses practised by the
samurai, with their hereditary incomes and privileges. But he does
offer striking comments on the evils of the passing system. A run
on shore, for example, brings him to Ibesu. "It contains about 2000
inhabitants, nine tenths of whom are blind, half blind, crippled,
or suffering from cutaneous diseases. The streets are narrow and
filthy in the extreme, and the sights that meet the eye and the effluvia
that attack the nose may not be described without an offence to
decency." And at Hakodate he sees instances of Japanese judicial
methods that (though sanctioned by an American consul) are far
too medieval to suit him.

The glimpses that Boyer's diary affords us of the coasts of China
and of the life in Hong Kong are so sharply etched that we wish
they were longer.

No reader of this striking record will doubt for a moment that
its value has been doubled by the painstaking editorial care lavished
upon its presentation. It is seldom that any historical document

receives such scholarly and discriminating attention. The work has plainly been a labor of love. It was begun by Dr. Barnes in collaboration with his wife; it has been continued by him as in part a monument to her memory. It will be an enduring testimonial to their laboriously careful partnership, and their personalities shine through introductions and notes as clearly as Dr. Boyer's gleams through the text. They have given American history a document of permanent value.

ALLAN NEVINS

The Huntington Library

The Setting and The Diary

The prosaic life of navy men in lonely vigil along the Atlantic and Gulf coasts is an almost forgotten chapter in the tragic war that convulsed the nation between April, 1861, and April, 1865. The mighty sweep of the armies as the blue and the gray pitched their tents and fought their battles along the Mississippi, in the valleys of the Cumberland and Tennessee, on the way to Atlanta, and on the roads between Washington and Richmond or in the region where Lee stretched his fingers into Maryland and Pennsylvania have in the records virtually submerged all but the most dramatic exploits of the naval personnel who deployed their ships and fought their duels over the seas and from the yards in Portland, Maine, to the far reaches of the Texas coast.

The fact that the Confederacy was for the most part a land of spreading fields where the people sent their cotton to foreign markets and to an appreciable extent bought their essential goods from their economic neighbors overseas made Federal naval operations a critical if usually an uninteresting factor in the war to preserve the Union —critical because the South could not be conquered unless it could be isolated and uninteresting because blockading duty was made up chiefly of merely waiting for an enemy who seldom let himself be seen. Rebellious complaints of dullness may have echoed up and down the Atlantic coast and around the Gulf at practically any time during the war. Except on relatively infrequent occasions when action blazed quick and furious or a chase led out to sea and stirred dreams of rich prizes that often disappeared with the enemy over the horizon, the routine duty was rarely broken. The arrival of mail was relished above all else; and even the sutler with his "villainous prices" was gladly hailed, for the flowing cup that followed his appearance washed away loneliness and brought at least for an evening grand visions of glory, though the gray morning after usually settled heavily on aching heads. Expeditions of various kinds and sightseeing and foraging excursions ashore too made for welcome diversion. Occasional shifts in station, the arrival of refugees (usually colored), special entertainment by ship personnel (particularly on holidays), and sometimes rumors hot from "Secesh land" served also to enliven the humdrum existence. For the most part each vessel sailed in a little world of its own, and small matters took on great import: such things as an item of food eaten, an incidental personal affair, a political discussion, and the perusal of a book assumed major proportions. But the blockade, tightening ever more securely its strangling hold, was vital in the winning of the war. Against the backdrop of its ceaseless operation the more spectacular yet no more essential actions of offensive warfare were carried out.

Naval Surgeon is the private journal of Samuel Pellman Boyer, Pennsylvanian, who, at the age of twenty-three years and eight days, entered the navy of the United States as a volunteer officer on temporary appointment shortly after his graduation from the medical department of the University of Pennsylvania in 1862. Volume one is in the main a day-by-day record of nearly three years on blockade vessels of war and a briefer postwar log of a year and a half on a supply ship. Notwithstanding the generally uneventful nature of the duty, with comparatively few high spots of interest, the story has its value, for it stands almost alone as a firsthand description of life in the fleet during the Civil War.

When Dr. Boyer received his naval commission as an acting assistant surgeon, the war had been in progress fourteen months. The outbreak of hostilities had found the navy of the United States poorly prepared for aggressive conflict. Of its ninety vessels at the beginning of 1861 only forty-two were in commission. Some of these were scattered in foreign waters, and others because of their size, draft, or lack of steam propulsion were not adapted either for fighting or for patrolling a land margin that was broken by countless shallow inland passages and that offered nearly two hundred places where cargoes could be landed. Moreover, foreign (especially English) adventurers lost no time in fitting out ships to carry goods in and out of the Confederacy, recognized early in the conflict as a belligerent. Immediate action was necessary if the commerce of the rebelling section was to be smothered.

Setting up a blockade of the thirty-five-hundred-mile coastline of the Atlantic Ocean and the Gulf of Mexico was a tremendous undertaking. Much of the vast distance was made up of a double shore where rivers and bays cut deep into the interior or carved out thin slivers of mainland and either left them hanging as peninsulas or else completely detached them as islands. In addition to the Potomac Flotilla, established at the start of the war primarily for the protection of the waterway leading from the sea to the national capital, and the Mississippi Squadron, formed shortly thereafter in conjunction with the War Department, two coastal blockading squadrons were organized—the Atlantic and the Gulf, each soon split into two separate squadrons.

Gideon Welles, Secretary of the Navy, applied himself with vigor to the task of building up his forces. Available vessels were allocated, steamers and sloops in far-off waters were ordered home, ships laid up in yards were repaired and commissioned, merchant bottoms and other craft of various kinds were bought outright or chartered at exorbitant rentals, and construction of new vessels was begun. Even small barks and worn-out sailing frigates—dependent altogether on wind or tow for mobility—were pressed into service. As time went on, some of the captured British-built steamers that had been used in the profitable, if increasingly risky, blockade-running trade were purchased by the government and converted into cruisers.

By the end of 1861 the navy had grown to 264 ships. A year later there were 163 more. Throughout the war the naval force continued to expand, totaling by December, 1864, 671 vessels of 4,610 guns and 510,396 tons. Naval manpower at the same time mounted from 7,600 men in service at the beginning of the rebellion to 51,500. The number of artisans and laborers in navy yards rose from 3,844 to 16,880. Technical improvements furthered the effectiveness of the fighting units: the change from sailing ship to paddle-wheel steamer and then to submerged-screw steamer, the use of armor plate for protection and of heavy ordnance for assault, the increase in size and, by means of more and more powerful machinery, in speed of vessels, and the development of the dramatic and useful, if unseaworthy, "cheese box on a raft" (Ericsson's *Monitor*) for harbor defense contributed greatly to the ultimate victory of the North.

The blockade, initially scoffed at by many Englishmen as an ineffectual attempt to interfere with thriving trade, grew in efficiency as time went on. At first many ships, both incoming and outgoing, slipped through the net, but the number seized as reported to the Navy Department tell of the fruit of diligent watching and occasional pursuit: 153 by the end of 1861, 543 by the end of 1862, 1,045 by the end of 1863, and 1,379 by the end of 1864, giving net proceeds of over thirteen million dollars.[1]

The first naval victory of the North was the capture in August, 1861, of Fort Clark and Fort Hatteras, guarding the principal channel for entering the sounds of North Carolina. Shortly afterwards the Atlantic Blockading Squadron was divided into the North Atlantic Blockading Squadron and the South Atlantic Blockading Squadron. The latter, to which Dr. Boyer was assigned on his entry into service, was placed under the direction of Flag Officer (later Rear Admiral) Samuel Francis du Pont, who remained in command until relieved in July, 1863, by Rear Admiral John A. Dahlgren. Its first major assault was a combined naval and military attack on the fortifications defending Port Royal harbor, South Carolina, on November 7, 1861. The successful outcome of this venture, in addition to proving the efficacy of the new Dahlgren guns mounted even on wooden steamers, provided the Federal forces a strategic coal, supply, and repair depot and prepared the way for further operations, by which the blockading forces eventually gained a firm foothold on the southern coastal area, with its inlets and "sea islands."

The fall of Port Royal was followed by the seizure of Tybee Island, in the Savannah River. The army thereby gained a base from which Fort Pulaski was subsequently reduced; it was able also to build entrenchments on Hilton Head and to occupy Beaufort, South Carolina, and nearby places. Step by step the navy spread its control over the sounds of Georgia and southward along the Florida coast and captured Fernandina (including Fort Clinch), Jacksonville, St. Augustine, and other towns. By mid-1862 the only important Atlantic approaches that were still in possession of the Confederacy were Savannah, Charleston (which still resisted even after the Federals had gained command of the harbor in July, 1863), and Wilmington, North Carolina. Even so, at unguarded points blockade runners continued to steal through the maze of inlets and island channels.

In February, 1864, Dr. Boyer left the South Atlantic Blockading Squadron and returned North to be examined for a permanent appointment as assistant surgeon. Soon therafter he joined the North Atlantic Blockading Squadron, which, under the command of Acting Rear Admiral S. P. Lee, had thus far been occupied chiefly in penetrating the rivers of Virginia and the sounds of North Carolina as well as watching and guarding the coastline of those two states. A successful naval attack in early February, 1862, on Roanoke Island, strategic point in the channel connecting Pamlico and Albemarle Sounds, together with the capture of Plymouth, Newbern, and other places, had put all the sounds of North Carolina under Federal control, making that state no longer an important Confederate supply base—Wilmington alone, most difficult either to blockade or to close entirely because of its several entrances and the shoalness of its approaches, being open to foreign traffic. At the time Dr. Boyer reported for duty, the squadron was in the process of expanding its activities.

With the tightening of the net along the entire coastline the Confederates were becoming more and more desperate to get munitions and supplies from abroad, and trade in contraband goods was increasingly lucrative. Blockade duty was accordingly becoming more detailed and more involved. Furthermore, extensive operations were being undertaken in cooperation with army forces in the vicinity, particularly in the direction of Richmond. Too, the construction of formidable Confederate ironclads in the Roanoke and Neuse Rivers constituted a real threat to Federal supremacy in the region and hence necessitated especially vigilant guard in Albemarle and Pamlico Sounds, outlets of these rivers. For the sake of efficiency the squadron was divided geographically into four separate units—one operating on the James River, two off the Cape Fear River, and one in the sounds of North Carolina. The last-named unit, to which Dr. Boyer was attached, was just beginning its most important work, which was complicated by the facts that Federal monitors could not get into the shallow waters of the sounds and that military support in the region was inadequate. In April, 1864, the Confederates besieged Plymouth, sent their ironclad *Albemarle* down the Roanoke to attack the wooden gunboats in the sound, carried the Federal defenses, and repossessed the upper sound. Thereupon Captain Melancton Smith was sent with a fleet of vessels of heavy armament (including the *Mattabesett,* to which Dr. Boyer was assigned) to destroy the ram. The excitement of the May 5 encounter in which his forces routed her, much relished by the diarist, was followed by a period of more or less uneventful and monotonous guarding and waiting; in October the *Albemarle* was torpedoed and Plymouth recaptured.

By the end of 1864 the North Atlantic Blockading Squadron had more vessels and more officers and men than any other squadron. Much of its force was now concentrated on Wilmington. An unsuccessful attack on the forts at the mouth of the Cape Fear River, made on December 24 and 25 by Rear Admiral David Porter and a bombarding fleet of thirty-seven vessels (including five ironclads) and a reserve fleet of nineteen more, was followed by a successful one on Fort Fisher on January 15 and immediate Confederate abandonment of all nearby forts; by February 22, 1865, the city of Wilmington itself was evacuated.

With enemy resistance on the wane and the end of the war in sight, the blockading squadrons were reduced in strength. All vessels that could be spared were withdrawn from duty and sent North for necessary repairs and disposition. Some were laid up in ordinary and some dispatched to foreign stations to help re-establish the protection of American "rights and interests" abroad. Many were returned to commercial use. By the end of May (the insurgent navy having surrendered in the Gulf on the tenth) the squadrons were ordered cut down to a hundred vessels, and by early July there were, aside from receiving storeships, only thirty steamers left on the Atlantic and in the Gulf. The Potomac Flotilla was broken up by the last of July, and the Mississippi Squadron, once composed of a hundred steamers, was discontinued by mid-August. In June the North Atlantic Blockading Squadron and the South Atlantic Blockading Squadron were consolidated; the East Gulf and West Gulf Squadrons, too, were thrown together. By the close of 1865 the squadrons had a combined strength of only twenty-nine vessels, carrying 210 guns, not including howitzers.

Acting Asssistant Surgeon Boyer had, of course, only a limited view of the Civil War. He wrote for the most part not of the great flow of events but of the things he did, the places he saw, the people he met, the cases he treated, the books and articles he read, the letters and papers he received, and the food he ate. Out of the detail emerges much information concerning life in the fleet, methods used in providing food for the blockading squadrons, the prices of goods that the sailors bought, the ways of obtaining postage stamps and of sending money home, treatment of the contrabands, medical service in the fleet, and a host of other things. Certain implications and omissions also are of import.

But the scene depicted is not wholly local. Dr. Boyer, like most of his fellows, was avidly interested in the progress of the war, even though he was often far from the theaters of active conflict. He made in his journal many references to occurrences in various fields of operation. The fall of New Orleans, the reduction of sundry points on inland waters, the sinking of the *Alabama* by the *Kearsarge*, and

the evacuation of Charleston are among the events noted. The diarist
was concerned, too, with politics, whether in Berks, his native county,
in Harrisburg, the capital of his state, or in Washington seat of the
Union that he was helping to defend. Political appointments of gen-
erals in the army, the Emancipation Proclamation, the use of
Negroes by the military, and many other things brought long and
sometimes explosive comment. The fact that there is no mention of
the close of the conflict is testimony to the completeness with which
the blockading squadrons had done their work by early 1865. That
Dr. Boyer was away in Norfolk being examined for promotion
lessens little the significance of the omission.

Unlike most of his fellow volunteer officers, Dr. Boyer at the end
of the war remained in the naval service. Promoted to the rank of
acting passed assistant surgeon, he was stationed on one of three
vessels used for carrying supplies, mails, and personnel along the
eastern and southern coast of the country. At the end of 1866, when
the first volume of his diary closes, there were in the entire navy 278
vessels (carrying 2,351 guns), of which 115 (carrying 1,029 guns) were
in commission. The Atlantic Squadron and the West India Squadron
were now consolidated into what was called the North Atlantic
Squadron, the South Atlantic Squadron taking in the southeast coast
of South America and the west coast of Africa. The Gulf Squadron
was still in operation, patrolling not only the United States coast
but also Cuban and Mexican waters; special vigilance was exercised
to intercept reported intentions to seize colored persons for the slave
trade in Cuba, and the French attempt to establish a monarchy in
Mexico was being watched with suspicion. A year later there was
little for the navy to do at home. Since attention was now almost
wholly on foreign service, it is not strange that Dr. Boyer soon found
himself in the Orient.

In the preparation of Dr. Boyer's journal for publication a con-
scious effort was made to keep to a minimum the liberties taken
with the original. It seemed expedient, however, to set up several
editorial policies in order to increase the readability of the text. The
manuscript was divided into as logical parts as possible, each given
a title descriptive of at least its most salient features. Within these
arbitrary divisions only minor deviations in form were made. Date
lines were shortened by means of abbreviations and of deletion of
place names except in case of change in location. Here and there

repetitious or meaningless words or passages were deleted. In no case was the reader deprived of a segment that might throw light on any part of the scope of the diary; even the routine accounts of letters written and received were for the most part retained in their entirety lest any omission tend to reduce the flavor of the humdrum in blockade duty and minimize the importance of correspondence as a palliative, and the ever recurring references to the weather were kept intact. In some instances changes were made in paragraphing; long passages were sometimes broken up, and brief sentences standing alone were, particularly in the postwar section, often consolidated. The word "and," frequently omitted in certain types of sentences, was inserted without the usual brackets denoting corrections or additions. Short omissions are indicated by the traditional three dots; longer ones by four.

Whatever incorrect sentence structure and blunders in grammar (such as the use of done for did, no one for anyone, left for let, learn for teach, lay for laid, seen for saw, and of for have) the writer indulged in were left untouched as expressions characteristic in part of his geographic origin.

Dr. Boyer's spelling, too, was for the most part respected. Word forms now obsolete, such as ordinance for ordnance, cosy for cozy, and sett for set, were retained as written, as were also such seldom-used variants as hale for hail and such individual variations as bladderdash for balderdash and Scotch free for scot-free. In case of obvious oversight corrections were made—as from unforseen to unforeseen, appropo to apropos, inflammed to inflamed, send for sent, finely for finally, and principle to principal—and when more than one spelling of a word appeared in various places, the first one used was usually kept throughout the text. On the advice of medical friends, the prescriptions noted by the surgeon are copied—except for capitalization—exactly as written. Habitual misspelling of names of individuals and of geographic locations was not changed; at the first instance of each case the correct form was indicated.

Punctuation was supplied, altered, or deleted whenever it seemed advisable to do so not only for readability but also for uniformity and even clarity. (Indeed, often it was impossible to know whether a hastily scrawled mark in the manuscript had been intended by the writer as a comma, a period, or a dash.) Many series, for example, were repunctuated; the semicolon, rarely used by the diarist, was often employed in an attempt to make long sentences clear while preserving the form. Periods after abbreviations were except in technical medical terms, inserted. In the interest of saving space, prescriptions, which Dr. Boyer nearly always wrote in the usual vertical form, were cast into running order, with commas separating the items. Superfluous quotation marks and underscores (often found in conjunction to set off the same word or group of words) were deleted; for simplicity as well as for uniformity italics alone were retained for vessels and quotation marks alone for the names of publications. For the sake of appearance of the printed page the symbol & was changed to the written and and &c. to etc., and an overabundance of capital letters, common at the time (though many no doubt had been written unthinkingly), was eliminated.

Insofar as possible individuals and places mentioned by the diarist were identified and historical factual material included was checked and sometimes elaborated by means of editorial notation. Material essential—at least in the minds of the editors—to an understanding by the general reader of certain particular entries by the diarist (such as those concerning geographic locations, plantations, mansions, military and naval incidents, and names and places of publications of books, newspapers, and magazines) is inserted in the text enclosed in brackets. Corrections and completions in names and titles are also supplied in bracketed form. References and additional explanations, interesting primarily to the specialist, are supplied in notes. Essentially, however, Dr. Boyer's journal is the same piece of work faithfully kept through long hours of duty on the Civil War blockade.

NAVAL SURGEON: *Blockading the South, 1862-1866*

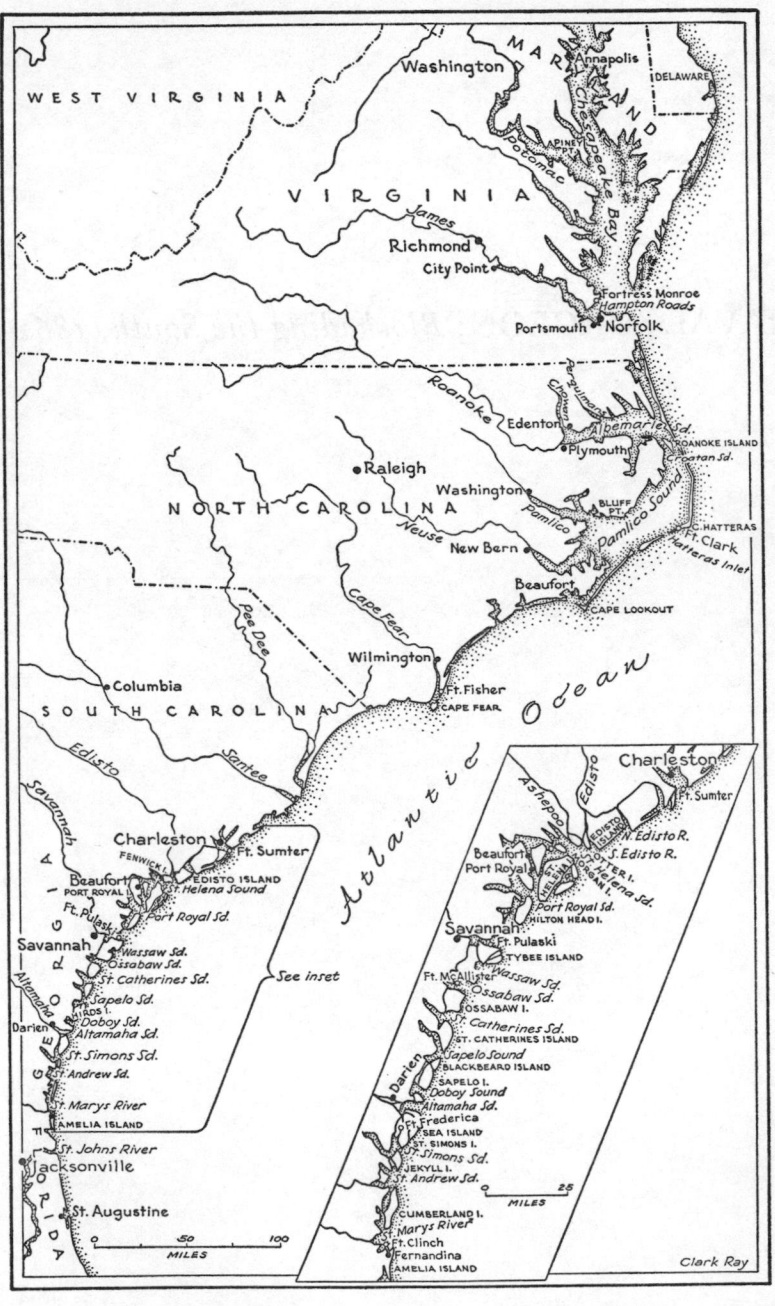

PART ONE

THE DOCTOR JOINS THE NAVY

1

Prelude to Naval Service

After studying hard from early morn to late at night for several years, attending three courses of medical lectures—two of which [were] in the Jefferson Medical College, Phila.—and claim [ing] the University of Pennsylvania, Phila., as my alma mater, I received my title of M.D. on the 13th day of March, 1862.

[The Medical Department of the University of Pennsylvania, oldest institution of its kind in North America, was on Ninth Street below Market. It and the Jefferson Medical College, on Tenth, constituted an important center of the medical profession not only of the city of Philadelphia but of the entire country as well. Both colleges, which drew many of their students from the South, suffered greatly during the Civil War. The diarist's class of ninety-two, the smallest since 1822, was only slightly more than half as large as the one of the previous year, and the next year's class numbered only seventy-eight. The subject of Dr. Boyer's thesis was "Scope of Surgery."]

The degrees were conferred on 92 students by the provost, Rev. [Daniel Raynes] Goodwin, in the Musical Fund Hall [used for the public commencements of the university medical school until 1866, when it was abandoned in favor of the Academy of Music], Locust Street [above Eighth], Phila., before a large and intelligent audience, two-thirds being of the fair sex, the remaining third "lords of creation." I claim this as one of the proudest events of my earthly career. On the 17th of March, 1862, I made my appearance before a naval board of medical examiners for the position of Asst. Surgeon in the U.S. Navy, consisting of Surgeons Greene, Wilson, Mayo and Shippen.[1] After a long and searching examination of 20 hours in all the branches of medical science as well as intruding on other sciences, operating on the "dead subject," visiting the medical wards of the naval asylum [Naval Home and Hospital], Phila.,[2] in company with Surgeon Greene, diagnosing cases, etc., I was told that I had been examined fully, etc. I left the city for home [Reading, county seat of Berks County, Pennsylvania, 59 miles northwest of Philadelphia], waiting patiently 4 or 6 weeks for my commission

—when lo and behold! I lacked 15 merits of entering the service. Nothing daunted, I immediately made preparations to follow the practice of my profession in the rural districts of my native, the Keystone, State.

My first object now was to find a location. Schuylkill County, Pa., being an anthracite-coal region and affording plenty of opportunities of practicing surgery, first attracted my attention. I arrived in the ancient village of New Castle on the 25th of May. Upon making inquiries as regards the prospects, I found that the locality was anything else than favorable to commence my career, being told that *probably* I *might* manage to pay my *board* and *horse feed* the first three years. Money was scarce, workmen out of employment— Irish all either drunk or too lazy to work. The best portion of the community—I mean the working class—had gone to war. Besides all this I found the country inundated with water, causing desolation and ruin, poverty and distress all around—so much, indeed, that I concluded to seek another region to hang out my "shingle."

I next heard of a practice that a doctor by the name of J. J. Comfort had to dispose of in the town of Conshohocken, Montgomery County, a place of about 1,000 inhabitants. I paid Dr. Comfort a visit; had a pleasant time while there, being taken up a high mountain so as to have a fair view of the surrounding neighborhood, which was attractive. I reminded Dr. Comfort of the devil and Christ when the former took the latter on a high mount, showed him all the beautiful valley below them, etc., trying to tempt him. The doctor smiled and said his idea was to advance his interests as well as my own. His practice amounted to $1,000 a year (so he said). Boarding was *only* $3.50 per week, horse hire or keeping $3.50 per week, office rent $1 per week. Wanted to have $250 for his good will etc. Told him I would think of the same. Returned to Reading; consulted my parents and brothers; finally concluded that a man was a —— fool to pay for a practice. Dropped Dr. Comfort a letter, stating that my banker—i.e., my father—concluded not to advance me the money, thinking it foolish to pay for what you can manage, by doing or attending to your business, to obtain yourself. The doctor answered by saying that he was very sorry (I suppose because he could not take me in).

My last attempt was successful as regards being satisfied with the terms etc., but an unforeseen event transpired, as will be seen by reading ahead some, that knocked that place all in a cocked hat.

AN ESSAY

ON

SCOPE OF SURGERY

FOR THE

Degree of Doctor of Medicine,

IN THE

UNIVERSITY OF PENNSYLVANIA.

BY

Samuel. P. Boyer

County **Berks.** State **Pennsylvania.**

Residence in this City, **1516. North. 4th. St.**

Preceptor, **David. P. Boyer. M. D.**

Duration of Studies, **Four. Years.**

Age, **Twenty Three**

Presented, **Feb'y. 3rd. 1862.**

Title page of Dr. Boyer's medical thesis at the
University of Pennsylvania.

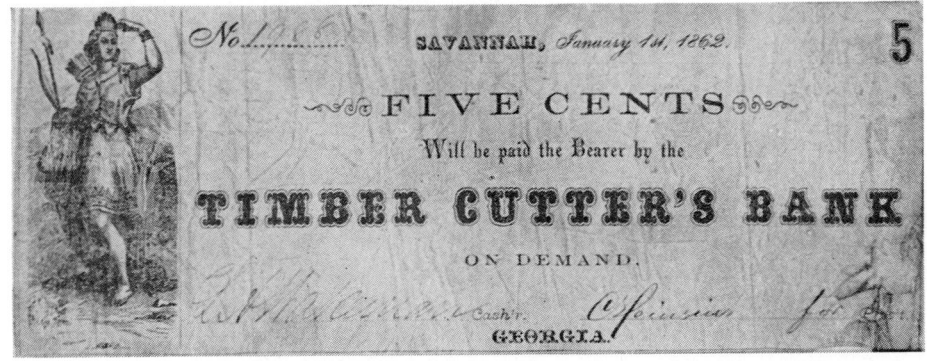

ST. JOHN'S COLLETON, *29 April* 18 *61*

Received, of *S. Jenkin, Mikell Esqr* the sum

of *Three hundred ninety* *90/100* Dollars,

amount of *his* Taxes for the year 18 *60*

General Tax................ $ *382 06*

Poor and P. B. Tax,- *7. 66*

N. I. Cut,.............

Total,................... $ *390 72*

G. W. Seabrook

Tax Collector for St. John's Colleton.

Tax receipt obtained by Dr. Boyer at Home Place.
(See diary entry, Dec. 12, 1862)

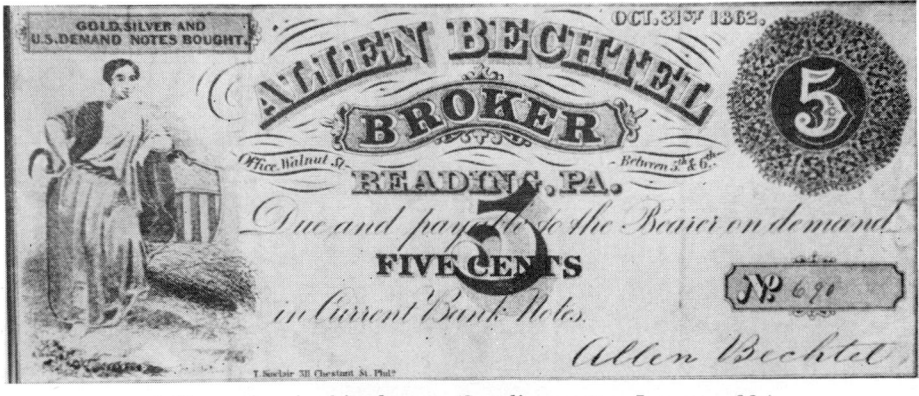

A Georgia shinplaster. (See diary entry, Jan. 27, 1863)

A Pennsylvania shinplaster. (See diary entry, Jan. 29, 1863)

Christ Church, St. Simons Island. (From Burnette Vanstory,
Georgia's Land of the Golden Isles)

Couper tombstones, Christ Church cemetery.
(Dr. Orrin Sage Wightman and Margaret Davis Cate)

BARKS ARTHUR, GRAZELERO, AMANDA, AND GEM OF THE SEAS.

TUGS SATELLITE AND PUTNAM.

PROPELLERS YALE, AND STARS & STRIPES

STEAMERS AUGUSTA, JAMES ADGER, FLORIDA, AND VALLEY CITY

PREPARING MERCHANT VESSELS FOR THE
BLOCKADE.

...put a rib through our screws — require some expense... fly — which caused Messrs Plunkett — Penett — & the rest of the wounded to be wounded — Besides any amount of damage done to our rigging — Still notwithstanding, taking all in all, We done Credit to ourselves — During the engagement & two hours afterward I was as busy as a bee attending the killed & wounded — Covered with blood from head to feet — I will here give the pen & ink sketch of said ram — So much for the Ram fight — Don't fancy such kind of fighting — Would prefer under Gunboat —

Sketch of the *Albemarle* by Dr. Boyer. (See diary entry, May 5, 1864)

The *Sassacus* ramming the *Albemarle*. (From *Harper's Pictorial History of the Civil War*)

Naval commanders of the South Atlantic Blockading Squadron: Rear Admiral Samuel Francis du Pont, Rear Admiral John A. Dahlgren. (From Robert Tomes, *The War with the South*)

Charleston, S. C.: Gillmore's explosive shells being fired from Fort Putnam, Jan. 3, 1864.

Plymouth, N. C., 1864. (From Benson J. Lossing, *History of the Civil War*)

Capture of Plymouth, N. C., October, 1864. (U.S. Naval Photographic Center)

... make them as comfortable as possible under the circumstances —

Wounded — 6 —

James L. Plunkett acting Master — Contusion of Right Thigh —
He fought his gun during the whole engagement & did not report himself to me until after the fight —

John R. Jewett — Sd. — 22 — Kentucky — Punctured wound of right fore-arm — He did not report himself until after the fight & then not until I sent for him — He has proved himself a hero in every sense of the word — Dressed his wound etc — Continues doing duty —

Greenbury F. Smith — Sd. — 31 — Tennessee — Contused wound of left shoulder — Rather a severe Contusion — Dressed with Cold water lotion medicated — Also administered Whiskey etc —

James I. Fulrehill — Ord. Sea. — 21 — New York — Contused wound of back & left elbow — Treated upon general principles — viz. Cold water dressings re—

Daniel Lamar — Capt. Forecastle — 42 — Scotland — Lacerated wound of Scalp in vicinity of right ear — pinna of right ear also wounded — Treated upon general principles — Cold water dressings &

Charles F. Wells — 1st Class Boy — 17 — Germany — Contusion of right knee, ankle and ecchymosis of right left eyebrow & lid — Apple Cold water dressings —

The Vessels of the fleet —
The Mattabesett done noble work — the Sassacus ran head on to the ram; dismounted some of the ram's guns &c confused — & received herself a shot which ...

Dr. Boyer's list of the wounded on the *Mattabesett* after the fight with the *Albemarle*. (See diary entry, May 5, 1864)

Having heard that the thickly populated township or districts of Hereford and Longswamp in the vicinity of Seisholtzville [Berks County] were in want of medical aid, I paid said region a visit. Found Mr. Chas. Gery, postmaster, landlord, and merchant of Seisholtzville, a good fellow. He spoke very highly of the neighborhood and recommended me to commence business there, telling me that I had a circuit in any direction from his stand 6 miles ere I came to any other doctor. He advised me to see Mr. Aaron Mull, the landlord of the Union House, ¼ mile from his stand, as regards room for an office etc., he not having any room. Mr. Mull also spoke very favorable of the place. Upon making inquiries, I found that I could obtain from Mr. Mull boarding, washing, office rent, horse feed, and stabling for the small sum of $3.62 per week—and the best of grub and accommodations at that. I immediately made arrangements for boarding etc. with Mr. Mull and told him to inform the citizens of said districts that Dr. Samuel P. Boyer, son of Old Michael K. Boyer [surveyor; prothonotary; member of the Pennsylvania House of Representatives from Berks County in 1836 and from Armstrong, Clarion, and Jefferson Counties in 1856; and a Democrat who was not always sympathetic with Lincoln's conduct of the war], would be at his house in two weeks ready to wait upon all who needed my services, whether young or old, male or female, rich or poor. I also ordered my saddlebags to be made by Mr. Zimmerman, saddler, of Kutztown. All my friends were highly elated at my good fortune in obtaining so good a place and at such reasonable terms, all wishing me success in Longswamp.

But never was the maxim of old more apropos than in the present case—viz., "Man proposes but God disposes"—for in the height of my glory I received the following news from Washington: Dr. Whelan of the Bureau of Med. and Surg. of the Navy Department [Surgeon William Whelan, chief of the bureau] wrote me a letter offering me the position of an a[cting] a[ssistant] surgeon in the Navy if I wished the same. I immediately answered the same, accepting an appointment if sent. This was on the 20th of June, 1862. On the 23rd of the same month I received the appointment [dated June 21, 1862] of a.a. surgeon in the U.S. Navy on temporary duty[3] and was ordered to report to Commodore [Hiram] Paulding [commandant of the navy yard at New York, which had the important function of handling problems of supply and repair for the blockading fleets] for passage in the first public vessel bound to Port Royal,

S.C. [base for supplying coal and other provisions and for refitting vessels since its capture by the Federals on November 7, 1861], and on my arrival there report to Flag Officer du Pont for duty on board the U. S. barque *Fernandina*.

[Samuel Francis du Pont, grandson of Pierre Samuel du Pont de Nemours, French statesman and author, and son of Victor, one of the early venturers of the family in powder making in America. A graduate of Annapolis, his appointment as flag officer of the South Atlantic Blockading Squadron in September, 1861, gave him the command of the nation's largest fleet to that time. The vessels assembled at the end of October at Hampton Roads, Virginia, rendezvous of the squadron, numbered seventy-five, including coal ships and army transports. In February, 1862, he received Congressional thanks for his services, and a few months later was promoted to the rank of rear admiral. He died before the war was over, bitterly disappointed at his failure to capture Charleston Harbor (see pp. 97, 157).]

At 3 A.M. on the 24th of June, 1862, I started for New York and arrived there at 8 A.M. After having obtained something to eat at Lovejoy's [probably Jonathon Lovejoy's Hotel, at 34 Park Row], I started for the Brooklyn Navy Yard. On my arrival there I reported to Commodore Paulding. He immediately acknowledged the same on my orders and ordered me to report to Lieutenant Commander A[aron] K. Hughes, captain of the U.S. steamer *Mohawk*, for passage to Port Royal. Did so; found the captain eating his lunch and drinking his grog. Capt. Hughes immediately signed my orders, certifying that I had reported to him. After drinking a glass of old rye with the captain, I left for the city again. Ordered my uniform, side arms, trunk, etc. Telegraphed home that I would be home same night. After having transacted my business, I left Jersey City at 8 P.M. on one of the New York Central lines. Arrived at Reading at 1 A.M. the next day. Packed my trunk, bid all my friends good-bye, and ate a breakfast prepared by my mother. Left home again for New York same day at 3 A.M., having had two hours to do all my business in at home, such as bidding adieu to friends etc. Arrived the second time in New York City at 8 A.M. Immediately proceeded to the Navy agent. Drew two months' advance as well as $13 mileage, amounting [to] $221 in all. [The pay of assistant surgeons on duty at sea was $1,250 per annum; on other duty, $1,050; and on leave or waiting orders, $800.] Paid for my outfit, took a last look at myself in citizen's, or civilian's, dress, then put on the uniform of the Navy of the United States of America, the finest country and best nation on the globe.

The steamer *Mohawk* left the harbor of New York on the 30th of June, 1862, and after a pleasant passage (I escaping from the [un]pleasant feelings of "nausea marina" whilst nearly all the rest on board suffered from the wrath of Old Neptune) of seven days we arrived in the harbor of Port Royal, S.C., Sunday, the 6th of July, 1862. After settling my mess bill on the *Mohawk*, which amounted to $12.50, I reported myself, same day, to Flag Officer S. F. du Pont for duty. He ordered me to report to Capt. Edward Moses, a[cting] m[aster] commanding, of the U.S. Barque *Fernandina* for duty as medical officer on said man-of-war. After returning to the *Mohawk*, bidding the officers adieu, I left with my baggage for my own craft, the *Fernandina*, at 3 P.M. of same day. I had the misfortune of having some of the men or crew of the *Mohawk* to be kind enough to appropriate my garrick, or overcoat, to their own use. In short, some of the sailors stole my overcoat.

PART TWO

SOUTH ATLANTIC BLOCKADING SQUADRON: THE U.S. BARQUE *FERNANDINA*

2

The Doctor Afloat

Upon my arrival on board of the *Fernandina* I reported to Capt. E. Moses for duty. He immediately approved of my orders and asked me to take a drink with him, which of course I did. Captain M. is a d— fine old boy—one who knows how to keep a hotel.

[This expression, which the diarist uses frequently, may possibly be a variation of the more common "to keep a good house," in the sense of supplying bountiful fare. Albert Barrere and Charles G. Leland in their two-volume *Dictionary of Slang, Jargon and Cant* (London: Printed for subscribers only at the Ballantyne Press, 1889-1890), I, 515, however, give possession of administrative capacity as the connotation, attributing the origin of the expression to a banjoist in a Negro minstrel troupe who revenged himself on the landlord of a Vicksburg, Mississippi, hotel who refused to reimburse him for an overcoat lost on the premises by making him the butt of a humorous dialogue in his act in which an enumeration of inconsequential virtues was anticlimaxed by the drawled statement, "Ya-as—but he ca-ant keep a ho-tell!"]

I found my messmates in the wardroom to be as follows: Acting Master Richard B. Hines, executive officer; Acting Master Levi L. Jump, sailing master; Acting Master Magnus Schow; Acting Assistant Paymaster Andrew G. Myers. After having a social chat, we commenced to talk about the mess bill. They, the rest of the members, had the audacity to charge me the sum of $40.75 as an entrance fee. Rather a salty dose to swallow—nevertheless, I paid the same without raising a dissenting voice.

After my stateroom, which is on the port side, was prepared for my reception and everything kept or placed in order, I made inquiries as regards a steward. I found that the former steward, Russell D. Adams, was in charge of the medical department of this craft for the last two weeks. He had Messrs. Jump—contusion of right arm; Henderson—secondary syphilis; Chas. Callon—ulcer of penis; Wm. Brown—constipation; and Kingsley—general debility on the sick list. Next day I commenced treatment of the above patients. Found that some of the boys were trying to play "old soger" so as to shirk duty. But having my eyes open, I generally in a day or two convinced them that it was better to do duty than to be blistered for every ache and pain. After the lapse of a week or so the boys all knew me and my plan of treatment and concluded not to play "old soger," as the inevitable consequences would be a large Spanish fly blister or else a dose of calomel and jalap.

After having our decks polluted with wood, we started [as per orders dated July 9] for our station off Charleston, S. C.,[1] where it took us the better part of a month to dispose of our cargo of wood, which was intended for the fleet. We lay at anchor off Charleston until the 7th of September, 1862, when we left said station for Ossabaw Sound, Ga., where we arrived on the 8th.

[Like other vessels in du Pont's squadron, the *Fernandina* was moved about from station to station among the coastal inlets. The main object of such continued movement, according to naval officials, was to reduce the monotony of blockade duty.]

Nothing of any interest transpired while we lay off Charleston except that Acting Master Magnus Schow was sent home by the orders of Rear Admiral du Pont for sleeping while on duty as officer of the deck, and Calvin C. Childs of Massachusetts, an acting master, arrived on board and took his place. Mr. Childs paid our paymaster the sum of $40 as an entrance fee, which Mr. Myers pocketed himself. I also while off Charleston sent a sailor by the name of Robert J. Tufts home, or rather to a hospital, affected with nephritis chronica. Also had our paymaster, A. G. Myers, who labored under general debility, condemned by a medical board of survey, which consisted of Drs. Gorgas, Holmes, and Atwood [Surgeon Albert C. Gorgas, stationed on the *Vandalia;* Acting Assistant Surgeon William H. Holmes, stationed on the *Augusta;* and Acting Assistant Surgeon R. N. Atwood, stationed on the *James Adger*], and recommended to go North for the benefit of his health. Besides this, Acting Master Levi L. Jump, the very essence of meanness and ignorance, was put under arrest for raising the very "Old Harry" in the fleet one night while we lay off Charleston, causing some of the vessels to be fired at by some of our own men-of-war. The principal cause was rum, he being drunk at the time—consequently like any other drunken fool he disobeyed the orders of his superior officers. No sooner was he placed under arrest than he feigned sickness. The way I physicked him was not slow; Spanish

flies were in great demand. He continued being sick until he was released from arrest at Ossabaw Sound on the 12th of September,
when he returned to duty, and the officers of this craft had the
pleasure of seeing him on the 17th of Sept. discharged from the
service forever.

[The liquor problem was at times acute. At least one officer in 1862
complained that the trading schooners serving the South Atlantic Blockading Squadron under permits of the Secretary of the Treasury were
"fast becoming in spite of every precaution more or less floating grog-
ships," retailing "almost poisonous liquors" to the sailors at exorbitant
prices—"two dollars a bottle and more for the most wretched stuff, worth
perhaps ten cents." Even the navy's own sutlers participated in the liquor
traffic. Efforts of the authorities to stop the lucrative practice resulted in
the smuggling of intoxicating beverages in cans supposed to contain
foods such as oysters and "milk drink."[2]]

We arrived in Ossabaw Sound on the 8th of September 1862.
Found the place to be a splendid place to lay at anchor. On Ossabaw Island [one of the six "Golden Isles of Guale," as they had
been called by the Spanish settlers, the other five being St. Catherines, Sapelo, St. Simon, Jekyll, and Cumberland. At the outbreak
of the Civil War plantation owners had fled to the mainland, leaving their productive fields and their beautiful mansions deserted
except for some of the former slaves who stayed behind[3]], on the
plantation of a certain McDonnald [Alexander McDonald, owner
of the middle portion of the island], live 7 contrabands [Negro
slaves who had escaped to Union lines or otherwise come under
Northern jurisdiction—so-called from being considered contraband of war], who supplied us with potatoes (sweet) at $0.50 per
bushel, corn and grits $.65 per bushel, chickens 25/100 dolls. per
pair, etc. Their names were March and his wife, Aunt Sally, a
wench weighing about 212 lbs.; Ceaser and his wife, Molly; Old
Peggy, 120 years old, an old widow; Bob, an old widower, but full
of sport and devilment; and John, a bachelor, who was affected
with ascites. They all lived on the McDonnald place, about 3 miles
from the sound, towards the mainland. They had about 1,000
bushels of corn, 500 bushels of sweet potatoes, plenty of sugar cane
and pumpkins, 5 or 6 cows, chickens by the hundred, and pigs not
a few. We found them without winter clothing and salt. We supplied them with both. I gave a pair of doeskin cassimere pantaloons,
cloth vest, and two shirts to some of them.

While in Ossabaw Sound our paymaster, A. G. Myers, left for

the North on the 17th of Sept. for the benefit of his health, as well as Levi L. Jump, who was discharged. Magnus Schow arrived at the same time to be tried by a court of inquiry. He was tried and found wanting. He was discharged as an acting master on the 27th of Oct. [our new] acting assistant paymaster, T[homas] N. Murray of Olean, New York, arrived on board on the 18th of Oct. We (the rest of the mess) charged him an entrance fee of $25, having at the time a large amt. of stores on hand. We had the misfortune to lose our gunner's mate, Lewis Lawson, on the 27th of Sept., who accidentally shot himself in the abdomen. He was buried with the honors of war on the west end of Ossabaw Island.

Oysters, clams, and fish were very plenty here. We had on the wardroom table either a dish of oysters, clams, or fish every day— so much indeed that they almost proved to be a bore. While we lay here, we paid the enormous sum of $6 for a barrel of apples, $4 for a barrel of potatoes, the same for onions and half rotten at that, $12 for a barrel of flour, 18/100 dollars for a lb. of pork in the shape of shoulder, palming them off for hams, $6 and $8 per hundred for cigars worth $1.50, and everything else in proportion. The sutler schooners knew that they monopolized all the business; hence they asked any prices that suited their fancy.

After spending, taking all in all, a splendid time at Ossabaw Sound from the 8th of September until the 12th of November, 1862, when we were ordered to proceed to Port Royal, S.C., we left this place on the 12th inst. and arrived at Port Royal on the 15th, and after taking on wood, grub, and water enough to last us three months, we left for St. Helena Sound, S. C. [a broad estuary above Port Royal considered "exceedingly valuable for a harbor, for its proximity to Charleston, and for the command it secures of large rivers, supplying interior communication with the State of South Carolina"], on the 21st of November [to relieve the *Norwich*] and arrived at said sound on the evening of the 22nd.

While we lay at Port Royal, I transferred two men to the U.S. ship *Vermont*—viz., Augustus Rose, lds. [landsman], affected with chronic bronchitis, and James Austin, sea. [seaman], affected with aneurism of the right external carotid artery. They both left in the *Massachusetts* for the hospital at New York, there [to] undergo a course of treatment which necessarily is denied them on board a man-of-war. At the same time the following persons were honorably discharged and sent home, their times of service having expired— viz., Francis Little, captain of the hold; Henry M. Brown, paymaster's steward; William Crocker, lds.; James Minor, lds.; William Summerville, lds.; also Minor B. Haggerton, who was dishonorably discharged from the service as being a nuisance and disgrace to said service—he was the yeoman while on duty. We obtained 9 men from the U.S. ship *Vermont* to take their places—3 sea., 3 o. sea. [ordinary seamen], and 3 lds. On the 17th inst., the day the above men were transferred, Acting Ensign Francis Bacon of the U.S. ship *Vandalia* was transferred for duty for a short space of time to this ship. Mr. Bacon is a young gentleman 21 years of age, of gentlemanly manners and of prepossessing appearance. Being a wardroom officer, of course he had to be taxed a "fee". We, at least I as the caterer, assessed him $25, which he paid without any objections—and well he might, for, considering the stores on hand, it was paying cheap for his whistle. While here, we lay in wardroom stores to the amount of $75.

On the 20th of Nov. at 8 P.M. Captain Moses, R. B. Hines, and myself paid Capt. [Richard G.] Shaw of Company D of the 7th Rhode Island Regt.[4] a visit, having been favored with an invitation in the early part of the day. Capt. Shaw's company was encamped on Bay Point, in the harbor of Port Royal, opposite to Hilton Head [headquarters of the Department of the South, and like Bay Point, used as a military base for expeditionary operations]. The object of said visit was to witness a theatrical performance got up by some of his men for his (Capt. Shaw's) and his officers' benefit. The performance was held in a large hall over the armory of the encampment. Said hall was prepared for the reception of visitors. At one extremity, occupying about ¼ of the space, was placed the "stage" and side passages. Footlights, side shifts, curtains, etc. were all "according to Gunter." The drop curtain consisted of the Stars and Stripes. A large domestic chandelier hung in the center of the hall, suspended from the ceiling. Everything, in short, was placed in apple-pie order. The front seats were reserved for the naval officers, so that I had the pleasure of occupying a front seat in the shape of a rocking chair. The performance commenced with the celebrated family of the Toodles. "The Toodles"[5] was well performed, and the soldier taking the character of Mrs. Toodles done nobly. This was followed by a piece styled "The Rudiments." The performance concluded by the singing of the following songs in fine style: "Paddy's Wedding," "Rale Ould Irish Gentleman," and one or two more Irish songs[6] the titles of which slipped my memory. After spending a happy time in the hall witnessing the performance, we adjourned to the captain's headquarters, where we endeavored for the rest of the evening to "drive dull care away." In short, after using up, or spoiling, a large quantity of claret, cigars, and tobacco, having a merry time of it, we all dispersed and retired to our respective vessels, well satisfied with Capt. Shaw's hospitality and the sociability of his officers—Lieuts. Barker [probably John M. Barker, who became a captain in the Third Rhode Island Heavy Artillery on January 16, 1864], [Edward F.] Curtis [in command of Company A of the Third Rhode Island Heavy Artillery], [Richmond A.] Rawson [who transferred in January, 1864, to the Fourteenth Rhode Island Heavy Artillery, United States Colored Troops, and died the following May of disease at Providence], etc. Thus the curtain drops as regards Ossabaw Sound and Port Royal, except to state that during the months of September and October it was *very* warm, and the mosquitoes and sand flies were as thick as the frogs in the days of Moses. I might also in this connection state that the crew on an average were healthy; consequently "ye doctor" had not too much business on hand.

3

Coastal Islands of South Carolina

We arrived at our present station on the 22nd inst. Find St. Helena Sound and vicinity to be a pleasant harbor to lay at anchor. Ottar Island [Otter Island, a small island at the mouth of St. Helena Sound, a strategic position in keeping possession of the harbor] can claim a small village, populated with about 30 contrabands, male and female, from Old Aunt Peggy, who is 100 years old, down to General ——, who is a youngster of 12 months. Sweet potatoes, oranges, peanuts, chickens, clams, oysters, curlew, ducks, sheep, cows, oxen, and hogs appear to be plenty around this region. Ottar island is the place upon which Fort Drayton, at least what remains of it, stands—which was built by the Rebels and captured from them the same time that Port Royal was taken. [Actually Commander Percival Drayton of the *Pawnee* on November 25,

1861, found the fort to be unoccupied. "The magazine had been blown up, and everything carried away or destroyed, the only thing left being the fragments of an 80-pounder rifle gun, which had been burst." Called Fort Otter by Commander Drayton, the fort was renamed Fort Drayton by Lieutenant J. W. A. Nicholson of the *Isaac Smith* (who had been left temporarily in charge) before he turned it over to the army on December 11, 1861. The place was "entirely abandoned by the land forces" in mid-July, 1862, leaving only gun boats to guard the area.[7]]
Large pieces of exploded ordinances lay around said fort.

[Here Dr. Boyer wrote: "This journal was commenced on the 1st of December, 1862. What has been written up to this day has been from memory. It is a short account of my adventures from the day I graduated to the present time. I shall continue the same."]

St. Helena Sound, S. C., Dec. 1, 1862. This morning at 10 A.M., or 4 bells, Mr. Bacon, an actg. ensign, started with an armed boat's crew with the mail for Port Royal, taking the inland route. He expects to return tomorrow, when all expect to hear from the dear ones at home. May he have a happy time of it. I had two patients to report to the captain in my morning sick report as unfit for duty—viz., John Lahey, landsman—sore hand, and John Collins—intermittens. Besides those I had 5 or 6 outdoor cases, such as require treatment, but still fit for light duty.

At 10½ A.M. Capt. Moses, Paymaster Murray, and myself took a stroll, or walk, around Ottar Island, armed with shotguns, ready to pop away at any curlew or ducks should we chance to come across some. Finding game anything than plenty, the captain took a ride on his favorite "charger," Dandy, along the beach, while Murray and myself strolled along the beach in search not of a father as Marryat's Japhet [*Japhet in Search of a Father*, by Frederick Marryat, captain in the Royal Navy and writer of novels of sea life; first edition 1836, followed by several others, including London: R. Bentley, 1854] but of shells and relics. In our perambulations we came across the last resting place of some soldiers of the war of 1861-2—brave patriots who died of disease while encamped on said island. From the inscriptions on their "tomb-boards" they proved to have been, with one exception, all Pennsylvanians. Peace to their ashes. . . .
[In February, 1862, 935 officers and men of the Forty-Fifth Pennsylvania Infantry had been stationed on the island; in April two companies remained. The occupants of the graves may have been malaria victims.

Both malaria and dysentery, often in combination, were prevalent among Northern forces in the South, and in May there had been reported "some indications of malarious diseases . . . amongst the troops" on the upper end of near-by Edisto, north of St. Helena Sound, and at Little Edisto.]

We finally concluded to return to our ship, or present home, which we did at 1.30 P.M., all fatigued and somewhat anxious for dinner. After I had dined, being weary I took a nap. Ate tea at 5.30 P.M. Took a Conchita and smoked away for a short time. At 6.30 P.M. I took said journal and noted down the above few items of today's work. In this connection I might state that we tarred down the rigging—i.e., the crew did—today. All were happy aloft as a young bride. Thermometer 64° Fahr. in shade.

Dec. 2, 1862. Today we have delightful weather. Everything has more the appearance of a morn in spring than a usually cold December day. All hands appear in the best of humor. My daily sick list contains the names of Charles Mowatt, boat's mate—intermittens; James M. Crusey, sea.—abrasio; John Collins—bronchi. acuta; John Lahey—abrasio, besides having several outdoor patients to prescribe for. Having attended to the sick, I sent a boat to the schooner *Wild Cat*, commanded by Jno. Pickle, for one of his officers, Jno. Smith by name, so as to dress a gumboil of his. After that I made 120 aperient pills—which I must say fatigued me not a little.

11 A.M., the thermometer 67° Fahr. The weather changed some in its aspect towards night—at 5.30 P.M. the thermometer stood 57° Fahr., or 10° lower than at 11.30 A.M. Since 3 P.M. we have all been waiting patiently for the 2nd cutter to "hove" in sight on its return trip from Port Royal with the mail, which we are all anxious to see, expecting news from the North. No signs of Ensign Bacon at 6 P.M. Supped at 6 P.M. on "leather clams," as the captain styles clams. He says we all will see a "horse" tonight on account of the indigestibility of said clams. He is not far out of the way. Notwithstanding the prospects of a "nightmare," I managed to lay in a cargo of two large platesful of said clam soup.

10 P.M., Ensign Bacon returned, but alas! *Fernandina's* mail had ere his arrival been sent to South Edisto; so we will have to wait for said mail until next week. Thank fortune, he at least brought books and illustrated and other papers of very late dates, so that we can read the war news as late as the 25th inst. [ult.] He also

brought with him that ever welcome article to a Navy or Army officer, postage stamps, as well as some good old sherry wine, $18 per doz. We drank his health in a bumber [bumper] of sherry. I relieved him of two bottles ($3). Sweet oranges to the tune of 100 he brought along. I bought the same for the mess. After reading a few items in the papers, I again turned in at 12 o'clock at night. . . .

Dec. 3, 1862. Terrible was the effect of our supping upon clams last night. All complained of a hard night's rest. We all suffered so much, indeed, that we concluded not to have any more clams for tea hereafter. The day commenced with a sort of drizzling rain—not enough fluid to constitute a shower but sufficiently to make it disagreeable. Report 5 sick today to the captain, they being, with the addition of Jacob Kingsley, lds.—adenitis, the same as yesterday. Read the papers and found that instead of "all being quiet on the Potomac" [from "All's quiet on the Potomac," so frequently repeated in bulletins of the Secretary of War that the expression came to be popularly used, finding its way into a number of songs as well as into ordinary conversation], our Army was on the forward movement. Also seen that a schoolmate of mine, Howard McIlvain of the Army, a commissioned officer [lieutenant, Independent Battery D, Pennsylvania Light Artillery], is numbered with the dead [killed in action "while firing one of his pieces, by the bursting of a 20-pounder shell directly in front of him" during an engagement at Warrenton Springs, Virginia, on November 15, 1862]. Poor fellow—he always was a good-hearted companion and died too soon for science. But such are the fortunes of war. . . .

That pleasant intruder, sand fly, has made its appearance in our midst today. Comment is not necessary. Thermometer 60° Fahr. Dull! Dull!! Dull!!! is the day. Nothing to do. Endeavored to kill time, and succeeded in consuming some, by reading two of ye light literature—viz., Chas. Lever's "One of Them" [New York: Harpers, 1861; a minor work of Charles James Lever, Irish novelist] and the work by Anthony Trollope styled "The Struggles of Brown, Jones, and Robinson. By One of the Firm" [New York: Harpers, 1862.]—both good and humourous works. Still making attempts to rain—drizzle! drizzle!! drizzle!!! all day long.

Morgan Island [between St. Helena Sound and the Morgan

River, possibly named after a prominent family that had lived on St. Helena Island, directly below, before the war] sent a delegation of contrabands today to our ship with sweet potatoes and peanuts for sale. On account of their high prices none felt too eager to purchase. So contraband crowd pushed off again in disgust. Well they might, for we are not overanxious to pay those innocent causes of the war big prices for their goods. 7 P.M., rains at last in earnest. 8 P.M., retired to my room, ignited my light, laid myself on my berth, and read Walter Scott's "Fair Maid of Perth" until 10 P.M., when I turned in for the night.

[*The Fair Maid of Perth;* or, *St. Valentine's Day* had appeared in a number of editions, American as well as English, of Scott's Waverley Novels. Dr. Boyer read several of these works while on board ship.]

Dec. 4, 1862. Still continues to rain. Besides it being a rainy day, it is also rather a cold one, thus making it doubly disagreeable. Our only comfort is that we have some reading matter. Reported 6 cases to the captain this morning besides those of yesterday, George Briggs, o. sea.—laryngitis, and William Pfander, lds.—scabies. The latter is rather an interesting case, both on account of its itching properties and difficulty of preventing it spreading itself. After washing the fellow from head to foot with soapsuds, I anointed his body with ol. olivae. Will apply an ointment tonight, compel him to live a retired life in the sick bay for some time to come, also keep his bowels in order as well as diet him some.

Today, we, the wardroom mess, dined on some game shot by our obliging captain, who is himself a fellow member. The game consisted of curlew, snipe, and sand pedes [probably sandpeeps, very small sandpipers]. I must confess that the dose is not disagreeable to our palates, and all hope for a repetition of same dose. The dose was taken in the shape of a pie. 4 P.M., the *Tiger* left for clams. 5.30 P.M., the *Tiger* has returned with some clams. When asked, for I am the caterer of our mess, whether we wished any for supper, I answered, having not forgotten the effects of a certain dish styled clam soup, which was taken in on the 2nd inst., I emphatically answered, "No! No!! No!!! But have some for breakfast and dinner tomorrow." "Aye, Sir!" answered our steward. So much for clams. Wrote a letter at 4 P.M. to Dr. D[avid] P. Boyer [brother of the diarist, who served at one time or another during the war as surgeon with the 24th, the 99th, and the 197 regiments,

Pennsylvania Volunteers], 926 North Sixth Street, Phila., in regard
to medical lore. The thermometer stood 52° Fahr. in the shade
today. Supped on cold game tonight, which Capt. E. Moses had
the kindness to supply me with. After tea I smoked a Conchita and
read Walter Scott's "The Surgeon's Daughter" until 10 P.M., when
I turned in for the night.

Dec. 5, 1862. Two days ago it was drizzle! drizzle!! drizzle!!! Now
it is rain! rain!! rain!!!—so much indeed as to constitute a gale,
nautically speaking. Cold as Christmas. Reported but 4 cases to
the captain today: same cases as yesterday, except two less—viz.,
Collins and Kingsley. My case of scabies appears to be improving
under the oil-and-soapsuds treatment. Since it has become known
that scabies is about, nearly everyone has been showing their hands
etc. to me, the doctor, for examination, to see whether they have a
right to scratch. Knowing that they are free from scabies but merely
have a slight eczema caused by indigestion, I generally order a dose
of mag. sulph. and cauterize one or two eruptions, which generally
pains them so much as to [make them] come to the conclusion that
they have no right to scratch and I know it, or else I would order
them to the sick bay and stop their "baccy" (tobacco), so that they
won't come to the doctor again unless they are really sick. One of
the w[ard] r[oom] o[fficers] is nearly frightened to death (having a
slight eczema) thinking he has the "itch." In order to keep him
quiet, I tell him nothing to the contrary. I even restrict his diet
and order him ol. ricini, sulphur, bitart potassa, etc., which he
takes (to correct his indigestion), as he thinks, for the cure of
"scabies." If he had any idea that it was not scabies, why, he would
not take any medicine to correct his digestive organs—hence my
silence.

The thermometer today is 48° Fahr. We dine on oysters and
clams today. Having had some clams for breakfast, we concluded
to have some more for dinner. 2.30 P.M. Weather has moderated
considerably. Thermometer 65° Fahr. Sun once again sheds his
refulgent rays all around. In short, it is almost as pleasant as a
spring morn. 5.30 P.M. Another change in the weather since 2.30
P.M. Rains and blows like thunder! Sent per captain's letter to his
wife $2.75 for gold lace, $0.75 for cologne, and $1.25 for a Prayer
Book of the Episcopal Church, or Creed. Commenced Scott's "Anne
of Geierstein." Expect to finish it ere I turn in. 11 P.M. Finished

the greater part of Scott's "Anne of Gierstein." Actg. Master C.C. Childs observed an eclipse of the moon from 2 A.M. to 4 A.M. last night.

Dec. 6, 1862. Stern winter stares us in the face this morning. The storm, or gale, of yesterday appears to have been the settling point between autumn and winter. Thermometer 38° Fahr. Cold! Cold!! Cold!!! is the wind that blows. Reported 5 cases to the captain this morning—same cases as last sick list with the addition of Lewis Benisole, 2nd-c[lass] boy—urticaria. There appears to be an epidemic of cases laboring under urticaria. I invariably order ablution with soap and water [and] order a laxative, followed with muriated tinct of iron in gtts vii doses ter in die and apply a lotion consisting of ammonia carb ℥ i, plumbi acetas ℥ i, aqua ℥ viii ter in die.

Today our steward went on shore to rusticate. Consequently we had decidedly the worst dinner on record. Beef (God forgive me for calling things by the wrong name! I ought of said "old horse") constituted the principal dish, which was followed by something in the shape of pie, the crust of which would have answered for a drumhead, so tough it was. D— such a steward, say we all, when we well know that he could of given us something better. Killed our piggy today and found her to have measles. Fate of body— thrown overboard, being as she was not fit for man to eat. Bought 5 more hogs today at $1 per head. Hope they are not in the same condition as Miss Mary Ann Crocker (our dead pig's name). If found to be so when butchered, overboard goes their bodies. 5.30 P.M., continued to be cold. Read Walter Scott's "Count Robert of Paris" until 10 P.M., when I turned in.

Dec. 7, 1862. The weather continues to be cold. Thermometer 34° Fahr. Nothing of any importance transpired today on account of it being the day of rest—Sabbath. Reported 5 cases to the captain this morning—same as yesterday. All improving slowly. Have considerable difficulty in those common cases of abrasio. They as a general thing take on a malignant aspect, consequently take some time in healing. Spent the greater part of the day in reading Charles Lever's "The Daltons' or, Three Roads in Life" [Lever's longest novel; London: Routledge, two volumes, 1852].

Dec. 8, 1862. Cold! Cold!! Cold!!! Thermometer 32° Fahr. 5 A.M., sent boat to Port Royal, in charge of Messrs. Bacon and Murray, for the mail. I sent a requisition to Fleet Surgeon Geo. Clymer for medical stores. Reported 5 cases sick today. Messrs. Briggs and Crusey discharged to duty; and John Murphy, o. sea.—intermittens, and Sheldon H. Hoyt, 2nd c. boy—furunculus, added. 9 A.M. Capt. Moses and myself went in schooner *Wild Cat* to pay a visit to the Seabrook place on Fenwick Island.

[A seventeenth-century grant "originally known as Cartwrights, then Seabrooks, and lastly Fenwicks; situated between the Rivers Ashepoo and So. Edisto," above Otter Island. Acquired by Captain Robert Seabrook (d. 1710), progenitor of a large and influential family that spread widely over the sea islands, and later for a time possessed by the prominent Dissenter family of Fenwick, by whose name it is still known. The "Seabrook place" referred to by Dr. Boyer was actually on Sampson's Island, a small island cut off by a creek of the same name from the main Fenwick Island.[8]]

Had a pleasant time of it. Secured a lot of castor-oil beans and plucked a small quantity of cotton on said place. Took a lunch on schooner at 1 P.M. Returned on board at 3.30 P.M. tired and weary. Supped at 5.30 on snipe and toast. In the interior of the remains of a fort erected by the Rebels is an old English gun of Geo. Rex style—an old 24-pounder. Beneath the English crown and coat of arms was marked George Rex. Said fort was made of sand and plank.

Dec. 9, 1862. Weather moderate. Thermometer 46° Fahr. The mail boat has not returned from Port Royal. Reported 7 cases to the captain sick in my morning report—viz., Murphy—improving; Hoyt—improving; Benisole—improving; Lahey—better; added James Sullivan, o. sea.—sore throat; Thomas O'Neil—febre; Michael Spain, lds.—chills and febre. Discharged to duty Wm. Pfander.

The captain and myself at 11 A.M. had a lunch on oysters and at 1 P.M. dined on roast duck etc. The carpenter commenced to make a few shelves for my medicine bottles, the medicine chest being rather unhandy. Messrs. Hines and Childs returned on board, having left in two cutters at 7 A.M., at 5 P.M., with about 25 bushels of sweet potatoes. 7.30 P.M., mail boat not yet returned. Read until 10 P.M., when I concluded to retire to my virtuous couch and seek repose in the arms of Morpheus.

Dec. 10, 1862. Reported Messrs. Lahey, Murphy, Hoyt, Sullivan, Benisole, O'Neil, and Spain to the captain sick in my morning report. The mail boat returned from Port Royal at 1.30 P.M. Our worthy paymaster purchased several heads of cabbage for the w.r. m[ess]. Received the celebrated dead pledge (judgment note) [a mortgage on land and goods] held against me by Messrs. M.K., M.P., and B.F.B. [Michael K., Michael P. (attorney), and Benjamin Franklin (attorney, often referred to as B. Frank) Boyer, father and brothers of the diarist] as cancelled, I having sent the amount of said note ($215) home about a month ago. I immediately tore the note to pieces and scattered the pieces to the four quarters of the globe by allowing them to be taken up by the wind, which was then blowing. Spent the better part of the day "yachting." Retired at 9 P.M.

Dec. 11, 1862. Reported Messrs. Lahey—improving; Hoyt—improving; Sullivan—improving; Murphy—improving; and Geo. Gray, contraband—sore foot, in my daily sick report to the captain. Messrs. Benisole, O'Neil, and Spain discharged from the sick list to duty.

Captain Moses, myself, and two boats' crews went in the schooner *Wild Cat* in search of beef. After running about Fenwick Island all day, returned minus beef. I obtained a fine cluster of oranges, which I hung up in my stateroom, there to remain until I reach a northern port (providing I can preserve them sound that long), when I expect to take them to "Old Berks" [Berks County, Pennsylvania] as a specimen of South Carolina oranges. The thermometer stood 65° Fahr. in the shade today at 1 P.M. After reading until 9.30 P.M., I concluded to turn in for the night.

Dec. 12, 1862. Reported Messrs. Lahey; Murphy; Gray; George Thompson, sea., Chile—constipation; and Wm. Donalson, sea., Boston—sore throat, sick today to the captain. Messrs. Hoyt and Sullivan return to duty.

At 9 A.M. the captain and myself with an armed boat's crew paid a visit to the place of I[saac] Jenkins Mikell, South Edisto. Found it to be a beautiful place. The mansion was a large one, with sandstone steps leading to the main floor. Green shutters surrounded the windows. Eight rooms. Fine furniture, statuary plenty —one of Sir Robert Peel. Large amount of theological manuscripts lying around the rooms. Obtained several medical works. Splendid orange groves in vicinity of the house. Everything indicating that the owner was a man of means. The name of the place was "Home Place" [now known as Peter's Point Plantation—considered a typical prewar plantation]. His taxes for 1860 amounted to $390.72. . . . After roaming about the place until fatigued, we set sail for the ship at 4 P.M. and arrived on board at 6 P.M. tired and weary. 9 P.M., turned in for the night.

Dec. 13, 1862. Reported same cases to the captain today sick as yesterday with the addition of my steward, who has a slight febrile reaction. The carpenter finished the medical rack for the sick bay today, which is quite an improvement. This being Saturday, a day set apart in the Navy for mending clothing etc., I concluded not to go to any place today, so as to let the boys do some of their sewing and have a good time on board. The weather is altogether lovely—thermometer 68° Fahr. in the shade. Nothing of any importance happened today. Read the better part of the time. Wrote a letter to father, an answer to one I received on the 10th dated Nov. 17, 1862.

Dec. 14, 1862. Another week has been and is gone. Sunday, the day of rest, set in with a bright and beautiful sun in the horizon, everything appearing today as man would wish for as regards the state of the weather. All appear happy on board. One thing only happened which put a damper on our spirits—viz., the leaving of Actg. Ensign Bacon for Port Royal, there to do duty on board the U.S.S. *Vandalia.* He being the very essence of honor, consequently beloved by all, we all felt sorry in bidding him adieu; but such being the fate of war, we have to bear it. In order to show him in what light we held him, we "cheered ship" as he left the side of the ship—an honor of no mean import. May his career in this life be a happy and prosperous one—plenty of prize money and fair women. The wardroom mess lost one of its best and brightest members. Adieu, Frank. "Fare you well."

Reported same old cases in my daily sick report to the captain at 9.30 A.M. with the exception of Thompson and Donalson. All improving slowly. Since my steward is unwell, I have considerable duty to perform—both the part of surgeon and surgeon's steward. Today at 1.30 P.M. we dined on a roasted pig (barbecue), clam pie, etc. etc. etc.—in short, had a good old-fashioned dinner, ending with sherry. At present the larder of the wardroom is well filled.

3 P.M., the mail boat, Actg. Master's Mate Jas. B. Henderson in charge, left for Port Royal, to return on Tuesday, the 16th inst. May she have a fair wind and a good tide. May she return with a

large mail and late newspapers. 4 P.M., Capt. Moses and myself paid the schooner *Wild Cat* a visit—or, more properly, Capt. Jno. E. Pickle of said schooner—in the *Tiger*, I pulling one of the oars, boy Hoyt the other, and the captain acted as coxswain. It was splendid exercise; I perspired beautifully. Thermometer 58° to 64° Fahr.

Dec. 15, 1862. Sick list of this day sports three names—viz., Murphy, Lahey, and Adams. The trio improving under the course of sprouts [punishment] through which they are being put. Adams is using as a gargle for his throat acidum hydrochloric ℨ i, syr simplex ℥ i, aqua ℥ viii, M̶. Use three times a day. Also takes internally port wine ℥ i ter in die. George Gray returns to duty which consists in being "Jack of the dust" [paymaster's assistant] for the paymaster's department, he being able to attend to that work even with his foot somewhat tender.

The weather is rather disagreeable, the day being cloudy and somewhat inclined to drizzle. . . . Thermometer 66° Fahr. at 4 P.M. Ottar Island sent a delegation of two to the ship with peanuts (groundnuts) for sale at the rate of $3.20 per bushel. They met with a brisk sale, everyone either buying or taking some. They also collected dirty wash, to be returned in a day or two clean. I bought some of said nuts; ate quite a large quantity and was blessed with a pain in my bowels, they, the nuts, causing indigestion. My only safe remedy is to grin and bear it. 4.30 P.M., commences to rain. 7 P.M., stopped raining.

7.30 P.M. The lights of the night are out in all their glory and seem to shed their rays, like so many small suns, over the "dark waters of the deep blue sea." In other language, it is a beautiful starlight night.

Read until 10 P.M. Miss Mulock's work, the title of which being "A Life for a Life" [by Dinah Maria Mulock (later Craik), English novelist; New York: Harpers, 1859]. I found it to be a very interesting tale on account of the hero being one of the medical fraternity, one Max Urequat [Urquhart] by name. The reading of light literature is carried on to a great extent in the service on account of the monotony pervading. No prizes to be seen or captured makes it rather dull work and poor pay. Oh, for a cruise on the briny deep! Hoping ere long to hear the words piped "All hands up anchor," I'll close for the night.

Dec. 16, 1862. A stiff northwester is blowing all day. Thermometer 55° Fahr. in the shade. Reported Messrs. Murphy, Lahey, and Adams in my daily sick report to the captain. All improving gradually, or slowly. Daniel Bailey, one of ye bright contrabands of Ottar Island, wishing to have some pork, ignited the tall grass on said island so as to drive the swinish portion of said settlement toward his palace, and I must say he succeeded beautifully. It was a magnificent sight to see several hundred acres of land all in blaze. Rather a novel mode of hunting game.

2 P.M., the mail boat arrived from Port Royal with a small mail and oranges on board. Our old master's mate, William H. Thomas, received an appointment of acting ensign, which is a well-deserved honor. It is quite an item in a pecuniary point of view: instead of receiving $400 per annum [actually $40 a month], as heretofore, he is the happy recipient of $1200 per annum. In the language of the poet I must exclaim, "Well done, good and happy old boy! Bully for you!" Our paymaster's steward also was one of "ye lucky dogs." He had the pleasure of being appointed an acting master's mate, which increases his pay from $30 per month as paymaster's steward [the complement being under a hundred] to $40 per month. I had the pleasure of receiving two letters—one dunning me for a V and the other for the small sum of $60.75—anything else than agreeable. We also received newspapers as late as the 2nd of December. After writing down roughly the items of today's doings and reading some of the papers, I finally turned in for the purpose of resting my weary bones. Recd. a letter from Beta and one from B. Frank today, which I shall answer in a day or two. . . .

Dec. 17, 1862. Still continues to blow. Weather somewhat colder than usual. Thermometer 48° Fahr. Reported one case sick—viz., R.D. Adams—in my daily report to the captain, Messrs. Lahey and Murphy returning to duty today. Nothing of any importance transpired today. I ate, drank, and read the best part of the time. Upon giving it a careful perusal, I find the President's Second Annual Message to Congress to be just the thing for the times, and I heartily endorse the sentiment expressed therein. Well done, honest "Old Abe"! You are the right man in the right place! I also was well pleased with Secretary Welles' report. Like his ideas about increasing the Navy, especially as regards the building of ironclads.

[The subject of ironclads, said Secretary Welles, was still "full of difficulty and doubt." Since the *Monitor's* engagement with the *Merrimac* at Hampton Roads, Virginia, on March 9, however, the hitherto lagging construction program had been hurried forward with enthusiasm. Most of the vessels were built on the plan of the *Monitor* (the popular "cheese box on a raft"), a turreted vessel designed by John Ericsson of New York, which, though slow and clumsy, could, because of its light draft and heavy armament, penetrate the inner waters of the coast. Though the North actually built more of the new-type fighter than did the South, Federal naval personnel was obviously alarmed by the threat of Confederate ironclads and by the raidings of the "pirate ship" *Alabama*.]

Secretary Chase is a financier of Old Man Morris' style of Revolutionary fame. He both understands and knows what he is about. Go in, Salmon! You're a trump!

[Salmon P. Chase, Secretary of the Treasury from March, 1861, to July, 1864. The press in general and financiers in particular were bitterly criticizing the secretary. Specie payments had been suspended in December, 1861, and United States Notes, commonly called "greenbacks," had become the basic money of the country. Inflation, though it aided in some ways the poor, particularly the farmers, brought many difficulties. The reluctant appointment of Jay Cooke of Philadelphia as subscription agent for the sale of government bonds, the setting up of a realistic though long delayed tax program, and the establishment of a national banking system helped appreciably—but condemnation of Chase still prevailed, and time has lessened it but little.]

Dec. 18, 1862. Stern winter has come at last. Jack Frost is about. Thermometer 31° Fahr. this morning at 6 A.M. and 34° Fahr. at 8 A.M. Reported one case sick today—viz., Geo. Parker, o. sea., Havre, 21 yrs.—otalgia. My steward, R.D. Adams, returns to duty. Wrote several letters—one to Beta, enclosing $2, and one to B. Frank, informing him that I would send him on Monday per Adams Express the sum of $100—$60 for his pile and $40 for M.K.'s pile. The peanut venders from Ottar Island paid us a visit at 3 P.M. and sold their trash like hot cakes. Sent some cotton picked on Fenwick Island home in a letter to father as a speciment of Confederate cotton. Capt. Jno. E. Pickle, quartermaster, commanding schr. *Wild Cat*, brought 8 curlew on board as a present to Capt. Moses. Pickle has become quite a Nimrod, something unusual for an old tar. He is our principal fisherman—a regular Izaak Walton.

Dec. 19, 1862. Thick shoes and heavy overcoats are all the go at present. Everyone that has anything of the kind wears it today, for the cold weather has come at last. Thermometer 37° Fahr. I have placed on my back one of "ye seamless overcoats" provided for the seamen by the Navy Department, in order to keep myself warm. Reported John Smith, ord. sea., affected with a large boil on his cheek, sick to the captain at 9 A.M. and discharged Parker to duty. Dull times here in St. Helena Sound. Nothing to see, do, read, or eat of any account except contrabands, physic some of the boys, old superannuated newspapers, and hard-tack and salt junk [hard salted beef supplied to ships].

Dec. 20, 1862. The boys are in good spirits on account of this being Saturday, the day for them to overhaul their bags, do their sewing, etc., no work as a general thing being demanded of them; in short, this is a holiday, or day set apart for sailors to loaf around the decks. I very seldom have a large sick list either on Saturday or Sunday; consequently I had but one man to report sick—viz., John Smith. The weather has moderated some—thermometer 45° Fahr. The paymaster paid me $75 on account of pay, which together with $25 I intend sending per Adams Express Company to B.F.B. Our new ensign, Wm. H. Thomas, intends going after the mail to Port Royal tomorrow; so I will send the money with him for to deposit it in the hands of said company's agents at Hilton Head. Bought four small porkers for the wardroom mess at 75/100 dolls. per head. We intend to fatten them and, after being fed for several weeks, have them barbecued one at a time. Killed, or butchered, one of our old stock, which our steward intends to roast for us tomorrow. Spent the latter part of the day in making out my yearly return of medicines, stores, etc. to the fleet surgeon —at least so much of it as to prepare the papers. I will fill them up on Jan. 1st, 1863.

Dec. 21, 1862. Actg. Ensign Wm. H. Thomas left today at 1 P.M. for Port Royal with the mail, accompanied as usual with an armed crew of six men, in the 2nd cutter. May he have a pleasant time and return with a large mail. Actg. Master R.B. Hines left in the schr. *Wild Cat* for Fenwick Island in search of bullock. May he return with two or three oxen so that all hands may have the pleasure of feasting on fresh beef on the 25th of December, or, more properly speaking, Christmas. The thermometer indicated the temperature to be 32° Fahr. at 7 A.M. and 40° Fahr. at 10 A.M. —rather cool for Dixie. John Smith on sick list.

Dec. 22, 1862. John Smith still continues to remain on the sick list. He is improving slowly. Temperature 39° Fahr. at 6 A.M. and 46° Fahr. at 9 A.M. At 9.30 A.M. heard heavy firing from the schooner *Wild Cat,* which was stationed in the Ashapo River [Ashepoo River, flowing into St. Helena Sound]. Sent Actg. Master's Mate Jas. B. Henderson with 12 armed men in the 1st cutter to ascertain the cause of said firing. Returned at 4:30 P.M. and reported the capture of Thos. Crummy and William Lahey, two of our men, by the Rebels. The firing was done by Capt. Pickle and crew of schr. *Wild Cat,* who were shelling the enemy on the mainland. He (Mr. Henderson) brought along the body of a beef, which Richard Costar, quarter gunner [petty officer who assisted the gunner—now called gunner's mate] had shot. I suppose his (the bullock's) weight was somewhere in the neighborhood of 1,000 lbs. Thus we have plenty of fresh beef, at the sacrifice of two good men—rather costly beef and dear amusement. I hope the poor boys will "fare well" in Dixie. 2 A.M. the second cutter with our ensign, Mr. Thomas, in charge arrived, having an actg. master's mate and paymaster's steward with him—also a large mail. I received a sporting paper—nary letter. Read some of the captain's papers from 2 A.M. until 4.30 A.M., when I turned in again.

Dec. 23, 1862. Added one patient more to, or on, my sick list besides John Smith, who is improving (I lanced his cheek the second time)—viz., William Price, coxswain of the gig—intermittens. Today was one of Nature's pet days, the sun being out in all his glory. All hands are rather down in the mouth on account of their messmates Crummy and Lahey being taken prisoners. Everyone pities them. Had some of the fresh beef for dinner. It is very tender and juicy.

Dec. 24, 1862. Three "sick sisters" (as the crew call them) today —viz., Messrs. Smith, Price, and Hoyt. Thermometer 57° Fahr. Took a sail in the schooner *Wild Cat* in company with the captain from 1.30 P.M. to 6 P.M. On account of tonight being Christmas

Eve, the captain gave forty of the boys liberty to spend a few hours on shore. So at 7 P.M. the captain, Paymaster Murray, Actg. Master Childs, Actg. Master's Mate James B. Henderson, and Actg. Asst. Surgeon Boyer with the above number of boys started for and landed on Ottar Island, the place occupied by King Ceaser. After we landed, the boys started on a double quick for one of the mansions, arousing up on their way King Ceaser and family, who were rather astonished. After the candles were all ignited, one John Brown (a darky) struck up a jig on his violin, and the boys commenced to dance, or rather make attempts. John Brown was mounted on a chair in one corner sawing away. Lewis Y. Close kept a bar in another corner, dealing out Adam's ale and cigars. The fair sex were represented by Aunt Peggy, aged 60 years, who danced every sett (at least 20 times); her daughters Maria and Rina; and Milie, Bailey's wife—all colored. The way the boys hugged the ladies was not slow. In short, to use their expression, they (the boys) had a *damn good time!* Thomas O'Neil, who is a wit, sang several songs and danced hornpipes not a few. Our carpenter, Chas. Callon, Quartermaster Scott, and Donalson, a seaman, also gave us several good songs, such as "Paddy's Wedding," "Och! Laroy," "Columbia, the Gem of the Ocean" [presumably by David T. Shaw, although Thomas A. Beckett also is said to have claimed ownership; frequently called "The Red, White, and Blue," which Boyer lists as a separate song], "Met Me by Moonlight" [probably "Meet Me by Moonlight Alone," a popular song by Joseph Augustine Wade, Irish composer, which appeared in *Fraser's Magazine* for October, 1834], "The Pretty Cabin Boy" [probably "The Cabin Boy," by W. H. Ware, words by T. Dibdin], "Red White, and Blue," and others both nautical and sentimental. I must confess that I also felt elated, for I danced several times myself. The boys gave three cheers for our, the best of, captain. Everything passed muster. All enjoyed themselves. After dancing, singing, etc. until all were fatigued, we came on board at 10 P.M.—rather an early hour. I doubt whether many young men up North retired as early on the same night.

Dec. 25, 1862. Christmas, as a general thing, on the blockade is a dull day, but I must say that the boys of the *Fernandina* had a pleasant time, or rather spent a "merry Christmas." The day was a lovely one, the sun shining in all its glory; thermometer 59° Fahr.

Barry University Library

Miami, FL 33161

The members of the wardroom had a dinner consisting of the following dishes: 1st course—clam soup; 2nd course—roasted pig, clam pie, sweet and Irish potatoes, rice, apple sauce, stewed onions, etc.; 3rd course—plum pudding; 4th course—gooseberry and raspberry pies, with ale; 5th course—cigars, pipes, and Lynchburg [tobacco]. The steerage mess also dined well. The crew all had roast pigs for dinner in their respective messes. At 6 P.M. the crew had a minstrel performance, the principal leaders being Jerry, Tommy, Dick, and Billy. Jerry made a temperance speech, which was rich, and sang the following songs: "Jeremiah's Lament" [probably "The Destruction of Jerusalem. Jeremiah's Lament," a sacred song, music by F. Hiller], "Mickey Free," etc. Tommy sang "The Happy Land of Canaan," "Paddy's Wedding," "The Union Forever" [no doubt "The Battle-Cry of Freedom," a Northern rallying song during the Civil War, the author of which, George F. Root, wrote also "Just Before the Battle, Mother" and "Tramp, Tramp, Tramp the Boys are Marching"], etc. Both Jerry and Tommy danced several dances, performed several pieces, and held several dialogues in the Irish language. Mr. Gibson had the kindness to play the violin for the boys. The riding of the jackass [hawse bag, a bag stuffed with sawdust or other substance for closing a hawse hole] by O'Neil and Riordan was rich. At 8 o'clock, when hammocks was piped down, the boys left, some to turn in, others to keep their watches—all well satisfied with their sport.

Reported Smith and Hoyt sick in my morning report. Paid my barber bill for two months in advance. Turned in at 9 P.M., fatigued.

Dec. 26, 1862. My sick list has dwindled down to one solitary patient—John Smith, still continuing to receive the benefits of the medical skill of *Fernandina's* "sawbones." Thermometer 54° Fahr. Foggy all the morning. One of the men captured a Secesh in the form of a snake, brought his serpentine majesty on board in a bottle, and presented him to me alive. I immediately transferred him to another bottle containing a little alcohol diluted, corked the bottle, covered the cork with a nickel, and over that placed a small piece of oiled silk. I will endeavor to take him up North, providing I can preserve, or rather keep, him in good condition until that time. Wrote a letter to father, in which I gave him a brief account of the way I spent my Christmas. Dissected the head of a curlew for the captain today—at least commenced the dissection; will finish the same in a day or two.

Dec. 27, 1862. John Smith, George Thompson, and George Briggs were reported in my daily sick report to the captain. Commenced to rain at 3 P.M. Weather somewhat cooler than yesterday—thermometer 49° Fahr.

Daniel Bailey, his father, wife, and son, Thomas Mathers and wife, and Miss Maria Grant, all denizens, or inhabitants, of King Ceaser's settlement on Ottar Island, came alongside at 10 A.M. to report themselves, they being on their way to the village on Camp Island. All were dressed in their best. Master Bailey was munching away on peanuts. He goes by the name of General or Colonel Webber, who was his godfather when he was baptized. Miss Grant looked as pleasant as a basket of chips. Tom Mathers had on his usual dry look. Bailey was as officious as usual—preaching honesty etc., at same time being an *honest* man himself. Old Man Bailey showed himself to be the same good-natured old darky.

At 4 P.M. a strange sail hove in sight, steering directly for us. All hands were called to quarters. Guns [were] trained and manned. I had the sick bay all ready for patients. Everyone felt elated at the idea of getting a prize. Some said she was the famous *Alabama* (290); others swore she never was built in America, being an English-rigged vessel. A few said she was a friend. I for one did not care a curse whether she was Union or Secesh, having confidence enough in our officers and men to be able to do some hard fighting. Finally we fired a gun, which was answered. The next scene was that our visitor was aground. As soon as it was dark, we signalized her, when she answered that she was the *Kingfisher,* come to relieve us, or rather having communications for us. Knowing who she was, we asked her (by means of signals) if she wanted assistance. She answered, "No!"—so we left her for the night by herself.

Dec. 28, 1862. Reported same cases sick as yesterday. All hands were called to muster at 10 A.M., when I read the Articles of War to the men. Sent the *Wild Cat* to the *Kingfisher* so as to communicate with her. The captain received orders to proceed to Port Royal, S. C., with the U.S. barque *Fernandina.* Whether we are bound homeward or not I cannot tell. All are anxious to know. I don't care a fig whether we go home or go to a new station, as long as my country needs my services. I like both the officers and the crew of the *Fernandina,* consequently would not like to leave them.   . . .

At 5 P.M. John W. Godfrey, actg. master, came on board to act as pilot on our voyage from St. Helena Sound to Port Royal harbor. Being short of staterooms, the captain and myself rigged up a berth on his (the captain's) sofa, the captain furnishing the mattress, sheet, and blanket—I supplied the pillow, pillowcase, and counterpane—which makes a comfortable bed, the only objection being that he has to lay amidships instead of fore and aft, but it will have to answer, as "necessity knows no law."

George Brown, the wardroom steward, transferred our "live stock," consisting of six porkers (pigs), from their former sty on Ottar Island to their present destination, the U.S. barque *Fernandina.* Upon their arrival on board the captain made the master-at-arms a present of one of the porkers; and I, the caterer of the wardroom mess, at the suggestion of the members of said mess, made the master's mates, or steerage mess, a present of another of said porkers so that they can have a barbecue on New Year's (the first of January, 1863). I understand from the tenor of the captain's conversation to me that we are to leave this place at 6 A.M. tomorrow—bound for Port Royal—which is one hour earlier than I usually turn out. The paymaster, T. N. Murray, who is a trump, informs me that he was made to understand by the paymaster of the *Kingfisher* that there was a mail for us at Port Royal, which we are rather anxious to receive. I expect quite a cargo of mail matter from home. Hope I will not be disappointed. The captain had a severe attack of cephalalgia this evening. I ordered for him pil. cath: comp. no. iv, which I think will correct his digestive apparatus and relieve him of said complaint. Today we were blessed with fine weather; the sun was out in all his glory. All appeared as merry as a young bride. In short, "everything is lovely and the goose hangs high," if I may use a common expression.

Dec. 29, 1862. The *Fernandina* is afloat, and that is all; the wind having left us, we are becalmed. Reported Smith and Briggs sick. Oh, for a breeze, so as to be able to anchor ere many hours in the harbor of Port Royal! 11 A.M. are compelled to let go our starboard anchor on account of having no wind and the tide being a flood tide. The male portion of Ottar Island settlement paid us a farewell visit at 4 P.M. They had quite a time collecting their money due them for washing, etc.

4

Interlude at Port Royal

At Sea, Dec. 30, 1862. No change in my sick list. Butchered one of our porkers last night so as to have a barbecue for dinner today. The 1st, 2nd, and 3rd cutters are towing us out of the harbor, there being no wind. 12 M. The *Fernandina* is out at sea at last. All her canvas is spread, and a fair wind is blowing. Dined hearty upon roasted pig. All appear lively. As usual, the wind is dead ahead.

Port Royal, S. C., Dec. 31, 1862. Same patients as yesterday. We are sailing around outside the harbor of Port Royal. After tacking ship about 100 times, we finally at 4.15 P.M. arrived near enough to the *Wabash* to let go our starboard anchor. The captain and myself went on board the *Wabash*, he to report and I to see the fleet surgeon. I also found out that we were bound for St. Simons, Ga., which just suits my fancy.

[According to U.S. Geographic Board ruling St. Simon; in official war records St. Simon's; usually in Dr. Boyer's journal and on the island itself St. Simons. The island, a beautiful place and long a center of plantation agriculture, was an important Federal rendezvous, "so near . . . the mainland that two or three rebel flags can be seen with the naked eye constantly floating, while the smoke of their salt manufactories blackens the sky day and night." After the war few of the former residents returned, and the island reverted for the most part to its precolonization use as a hunting and fishing area. A half century or more later it began to be developed and is today a popular summer resort.[9]]

Nothing of any importance transpired today except to find that I happened not to receive any letters from home when the mail came on board. Rather agreeable!

Jan. 1, 1863. A happy New Year to all. This was decidedly the dullest New Year's Day that I ever experienced. Nothing to see, do, or eat of any account. I happened to come across 1 doz. of champagne cider for the small sum of $5, which elated some of the officers. Reported Smith and Briggs sick today. Paymaster paid me $25 on account.

Jan. 2, 1863. Miles Powers (sprain) and Chas. Callon (piles) are added to the sick list, making four cases in all. Paid a visit to Capt. Chas. McIlvain, 97th Regt., P. V.

[The Ninety-seventh Regiment, Pennsylvania Volunteers, was ordered to Port Royal in late 1861. In January, 1862, it was sent to Wassaw (sometimes Warsaw) Sound for diversionary purposes, and in March it landed at and took Fernandina, Florida, and went on to Jacksonville, returning to Hilton Head when the evacuation of Florida was ordered. A serious epidemic of fevers led to the removal in November of almost the entire regiment to St. Helena Island, directly across the harbor entrance. In the table of organization of troops in the Department of the South dated December 31, 1862, the Ninety-seventh Regiment under Colonel H. R. Guss is listed as a part of the military force stationed at "St. Helena Island, Hilton Head, S. C.," under the command of Brigadier General A. H. Terry. Charles McIlvain, mustered into service on October 17, 1861, for three years and resigned on June 10, 1863, was captain of Company H, recruited in Chester County.[10]]

Found him to be one of my old chums; had a lively time. He knew all my friends, both male and female, at Reading; consequently we had a pleasant chat over olden times.

Had our bottom cleansed today.

Jan. 3, 1863. We are alongside the *Vermont,* taking in water and provisions. Paid the fleet surgeon a visit; had a medical chat with him. Received a few medical stores today. Capt. Moses, Paymaster Murray, Ensign Thomas, and myself went to Hilton Head in the afternoon. Became acquainted with Colonel [J. H.] Jackson, N. H. 3rd.

[The Third New Hampshire Regiment, the second raised in New Hampshire under President Lincoln's call for three-year troops, was recruited throughout the state after the governor's offer of a ten-dollar bounty for enlistment. It rendezvoused 1,047-strong at Camp Berry, Concord, in August, 1861. Sailing south in October on General Sherman's flagship, the *Atlantic,* it reached Port Royal on November 4, but did not land until the ninth, two days after du Pont's gunboats had taken the Confederate forts guarding the entrance to the harbor. In early July, 1862, it was sent to Hilton Head, which became its base.[11]]

Drank a glass of cider with him that was made in the Granite State. Also was introduced to and drank a glass of whiskey with Capt. [Rufus F.] Clark [of Company A] of same regt. They are jolly boys. Purchased some lace for my coat, which cost me $4.37, some books $1.00, postage stamps $1.00, etc. at the post office in Hilton Head.

One has to pay four prices for everything that you buy here. The weather all along has been beautiful. . . .

Jan. 5, 1863. Reported Messrs. Callon, Gray, Briggs, and Smith sick today. A dense fog covered the harbor all day. Wrote a letter to Brother Mike. Sent the Reading *Gazette and Democrat* to Capt. McIlvain. Paid, in company with the captain, Capt. Beers [Acting Master James R. Beers] of the U. S. schr. *G. W. Blunt* a visit. As caterer of the wardroom mess I bought stores for said mess to the tune of $60. Read Dumas' "Three Strong Men" and Reynolds' "Palace of Infamy; or, White Slave of England" and found both splendid affairs in that line of literature.

[A number of Alexander Dumas' works, several of which Dr. Boyer read while on blockade duty, were published in translation by British and by American firms, some in inexpensive paper-covered editions. The subtitle of George William MacArthur Reynolds' *Palace of Infamy* is *The Slave Women of England.* The *White Slave of England* is listed in the British Museum and the *Dictionary of American Biography* as the subtitle of *The Seamstress* by the same author, although Roorbach gives *A Tale of Domestic Life* as the subtitle of this work.]

Turned in at 10 P.M.

Jan. 6, 1863. The same names grace my sick list as yesterday—all improving. I expect to discharge some of them ere long. The day was rather stormy. Rain and wind predominate. Heard today by means of Madame Rumor that there has been an armistice declared for 90 days between the Federal and Rebel governments.

[On November 10, 1862, Emperor Napoleon III of France proposed that his government and England join in suggesting to the American belligerents a six-months armistice and cessation of the blockade, but the British declined to intercede. Shortly before this time Confederate General P. G. T. Beauregard, commanding the Department of South Carolina and Georgia, had wired Governor Francis W. Pickens of South Carolina "urging the propriety of Southern Governors meeting the Northwestern Governors at Memphis, to see if propositions of peace could not be suggested." While doubting the practicability of the proposal, Governor Pickens had written to Governor Harris of Tennessee and Governor Brown of Georgia, asking their opinions. Peace talk and rumors of peace were unceasing, but even the most vigorous antiwar Northerners were somewhat fearful that an armistice agreed to while the Confederates were powerful might be interpreted by the South as a virtual victory when final settlements came to be made.[12]]

We obtained the news by, or through, our pickets, who had the same from Rebel pickets. Whether this is true I cannot tell. If so, I hope for the best. Once united under the "Old Flag" (the Stars and Stripes), we'll be able to defy the world and the rest of mankind— New Jersey included. Some pretend to say that our cause is lost. Others, and I think the most sensible, say that we never were on better footing. All we at the North lack is activity! activity!! activity!!!—more fighting and less talk! We have no mean foe to contend with—on the contrary, Americans like ourselves. So let us drop politics and put our shoulders to the wheel. What matters it whether Tom, Dick or Harry is a Democrat, Republican, or what not, only so that he is a good loyal man, able to lead an army to battle? This changing of commanders for mere politics is doing more harm than good.

Jan. 7, 1863. Charles Mowatt—sores on right inferior extremity was added to my sick list, thus making 5 cases. Capt. McIlvain, Penna. 97th, paid me a visit at 2 P.M. We spent a happy afternoon together. At 5 P.M. I accompanied the captain to Hilton Head, where he is at present staying, being a member of a court-martial convened there to try "all poor devils," as he says. I became acquainted with quite a lot of Army officers, amongst which were Captains [George C.] Newman and [probably David R.] Allen of a New York regt. [the Forty-seventh], both "hale fellows well met." For the first time since June, 1862, I had the pleasure of supping in company with one of Eve's fair daughters—Lieut. Stickler's wife—at the Port Royal House, the Continental [no doubt a reference to the Continental Hotel in Philadelphia, an impressive building at the southeast corner of Chestnut and Ninth Streets, said by *The Stranger's Guide in Philadelphia* (Philadelphia: Lindsay and Blakiston, 1863), to be "the newest, and being furnished with all the modern appliances for comfort, . . . probably the finest hotel now in the country"] of Hilton Head—and must say I felt rather awkward. Remained on shore all night. Paymaster paid me $25 on account.

Jan. 8, 1863. Discharged to duty Callon and Gray. Returned on board at 10 A.M. At 2 P.M. the captain and myself paid Capt. Shaw,

Company G [D], Rhode Island 3rd, Bay Point, S. C., a visit. Found Capt. Shaw, lady, and son, Lieut. Rawson, lady, and daughter, and Lieut. Barker and lady all at home. All were well and lively. The ladies were both pretty and sociable. After chatting etc. until 4 P.M., we left, after shaking hands all around, for our craft. I must confess I felt good when I had the pleasure of taking a lady once again by the hand. So much for the influence of ye tender sex over ye "lords of creation." After reading until 8 P.M., I turned in, being somewhat fatigued.

Jan. 9, 1863. One of the 2nd-class boys, Sheldon H. Hoyt— tonsillitis, was admitted on and Chas. Mowatt discharged from the sick list. Actg. Master Richard B. Hines left the ship; he was transferred to the U.S.S. *Vermont.* Actg. Ensign [Christopher] Flood came to report himself for duty on board this ship. Actg. Master C. C. Childs, being the only master on board, was appointed executive officer, an honor well conferred, as Mr. Childs has had considerable experience at sea. May he be successful in carrying out the duties of said capacity. I invested the sum of $4 for a pipe today. The seller pronounced it a meerschaum. Whether or no it is one I am not altogether certain, but time will tell. Received a letter from father dated Dec. 29, stating that all were well at home. Also received a note from the office of Adams Express Company, Hilton Head, S. C., informing me that there was a package in their possession marked to my address. Not having time myself to go after it, I sent three dollars to Actg. Master [Townsend] Stites of the flagship *Wabash,* asking him to obtain said package etc. and send to me by the first opportunity. After reading until I was tired of so doing, I turned in at 1 A.M.

At Sea, Jan. 10, 1863. No change in my sick list. Weather cloudy and raining. Set sail for St. Simons in fine style at 9 A.M. Thanks to the powers that be, we are afloat and out of Port Royal harbor. Nothing of any account transpired today. Read Dumas' "[The] Man with Five Wives" [published in translation by Petersons, Philadelphia, between 1858 and 1860] the better part of the day and found it rather interesting. Turned in very early tonight— 8 P.M.

Jan. 11, 1863. Sabbath Day. Nothing of any importance transpired today. We sailed along the coast of Georgia. Same sick as last report.

5

Desolation and Plunder
on St. Simons Island

St. Simons Sound, Ga., Jan. 12, 1863. Sheldon Hoyt returns
to duty; hence I have only three patients to report. The U.S.
steamer *Paul Jones* took us in tow outside of St. Simons Sound and
towed us into said sound, our station, at 10 A.M. It appears to be
a beautiful harbor to lay at anchor. There is said to be some venison
on shore—also beef. Not having been ashore, I cannot give any
account of the place. Resigned the caterership of the wardroom
mess today. Mr. Thomas, actg. ensign, was elected. May he have
a happy time of it. There are more cares than honors attached to
the caterership. The thermometer is 65° Fahr. in the shade—rather
warm for January.

Jan. 13, 1863. Messrs. Briggs and Grimes return to duty today.
Poor Briggs has in my estimation entered upon or into the domain
of phthisis pulmonalis; he still continues his expectorants. My
list sports one patient—viz., Jno. Smith. Weather still warm and
pleasant—thermometer 67° Fahr.

The island next the ship is called St. Simons, upon which is situated the mansion of the celebrated nabob of the South, Thomas
Butler King, who before the war was in possession of from 600
to 800 contrabands [slaves]. The mansion is built of lumber, being
a frame one, on the Southern style—viz., with large porticos,
porches, or verandas surrounding the same; in other words, it is
a beautiful villa. Fine orange groves in vicinity of the house. A
large avenue or park leading from one end of the island to the
other, of white or live-oak timber, making a beautiful shady drive.
Mr. King had two mansions, one at each extremity of said avenue.
Everything in and around the main mansion indicates that the
former occupant was a man of means.

[Thomas Butler King—lawyer, planter, state senator and later national
congressman, and diplomat—was important politically and economically.
As chairman of the House Committee on Naval Affairs he was instru-
mental in the reorganization and modernization of the United States Navy

in the early 1840's. A native New Englander who had become an adopted son of Georgia and a staunch Whig, he loyally supported the Confederate cause even though he had opposed secession. On Georgia's withdrawal from the Union he was sent abroad to establish direct trade with Europe, but his efforts were made fruitless by the blockade. After two years as commissioner of the Confederacy in Europe he returned to Georgia, where he died in May, 1864. At the time of the above diary entry King's estate, a large cotton plantation called "Retreat" at the south tip of the land (acquired by marriage to Anna Matilda Page, daughter of Major William Page) was, like others on the island, abandoned. Today a part of the land is occupied by the Sea Island golf course. Ruins of the tabby (a mixture of burned oyster shells, lime, and sand) slave hospital built by Page and a part of the avenue of live oaks planted under the supervision of Anna Page King may still be seen. Nowhere in the Old South in the days before "The War Between the States" did the gossamer mantle of romance fall more gently than on "Retreat." After Reconstruction the three daughters attempted to recapture the days that were past, even though they had to ride to church in an oxcart.]

At present no one lives there [on the Butler plantation] except 4 or 5 superannuated contrabands, who do the washing for the officers of our men-of-war that may be stationed here. Their prices are $0.50 per dozen, you find soap etc., or $0.75 per doz., they find all the material such as soap, starch, etc. There used to be, about three months ago, upwards of 200 contrabands living on St. Simons Island, but they were all, with the exception of the few above mentioned, sent to Hilton Head, S. C., by orders of the commanding general stationed there.

[Transfer and concentration of Negroes under the guardianship of Federal forces was not uncommon; at times parts of the "overpopulated field" in the coastal region were extremely congested. Despite the government's attempts to provide systematic labor at fixed compensation, the rapid shifts often resulted in poor living conditions and inadequate employment. According to Brigadier General Rufus Saxton, assigned in April, 1862, to special duty in the Department of the South "for the purpose of occupying, cultivating, and taking care of the plantations" under Major General David Hunter's command and "protecting, employing, and instructing the inhabitants who have not hitherto been accustomed to self-protection," the number of refugees in the colony on St. Simon Island in mid-August, 1862, was double that mentioned by Dr. Boyer. These had been "gathered and protected by the Navy alone, and thus far sustained without any expense to the Government." With "some marked exceptions," noted a naval officer in late June, "idleness, improvidence, theft, and a disposition to vagrancy" were "the besetting sins of the contraband race on the island.[13]]

Those poor innocent causes of the war (contrabands) cost the government a large sum of money, and I am afraid that the Gideonites, as the agents are called, are imposing somewhat on the government—in other words, making money. But I hope all may be for the best.

[The "Gideonites" (commissioners sent down by the Treasury Department to claim abandoned property for the government) were intensely unpopular. Military personnel resented supersession, and "cotton agents" believed "their interests, and their personal use of negroes, horses, and houses" to be "hurt." Not only was there duplication in the War Department of some of the prerogatives and duties assumed; there were "two sets of treasury agents here with equal and sometimes conflicting powers."[14] Dr. Boyer sometimes refers to the Negroes themselves as Gideonites.]

Our Nimrod, Jno. Pickle, started on a hunting trip this morning and returned in the afternoon with four curlew, five plover, and two ducks, after using up considerable shot. May he continue his sport, only have better luck next time. Capt. Moses dined with Captain [Charles] Steedman of the *Paul Jones* today on venison, rather a luxury. He appeared to have had a pleasant time of it. While writing up today's journal, 7 P.M., I hear Old John Brown, our musician, sawing away on his violin and some of the boys dancing to his lively tunes, which are nothing more or less than one tune—viz., "Plantation Walk Around" [written by Daniel Decatur Emmett, composer of "Dixie," "Old Dan Tucker," etc.]. He appears in all his glory. Every one of the boys likes Brown or at least appreciates his music.

Jan. 14, 1863. Continue to have one case on sick list. Weather same as last report—viz., 67° Fahr. Paid a visit to St. Simons in company with Capt. Moses and Paymaster Murray. A poor forlorn being in the shape of a female with a female child and two slaves (now free) escaped from Secesh and came to our fleet. She is the wife of a Rebel soldier and said that she could not stand it any longer in Rebeldom on account of the hard times. She was without money and food. We (the officers) immediately made up a purse for her; also supplied her with food and raiment. As soon as

"Jack Tar" heard it, they (the boys) also made up a purse, not wishing to be outdone by no one as regards charity. She talks anything but favorable of the Rebel cause; from her account starvation stares the poor class in the face. Well might we say, when asked the cause or effects of civil war, that the effects are "desolation and ruin; poverty and distress; anarchy and confusion."

The *Paul Jones* left for a short cruise. The *Potomska* arrived here after coal at 1 P.M. As soon as she has taken in enough black diamonds, she will leave again for her station, a few miles north of St. Simons. 5 P.M., a schooner in the employ of the Coast Surveying Department came into our harbor so as to be out of danger, it blowing a hard gale outside.

Jan. 15, 1863. Two cases to report sick—viz., John Smith and George Parker—intermittens. Thermometer 67° Fahr. Our obliging executive officer, Mr. Childs, ordered the carpenter to make me a new binnacle list [a sick list posted at or near the binnacle for the use of the officer of the deck], or board, and I must say it is a splendid affair. Paymaster Murray being rather costive, I ordered him a dose of calomel and jalap, which opened his bowels to his heart's content. Blowing a heavy gale at 8 P.M. Turned in at 9 P.M.

Jan. 16, 1863. Master James Holliday, 1st-class boy, became one of my patients today, affected with catarrhus, thus making three cases to report to the captain in my morning report. Blowing a cold, heavy gale all day. Thermometer 38° Fahr.—rather cold for the "sunny South." Overcoats were quoted at a high figure today. All complaining of the cold. I for one am compelled myself to admit it is *cold* for this climate. Up North this would be considered a warm day, but to have a change of 30° is rather too great a change. The U.S. steamer *Bibb* came into the fleet tonight, or rather this evening, at 5 P.M. What her business is I am not able to tell at present. [The *Bibb* was on her way southward to assist a lighthouse engineer in a survey of sounds and harbors with respect to coastal navigation aids.] Hope she may have a mail for us. If so, I also hope that I may be the happy recipient of several letters and newspapers. Our paymaster says that the dose consisting of hydrarg chlorid mitis et jalapa pulv is rather a tough pill to swallow and that he has had plenty of said article for the next ten years to come, so effectually has the powder done its duty—viz., physicking him almost to death, as he says. At the same time he is willing to admit that it done him good. Well he might, for it is the *ne plus ultra* of cathartics in this latitude. After having a social chat with the rest of the members of the wardroom, telling yarns (or rather spinning them), smoking, and reading, I finally concluded to lay my head on my pillow and court "tired Nature's sweet restorer". . . .

Jan. 17, 1863. Cold! Cold!! Cold!!! Thermometer at 7 A.M. 32° Fahr., at 1 P.M. 48° Fahr., at 5 P.M. 45° Fahr. Reported Messrs. Smith; Parker; Benisole, 2nd-class boy—intermittens; and Birdsall, 2nd-class boy—catarrhus sick, and discharged James Holliday. Received my wash from shore, all clean. I was surprised to see it done up so nicely. Will patronize said wash firm hereafter, at least as long as we are stationed here. At 8 A.M. the steamer *Bibb* and her tender put to sea. At 5 P.M. *Paul Jones, Sr.,* and *Paul Jones, Jr.,* arrived in the harbor. From the *Paul Jones, Jr.,* we learn that [on January 1] the *Harriet Lane* was captured by the Rebels, also that the Rebels had recaptured the city of Galveston, Texas—rather bad news. The Secesh lady on shore has left the "cat out of the bag"—i.e., from her manners and actions she turns out to be nothing better than a harlot. We will send her to Port Royal tomorrow so as to be relieved of her company. So much for Secesh lady. Wrote a letter to father; also wrote a few lines to Captain Chas. McIlvain of the Penna. Vol. 97th Regt., stationed at Hilton Head, concerning some ale etc. which the captain had the kindness to send me.

Jan. 18, 1863. George Parker returned to duty today, and Peter Quinn with a sore arm was added to the list. The weather is about the same as yesterday, only blowing more of a gale. The *Paul Jones, Sr.,* left this morning at 4 o'clock for Port Royal but returned again at 5 A.M. on account of the heavy gale blowing outside. The port watch had liberty on shore today. One of them, Geo. Briggs, brought me a work on cholera morbus which he found on shore. Our quarter gunner, Richard Costar, brought me the skull of a raccoon, and boy Allen brought me a cane and the antlers of a deer—quite a budget of relics. Dull and dreary on board today.

Jan. 19, 1863. I made my appearance on the quarter deck at 8 A.M. and found it raining. At the same time the weather had moderated some. Thermometer stood from 46° to 50° Fahr. all day. Messrs. S., B., Q., and B. still on the list. Sent $1 for postage stamps, with Capt. Steedman, to Port Royal. Took a stroll at 5 P.M. on St. Simons Island. Commenced at 8 P.M. to read Victor Hugo's great romance "Hans of Iceland; or, The Demon of the North" [English translation published in 1825, two years after anonymous appearance of the work] and read until 11.30 P.M., when I turned in, having finished the same.

Jan. 20, 1863. Still continuing to rain. Thermometer 60° Fahr. Same patients as last report on the list. Nothing of any importance transpired today. 3 P.M. ceased raining, and from all appearances there is evidently a going to be a spell of fine weather.

Jan. 21, 1863. Discharged all my cases on the sick list with the exception of Peter Quinn. Capt. Moses and myself went to the island with the intention of taking a ride, but finding that the carriage needed repairing, we postponed the same. Upon our return we found Capt. [Nicholas] Kirby, a.m. cmdg., U. S. barque *Midnight*, and his [acting assistant] paymaster, Mr. [Franklin] Miller, on board. They brought a mail for us to send North. Both staid to dinner. Found Paymaster Miller to be a jovial sort of a boy— splendid company and a "hale fellow well met." He has been on blockade duty for fourteen months and in that time had a leave of absence for the long period of *seven days*. Rather a tough pill to swallow!

Jan. 22, 1863. No cases on the sick list. All are well and in good spirits. The sun shed its refulgent rays in good earnest today. Thermometer 67° Fahr. Took a short stroll on St. Simons. While there, cut an orange twig for a cane and paid a visit to the last resting place of the late Asst. Surgeon U. S. Navy Dr. [Charles H.] Pile, who performed the duties of medical officer on the U.S. steamer *Paul Jones* prior to his demise. He died from the effects of chloroform, which he used to inhale at night, it being an old habit of his. Peace to his ashes. I understand that he is, or rather his body is, to be removed to Philadelphia, there to be buried in the family vault. I was personally acquainted with the doctor— made his acquaintance off Charleston while on blockading duty at that station. He was a pleasant companion and a skillful physician.

Made boy Allen a present of a blacking brush and a box of

blacking, in return for the relics presented by him to me on the 18th inst. He was well pleased with the same. A native of St. Simons, a white man aged 30, paid us a visit today and took along with him quite a load of provisions etc. He had a long history to relate about the former occupants of the island; says that he never saw better people than what we were—always ready to give and not take, as the Rebels used to do. From all accounts he had rather a tough time with the Rebels when they skedaddled for the mainland. He lives about seven miles from the ship in company with his parents, two old people aged 80 years, and a little daughter.

Our Nimrod, John E. Pickle, in company with two contrabands went in search of beef, venison, and turkeys. Hope they may be successful. Being somewhat fatigued, I turned in at 8 bells.

Jan. 23, 1863. None to report sick today. The boys have concluded to remain off the list as long as the weather continues to be so salubrious. All hands went to general quarters at 9 A.M. and remained there until 10 A.M. Read Watson [Thomas Watson, M.D., *Lectures on the Principles and Practice of Physic* (commonly called Watson's *Practice of Physic*) the second American edition of which, from the second London edition, revised, with additions, by D. Francis Condie, M.D., was published by Lea and Blanchard, Philadelphia, in 1845 and the third in 1857; a "comprehensive work," made up of a series of "celebrated lectures" delivered at King's College, London, during the session of 1836-1837, said to be exceedingly valuable as a textbook for medical schools, as a guide for young practitioners, and as a reference book for the "more advanced brethren" in the profession] and talked medicine to my steward the better part of the forenoon. Took a walk on the beach from 2 P.M. to 4 P.M. seeking sea shells etc., but was not successful as regards the shells. I did find a primer, Brown's "Primer" [probably Goold Brown, *The Child's First Book; Being a New Primer, for the Use of Families and Schools,* the sixth edition of which was published by M. Day of New York in 1827], which I will give to one of the boys so as to be able to learn to read. It will be just the thing, as primers and spelling books are rather a scarce article on a man-of-war.

The thermometer ranged from 55° to 65° Fahr. today. On shore the trees are beginning to bud anew, the grass is springing forth, and everything in the vegetable world indicates the approach of spring. Taking exercise on shore is a great blessing to us naval officers and is a luxury that few on blockade duty enjoy.

Jan. 24, 1863. Lewis Y. Close, lds.—sore foot was admitted on the sick list. All hands to quarters at 9 A.M. The suspected enemy proved to be the Army transport *Ben De Ford* with the 1st Regiment of South Carolina Volunteers on board. Col. Higginson and the surgeon paid us a visit. At 4 P.M. the *John Adams* also arrived with a part of same regiment. It must be remembered that this regiment is composed of ye intelligent contrabands, the commissioned officers being the only whites. From what I have seen of the contrabands, I must confess that in my estimation they are small potatoes. Their dress is blue coat and red pantaloons. Where they are bound for I cannot tell; in fact, I don't care. I have the smallest opinion of said Gideonites.

[The expedition, consisting of 462 officers and men of the First Regiment of South Carolina Volunteers (colored) under the command of Colonel T. W. Higginson, was on its way southward from Beaufort, South Carolina. Major General Hunter had in May, 1862, ordered the emancipation of slaves in Florida, Georgia, and South Carolina and authorized the arming of all able-bodied Negroes in those states. Three months later Brigadier General Saxton had been at his own suggestion authorized by the War Department to employ up to five thousand "colored persons of African descent" as volunteer laborers in the Quartermaster's Department, not more than five dollars a month to be paid to common laborers and eight to mechanical or skilled laborers in addition to clothing and subsistence, and also to enlist and train up to the same number of Negro volunteers in the army as regular soldiers for the purpose of guarding the plantations and settlements under Federal occupation and protecting the inhabitants from "captivity and murder by the enemy," turning over to the navy "any number of colored volunteers that may be required for the naval service." By November 12 more than a thousand able-bodied Negroes had come into the employ of the Engineer and Quartermaster's Departments, and the First Regiment of South Carolina Volunteers was filling up rapidly, five hundred and fifty being already enrolled. The troops, carrying "the regimental flag and the President's (emancipation) proclamation far into the interior of Georgia and Florida," demonstrated, it was said, superior fighting qualities.[15]]

Recd. the "Tribune" [probably the New York *Tribune*] of the 17th inst. and the "Free South" [a weekly paper published at

Beaufort, South Carolina, first appearing on January 10, 1863, and being discontinued sometime the next year] of the 24th (today) from the colonel.

Our Nimrod, John E. Pickle, has returned from his hunting excursion, having one hen and two ducks, as trophies of said hunt, in his possession. Rather unlucky. Nothing at all abashed by his failure, he one hour afterwards started on a fishing and clamming trip and returned at 7 P.M. with any amount of clams and fish, saying that where he obtained this load he could get as many clams and fish as our first cutter could carry. He is rather pleased with his success. "Bully for Pickle" can be heard all over the ship; "Pickle is the boy for us," and other expressions. Finally all his messmates gave three cheers for Capt. John E. Pickle, ex-quartermaster commanding, of the schooner *Wild Cat*. Pickle stock is high at present. I hope that he will drop the gun and return once again in good earnest to carry out the precepts of Izaak Walton—i.e., to his dinky, rod, net, and line.

I took a long walk today on St. Simons Island in company with Paymaster Murray. We had a pleasant time of it searching for relics; but finding none, being fatigued, we finally returned on board at 3.30 P.M. The black regiment are having a gay time of it on shore, singing "Glory, Hallelujah!"—a tune which I understand cost the government $200,000 to learn said contrabands to sing it—so says Father French.

[The Reverend Mansfield French, army chaplain, who was active in the work among the colored people under the protection of the military in the Department of the South. In October, 1865, he became chaplain of the 136th Regiment of United States Colored Infantry, organized at Atlanta the previous July. The diarist's reference to cost may be an allusion to some of the expense incurred by the government in its experiment in "instruction and management of the negroes within the lines of the United States army, at Port Royal and its vicinity"; according to one estimate quoted shortly afterwards, "the cost of rations . . . a part of which were consumed in this experiment, was . . . $100,000 per day."[16]]

Jan. 25, 1863. Same sick as last report. Being the day of rest, Sabbath Day, today, the starboard watch had liberty on shore. The Gideonites appear to be on a plundering expedition. They are removing everything from the Butler King place; even the window sashes and panes are taken on board their steamer. When asked the question by what right they plunder, they answer, "We take those things for the government"—as though Uncle Sam depended upon the sale of old iron, window sashes, etc. for the purpose of carrying on the war! The black cattle were working all day, plundering etc, not having the least regard for the day. I sincerely hope that a day of retribution "am a coming" so that the Gideonites will receive their just dues. I, for one, do not consider the officers of said regiment worthy the respect of gentlemen.

Took a stroll over the island in the forenoon, but finding too many "mokes" [Negroes] about, I cut a bee line for the good old ship *Fernandina*. Feeling rather unwell, I took pil. cath: comp. no. iii. They had the desired effect somewhat; hope by morning to be relieved of my cephalalgia. Read until 9 P.M., when I turned in, the work of Frank Forester [pseudonym of Henry William Herbert, editor] titled "Mr. Sponge's Sporting Tour" [Robert Smith Surtees (New York: Stringer and Townsend, 1856; first issue of Frank Forester's edition, and first American edition of "Mr. Sponge")], which I find to be both humorous and interesting. The day has been rather disagreeable—rain one hour, sunshine another, foggy the next, and ending up with a cold drizzly rain and wind.

Jan. 26, 1863. Messrs. Close and Birdsall reported sick. The Captain and myself in the 1st cutter (Dick Welsh, coxswain) paid a visit to Jakel Island.

[Jekyll (U.S. Geographic Board ruling; Jekyl in official war records; Jakyl and Jekyl in coastal usage; and Jakel or Jakell in Dr. Boyer's journal) Island, immediately south of St. Simon, was presumably given the name by General Oglethorpe in honor of Sir Joseph Jekyll, benefactor of the colony of Georgia. There are stories, however, that the name (through corruption) came from a Frenchman called Jacques, who in the 1600's operated there a supply and receiving station for pirates and buccaneers. The last slaves brought directly to the United States from Africa were disembarked on the island. The Captain Lamar referred to below by Dr. Boyer—Captain (later Colonel) Charles A. Lamar (killed in Wilson's raid in Alabama and Georgia in June, 1865), commander of the Seventh Battalion, Georgia Mounted Rifles, comprising seven companies—was the owner of the slave yacht *Wanderer*, which landed a cargo there on November 28, 1858. Its past glories ended by the war, the island was bought in 1886 by a group of America's richest business men. The lesser financiers lived in their "cottages" of twelve to twenty rooms, but the great club house was presided over by J. Pierpont Morgan. There financial strategies were planned, there decisive political decisions of the Republican party were made, and there, it is said, was written the Aldrich-Vreeland Act of 1908. In 1947 Jekyll became a State Park of Georgia, open to all who wish to enjoy its incomparable beauty.[17]]

Found there [on the island] the ruins of an old camping ground. From the inscription on the boxes laying around the camp, I seen that a Rebel company commanded by Capt. Lamar of Savannah, Ga., occupied said ground ere the arrival of our gunboats. The walls of a large building also can be seen on said place. Adjoining said building, say 40 rods from the house, is a family graveyard. Therein are buried three persons by the name of Dubignon, one age 70, one 76, and the other 36 years.

[Le Sieur Christophe Poulain du Bignon, French adventurer, had acquired Jekyll Island in the 1790's, and his descendants held possession until 1886. Poulain du Bignon lay at rest "near du Bignon Creek with a live oak tree as his only monument," but other members of the family were buried in the family graveyard.]

All three are entombed in fine graves, or tombs, with the tomb-stones horizontal and consisting of marble.

After our return we dined, after which we took a tramp on St. Simons Island. Found the place drained of almost everything of any value, the Gideonites having taken all along. They left this morning—all three [Army] steamers, consisting of the *Ben De Ford, John Adams,* and the *Planter.* Thank fortune they are gone. I am told that they were ordered to do so as they have done by the government. If so, I take back, or retract, what I have written yesterday as regards them.

7 P.M. The *Paul Jones* has arrived from Port Royal with a large mail etc. Captain and myself went on board. While on board I had a pleasant time of it. Doctor Hazleton [Assistant Surgeon J. H. Hazleton] and [Acting Assistant] Paymaster [J. Appleton] Berry both being old acquaintances of mine, consequently we had a social chat of old times etc. Bought some tobacco from the sailing master at $1 per lb (5 lbs. in all). Received a letter from B.F.B. enclosing satisfied notes to the tune of $60.75, also a receipt from M.K.B. for $40. Fleet Surgeon Clymer honored me with a few lines as

regards some reports etc. Ex-A.A. Paymaster A.G. Myers sent me several newspapers. Read letters and newspapers until 12 M., when I turned in.

Jan. 27, 1863. Two sick men were transferred from the *Paul Jones* to this ship for a day or two, then to be transferred to their destination, the *Madgie.* One has a beautiful chancre; the other has rheumatism. Both are on my list and undergoing treatment. Messrs. Close and Birdsall still continued. The *Paul Jones* left for St. Johns River this morning [for the purpose of reconnaissance up the river to Jacksonville]. Dr. Bacon [Acting Assistant Surgeon James G. Bacon] and [Acting] Master's Mate [Allen K.] Noyes of the *Midnight* came in their 2nd cutter after the mail. Found the doctor to be a pleasant young man and a physician in every sense of the word. After dinner both left again for their craft. Wrote a letter to Asst. Surgeon [Henry F.] McSherry of the *Wabash* as regards reports etc., sending at same time, or rather enclosing in same envelope, a duplicate quarterly report for 4th qr., 1862, also a voucher for some groceries recd. from Paymaster Myers. I will send said letter whenever the mail leaves for Port Royal. Rained and blew hard all day. Spent part of the time reading "Mr. Sponge's Sporting Tour." Turned in at 10 P.M.

P.S. Upon reflection I have concluded to address my letter as regards my quarterly report etc. to the fleet surgeon instead of the asst. surgeon, Dr. McSherry, of the *Wabash,* as above stated. The above Secesh shinplaster, pasted on this page, I received from one of the escaped contrabands. It is a fair specimen of the Confederate bank notes.

Jan. 28, 1863. The man with the "white hat" showed himself to the boys at 5 A.M. while they were washing or scrubbing decks. "Jack Frost" made his anything but welcome appearance this morning. In short, stern old winter is come at last in the shape of a few flakes of snow and a cold northwestern wind (nor'wester). It has been blowing a stiff breeze all day. Thermometer ranging from 37° to 45° Fahr. Reported same cases sick—all improving. Took a run on St. Simons Island in order to take exercise and by so doing equalize the circulation of my blood, which was rather stagnant, if I may use the term. After causing all my pores to pour forth freely their secretions, I paid the guardhouse a visit and took a lunch consisting of a cup of coffee and two sea biscuits, after which

I tried my hand at cutting wood; finally, being somewhat fatigued, I returned on board at 3 P.M., well satisfied with my stroll. Finished "Mr. Sponge's Sporting Tour," which is a splendid work, showing the adventures of a sporting character or gentleman. 5 P.M., all hands to general quarters; 5.30 P.M., tea; and 9.30, turned in.

Jan. 29, 1863. Cold! Cold!! Cold!!! Thermometer from 4 to 8 A.M. 32° Fahr. Reported same cases except Birdsall, who returned to duty, sick. 12 M. thermometer 45° Fahr.; 3 P.M. thermometer 55° Fahr. Took a stroll on shore today; walked about 12 miles. Found a small book in one of the deserted mansions on St. Simons Island, the title of which is "Sermons by Wesley," vol. vi.

[The usual listing of Wesley's sermons run no more than four volumes. Volumes five to seven, however, of a fourteen-volume set of Wesley's *Works* the third edition of which was published in London in 1829-1831 are devoted to sermons.]

Received the above shinplaster from home, which I paste herein, as a specimen of the want of specie up "to hum." Capt. Jno E. Pickle, ex-quartermaster, returned from a hunting tour with 5 dead deer, 1 dead cow, 12 live hogs, and 8 dead duck—quite a budget, or load, of game. Pickle is in high glee. Won't we live high for a short time!

Jan. 30, 1863. Wm. H. Thomas, actg. ensign, became a member of the sick list today, laboring under odontalgia. ℞ ulmi cataplasm. Hence I have two cases to report to the captain. Dissected the head of a buck on St. Simons Island, and at 3 P.M. the captain and myself took a ride in a carriage and two, having the celebrated darky Dublin to drive us. We paid Old Man Cole a visit, who lives 7 miles in the interior; found an old man sick at the house who is going to his last home, he being beyond all medical skill, aged 80 years. Poor soul—all by himself and not a female hand to smooth his pillow for him. On our way we entered the graveyard of the Episcopal Church and found several splendid tombstones.

[Christ Church at Frederica, named for Christ Church in Savannah, stood in the grove of oaks that had sheltered Charles and John Wesley as they had preached to the colonists; there George Whitefield, William Norris, and Thomas Bosomworth had also ministered to the people. The structure visited by Dr. Boyer was built in 1820 from income from lands granted by the legislature in 1808. The church not only suffered much damage during the Civil War, but when the planters who had supported it had to flee from the island, funds from the sale of glebe lands were lost also. The present church, "hardly larger than a chapel," was built in 1884.[18]]

I suppose there are about 50 persons buried there; the following are some of the names on the stones—viz., Couper, Gould, King, Grant, Hamilton, Cater, Fraser, etc. One Dr. Fraser, surgeon in the Royal Navy of his B. Majesty, who died in 1836; a young lady, Rose Grant, aet. 15 yrs., buried in 1860; a young man aged 32 years, Couper by name, "who fell a victim to his generous courage"; a lieut. col. of the British Army, aged 50, who died while stationed on this island in 1812; and others.

[The names mentioned by Dr. Boyer are prominent ones in the annals of Georgia. John Couper (1759-1850), who, with his wife Rebecca and several descendants, lies buried in the Christ Church burying ground, emigrated to Georgia from Scotland, acquired extensive holdings, and became an influential leader in his community; the Couper family name Hamilton was derived from his friend and partner, James Hamilton, important in local affairs, both social and economic, before his removal to Philadelphia. James Gould, from Massachusetts, built the first lighthouse on the island (destroyed by Confederate soldiers in early 1862) and was appointed its first keeper by President Madison.

[Mrs. Thomas Butler King (see pp. 42-43) was famous for her skillful management of "Retreat"; her careful attention to the welfare of its hundreds of slaves, on whom an average of a thousand dollars a year was spent for medicines and care; the superior quality of the Sea Island cotton produced; the beauty of her horseshoe-shaped rose garden, which contained nearly a hundred variety of roses; and the ease and grace of her hospitality. Benjamin Franklin Cater, whose remains joined those of his wife Anne in the graveyard in 1839, inherited from his father, Thomas Cater, a tract of land that included the site of the momentous Battle of Bloody Marsh on the west side of the island, where General Oglethorpe turned back the invading Spanish.

[The Fraser family, originally from Scotland, was connected with the Couper family through marriage. The Dr. Fraser referred to by Dr. Boyer was Dr. William Fraser, mayor of Darien, who died at West Point, New York, at the age of forty-three and to whose memory a tablet was erected by his brother in 1837. The Rose Grant—"our darling Rose"—was Buford Rose Grant, youngest daughter of Hugh Fraser Grant. The young man "who fell a victim of his generous courage" at the age of thirty-two was not a Couper but John Armstrong Wylly, brother-in-law of James Hamilton Couper, killed in December, 1838, by a neighboring planter with whom he had had boundary-line differences, and the British army officer who died at the age of fifty in 1812 was Lieutenant Colonel Wardrobe.[19]]

After spending an hour in the "city of the dead," we left for the ship in our coach and two and arrived on board at 5.30 P.M., rather fatigued and hungry. I might mention that the church was a frame one, painted white, shutters green, with a belfry on top. The bell, however, is removed, the organ smashed all to pieces. The church is built in a beautiful grove of live-oak timber, the enclosure being surrounded by a fine fence (at least it looked well before it was abused by the "mokes").

[A few months later—on the morning of April 17, 1863—men from a Federal gunboat found on a stick in a prominent place in a road on the island a note, apparently left by a Confederate visitor from the mainland the night before, in which the desecration of graves in the churchyard by Union troops was bitterly protested. The outrages were attributed to the colored regiment that had stopped en route to Beaufort, South Carolina (see pp. 49, 50-51). "From information that has reached me," wrote the Union officer transmitting the protest to du Pont, "I am fearful the complaint of the writer is but too true. I have been told that the negro troops who were at one time stationed upon this island committed grave outrages, firing upon the church, pulpit, gravestones, etc., conduct that can not be too highly reprobated."[20]]

Everything in and around the church indicates that the congregation was an aristocratic one. The weather all day was beautiful. Turned in at 10 P.M.

Jan. 31, 1863. No additions to my sick list; continue same old two cases. The *Paul Jones* arrived today from St. Johns River. The transport *Planter* (of Small notoriety) [the name of the Negro pilot who delivered the ship to the Union blockading fleet being Robert Smalls, sometimes written Small] with part of the 1st South Carolina Regt. on board also arrived in the sound today. At 9 A.M. Paymaster Murray and myself took a ride, in the same carriage that the capt. and myself used yesterday, on an exploring expedition in the interior of St. Simons Island as far as the plantation of J. H. Couper, Esq., a distance of 15 miles.

[The Couper plantation at Cannon's Point, in the northeast part of the island—often called "Georgia's first agricultural experiment station"—had in its gardens rare plants from all over the world. John Couper, who built the handsome mansion described below by Dr. Boyer, not only developed the finest grade of long-staple cotton but also experimented successfully with the production of sugar cane, oranges and lemons, dates, olives, and grapes. After his death his eldest son, James Hamilton Couper, graduate of Yale and student of methods of water control in Holland, continued the work. He was responsible for the introduction of such plants as Bermuda grass and for progress in the production of sugar cane, cottonseed oil, and olive oil. At one time he had fifteen hundred slaves under his supervision. Like his father, he was known at home and abroad for his wise and constructive husbandry, his treatment of his Negroes, his fine hospitality, and his wide range of interests, which included the fields of geology and conchology. He opposed secession, but all his sons served in the Confederate army.[21]]

The mansion is, or rather was, a beautiful one, three stories high—fine verandas, green shutters, and plenty of shrubbery around the house; orange groves, bearing fruit, in vicinity of house; any number of outhouses such as bath, boat, gin, and other minor houses; large amount of books and manuscripts strewn around the rooms of the main mansion, such as geological, theological, philosophical, horticultural, etc., etc. In the basement large quantities of bones and minerals of all sizes and kinds are scattered around the floor. Broken furniture, dilapidated paintings, and broken crockery by the boatload are strewn around the rooms. I suppose there are about 25 or 30 rooms in the mansion; from the nature of the manuscripts I judge Mr. Couper to have been quite a scientific man. He was in possession of 700 Negroes ere the war. I obtained several old medical works and other books. On our return we stopped at Mr. Cole's place and found that the old man had gone to that "bourne from whence no traveller returneth." Peace to his ashes.

The captain obtained quite a relic today in the shape of a pianoforte. I might mention that while on the top of the Couper mansion I saw in the distance, say 4 miles, a Rebel schooner under way. Where she was bound to I cannot tell. We returned on board, tired and weary, at 5 P.M. The day was a beautiful one. The U.S. transport *Ben De Ford* arrived at 5.30 P.M. and let go her anchor opposite the ruins of a fort on Jakel Island.

Feby. 1, 1863. Messrs. Thomas and Close improving. Executive Officer Childs read the Articles of War, and Paymaster Murray acted the part of chaplain by reading the Episcopal service when all hands were at muster. The port watch had liberty today on shore. My steward, Russell D. Adams, being on shore, having violated orders, was put under arrest by orders of the senior officer commanding, Capt. Charles Steedman of the U.S. steamer *Paul Jones,* thus depriving me of the benefits of a steward. So much for disobeying orders. Hope it may have a beneficial effect. Wrote a letter to brother Frank concerning money affairs etc. Spent the better part of the day reading "A Report to the City Council of Savannah, on the Epidemic Disease of 1820," by William R. Waring, M.D., published by order of council [printed by Henry P. Russell, 1821], which I had the pleasure of finding in the deserted mansion of J. Hamilton Couper yesterday, and have found it to be both interesting and instructive.

The U.S. transport *Ben De Ford* left the sound for Port Royal at 4 P.M. The *Planter* followed in the rear of the *Ben De Ford.* Adieu, ye colored gentry of the 1st South Carolina Regiment of Volunteers. No serious objections to your remaining at Beaufort, S. C.

[Before the Civil War Beaufort, an old town on Port Royal Island founded in 1710 and named for the Duke of Beaufort, one of the lords proprietors, was a great Southern social center. When the Federal fleet attacked the harbor fortifications on November 7, 1861, its inhabitants went down the river in boats to witness what they were sure would be a Confederate victory. On the fall of the defenses they quickly fled from the area, and gunboats sent by du Pont found the town deserted by all the white residents but two—"abandoned to the negroes, represented . . . as in a lawless condition," allegedly "committing excesses and destroying private property." "AN AMERICAN NAVY OFFICER" posted on the principal house this notice: "Every effort has been made by us to prevent the negroes from plundering their masters' houses. Had the owners remained and taken care of their property and negroes, it would not have occurred. I only trust that we will not be accused of the vandalism."[22]]

Renew your visit the day after we leave this station.

The paymaster and surgeon of the U.S. barque *Midnight* were passengers on the *Ben De Ford* on a visit to Port Royal, the former in search of stores for the ship and the latter to report to the admiral for passage North, having been condemned by a medical board of survey and recommended to take a trip North for the benefit of his health. Not feeling well myself, I took pill hydrarg no. i (a gr v pill) at 7 P.M. and intend taking a Seidlitz powder in the morning.

Feby. 2, 1863. My cases are improving slowly but surely. None to add to the list today. Finished the dissection of the skull of the buck that I commenced on the 30th of January, after which I had it suspended underneath the crosstree of the mizzenmast, there to dry and bleach. Made an ointment composed of ol olivae, suet āā ℥ ii, creosote ℨ i: melt the suet and ol olivae, adding while cooling the creosote. I intend the same for a chronic case of cutaneous affection. Hope I may be successful in treating the case, as the patient is a fine and good-natured sort of a tar, being our master-at-arms, the terror of evildoers on board.

Dined on venison today, rather a choice dish for seafaring boys. Read some part of Dr. Waring's report of the 1820 epidemic. The boys are scraping the sides of the *Fernandina,* working today on the starboard side, finishing tomorrow on the port side, preparatory to giving her a coat of paint—not a coat of black, as heretofore, but a coat of lead so as not to be so prominent a mark for the Rebels. Bully for us. Won't we feel proud of the good old ship *Fernandina* after she has on her new coat!

4 or 5 contrabands made their appearance, having escaped from servitude. We intend taking one of them in the wardroom as one of our boys. My steward, Russell D. Adams, has been released from being under arrest with the caution of never violating the regulations again. May he profit by the same. I am very glad that he has been released, for I missed him considerable while he was under arrest. The case of chancre which was transferred temporary on board is improving under my hands. Will not be sorry when the *Madgie* comes and relieves me of the same nuisance. Today the body of Surgeon Pile, formerly the doctor of the *Paul Jones,* was disentombed and incased in a leaden coffin, to be sent up North. The original coffin was in a splendid state of preservation, not even moist; the coffin was not opened, so as not to expose the body to the air, but was immediately transferred, body and coffin, to the metallic one. Thermometer 58° Fahr. and raining slightly all day.

In order to show how great a change 7 months can make as regards the officers of a ship, I will quote the officers of this ship in the month of July, 1862, and those of the present time.

July, 1862	February, 1863
Captain—Edward Moses	*Captain*—Edward Moses
Executive Officer—R. B. Hines	*Executive Officer*—C. C. Childs
Sailing Master—L. L. Jump	*Sailing Master*—Christ. Flood
Actg. Master—Magnus Schow	*Actg. Ensign*—Wm. H. Thomas
Surgeon—Samuel P. Boyer	*Surgeon*—Samuel P. Boyer
Paymaster—Andrew G. Myers	*Paymaster*—Thomas N. Murray
Master's Mate—Wm. H. Thomas	*Master's Mate*—Wm. C. Gibson
Master's Mate—Jas. B. Henderson	*Master's Mate*—Jas. B. Henderson
Master's Mate—Wm. R. Morton	*Master's Mate*—Alonzo Townsend
Surgeon's Steward—R. D. Adams	*Surgeon's Steward*—R. D. Adams
Paymaster's Steward—H. M. Brown	*Paymaster's Steward*—Chas. Shaw

R.B. Hines was transferred to the *Vermont* and C.C. Childs made executive officer in Jan., 1863; L.L. Jump discharged forever from the Navy in Sept., 1862; Magnus Schow discharged in Oct., 1862. C.C. Childs came on board in August, 1862. Paymaster Myers was condemned, by my orders, by a medical board of survey and recommended North on the 17th of Sept., 1862. Paymaster Murray came on board in Oct., 1862. Wm. R. Morton resigned in July, 1862. H. M. Brown, time being up, went home in November, 1862. Wm. H. Thomas was appointed an actg. ensign in Dec., 1862. Wm. C. Gibson was appointed a master's mate in Dec., 1862. Alonzo Townsend came on board Dec. 22, 1862. Chas. Shaw, paymaster's steward, also came on board Dec. 22, 1862. Christopher Flood, actg. ensign (and sailing master at present), came on board Jan. 9, 1863. I might mention that R. B. Hines was and still is an actg. master. Calvin C. Childs, our present executive officer, also is an actg. master. Capt. Moses is an actg. master commanding. Surgeon Samuel P. Boyer is an actg. assistant surgeon. Paymaster Thomas N. Murray is an actg. assistant paymaster. The former paymaster, Andrew G. Myers, was an actg. assistant paymaster while in the service. He has, since he was sent North for the benefit of his health, recruited sufficiently to take unto himself a partner for life (a wife). I was pleased to hear that he was a sound man again, for he was very feeble when sent home. He also has resigned his position as an actg. asst. p.m. in the U.S. Navy and is now holding a position in the Naval Department at Washington as a clerk. I wish him all the good and prosperity that a man can obtain on this terrestrial globe, for he used to be a pleasant companion and a "hale fellow well met." Wrote a letter to him today, giving him "fits" for not answering my last.

The U.S. steamer *Madgie* arrived tonight from St. Catharine's Sound [St. Catherines according to U.S. Geographic Board ruling; St. Catherine's in official war records; St. Catharine's consistently in Dr. Boyer's diary]. I shall get rid of my case of chancre tomorrow. After noting down the above items, I turned in at 10.30 P.M.

Feby. 3, 1863. A cold northeast wind blowing. No additions made to sick list. The *Madgie* relieved me of the sick man, named Faunce. Poor fellow—he is sick enough to go home. The new wardroom mess boy came this morning. He looks more like a white boy than a contraband. I think he will make a good boy.

[Secretary Welles authorized du Pont on September 25, 1861, to enlist "persons of color, commonly known as 'contraband,' " for naval service "when their services can be made useful . . . under the same forms and regulations as apply to other enlistments" but at "no higher rating than boys, at a compensation of $10 per month and one ration a day." The Navy Department, he said, had found it necessary to adopt a regulation "with respect to the large and increasing number" of such individuals "now subsisted at the navy yards and on board of ships of war" since they could neither be expelled from the service to which they have resorted nor . . . be maintained unemployed," and it was not proper to compel them to "render necessary and regular services without a stated compensation."]

The news came on board that the *Alabama* had sunk the U.S. steamer *Hatteras* off Galveston, Texas. All on board were lost except four men, whom the *Brooklyn* rescued from a watery grave, having set the pirate to flight—she being afraid of the *Brooklyn's* bulldogs, I suppose.

[On the afternoon of January 11, the "poor little good-for-nothing" *Hatteras* was sent out by the flagship *Brooklyn* to investigate the *Alabama*, approaching off Galveston under British colors. Decoyed twenty-eight miles offshore, away from the rest of the fleet, the "frail iron shell" was engaged after nightfall in unequal combat that resulted in swift disaster for her, and her captain requested the Confederate commanding officer to send his boats to rescue the crew. The prisoners, 130 in number, were taken by the *Alabama* to Port Royal, Jamaica, where they were given a chilly reception by the English residents, and paroled. They were shortly sent home by the American consul. The *Brooklyn* may actually not have "set the pirate to flight" at all, though her presence may have hurried the withdrawal of the *Alabama*.[28]]

I sincerely hope that the *Alabama* and all her hellish crew will be sent to hell ere long. She has done more harm than we well can bear. Oh! for some fast steamers to come to the rescue and destroy the pirate—for in no other light can she be viewed; all her actions prove her to be a pirate, and as such she ought to be wiped out of existence.

Read Jeff Davis' message to the Senate and House of Reps. of the so-called Southern Confederacy—and a bombastic affair it is. It is just the thing to gull the misguided portion of the Southern States, consisting of nothing but false statements and absurd ideas —lauding the actions of the pirate Semmes etc., etc.

The *Madgie* left at 5 P.M., sailing down the coast—where bound I am not able to tell. The surgeon of the *Madgie* does not like the idea of having a sick man transferred to his care and coincides with me in thinking that he ought to have been sent to a hospital ship instead of a man-of-war doing active service. I understand that he intends sending him to the hospital for treatment. If so, it is a wise conclusion that he has come to, for I should have done the same, were he one of my patients, on account of the accommodations being too meagre for the treatment of a bedridden patient on board of us small gunboats.

Read part of a work by Jabez W. Heustis, M.D., late surgeon in the Army of the United States etc. titled "Physical Observations, and Medical Tracts and Researches, on the Topography and Diseases of Louisiana" dedicated "To His Excellency Daniel D. Tompkins, Governor of the State of New York," in 1816 [published in 1817 by T. and J. Swords, 160 Pearl Street, New York]—and I have found it rather interesting as well as instructive. He treats of yellow fever, dysentery, and scurvy. His treatment of yellow fever differs from that of Dr. Waring of Savannah in 1820. The pamphlet of Dr. Heustis I found in the deserted mansion of J. Hamilton Couper, on the island of St. Simons. I intend to continue reading old medical pamphlets until the arrival of the mail boat from the North, when I expect to be the happy recipient of a batch of late dates (newspapers and letters). We expect the

U.S. transport, or supply steamer, *Union* every day to make her appearance in St. Simons Sound with fresh beef and sutler stores for the fleet. With longing eyes we await her appearance.

[When the *Union* finally arrived she did not have the expected stores. On February 9 du Pont complained to Secretary Welles that he was not receiving needed supplies. "We have been out of oil for machinery," he wrote, "and coal is not more essential." He had, he complained, been purchasing from transports or wherever it could be found, 2 or 3 barrels at a time." Even when the *Union* came with oil, he continued, "it was stowed under all her cargo and the captain wished to defer its delivery until his return from the Gulf, which, however, I would not allow." Furthermore, "important parts of the ration, such as sugar, coffee, flour, butter, beans, and dried fruit, with clothing, . . . exhausted on the storeships of this squadron," were not on board.[24]]

Feby. 4, 1863. The schooner *Hope* arrived this morning with a mail. I received a letter from father—all well at home; one from Ex-Paymaster Myers, Washington—he is as happy as a mud turtle since his marriage, he says; one from Sailing Master Stites of the *Wabash,* enclosing me the package at Port Royal . . . , which proved to be some money sent by Magnus Schow . . . Several newspapers came by same mail to my address. I answered father's, Myers', and Stites' letters; also refunded the money to Schow by Adams Express. Today I was the happy recipient of a penwiper, which Capt. Moses' daughter had the kindness to make me a present of. We, the captain and myself, received our lace and cologne and I my prayer book, which we sent home, or rather to the captain's wife. On the 5th of Dec., 1862, I had sent $2.75 for the lace, $0.75 for the cologne, and $1.25 for the prayer book, but they cost me as follows: lace $3.81, cologne $1.00, and prayer book $2.25; express $1.25—in all, $8.31. Having paid $4.75, there still remains a balance of $3.56 due the captain, which I will pay over to him. The prayer book is a splendid affair, and Mrs. Moses deserves great credit for her taste, as well as her taste in selecting the lace and cologne. Mr. Charles A.A. Kerman, a friend of the captain's, also made me a present, for which I will thank him kindly by letter. I hope to have the pleasure of making his acquaintance some day. If all accounts are correct, he must be a "prince of good fellows," a "hale fellow well met." Long may he live to enjoy the pleasures of bachelordom. I read until 8 bells, when I turned in. A strong northeast wind has been blowing all day; also raining part of the time.

Feby. 5, 1863. Acting Ensign W.H. Thomas returned to duty. One man to report sick, and that is Close. Rain! Rain!! Rain!!! Thermometer 60° Fahr. A southeast wind blowing all day. The schooner left with the mail this afternoon—i.e., the schooner *Hope*. The *Madgie* arrived and left again today. Took a run on shore. Nothing of any account transpired today.

Feby. 6, 1863. Still continues to rain. Three cases on the sick list—viz., Messrs. Close, Hoyt, and De Cruiz—the first a sore foot, the second a sore throat, and the third chills and fever. The first is using cerate simplex, the second capsici gargle internally and ol terebinthinae externally, the third pill hydr no i last night and mag. sulphas ℥ i this morning, to be followed by nitrous pulvs.

Finding the tobacco I bought of an officer on the *Paul Jones* to be too strong for me, I sold three dollars' worth and gave the balance away. I intend buying some mild tobacco from the next supply ship that pays us a visit; in the meantime the captain promises to supply me. Took a stroll on shore today. Stopt into the "sanctum sanctorum" of Blind Jack (a poor blind contraband on St. Simons Island). Found him as happy and snug as a bug in a rug. Had a lively chat with him about his past life. All that he wants now is his wife, who is in Secesh, to complete his happiness, he says. Poor fellow—I pity him. The weather is somewhat milder at 7 P.M. than what it was at 9 A.M.—not as cold. Ceased raining at 11 A.M. and less wind.

Feby. 7, 1863. Close returns to duty today; Hoyt and De Cruiz are improving. Thermometer at 5 A.M. 32° Fahr. Cold as Christmas. 10 A.M., the weather moderated some. Paymaster Murray, Captain Moses, and myself left the ship in the gig at 10 A.M. for the shore. On our way we dropped alongside the flagship *Paul Jones* and took the senior officer commanding, Capt. Steedman, along with us on shore. After we landed, the paymaster and myself took a tramp. In our perambulations we came across a swamp, in which we saw a path. Thinking it to lead to the beach, we followed said path, and after travelling about a mile over ditches and through the mud, we finally saw a house in the distance. Being somewhat of an inquisitive turn of mind, we concluded to take a bee line for said mansion, which we reached after going through mud up to our ankles, tearing our clothing while passing through briars and bush, our feet all wet and our faces scratched. We found said place

drained of anything like relics. Not wishing to return by said route
—viz., the swamp—we attempted to return on the beach. After
walking a mile, we run afoul of another swamp full of water and
mud to our knees. Consequently we had to retrace our steps and
return by our former route—swamp number 1, where the mud was
only ankle deep—which we did, much to our chagrin. We reached
the wharf, or landing, at 1 P.M., tired and hungry. After we came
on board, we had to change our pants, shoes, and stockings, which
were all one mass of mud and thistles. Murray and myself concluded that we had enough of Southern bogs and swamps.

One of the contrabands on shore, Tom by name, is confined in
our brig in double irons for theft, the stolen property being found
in his room under his pillow. Actg. Master Edwin Coffin and Master's Mate Noyes of the *Midnight* were on board for a short time
today, having come for the mail. Mr. Coffin is an old sea dog,
and a jolly one at that. Actg. Ensign and Caterer of Wardroom
Mess Mr. Thomas went on a hunt with Pickle on Jakel Island
today, intending to return Monday or Tuesday. Hope he may get
some game. Sold my pipe, which I bought at Port Royal on the
9th of Jan. for $2.50 or $1.50 less than what I paid for it, the reason
being the want of good tobacco. Rather not smoke at all than
smoke bad tobacco. I am reading the Tauchnitz edition[25] of "The
Last of the Cavaliers" by Rose Piddington; two volumes, 1862,
which is interesting.

Feby. 8, 1863. The holy day of rest has come again. Another
Sabbath day has to be spent in St. Simons; hope to have the pleasure of spending many more Sabbaths at this anchorage, it being
so lovely a place to be at. Paymaster Murray read the service at
10 A.M. Antonio the cook returns to duty. None to report sick today. Actg. Ensign Thomas returned on board at 7 A.M., being disgusted with hunting. Dined on a roasted pig today. The starboard
watch being on liberty today, one of them, Dowd by name, brought
me an owl, a live one, he calling it a St. Simons canary. My steward,
clipping its wings, intends to keep it in the sick bay as a pet. The
day was rather cool.

Feby. 9, 1863. None to report sick to the captain. I have 3 or 4
"outdoor" patients. One has a slight catarrh, one is affected with
hemorrhoids, and two of them are laboring under what they call
"relics of old decency," I calling it venereal. Pickle, our Nimrod,

returned with 6 deer, 1 bullock, and 1 hog. Well done for two days' hunt. Took a short run on shore. We had some of the beef for tea, and I must admit it was anything else than tasty, being as tough as an old bull of twenty-six years. A coal brig arrived in the sound at 5 P.M. with coal for the fleet. From the captain we ascertained that our steamers off Charleston captured another Rebel steamer, making two prizes in the space of six weeks. Bully for the boats off Charleston.

[On January 4 the Confederate sloop *Mercury*, coming out from Charleston loaded with seventeen barrels of spirits of turpentine, was captured by the *Quaker City*, and on January 21 the Confederate schooner *Etiwan*, trying to leave Charleston carrying ninety-nine bales of cotton, was taken by the *Ottawa*. On January 18 another Confederate vessel, the steamer *Tropic*, loaded with 326 bales of cotton and "a quantity of turpentine," took fire while attempting to run the blockade off Charleston. Somewhat later two British vessels were captured: on January 27, by the *Hope*, the schooner *Emma Tuttle*, carrying an assorted cargo, most of which was reported to be contraband; and on January 29, by the *Unadilla*, the steamer *Princess Royal*, whose cargo, consisting of machinery for gunboats, arms, ammunition, medicines, and other items, was said to be an extremely valuable one.[26]]

Sold my lace for $3.75, having no need of the same. Finished the Tauchnitz edition of "The Silver Cord," by [Charles William] Shirley Brooks, [Leipzig: B. Tauchnitz, 3 vols., 1862] at 9 P.M., which I commenced on the 8th inst. The weather all day was lovely.

Feby. 10, 1863. The sick list appears to be slighted today as well as it was for the last two days, I having none to report sick today. I am glad that the boys are so well and hearty; hope they may continue so. Paymaster Murray and myself took a stroll on St. Simons Island from 2 to 5 P.M. searching for shells, etc. but found nothing of any account, only coming across any amount of marshes and sand banks. Actg. Master's Mate James B. Henderson, being under the weather some, asked me for and received a dose of magnesia sulphus, say ℥ i, which had the desired effect to such an extent as to cause him to remark that the "d— thing almost physicked him to death," and he had to be very sick hereafter ere he could be tempted to take any more of my "bitter lemonade." Poor boy—he'll feel the better for it tomorrow. Patched my pantaloons astern at 8 P.M. Turned in at 9 P.M.

Feby. 11, 1863. Nary patient made his appearance at 9 A.M., consequently no sick to report. Took a stroll in company with Paymaster Murray from 9.30 to 11 A.M. on St. Simons Island in search of shells etc. We obtained few shells and bespattered ourselves with mud. A regular "London fog" pervades the atmosphere all day. At 2 P.M. Paymaster Murray, Master's Mate Henderson, and myself took a sail in the yacht *Old Greeley,* nee *Old Abe,* and notwithstanding the fog had a pleasant time of it. Sold my revolver to Mr. Henderson for $13; being out of cartridges, I found the same to be useless. Commenced to read "The Twin Lieutenants; or, the Soldier's Bride," by Alexander Dumas [a translation by H.L. Williams (Philadelphia: 1862) of *Le Capitaine Richard*]. The *Paul Jones* towed the coal brig up to the coal wharf at 5.30 P.M. The coal wharf is about 2½ miles up the stream from our anchorage. Finished Dumas' "Twin Lieutenants" by 1 A.M., when I turned in for the night—rather an *early* hour!

Feby. 12, 1863. No sick today. Paymaster Murray, Master's Mate Henderson, and myself went a yachting in the *Old Greeley,* nee *Old Abe,* from 9 A.M. to 2 P.M., ascending the river [the Frederica, running along the west side of St. Simon Island] as far as the coal wharf, a distance of 2½ miles, where the coal brig is unloading her cargo of "diamonds"; landed there and strolled around the plantation, another beautiful place deserted by its former occupant, a Rebel.

[Hamilton Plantation, property of James Hamilton and later of James Hamilton Couper, was described by Fanny Kemble in 1839 as "by far the finest place on the island." The wharf at Gascoigne's Bluff was the island's chief cotton and lumber shipping point. After the war the estate was purchased by a lumber company, and a mill community sprang up along the Frederica. In 1927—the timber supply long having been used up—the plantation was bought by Edward W. Lewis, Detroit banker and automobile and aircraft pioneer, who as a "gentleman farmer" restored it and put it under large-scale vegetable cultivation, which he continued as long as economic conditions permitted. In 1949 it became a Methodist conference center—"Epworth-by-the-Sea."[27]]

We had a pleasant time of it. We went about, or tacked ship, no less than 30 times, the tide and wind being against us, so that we had to do the best we could.

The steamer *Flambeau* arrived at 11.30 A.M. and brought a small mail, some stores for the *Midnight,* and a 24-pdr. rifle howitzer for us, which we intend to place in the after part of the ship, thus making our armament amounting to 8 guns, or six medium 32-, one 20-lb. rifle, and one 24-lb. howitzer. I received a letter from Sailing Master Townsend Stites of the flagship *Wabash,* Port Royal Harbor, S. C., informing me that he had received my last enclosing the Schow money, also that he had attended to the same etc. The *Flambeau* left again at 3 P.M. At 5 P.M. the steamer *Madgie* arrived.

Feby. 13, 1863. Sick list without a name. Although the month of February is here—a cold month North—the weather for the most part is delightful, very like such as we find at home in early October. Such glorious sunrises and sunsets as we have here! Everything is altogether lovely, and the goose hangs high. Wrote a letter to father. Took a stroll on St. Simons Island. Capt. Kirby of the *Midnight* paid Capt. Moses a visit, also presented him with a bag of oysters, of which I had a taste. The *Flambeau* arrived in port again at 7 P.M.; will leave at daybreak tomorrow with the mail. Read a Savannah paper today of the 29th of January and found butter quoted at 85 cents per lb., tea $7.50 per pound, salt 25 cents per pound—rather tough prices. Wrote a letter to Captain Freeman, U.S. Navy [probably Acting Master Simeon N. Freeman, commanding the mortar schooner *C.P. Williams,* on duty in Ossabaw Sound but temporarily at Port Royal].

Feby. 14, 1863. Took a stroll on St. Simons in company with the "nipcheese" [paymaster] of the ship. While on shore I met Dr. Louis Michel, a.a. surgeon of the U.S. steamer *Madgie.* Had quite a pleasant chat with the doctor; subject—medical treatment of sailors. We both agreed as regards the mode of administering remedies to a certain class of patients—viz., malingerers. Promised to call on him tomorrow. Our mess bought a cow from King [one of the Negroes on shore], for the sum of $5, which we intend to fatten so as to be fit to butcher by the latter part of April. The *Madgie* was condemned today. She will go to Port Royal on Tuesday.

[Du Pont had written Secretary Welles three days previously that the *Madgie,* the *Mohawk,* and the *Potomska* were broken down. On March 7 he reported that the repairs the *Madgie* was undergoing at Port Royal could be only temporary. He requested—though not "in a spirit of complaint"—replacements for a number of other vessels in the squadron that also needed attention. "No one knows better than I do," he continued, "how unprecedented have been the requirements and tests on steam machinery brought out by this war and this blockading service."[28]]

The *Flambeau* left again at 7 A.M. for Port Royal. No cases on the sick list. Another one of our porkers lost his life today. Cause of death? Knife of butcher. Reason for same? Wanted on the mess table of the wardroom tomorrow, roasted, etc., for the benefit of the members of said mess. Am reading "Agnes Sorel" by G. P. R. James, Esq. [New York: Harper and Brothers, 1853], the author who generally commences his novels by giving a description of "the lone Cavalier riding on horseback," find it rather interesting.

Feby. 15, 1863. Today being the Sabbath day, the port watch had liberty on shore, and they enjoyed themselves hugely. Harry (one of ye intelligent contrabands) served them a dinner at 50/100 dolls. per head, consisting of fresh pork, chickens, rice, greens, potatoes, etc. All were well satisfied with both the price and grub. From 16 to 20 dined at his table today. Harry done right smart; he intends to serve them a dinner every Sunday. Bully for Harry and his dinners. Took a stroll as usual on St. Simons, in company with the executive officer and paymaster. Had a pleasant time of it. Dined on a barbecue today. None sick today. Had the Episcopal service read at muster by the paymaster. Foggy all day. Weather rather cool. Finished James' "Agnes Sorel" at 9 P.M., when I turned in.

Feby. 16, 1863. John Galleghar, lds., became a member of the sick list today, laboring under the effects of an anthrax located on nape of neck. I lanced said carbuncle and applied lini cataplasm. Paid Dr. Michel of the *Madgie* a visit and obtained from him iodine ℥ ¼, cerate simplex ℥ iii, pil cath comp no 50, and a small quantity of white wax—articles that I needed in my dispensary, being short of said drugs, I must admit that the quarters of the *Madgie* are anything else than comfortable. The berths in the wardroom open into said room, she having no staterooms. The doctor and paymaster are completely disgusted with her. Well they might be, for she is nothing of any account, compared with the *Fernandina*.

Took a stroll on shore; had a pleasant chat with Miss King, who is a good-looking Negro wench. Captain Moses, Paymaster Murray, and Doctor Boyer had a sail in the captain's gig. The tide and wind being favorable, we sailed through the water at the rate of 10 or 14 knots—so fast, indeed, as to cause the water to lap the gunwales, almost swamping the gig. The paymaster felt rather squeamish and concluded that the sea was rather rough for sailing. The captain and myself enjoyed the sail. In short, we felt as happy as dogs. The weather was rather changeable—sunshine one hour, rain another, and foggy the next. By visiting Dr. Michel, taking a stroll on St. Simons, and sailing in the captain's gig, I managed to kill time and drive dull care away.

Feby. 17, 1863. Reported one case sick—viz., Galleghar, who is improving. The *Madgie* left for Port Royal at 10 A.M. The *Paul Jones, Jr.,* with Paymaster Murray on board, left for Port Royal at 2 P.M. She had a mail on board for the North and intends to return with a mail for us. I hope that Mr. Murray may have a pleasant time of it. Sent a letter to father, also one to Capt. McIlvain. . . . John Pickle returned from a hunting tour with one deer and one bullock. The captain sent a deer to the admiral and a string of ducks to Fleet Captain [Commander] C. R. P. Rogers, Paymaster Murray having said "game" in charge.

At Sea, Feby. 18, 1863. Galleghar is improving. The U.S. steamer *Wamsutta* arrived at 9.30 A.M. from Port Royal with a mail. I received a letter from Actg. Master Stites, also a New York "Clipper" [a sporting and theatrical weekly, established in 1853] from Bassler Boyer [son of Dr. David Boyer, older brother of the diarist]. She also brought orders for us to set sail for Doboy Sound, Ga. 1.30 P.M., under way, the *Wamsutta* having us in tow.

[The *Wamsutta,* having been North for repairs, was on her way to her station at St. Simon, delivering mails for the vessels there. She was ordered by Commander Steedman to proceed to Doboy Sound, taking the *Fernandina* in tow and placing her at the entrance.]

Adieu, St. Simons. King and his family (all contrabands) left in the coal brig today for Phila., Penna. 5 P.M. still under way. The old *Fernandina* is rolling and rocking like an old washtub. Several of the crew are laboring under the effects of "nausea marina" and vomiting right and left. Saw a whale, on our port quarter, for the first time. He was about 60 to 70 feet in length—so says our executive officer, who is an old whaler. Mr. Whale was floundering about, or playing in the water. 5.11 P.M., let go our starboard anchor. We are outside of Doboy Sound. The *Wamsutta* made tracks for the sound. We remained all night outside.

6

Expeditions About Doboy Sound

Doboy Sound, Ga., Feby. 19, 1863. We started for Doboy Sound at 7.30 A.M., the *Wamsutta* having us in tow, and arrived at our anchorage in said sound at 8.30 A.M., when we let go our starboard anchor. We are anchored opposite the Doboy lighthouse. From present indications I would prefer St. Simons Sound as a station. I may change my mind in a day or two, after I have seen more of the station. Captain Moses and myself went on board the *Wamsutta.* I had the pleasure of seeing a college chum of mine, Dr. Edward R. Hutchins, acting asst. surgeon, U.S. Navy.[29] He informed me that my friend A. A. Surgeon Passmore Treadwell, formerly of the *Vixen,* was at present an occupant of a Secesh prison, having been captured on the coast of North Carolina. Poor fellow—I pity him.

[One of the twelve officers and twenty-eight men taken prisoner by the Confederates when their ship, the *Columbia* (see p. 106), was wrecked off Masonboro Inlet, North Carolina, January 14, 1863. Paroled in March, his name was included in a list of officers reported to the Secretary of the Navy by the former commander of the *Columbia* as guilty of "insubordinate and discreditable" conduct. Among the charges were "entire disregard of all the regulations and discipline of the service . . . vituperative language in the hearing of our enemies in reference to the President of the United States and the policy of his administration . . . affiliation and constant fellowship with rebel officers at Salisbury . . . communication with rebel functionaries on the subject of spirituous liquors, after having solemnly pledged their word of honor as officers and gentlemen not to use any so long as they remained prisoners of the South."[30]]

I had quite a pleasant time of it while on board. The paymaster and doctor both are damn good boys. I must say that I do not fancy their craft. Their wardroom is rather small, the doctor has no sick bay, and the berth deck is a small affair. In short, I prefer the *Fernandina,* if she is a sailing vessel, to the *Wamsutta,* though she be a steamer. The islands forming this sound are Doboy [one of the sea islands of McIntosh County, Georgia], on which is a beacon light; Sapelo [Zapala in the days of the Spaniards; one of the six "Golden Isles of Guale" (see page 15)], on which is a light-house [erected on the beach at the south end of the island in 1820] —and a beautiful one at that; and Wolf Island [sometimes described as a bar of Sapelo Island].

Feby. 20, 1863. The *Wamsutta* left this morning. She made tracks for the outside. No one on the sick list. Took a tramp on Sapelo Island; while there, I mounted the lighthouse, ascending 76 steps, each one 12 inches high, and ere I reached the cupola I had to ascend a ladder 12 feet high. The cupola is about 14 feet high. 156 panes of glass form the lights of said cupola, outside of which is an iron railing. The tower is built of brick. In short, it is a splendid affair. The carpenter killed a snake in the vicinity of the tower. Some call it a "calico snake," for it looks very much like a fancy calico pattern. I preserved said snake in alcohol and intend to take it North with me. 5 P.M., the *Wamsutta* arrived in port, having been to Sapelo Sound. Visited Dr. Hutchins of the *Wamsutta* at 6 P.M. Had a pleasant time of it. Retired at 8.30 P.M.

Feby. 21, 1863. Capt. [Acting Volunteer Lieutenant] J. W. Kittredge of the *Wamsutta,* his doctor and paymaster, and Capt. E. Moses, Ensign Thomas, and myself of the *Fernandina,* accompanied by 12 armed men, took a tramp in the interior of Sapelo Island. After travelling six miles through swamps, briars, etc., we arrived at an old hut inhabited by 7 superannuated contrabands and one cripple—all as poor as Job's turkey. From them I learned that a man by the name of Randolph Spalding used to live on this island and occupied the large mansion, which is built in the Corinthian style.

[Spalding, one-time member of the Georgia state senate (1851-1852) and a colonel in the Confederate army, was less noted than his father, Thomas Spalding. The latter, a scholar, statesman, scientific agriculturist, and noted host, had developed a fine plantation on the island, calling his beautiful mansion "South End House." Damaged beyond use during the Civil War and Reconstruction, South End House with its recessed columns, square-hewn timbers, and thick tabby walls was in the twentieth century restored by Howard Coffin with Hudson Motors profits and for a time once again became a center of island hospitality.]

He was in possession of 300 darkies ere the war, but they have all been removed to the mainland. Finding or seeing nothing of any importance, we finally concluded to go about and return to our respective ships. We reached the landing at 1 P.M., all tired and hungry. I might state that Ensign Thomas managed to buy 11 eggs for twenty cents from the contrabands. I had no one to report sick this morning. Mr. Henderson is about the same, the master-at-arms no better, but still both fit to do duty—hence my not reporting them. Being somewhat fatigued, I'll turn in early—say 9 P.M.

Feby. 22, 1863. My steward being somewhat under the weather, I had him excused from appearing at muster this morning. It being Washington's Birthday, we, in order to commemorate said event, had our ship dressed with flags. Captain Moses read service today. Took a stroll in company with Capt. Moses on Sapelo Island; had a pleasant time. Turned in at 9 P.M.

Feby. 23, 1863. A cold wind blowing all day. None on the sick list. A sutler schooner has arrived. The messes bought potatoes etc. from him. I bought some cigars at $3.50 per box—rather high, but "necessity knows no law." I had the pleasure of taking a glass of ale with Mr. Henderson, he having bought said ale from the sutler at $3.50 per doz. pint bottles.

Feby. 24, 1863. Mounted the howitzer on the poop this morning. No more danger of boarders boarding aft. The way we can rake them by means of our 24-pdr. will not be slow. None on the list. Messrs. Henderson and Eldridge, two so-called outdoor patients, are about the same. Had quite a pleasant sail in the captain's gig this afternoon in company with Capt. Moses. The sutler schooner sold stores to this ship to the amount of $200—quite a small bill.

Feby. 25, 1863. None to report sick. Messrs. Henderson and Eldridge about the same. Took a stroll on Sapelo Island from 8 A.M. to 10 A.M. 11.45, the U.S. steamer *Paul Jones* arrived, bringing our paymaster, Thos. N. Murray, back on board again, also a mail. I received a letter from father dated the 9th inst., which I answered. I also wrote and sent a letter to B.F. Boyer. Bo't 1 doz. ale, $3, from schooner.

Feby. 26, 1863. Mr. Henderson is improving slowly. The master-at-arms is about the same. None to report on list. The *Paul Jones* left with the mail at 11 A.M. Sutler schooner *J.L. Curtis* left the sound this morning. A heavy fog prevailed the early part of the day. Bought a pair of heavy boots from the paymaster's department for the small sum of $3.80—rather cheap. Thermometer 70° Fahr.

Feby. 27, 1863. None to report to the captain. My medical duties at present are light. Nothing of any account to do. Two contrabands "all the way from Darien, Ga.," made their appearance today on board, having cut the Southern Confederacy.

[Darien (twelve miles away), founded as a military colony in 1736 and peopled by Scottish highlanders recruited for aid in the protection of the southern frontier, was before the Civil War a thriving town. It suffered grievously from the ravages of the conflict; by mid-March of 1863 it was deserted (see March 17 entry), and a few months later it was burned (see June 11 entry).]

Starvation, from the tenor of their conversation, stares them in the face. Captain Moses landed them on Sapelo, where they have a house to live in and be protected by our guns. Our paymaster will attend to their grub—i.e., ration them. They were in high glee when they arrived up to our ship. "Bress de Lord!" etc. fell from their lips. It was "Massa!" here and "Massa!" there all the time. The old wench is a terrible talker. In short, they felt good. We all felt thankful that they came, for now we can get some washing done. Paid a mess bill of $10.68 today to our caterer, Ensign Thomas, who is a "caterer as is a caterer."

Feby. 28, 1863. None to report sick. The U.S. steamer *Paul Jones* arrived. At 2 A.M. two cutters, the 1st and 2nd, with 18 men, all armed with a cutlass, pistol, and musket or rifle, and two officers, Master's Mate Mr. Henderson and Ensign Wm. Thomas, who also were armed, from our ship and an officer and boat's crew of the U.S.S. *Wamsutta*, making in all 30 men, started on an expedition to capture some Rebel pickets stationed several miles from here on the Darien River. At 4 A.M. the *Wamsutta,* Captain Moses and myself on board, started up the river to aid said expedition. Our boats passed along all quietly until they came to the landing place, when the first thing they heard was a volley of musketry, or about 25 men firing at them. Our men could hear them talk. They immediately opened fire on the enemy, but, finding themselves too weak and the enemy prepared, they immediately, thinking prudence the better part of valor, retreated and met the *Wamsutta.*

We were all happy to hear and see that all escaped without receiving any wounds. Whether anyone was scared or no I cannot tell. Taking all in all, it was quite an affair. I might mention that I had forethought enough to supply our boats with 6 tourniquets—2 petits and 4 field—ere they started, not knowing whether or no anyone might have occasion to use a tourniquet; but, as stated before, none had occasion to use any. At 4 P.M. Captain Moses and myself arrived on board the good old ship *Fernandina.* All hands on board were happy to see all safe and sound. My steward informed me that none made application for any physic this morning—hence I have none to report sick. 4.30 P.M., commenced to rain—rather a cool rain. Sail in the offing. Steamer *Wamsutta* made tracks outside so as to speak her. She looks like the schooner *Hope.* I hope it may prove so, for then we can expect a mail.

March 1, 1863. None to report sick. The *Paul Jones* left for St. Simons Sound. The *Wamsutta* arrived in the sound at 8 A.M. and reported said schooner in the offing to be a sutler schooner and not the *Hope,* as we all hoped. Rained all night. Cleared up at 7 A.M. today. 9 A.M., all hands to muster and divine service, Paymaster Murray officiating as chaplain.

March 2, 1863. None to report sick. Weather springlike—thermometer from 65° to 70° Fahr. Took a stroll on shore today. While building a chicken coop, Captain Moses, attempting to drive a nail, accidentally sent the nail into his eye, contusing the conjunctiva, causing great pain and redness. I applied an ulmus cataplasm and administered a morphine powder. Hope to find him better in the morning. Having a severe headache, I took pill cath comp. no iv tonight. Erected a target on the island of Sapelo about 500 yards from the ship, which we intend to use as a mark for our heavy guns on Thursday. The *Wamsutta* went to sea this evening.

March 3, 1863. No sick to report. The captain's eye is somewhat better. 7.30 A.M. steamer *Potomska* arrived and anchored. She went to sea at 4 P.M.

March 4, 1863. Confined the captain to his room, having it darkened at same time, and kept lead water applied to his eye, Spanish fly blister to temple, and pil. cath. comp no iv internally. Weather stormy. Painting ship. *Potomska* arrived at 8 P.M. with mail matter. I received several papers from A.G. Myers, Esq. Mr. Schow sent me a Dutch letter which I cannot read, so that I am in rather a bad fix. D—n his Dutch ideas! Heard that the Rebel steamer *Nashville* was sent to the devil by the *Montauk*—i.e., blown up (Bully for us!)

[On the evening of February 27, 1863, Commander John L. Worden of the *Montauk,* who had made two attacks—one on January 27 and the second on February 1—on Fort McAllister to test the efficacy of his vessel, observed the *Nashville* (renamed *Rattlesnake*), bottled up in the Ogeechee River for eight months by Federal gunboats, in motion above the Confederate battery. Immediate reconnaissance disclosed that she was grounded. At daylight the next morning the *Montauk,* accompanied by the *Seneca,* the *Wissahickon,* and the *Dawn,* moved up close to the obstructions that had been planted for the protection of the privateer and, although under heavy fire from the fort, approached the enemy ship within 1,200 yards and attacked. The *Nashville* caught fire in several places and was soon completely destroyed. The *Montauk* suffered slight damage from a torpedo explosion.[81]]

Also heard that our Navy done wonders in the Mississippi River. Huzza for our gallant tars!

March 5, 1863. No sick today to report. U.S. steamer *Potomska* went to sea, and U.S. steamer *Wamsutta* arrived. Nothing of any account transpired today. Weather moderate.

March 6, 1863. The captain, for the first time since his accident, took a stroll on Sapelo. His eye is improving rapidly. Continue lead water. Made, or rather ordered to have one made, a shade covered with Florence silk for him to wear so as to protect his eye, which will be rather weak and delicate for some time to come. I found all hands well this morning except Mowatt, who, I think, is trying to play "old soger." I ordered tartar emetic and a Spanish fly blister, which will bring him to his senses, I hope. All hands painting ship. The *Fernandina* looks as neat as a pin since she has a coat of lead; the change is great and for the better. She looks like a new craft—

and with our 24-pdr. aft as saucy as "Old Nick." The weather was lovely today. Thermometer 65° Fahr. The *Wamsutta* took the inland passage for St. Simons at 4 P.M. Consequently we will be alone to blockade Doboy Sound until she returns. Read [Dr. John Mason] Goods's "[The] Book of Nature" [a series of lectures published in three volumes in 1826 and subsequently issued in a number of editions, including one in 1845 by Belknap and Hamersley, Hartford, Connecticut] until 10.30 P.M., when I turned in.

March 7, 1863. No sick to report today to the captain. 10 A.M., all hands to muster. Mr. Childs, executive officer, read the "fire bill," stating to each man his station during a case of fire. My station appears to be the same as during quarters—viz., sick bay—so as to be ready if necessary to destroy any combustible or inflammable drug in my stores. Taking all in all, the "fire bill" is a splendid idea. Hereafter, in order to become accustomed to our various duties in case of fire, we will be called to fire quarters once per week. I sincerely hope that we may never have occasion to go to fire quarters in real earnest, for I don't anticipate it to be very pleasant. The idea of a ship on fire may look well on paper, but to realize said state of affairs is not very agreeable.

Paid a visit to George and his wife, Mary, two intelligent contrabands who reside on Sapelo Island, and found them as happy and "snug as a bug in a rug." Had quite a pleasant chat with Mary, who is as loquacious as Mrs. Partington [an old lady known for her ludicrous misuse of words, a prominent character of Benjamin Penhallow Shillaber, nineteenth-century American humorist] and almost as smart. Read aloud for the edification of the captain, who is unable to read at night on account of his wounded eye, "The Bees," from the Latin of J. Vaniere; being the fourteenth book of [his] "Praedium Rusticum," by Arthur Murphy, Esq., [Middleton, Connecticut: Printed for I. Riley, New York, 1808] until 10.30 P.M., when we both turned in. The poem is both interesting and instructive. Rained part of the day. Weather warm.

March 8, 1863. Sabbath Day, the holy day of rest, found all hands of the good old ship *Fernandina,* with a slight exception all able to do duty—consequently I had no one to report. The starboard watch are on shore, it being their day of liberty. 9 A.M., all hands to muster. Paymaster Murray read the Episcopal service for this day, ending with a prayer for the President of the United States.

Sand flies are as plenty as politicians up North; whether they are as dangerous or no I cannot tell. This much I do know—that they are anything else than agreeable. Thermometer from 65° to 70° Fahr.

At 7.30 P.M. a boat's crew of 11 men, well armed, commanded by Actg. Master's Mate Wm. C. Gibson left the ship on a secret expedition [which with subsequent ones had as its purpose to capture a Confederate vessel loaded with cotton that was believed to be trying to run the blockade of the Darien River; the vessel was captured by an army ship on June 11, on which day also Darien was burned]. After reading aloud to the captain for a few hours until he felt drowsy, I turned in at 10 P.M.

March 9, 1863. The expedition commanded by Mr. Gibson returned at 2 A.M. At 9 A.M. I attended to my duties as surgeon and found no one to report in my daily report of sick. Landsman Carey is on the binnacle list, having caught a severe cold. My steward, R. D. Adams, is taking a stroll on Sapelo Island. The captain at my request granted him leave so to do. Adams is somewhat indisposed —cause, homesick. Poor d—l —he is tired of the service and wants to go home. I think I will have to get him discharged, for he is very anxious to have a discharge, consequently is not of much use to me, being as he is complaining of ill health all the time. The *Wamsutta* arrived this morning at 11 o'clock. At 2 P.M. all hands to quarters for the purpose of target practice with our heavy guns. Some fine shots were fired. All passed along merrily.

Read Fred Douglass speech, delivered on the 6th of Feb. '63, at the Cooper Institute, N.Y., on the subject of the President's Proclamation of Emancipation and the arming of the black man—and I must say that it was a "damn black affair," from the tenor of his remarks, but I suppose Horace Greeley was tickled almost to death with "Brudder" Douglass' bladder-dash or rigamorole [balderdash, or rigmarole] of a speech. Wool must of been in the ascendency about that time and *white trash nowhar.* I always had an idea that I was as good as a black man, provided I behaved myself—but from Brudder Fred's remarks I calculate that we poor white trash will have to take the outside seats hereafter and let Sambo take the inside and best places. So much for Fred Douglass and his powwow. One consolation is left, and that is that Fred Douglass and his whole clique are of no account and small potatoes, and the whole affair is "big cry and little wool."

[Frederick Douglass (1817-1895), mulatto, learned to read and write while a house servant in Baltimore, escaped from servitude in 1838, married a free colored woman, worked in New Bedford as a common laborer, and became an agent of the Massachusetts Anti-Slavery Society and a central figure in the "One Hundred Conventions" of the New England Anti-Slavery Society. After spending two years in Great Britain and Ireland he returned to the United States in 1847 with enough money to purchase his freedom and set up a newspaper, the *North Star*, which he published for seventeen years. A prominent orator as well as journalist, he assailed slavery as the real cause of the Civil War and urged his fellow Negroes to enter the service of the United States.]

Weather splendid. Thermometer 67° Fahr. Sand flies plenty. Took a stroll on Sapelo in company with the captain. Found George preparing some ground for planting. He appeared in the best of humor.

March 10, 1863. Landsman Michael Spain came to me this morning complaining of aches and pains. I, being of a charitable turn of mind, excused said Spain of duty today, also prescribed for him after which I paid Sapelo a visit and found all things there lovely. Our porkers and chickens are coming on finely, the latter so much, indeed, that our caterer, Mr. Thomas, built another hencoop today, in which he intends confining two hens that have a notion of hatching, so that ere long we will have plenty of young chickens. The captain is preparing one of the rooms in one of the deserted mansions on shore for a resort during the warm season, such as erecting a bathtub, table, berth, etc., so that he can take a bath occasionally in the tub and lounge on the berth, or cot, protected from mosquitoes by means of a mosquito bar during the day, smoking etc. In short, the captain and myself intend to spend a pleasant summer while in Doboy Sound, but I am afraid that by the time everything is prepared *à la* Gunter, orders will come from the powers that be for us to weigh anchor and make sail for either some other station or the North, for such has been the case heretofore—by the time we were snug and cosy in our other stations, we were ordered to leave. But such being the fortunes of war, we will have to grin and bear all disappointments.

My steward appears to be no better as regards his homesickness. I will try to ship him North as soon as possible so as to gratify him and make room for a more congenial steward. The master-at-arms,

Chas. Eldridge, is about the same; him also shall I send home by means of a "hospital ticket," for he is worthy of hospital treatment. Poor fellow—I am afraid that he will not get rid of his complaint very easy, he having suffered more or less from said complaint, which is a skin disease of the squamous variety, for the last 4 or 5 years. Read until 9.30 P.M. Turned in at 10 P.M. The thermometer ranged from 62° to 72° Fahr. during the day.

March 11, 1863. From 6 to 8 A.M. quite a squall was prevailing. Old Neptune appeared to have been on a lark. Nothing of any interest as regards the medical department transpired up to 10 A.M.; so at 9 A.M. my morning report to the captain read, "No sickness worthy of reporting." Our Nimrod, Jno. E. Pickle, started on a hunt early this morning, accompanied by his two dogs, "Black" and "Yellow," and his never-failing musket, to which he has given the name of "Death"—for, says he, she never fails to be true. He is death to all varmin [dialectic variant of vermin; used loosely by Americans in referring to various animals and even, earlier, to Indians] from a deer to a rattlesnake, as he says, and is not afraid of anything mortal. . . . .

3 P.M., signalized a steamer in the offing. 3.30 P.M., steamer *Wamsutta* hove up anchor and steamed outside the harbor so as to speak said steamer. From her general appearance, I think she was the U.S. steamer *Flambeau*. If so, why, we will be the happy recipients of a mail. I hope that she had a mail. 5 P.M., *Wamsutta* coming into the sound, and the strange steamer sailing north. The *Wamsutta* spoke her in the offing. 5.45, *Wamsutta* arrived and let go her anchor. Captain Moses went on board of her, and in less than no time he returned with a budget of letters and papers, of which I was the possessor of not a few—4 letters, three papers, and one doc[ument]. One of the letters was from brother Mike of "ye armie," commanded by "Fighting Joe Hooker"—and a letter it was.

[Michael P. Boyer was a first lieutenant in Company H, 128th Regiment, Pennsylvania Infantry, recruited in Berks County and ordered on August 16, 1862, to Washington. The company was mustered out in May, 1863, at the expiration of its nine-months term.]

Mike appeared in the best of humor although, as he stated, being blockaded by mud. Ex-Nipcheese Andy also honored me with an epistle teeming with both nonsense and common sense. Hope he may continue living in clover with his lovely "better half." Andrew Gackson Mysers, as we used to call him, is a diamond of the first water as regards wit and sociability. He can look out for a stunner from his good friend "Sawbones" (as he used to call the M.D. of the *Fernandina*) in return. Sailing Master Stites wrote me a few lines as regards the Magnus Schow affair, in which he closes his remarks by saying that if the "fool killer" has been round since, poor Magnus is now no more! Peace to his ashes!!!—which were very appropriate remarks. Dr. [Theoron] Woolverton, asst. surgeon, U.S.N., at the suggestion of Fleet Surgeon Clymer, wrote me a letter acknowledging the receipt of my yearly return etc., which were all O.K. Bully for me! I shall most assuredly as in duty bound answer all the above. Father sent me a "Gazette" [probably the Reading *Gazette and Democrat*], which was read with pleasure, it containing local news from home, hence a welcome sheet. Brother Jeff sent me the "Report of the Surgeon General of the Commonwealth of Pennsylvania, for the Year 1862," which is rather an interesting document. Ex-Paymaster A.G. Myers . . . sent me two papers, the contents of which were partly read and will be all read ere many days. In short, I am well pleased with my share of today's mail; hope I may be as successful the next time. 9 P.M. wrote a letter to Sailing Master Stites of the U.S. flagship *Wabash* in answer to one the 27th inst., received today. Read some of the papers etc. until 10 P.M., when I concluded that it were time for me to turn in for the night. . . .

March 12, 1863. None made application for a place on the sick list today. My outdoor patient, the master-at-arms, is about the same. The doctor of the *Wamsutta* having paid me a visit at 9 A.M., I showed him Eldridge's leg, upon which he exclaimed, "Why don't you send him to the hospital?" I felt rather well pleased with his ideas of the same as I intend sending him North at the first opportunity. The thermometer at 4 A.M. was 38° Fahr., at 12 M. 72° Fahr., and at 5 P.M. 56° Fahr.—rather changeable, but nothing strange for the stormy and cold month of March. Wrote a letter to Lieutenant M.P. Boyer of the U.S. Army, in which I gave him a description of the state of affairs of our *drinking larder,* or liquor establishment, which consisted of 4 beverages—viz., coffee, tea, chocolate, and water but nary a drop of whiskey, brandy, gin, wine, porter, or ale—rather a temperate bill of fare. From the tenor of his letter which I received yesterday, I take it for granted that he is as hard up as myself, having [had], as he says, nothing to drink for 22 days. But such being the fortunes of war, why! we will have to grin and bear it.

Read the speech of Mr. Funk [Isaac Funk, state senator] of Illinois delivered in the legislature . . ., in which he gives the Copperheads particular jessie, or hell. He appears to be an old patriot of the good old '76 standard—one of Nature's noblemen, a self-made man, and a true pillar of state—one in whom everyone can place confidence, and a fit subject for purposes of legislation. May he represent his district in Congress as soon as a member has to be elected in his district, is the wish of the writer of these lines. . . . After considerable conversation on the subject of Funk we all finally concluded that he was "trumps" and that it was time to disperse, or adjourn the meeting, and turn in, it being 9 P.M. So we all turned in at 9.30 P.M.

March 13, 1863. A cold and raw wind prevailing. 2 A.M. all hands were called to quarters by the springing of the rattle [sounding of the watchman's rattle]. In less than 5 minutes all were ready for action. 2.15 A.M., piped down. Several cases of colica and diarrhoea presented themselves for treatment at 9 A.M. All received ol ricini ℥ i et opii tinctura gtts vi as a dose. Our worthy and efficient executive officer, Calvin Childs, was one of the cases of colica. The paymaster, Thos. N. Murray, also complained of a griping sensation in his bowels. Both took a dose of medicine—Mr. Childs ol. ricini ℥ i et opii tinct gtts vi, and Mr. Murray preferred a carminative to a purgative dose.

3.45 P.M. Both the paymaster and executive officer have turned in, feeling anything but pleasant. Extracted a canine tooth for boy Short. Mr. Tooth was rather too prominent for him—so much indeed as to disfigure him—and, rather proud of his looks, he concluded to undergo the pain of having the tooth extracted rather than not to have the pain and retain the disagreeable ivory, as he called the tooth. I must say that the boy underwent, or stood, the operation like a soldier. Everyone on deck congratulated him for his spunk and pluck.

Austin Burroughs also came to me to have a tooth extracted. Upon examination I found the tooth broken; hence I merely had to extract the remaining portion—viz., the root. It appears that Austin, being of a restless disposition, during fire quarters run his tooth against a fire bucket and broke it off, consequently came to me for advice. I, as in duty bound, advised the extraction of the remaining part, to which he submitted bravely. I might mention that Austin is one of ye intelligent contrabands, formerly of North Carolina. His rate is 1st-class boy. At one time he was a wardroom boy but for certain reasons was displaced by the appointment of Thomas Bust, also a contraband, a native of Savannah, Georgia. Bust is a good boy and attends his duty. The remaining wardroom boys are Ellis Scarlet, who attends to the rooms of Mr. Childs and myself, and Henry Freeman, who attends to the captain's quarters—both very good boys. 6 P.M., Paymaster Murray took pil hydrarg no i (grs v) at my request.

My steward had a gay and happy time of it today. I allowed him permission to take a stroll on Sapelo Island. He remained 4 or 5 hours on shore and upon his return expressed himself well satisfied with his ramble. Hope it may have a beneficial effect, for he requires exercise and fresh air. During his sojourn on shore I, of course, attended to the duties of steward as well as surgeon, consequently had plenty to do. The pair of boots that I purchased from the paymaster on the 26th inst. for the sum of $3.80 have passed into the possession of boy Allen, who has been dunning me for them ever since I bought them. Upon making inquiries I found out that the boy needed a pair of boots and that by me letting him have said boots I would be doing an act of charity, as the paymaster had no more boots of said size—viz., no 6—so I, as one who is always ready to help his fellow man, left him have said boots for the original cost, or price. Boy Allen feels as proud as a peacock, and the way he struts about deck is not slow.

Read in the New York "Herald" of the 5th inst. that gold had fallen and that ere long it would be par again. Huzza! Huzza!! Huzza!!! for that. I suppose Wall Street is in a d—l of a flutter. Thank fortune that the biter is bit this time. The speculators in gold find that they are carrying "coal to New Castle." Serves them right. Ere long the jingle of the "Almighty Dollar" will be heard again, and shinplasters will be *nowhar!* Canada won't be so anxious to receive our specie now as she has done for the last 6 months, for the simple reason that she cannot get it. In short, the good old times of '58, '59, and '60, when gold and silver was plenty, are returning. It is enough to make the heart of every American feel jubilant.

[Since specie payments had been suspended, gold, like any other commodity, was bought and sold at the market price in greenbacks. The pinch of rising prices brought intense hatred of the gold speculators. Gold and silver, however, had never been plentiful in the circulating medium, (state bank notes, sometimes of doubtful value, had for the most part been used) and '58, '59, and '60 (in the shadow of the panic of '57) were good only in comparison with the inflationary situation during the war.]

March 14, 1863. Paymaster Murray on turning out this morning took a soda powder, which had the desired effect—viz., evacuated the contents of his alimentary canal. When asked how often he visited the "transit house," he answered, "A baker's dozen." Feels, at 5 P.M., as lively as a cricket. Executive Officer Childs, considering the ol. ricini which he took yesterday to be rather slow in its action, took last evening three pills and on turning out this morning two more, so that by 4 bells (10 o'clock) he was compelled to give up the flight and seek refuge in the "roundhouse" [a privy on deck near the bow]. 5 P.M., he says that he feels as spright as a young colt.

The delegation this morning at the sick bay was of no account. My report read, "None on the sick list." 10 A.M., had a delightful sail in the 1st cutter, Coxswain Welsh commanding. The boys are having a gay time on deck airing their duds, it being the day appropriated for "all bags on deck"; hence our spar deck looks more like the "sanctum sanctorum" of a tailor than the gun deck of a man-of-war.

7 P.M. A gay and happy time the boys are having. The drum, fife, violin, and accordion are being played at the same time; besides that hubbub several are dancing and laughing, while others are singing. In short, they all appear to be a merry set of tars. Jeremiah Riordan and Thomas O'Neil, both landsmen, are in their element, for singing, dancing, and laughing appear to be their delight. Both are particular favorites with their messmates. . . . .

March 15, 1863. All hands were called to muster at 9.30 A.M. to attend divine service, which was read by Paymaster Murray. None to report on the sick list. 10 A.M., Executive Officer Bryant [probably either Acting Ensign Charles R. Bryant, or Acting Ensign John L. Bryant] and Paymaster Winslow [probably Acting Assistant Paymaster W.R. Winslow] of the *Wamsutta* came to pay us a visit. They both dined with us and were well pleased with our accommodations etc. We had quite a pleasant time. Mr. Bryant is a very quick-witted man; hence he had plenty of yarns to spin and jokes to crack. I for my part, having a severe attack of cephalalgia, did not enjoy the sport, or yarns, as I should have done had I not had the headache. After tea the wardroom and steerage officers assembled on the spar deck in front of the cabin and under the poop, where chairs had been placed for their reception, to take a comfortable smoke and have a sociable chat. While there, many a yarn was spun by the old salts, Mr. Childs and Mr. Thomas, two ex-captains of the merchant service. The younger portion of the company of course done their duty, so that we drove dull care away and spent a pleasant evening.

March 16, 1863. None on the sick list. Took a stroll on Sapelo Island. Dined on board of the *Wamsutta*. Mr. Bryant was as witty as ever. The doctor and paymaster were on shore on a rabbit hunt and returned at 3 P.M. with 27 rabbits—rather a good day's hunt. The doctor made our mess a present of some of the game, for which he received the thanks of the members of said mess. Retired at 8 P.M.

March 17, 1863. At 2 A.M. Captain Moses and myself, in the 1st and 2nd cutters with 18 armed men, commanded by Acting Ensign Wm. H. Thomas and Acting Master's Mate Wm. C. Gibson, left the ship and proceeded on board of the steamer *Wamsutta*. 2.15 A.M., the *Wamsutta* got under way and started up the River Darien for Darien, Georgia. 5.30 A.M., we arrived opposite the deserted town of Darien (save for a few contrabands). Ere any of us landed, we first trained our port battery on said place, after which Executive Officer Bryant of the *Wamsutta* and Mr. Gibson of the *Fernandina* with 20 armed men landed and entered said town of Darien and found one man skedaddling like thunder. Not wishing to rouse up any Rebel pickets in case any were in the vicinity, so as to give them the alarm, thereby causing them also to skedaddle, they did not fire upon said running fugitive but proceeded in their search for Rebels etc. Six superannuated darkies, hogs, chickens, cattle, and sheep, besides plenty of fine buildings, which were locked, was all that remained in the once flourishing and striving town of Darien. About one-half hour or more [later] the exploring party returned with one venerable darky. Out of him came damn little intelligence. Upon their return Captains Kittredge and Moses, Surgeons Hutchins and

Boyer, Paymaster Winslow, and Actg. Master's Mate Gibson, with two boats' crews of armed men, proceeded to take a look at said town of Darien. We ascertained from some of the contrabands that a squad of men, Rebel pickets, were camped at the Ridge, a distance of 5 miles, and that some of them had been in town early in the morning but took to their heels upon the approach of our gunboat. None of the darkies were anxious to come along with us; so of course we left them remain where they were. Capt. Kittredge and Captain Moses each purchased a pig (small shoat) at a dollar a head from one of the decrepit darkies. They appeared to have a holy horror of us Yankees, supposing us to be vandals etc. I suppose the Rebs poisoned their minds against us.

Not finding anything of any account, nor being bent on a plundering expedition, we left Darien as we found it, at 7 A.M. I counted as many as 15 warehouses or stores on the river bank, all large buildings painted with a solution of lime, which we Yankees at home call whitewashing. Upon one is the name of "Mitchell and Smith" painted in large black letters, who I suppose were at one time quite an extensive firm. 4 or 5 large sawmills were on the river bank. The houses comprising the town were principally built of lumber, all painted, white and green shutters. Some fine country seats or villas in vicinity. Upon the door of the residence of the former consul of Mecklenburg, Carl Epping,[32] was pasted a notice, signed by said Carl Epping, consul, stamped with his seal of office, "warning all civil and military authorities from molesting said building, the wharves on the river bank of the Darien side," etc., as they belonged to and under his control. From the tenor of said notice I suppose that the said Carl Epping, consul, must have been a man of some "pumpkins" in Darien. In short, I think that in times of peace Darien must of been a beautiful, flourishing, and striving town. On our return trip we passed the mill, where a party of men fired upon an expedition which had been fitted out for the purpose of capturing said men on the 28th of Feby., 1863. (See Feby. 28th of said notes), While so doing, we fired a few shells into said mill—at least attempted so to do—so as to arouse anyone who might be concealed therein, but done no damage to said mill.

10 A.M., arrived on board of the *Fernandina* somewhat fatigued and drowsy. I for my part am not anxious to make any more such trips; expecting to see some bombarding, I was rather disappointed in finding nary Reb, but suppose it to be for the better. So much for expedition no. 2.

None to report sick today. Feeling fatigued and drowsy, I took a nap after dinner. Read part of Victor Hugo's "Les Miserables"— "Fantine," or vol. first—until 8 P.M., when I commenced to note down the items of this day in my journal. In my estimation Hugo is a splendid writer, and his "Les Miserables" cannot be excelled. The preface to this remarkable portraiture of society of the nineteenth century, to which Victor Hugo has given the richest twenty-five years of his life, is worth the price of the work itself.

March 18, 1863. None on sick list. I have 5 or 6 so-called outdoor patients who require medicine but are fit for duty. Ate a hearty breakfast this morning consisting of ham and eggs—quite a treat for blockaders, especially the eggs. Reading "Les Miserables." The further I advance with said novel, the more I like it. Hugo's Jean Valjean is quite a character, and his description of Waterloo is sublime. Commenced to rain at 4 P.M. Wrote a letter to A. G. Myers, Washington, D.C.

March 19, 1863. None on the sick list. 6.30 A.M., *Wamsutta* went to sea, with Paymaster Murray on board, to speak the so-called transport *Massachusetts*. 12 M., *Wamsutta* arrived and anchored. After having communicated with the *Massachusetts,* Paymaster Murray obtained some fresh beef, potatoes, and onions, for which he has the thanks of all on board the *Fernandina.* Also brought a mail. I was the happy recipient of two letters (one from M.P.B. of the Army and one from father, both containing matters interesting to me), one paper from father, and several documents from A. G. Myers. I will acknowledge the receipt of said letters etc. "Les Miserables" still takes up my leisure time. . . . . 7.54 P.M. Stormy! Southern wind prevailing. 9 P.M., turned in.

March 20, 1863. Rather a cold wind prevailing. Thermometer 40° to 53° Fahr. None on the sick list. Charles Eldridge continues about the same; still taking liq potassae arsenitis gtts v ter in die. I will send him to the hospital ship *Vermont* by the first opportunity which presents itself. Nothing of any interest transpired today worthy of note.

March 21, 1863. John Murphy was placed on the binnacle list today, being affected with a tumor in the popliteal space of right leg. Painted tumor with iodine tinct. and internally potassii iodidii grs v ter in die. None in sick report. Took a stroll on Sapelo today. Raining the better part of the day. Made a requisition on the paymaster for sugar, lbs. 3—$0.48—for the medical department of this ship. Turned in at an early hour.

March 22, 1863. "Sol" was out in all his glory today. All Nature smiled serenely. Paymaster Murray read the service today at 9.30 A.M., when all hands were mustered to attend divine service.

March 23, 1863. Today I finished Victor Hugo's masterpiece, "Les Miserables." . . . . It is splendid. None on sick list. Commenced a letter to C. C. O'Kerman, Esq., Portsmouth, N. Hampshire.

March 24, 1863. Expedition No. 3. At 5 A.M. Captain Moses, myself, Actg. Ensign C. Flood, and Actg. Master's Mate Townsend, with 18 armed men, left the ship for the *Wamsutta.* Upon our arrival we started up the Darien River to Darien Ridge for some lumber. Upon our arrival there Capt. Kittredge, Captain Moses, and Surgeons Hutchins and Boyer, with some men, landed with the intention of making observations. We found several contrabands, who informed us that no Rebels were about. So we searched some of the houses for relics etc., and while so doing we heard the sound of a bugle, also that of musketry, upon which we formed in a body and made an orderly retreat for the steamer, firing as we retreated. I was armed with a cutlass, pistol, and musket. The enemy proved to be Rebel cavalry—of what force we cannot tell, but of sufficient force to justify our retreating, they having the advantage of woods and cover of the houses.

After retreating a short distance, the doctor of the *Wamsutta* and myself with 4 men made an advance on the largest mansion with the intention of securing, if any could be found, medicines. While the doctor and myself were overhauling the bottles etc., "Bang! bang!! bang!!!" went several muskets, and our men crying out, "Away! Away!! They are upon us again!" Of course we two surgeons descended out of said building in less than no time and retreated with the rest, firing as we backed for the main body of men, they (the Rebels) firing at us all the time. After we reached the main body and reported the circumstances etc., we all concluded to make a bee line for the ship, which we done. As soon as we arrived on board, we—at least Capt. Kittredge—left them (the Rebels) have the contents of two guns loaded with shell. Not wishing to destroy the houses, we hove up anchor and started down the river.

I might mention that the darkies were all satisfied with their condition, none wishing to come along with us. We stopped for lumber at the Palmetto Mills, on Herds Island [Hird's (sometimes spelled Herd's, Hurd's, or Herd) about a mile east of Darien; named for Mark Hird, early Frederika settler, one of the first converts baptized by John Wesley]. The proprietor of said mills was one Isaac M[eans] Aiken [a native South Carolinian who moved to Georgia in 1854, served in the Confederate army as captain of Company B, Forty-seventh Georgia Regiment, and after the war lived in Pensacola, Florida]—at least, he was on January 1st, 1860, as [is shown by] the following Rules and Regulations, . . . found . . . pasted up in what used to be his office.

Rules & Regulations of Palmetto Mills.

1st Persons on entering the Mill are expected not to interfere in any way with the affairs or hands of the Mill.

2nd Persons are warned against hiring trading or talking with any of the negroes on the place, *under penalty of the law.*

3rd Masters of vessels, having one or more colored persons in their crew, are expected to report the same on their arrival at the wharf, or else *abide the law made for such cases.*

4th Masters of vessels wishing stowage or any alterations made in their cargoes are requested to apply to me.

5th Sailors are not allowed in the negro houses *at any time, or with the negroes,* and are also prohibited coming on the wharf after dark.

6th Smoking in, or about the Mill *is at all times positively prohibited.*

"Herds Island"   ISAAC M. AIKEN
January 1st 1860

We obtained plenty of lumber, several grindstones, chains, etc. Arrived on board the *Fernandina* at 12 M., tired and weary. I must not forget to state that one of the men received a bayonet wound in his thigh while skedaddling. It was a slight one, merely a flesh wound one inch in length and 1½ inches deep. His own bayonet done it. It merely required the insertion of one stick of the interrupted suture. All the rest escaped Scotch free. Some say they saw as many as 100 men. Some only saw 96 men. I for my part saw none but heard the bugle and the guns, both of which I consider self-evident to justify me in stating that they outnumbered us three to one; besides, as stated before, they had the advantage of the

woods etc. They continued their firing after we were on board of
the *Wamsutta*.

The following is said envelope, or at least part of it, mentioned
on the other page. It was addressed to Col. Isaac M. Aiken, Darien,
Ga. The writer was one Dr. E[dward] L[ewis] Baker [who died in
1862 and was buried in Darien] of Darien, Georgia, a young doctor
whom I met at the Jefferson Medical College, Phila., during the
term of 1859-60—at least I think it is the same one, for I met and
became acquainted with a Dr. Baker of Georgia during said session.
The letter was a dunning one for a medical bill.   . . .

None to report sick today. The master-at-arms is about the same.
He is waiting anxiously the arrival of a steamer so as to be able to
go North. 5 P.M. Miles Powers, the carpenter's assistant, captured
two black snakes, each 4½ feet in length, on the island of Sapelo
and brought them on board in a jug. After playing with them for
some time, he put them in a bottle, which required considerable
skill, as they did not feel inclined to enter said bottle, and sent
them adrift on the briny ocean. The bottle filling, they all sank to
the bottom. Whether they perished or no I cannot tell; but this
much I can say—that all felt pleased to see them go over the side
of the ship, for none considered them pleasant playthings.

March 25, 1863. I was compelled to place John Murphy, o. sea.,
on the sick list today, affected with a tumor in the popliteal space
of right leg, the nature of which I cannot positively diagnose, but
am partly inclined to think it of the enchondroma species, or
variety. Paint with tinct iodine, and potassii iodidii grs iii ter in
die. He is the first patient reported on sick list for three or four
weeks. My steward took a run on the island and returned well
pleased. Took a stroll myself this afternoon, in company with Paymaster Murray, on Sapelo. We had a pleasant time of it. Being
short of tobacco and rather fond of smoking, I was compelled today
to buy some hard tobacco from the paymaster until I can purchase
some Lynchburg or killikinick [kinnikinnick, a mixture of dried
leaves and bark of certain plants, used by the Indians for smoking].
Large signal fires burning all day on the mainland. I suppose the
Rebs are signalizing to each other or else are clearing some of their
land for planting.

7 P.M. The boys on deck are having a jolly time playing leading
the pig by the ear, which appears to be quite an amusing game.

Our crew are noted for their sociability and wit. I am rather partial to the boys and only hope that they may continue to be in such good spirits for the rest of the cruise.

March 26, 1863. Chas Mowatt was admitted on the sick list today, affected with a contusion; hence my list sports two names today—viz., Murphy and Mowatt. Steward took a run on shore. Thermometer 65° Fahr. The lighthouse lookout signalized a schooner in the offing sailing northward. He supposes it to have been the *Hope* returning from St. Simons Sound. I sincerely hope it may be the *Hope,* for then we can expect a mail. Took a run on shore.

March 27, 1863. The *Paul Jones, Jr.,* arrived from St. Simons with a mail. I received one paper but nary letter. Mowatt and Murphy on sick list. . . .

March 29, 1863. All hands to muster at 9.30 A.M. to attend divine service. Raining all day; a heavy storm brewing the better part of the day. Read Dumas' "Conscript" to kill time. [*Conscript, A Tale of the French Empire* (Philadelphia: T.B. Peterson, 1855-58); *Conscript; A Tale of War* (Philadelphia: T.B. Peterson, 1863).]

March 30, 1863. The old adage "March makes its appearance like a lamb and its exit like a roaring lion" appears apropos the present year, for on the 1st and 2nd inst. the weather was springlike and altogether lovely, whilst yesterday and today it was cold, stormy, and rainy. Mowatt is improving, and Murphy's tumor appears about the same. The caterer handed me a bill of $12.72, which I, in the politest manner possible, cashed. The *Wamsutta* is condensing water for us. We took in about 800 gallons of water today. Paymaster Murray opened his heart and handed me $16.56 today, which appeared due me on the account of the mess. Everything appears dull and dreary about the ship today on account of the inclemency of the weather.

March 31, 1863. The U.S. steamer *Wamsutta* left for St. Simons Sound. The *Paul Jones, Jr.,* arrived and also left again for St. Simons Sound. Sent Chas. Eldridge and John Murphy to the U.S.S. *Vermont* at Port Royal with "hospital tickets." They both left in the U.S.S. *Wamsutta.* Reported Mowatt sick this morning. Quartermaster Pickle was appointed master-at-arms in place of Chas. Eldridge, who was sent home sick. The captain of the afterguard [seamen stationed on the poop or after part of the ship to attend the after sails], George Briggs, was appointed acting quartermaster in place of James Johnson, promoted; James Johnson, actg. quartermaster, was appointed quartermaster in place of John Pickle, promoted; and Jeremiah Riordan was appointed captain of the afterguard in place of George Briggs, who was promoted. All appear to enjoy their new stations. Hope they may all give universal satisfaction.

A contraband made his appearance this morning in a canoe with a flag of truce flying, having made his escape from Darien Ridge last night. He reports them ready for us in case we should happen to make another visit to said place—also that there were 300 soldiers stationed at the Ridge. His reasons for escaping were that they (the Rebels) had promised him a flogging, and, not feeling anxious to undergo said pleasant exercise, he concluded to skedaddle, which he did last night.

April 1, 1863. The blessed first of April, set apart as "All Fools' Day," set in beautifully, and I was fooled rather beautifully at 5 A.M. by some of the officers in the following manner—viz.: At the hour of 5 o'clock this morning one of the wardroom boys roused me up and informed me that a schooner was attempting to run the blockade, upon which I turned out in double-quick time and commenced hauling on my trousers, when lo and behold! the magic word "April fool" was whispered in my ear by said boy. Of course I had to acknowledge the coin—in other words, admit that I was caught napping. My only remedy left was for me to turn in again. After breakfast I concluded to take a smoke; consequently in order to obtain a light I was compelled to call upon the messenger boy for a light. He very smilingly brought me the lantern used for that purpose, but to my astonishment when I opened said lantern, I found nary light. My first impulse was to frown upon the boy and demand an explanation, but ere I uttered a word, he smiled and said, "I guess I rather caught you, Doctor, this time." I again was compelled to utter the word or sentence "April fool" and in a pleasant manner order a lantern with a light, which was brought to me O.K. As a matter of fact, all the rest of the officers and men came in for their share. . . . .

The steward of the steerage mess played the sharpest trick on record. It is as follows—viz.: When the officers sat down to breakfast, they found one of their dishes to be a plate of fine biscuits, all warm and ready to eat. Anticipating a treat, they all took a biscuit, having first supplied themselves with butter on their plates to butter said biscuits, and commenced to divide them in two; but to their astonishment and chagrin they proved to be, instead of biscuits, nothing but potatoes rolled in flour and baked like biscuits. Like sensible persons, they burst out laughing and told their steward that he deserved the "champion belt." I might mention that the steward is a contraband, formerly of North Carolina—a smart boy withal; he is in every sense of the word one of ye intelligent darkies, or contrabands. I doubt very much whether that can be beat in the States. So much for "All Fools' Day."

Reported one man sick—viz., Chas Mowatt. Made out my 1st quarterly report for 1863. During the quarter I admitted 23 cases, discharged 22 cases, and had 1 case remaining, consisting of the following diseases: intermittens, erysipelas, scrofula, bronchitis chronica, ulcus, anthrax, tumor, psoriasis, vulnus contusum, contusio, abrasio, furunculus, syph: secondary, catarrhus, paronychia, odontalgia, tonsillitis, and haemorrhois. The average no. of ship's company 86, average no. of sick days 126, expenses in medicines $8.02, daily average no. of patients 1 36/90, and daily average cost per man $0.06 46/126. My report speaks well as regards the health of the ship's company. I sincerely hope that the boys may continue enjoying the same good health.

April 2, 1863. The sick list sports one name—viz., Chas. Mowatt. The weather is lovely. Took a nap from 2 to 4 P.M. Actg. Ensign Wm. H. Thomas and Quartermaster Wm. Scott started on a bullock hunt at 5 P.M. Hope they may be successful. Nothing of any account transpired today.

April 3, 1863. Spent part of the day on Sapelo burning weeds, old boats, etc., at same time roasting some oysters. 3 P.M., Mr. Thomas returned and reported that he had shot a beef. Bully for him! All hands will have fresh beef for a day or two. The weather was splendid all day.

April 4, 1863. Mowatt returns to duty. None to report sick. Weather lovely. Received a letter from Captain Beers, enclosing his *carte de visite*,[33] also a long and interesting epistle from sister Beckie. Nothing of any account transpired today. 8.30 P.M. Will turn in early.

April 5, 1863. Sabbath, the holy day of rest, set in beautifully. All nature smiled serenely. 9.30 A.M., all hands to muster to attend divine service and hear the Articles of War read. In the afternoon the executive officer, paymaster, and myself took a walk in the direction of King Sampson's settlement, a distance of 2 miles from the beach. Found Sampson, his wife and grandson Ceaser, Billy and his wife, Harry, and two other superannuated contrabands lively and in good spirits. Their corn looks well—the stalks measure from 4 to 5 inches. After chatting with the darkies for an hour or two, we left again for the ship. We arrived on board at 5.30 P.M., well satisfied with our tramp. Our caterer has been preparing, or manufacturing, some slop for our porkers. He said it were better to relieve a sheep in the ditch on the Sabbath day than to let it perish, intimating that it was necessary to boil his slop today or else the materials would spoil, so mote it be.

April 6, 1863. All hands well today. The weather lovely. Took a stroll on Sapelo Island. Gave George, the contraband on shore, a few doses of ol. ricini, also an anodyne mixture for his wife Mary, composed of tinct. capsici, tinct. zingiber, tinct. opii, and aquae. Retired at an early hour. An armed boat's crew, commanded by Actg. Ensign Wm. H. Thomas, left the ship at 7 P.M. on a secret expedition.

April 7, 1863. I started in company with Quartermaster Wm. Scott, armed with a musket, on a hunt after pelicans at 1 P.M. We landed on the east end of Sapelo Island and after a short stroll succeeded in obtaining a pelican, which was all that I wanted. I immediately separated the head from the body and commenced dissecting the head, which I intend to preserve as a relic, for it will be quite a curiosity up North. We returned on board at 6 P.M., tired and weary. The weather was splendid all day. My morning report reported, "None on sick list." 7 P.M., Actg. Master's Mate James B. Henderson with an armed boat's crew left the ship on a secret expedition.

April 8, 1863. Finished the dissection of the pelican head today. All hands pronounce it a splendid affair. I must admit that I feel proud myself of it. Took a run on shore; found Aunt Mary as loquacious as usual. Reported Wright and Donnelly sick this morning, the former affected with abrasio of right hand and the latter suffering from the effects of paronychia. Bought flannel yds x today of the paymaster at $.50 p. yd. I intend getting pantaloons etc. made of it. I also bought canvas duck yds. iiiss. [3½], $0.31 p. yd., which I intend for a cloth bag. 7 P.M., Actg. Master's Mate Wm. C. Gibson with an armed boat's crew left the ship on a secret expedition.

April 9, 1863. John Donnelly returns to duty, and Geo. L. Wright continues on the sick list. Took a run on shore in the forenoon, and in the afternoon my steward, R.D. Adams, had my permission to take a run on Sapelo. I enjoyed myself while on shore chatting with Aunt Mary and strolling about. My steward also had a pleasant time of it. The weather was lovely. Oh, for the ever welcome arrival of a mail boat! Mr. Townsend is in charge of the secret expedition tonight.

April 10, 1863. Two of our crew, Scott and Carey, started yesterday after some beef. They returned this morning with two head of beef. All hands feel jubilant over the idea of having fresh beef for the next two or three days. Paymaster Murray, Ensign Flood, and myself took a tramp in the direction of Sampson's plantation. We walked no less than 10 miles; had a pleasant time of it. Killed a moccasin snake. Saw a black snake, which we did not kill because he skedaddled ere we could apply the rod. We returned on board at 1 P.M., rather fatigued. The lighthouse man signalized the schooner *Hope* in the offing, sailing into St. Simons Sound. If she proved really to have been the *Hope,* why we can expect a mail tomorrow. We all hope to have the pleasure of seeing the *Paul Jones, Jr.,* tomorrow.

April 11, 1863. With anxious minds and longing eyes we were all looking for the appearance of the *Paul Jones, Jr.,* but nary *Paul Jones, Jr.,* hove in sight. At 5 P.M. a steamer looking like the *Massachusetts* was seen at the outer buoy sailing south. All are anxious for a mail.

Of all places in the States I think that Sapelo Island, Ga., is the greatest place for snakes, for no less than one hundred have been seen this season. . . . The weather was rather warm today. Mosquitoes and sand flies plenty. Paymaster paid me $20 on account.

April 12, 1863. All hands to muster and attend divine service at 9 A.M. None to report sick. 11 A.M. Messrs. Gibson and Flood, the former a master's mate and the latter an ensign, being out sailing in the *Greeley,* nee *Old Abe,* capsized said boat and received a ducking. The 3rd cutter picked them up. They say the water is rather cool. Both escaped Scotch free as regards wounds etc. The weather was lovely all day; hence all hands were in good humor and seemed to enjoy themselves. The captain, paymaster, and myself took a stroll on Sapelo so as to aid the digestion of our dinner, which consisted of roast beef, etc. We found George and Mary having a gay and happy time preparing a dinner for the port watch, who were on liberty on shore today. The dinner consisted of beefsteak; fried fish; stewed, fried and raw oysters; apple pies; and sassafras beer—the whole served up at 25/100 dollars per head. The boys enjoyed the dinner, and George and Mary put the "greenbacks" in their pockets.

The secret expedition tonight was commanded by Actg. Master's Mate James B. Henderson, a promising young naval officer, who deserves to succeed in the world. He has my best wishes. Turned in at an early hour.

7

Idle Hours in Doboy Sound

Doboy Sound, Ga., April 13, 1863.   . . . .   I had the pleasure of reporting "None on the sick list" in my morning report to the captain. At 1 P.M. a boat from the *Potomska* in charge of Actg. Master Basil W. Leary having some fresh beef, potatoes, and onions on board arrived and reported that our mail was at St. Simons Sound. Capt. Budd [Acting Volunteer Lieutenant William Budd of the *Potomska*] sent Capt. Moses dates [newspapers] to the 7th inst., in which we saw that demonstrations were about being made on Charleston. Mr. Leary informed us that the *Keokuk* had been sunk by some of Fort Sumter's guns—at least it was so reported. I only hope that the report will not be confirmed. I also hope to hear ere long that that hotbed of treason, Charleston, was destroyed root and branch by our Navy. In the meantime we'll "trust in Providence and keep our powder dry."

[On the afternoon of April 7, 1863, after some delay because of tide conditions and hazy weather, du Pont attacked Fort Sumter as a preliminary to a long-planned attempt to take Charleston, "cradle of this wicked rebellion." "Our armies have been a dead failure," he wrote a fellow officer the previous October, "and but for the Navy the nation would now be in sackcloth and ashes, perhaps suing for peace; certainly foreign intervention would have been upon us." The admiral strongly felt that whereas a joint operation against Charleston by army and navy forces shortly after the capture of Port Royal would have resulted in easy victory, the difficulties had since increased to such a marked extent that the outcome of an expedition made by naval forces alone would be, to say the least, questionable. In contrast, the Navy Department and the general public had a great deal of confidence in the offensive powers of the new ironclads, ordered south for the specific purpose of assisting in the enterprise, and were very anxious for the undertaking to be begun, although Secretary Welles feared that du Pont's hesitancy "jeopardizes the whole." When du Pont, in an effort to satisfy what he called the "morbid appetite in the land to have Charleston," finally tried "to take the bull by the horns," the bull "was too much for us."

[The fleet that made the attempt consisted of eight ironclad vessels besides the flagship, including the eagerly awaited and very recently acquired *Keokuk,* considered valuable particularly for "her less draft than the others." A plan to pass the fort and start action to its rear, placing the town "under the guns of the ironclads" and so forcing the Confederate military to come to terms, was thwarted by heavy fire and by obstructions in the water, and the approach of evening found no apparent impression made on the enemy stronghold. After less than an hour's concentration of fire from a number of batteries five of the monitors were disabled in whole or in part; the *Keokuk* had to retire altogether, sinking the next morning near Morris Island—the greatest single loss sustained. Du Pont in withdrawing the fleet for the night had in mind renewal of the attack, but after hearing the individual commanders' reports as to the injuries suffered by their ships he decided not thus to convert "a failure into a disaster." The ironclads, he said—"miserable failures where forts are concerned"—had proved their inability to endure "any weight of fire to which they might have been exposed" and consequently had not been able even to try to overcome the obstructions or test their torpedo power. Persistence in the objective, he wrote the Navy Department the next day, would have meant only greater casualty; Charleston could not possibly be taken by naval forces alone.

[Thus ended what "constituted originally the great feature of his command"—an achievement that, according to Welles, "the country expects and demands . . . from him." Relieved soon afterward, du Pont died before the end of the war.[34]]

I spent part of the day on shore and part in dissecting a pelican head and bill for the captain. At 7 P.M. John Denny, boatswain's mate, fell overboard and cut his chin. My steward dressed the wound by applying a few stitches and adhesive plaster, after which he reported himself to me. Upon examination I found that the wound had been properly attended to by my steward and that nothing remained for me to do but to tell him to apply cold-water rags so as to favor the union of the cut by the first intention. The secret expedition was commanded by Mr. Gibson tonight.

April 14, 1863. Reported John Denny, who received the wound last night, sick in my morning report, affected with vulnus incisum. The weather today was rather warm, so warm indeed as to bring the snakes out of the dens, for the boys killed no less than 9 snakes in the small space of 5 acres in the vicinity of the lighthouse, consisting of 1 rattlesnake, 2 coachwhips, 2 moccasins, and 4 black snakes. On account of the rarity of the coachwhip snake up North I skinned one of them and stuffed him.   . . .   The expedition tonight was in charge of Actg. Master's Mate Alonzo Townsend.

April 15, 1863. At 3.30 A.M. the 1st cutter with an armed crew commanded by Acting Master's Mate Jas. B. Henderson left the ship for Sapelo Sound to communicate with the *Potomska* and obtain from her some potatoes left in charge for us by the supply steamer *Massachusetts*. Mr. Henderson had a pleasant trip; found the officers of the *Potomska* to be all jolly boys. He returned at 5 P.M., having the potatoes on board. I reported John Denny, in my morning report to the captain, improving. He continues on the sick list.

Spent the greater portion of the forenoon in cleansing the pelican head which I commenced to dissect on the 13th inst. and finishing the stuffing of the coachwhip snake. In the afternoon I had a run on shore. The weather was lovely all day, a cool wind blowing, which made it pleasant on board. I had the pleasure of seeing a ripe blackberry and plenty of red and green ones today. The prospects as regards blackberries are favorable, for in one week more there will be plenty of them fit to eat. I consider it rather early for them to appear, not being accustomed to see them at this season of the year up North.

Mr. Flood was in charge of the secret expedition tonight. Read until 12 M. the "Misteries of the Court of Queen Annie," by Ainsworth [William Harrison Ainsworth, *Mysteries of the Court of Queen Anne* (Philadelphia: Peterson, 1852-1855], which is pretty good for a court story.

April 16, 1863. At 4.30 A.M. Mr. Henderson, in charge of the 1st cutter, started with the mail for St. Simons Sound, Ga. I sent per him my 1st quarterly returns for 1863, also letters to father, sister Beckie, and A.G. Myers. We all expect to receive a large mail from St. Simons Sound. 1 P.M. practiced target fireing with our heavy guns. Some of the shots were splendid line ones. The boys deserve great credit for their skill in handling the guns. I have no fear but what they will do their duty in case of an action with the enemy.

The captain made some improvements as regards the lighthouse signal station of such a nature as to facilitate the signaling of any sail etc. which may appear in the vicinity of Doboy Sound. 8 P.M., Mr. Henderson sent up a rocket in the vicinity of Wolf Island so as to inform us that all was O.K. We answered him in return with a rocket from the ship. After waiting for the mail boat until 11 P.M., I concluded to turn in for the night, for no mail boat came. Mr. Thomas had charge of the secret expedition tonight.

April 17, 1863. Mr. Henderson arrived at 8 A.M. with the mail etc. from St. Simons Sound. I received a letter and paper from Dr. T.J. Boyer [Thomas Jefferson Boyer, brother of the diarist], member of the legislature [general assembly, 1859 and 1863-1864; state senator from Clearfield, 1876]; a letter from Capt. McIlvain . . . also a box of medical stores, sent as per requisition of April 1st, 1863, from the U.S.S. *Vermont,* Port Royal, S.C. Mr. Henderson brought the news of a report that Admiral [David G.] Farragut of the Mississippi Squadron[35] was killed, which, if true, is a sad blow for us. I only hope that the report may prove false. Wrote an answer to Dr. T. J. Boyer's letter; also wrote one to Miss Amanda Carlisle, Luthersburg, Clearfield Co., Pa., a young lady with whom I had the pleasure of spending many a long and happy evening.   . . . I also wrote a letter to Dr. S. Chester Smith [acting assistant surgeon] of the U.S. steamer *Potomska* and at the same time sent him a few medical blanks. Mr. Gibson is in charge of the secret expedition tonight.

April 18, 1863. At 4.30 A.M. Actg. M. M. Henderson in charge of the 1st cutter started for Sapelo Sound, there to communicate with the *Potomska,* having some official docs. for Capt. Budd. He took a mail with him being as the *Potomska* will be enabled to speak the *Hope* or other mail boat. I sent the letters which I wrote last night. 11.30 A.M., Capt. Moses, A.M. Mate Gibson, and myself started on an expedition in the *Old Greeley,* nee *Old Abe.* While leaving the ship I commenced to sing, "I'm afloat! I'm afloat on the fierce rolling tide," but alas! at 12 M. I was compelled to sing as follows, viz., "I'm sticking! I'm sticking in the mud ever so tight," on account of our getting, or running, into a sand bank high and dry—and the tide leaving us every moment—where we were compelled to remain until 4 P.M., when the flood tide carried us off again, when I again hummed the words "I'm afloat! I'm afloat on the fierce rolling tide" etc. At 4.30 P.M. we anchored our craft, and at 5.15 P.M. we arrived back on board of ye *Fernandina,* rather fatigued and feeling somewhat sheepish. Between 12 M. and 4 P.M. we passed the time in eating a cold snack, drinking sassafras beer, smoking, and telling yarns. 7 P.M., Mr. Henderson returned from Sapelo and handed me a letter from Dr. Smith of the *Potomska* in answer to mine of the 17th inst., also a few pill. cath. comp. which the doctor sent me. From the tenor of his epistle he appears to be a fine young man.

April 19, 1863. Sabbath Day, and all is lovely. At 9 A.M. the boatswain's mate piped all hands to muster and divine service. Paymaster Murray officiated as chaplain, and our executive, Mr. Childs, read several Navy orders, after which the roll was called, and all answered to their names; and at 9.45 A.M. the boatswain's mate piped down. I had the pleasure of reporting all hands well in my daily morning report of sick to the captain. . . . .

Took a swim on shore in the afternoon; found the contrabands in the best humor. Read "Harper's Magazine" for Feby. and March, '63, until 11 P.M., when I turned in. The weather was rather warm all day—thermometer 83° Fahr.

April 20, 1863. The weather continues warm; at 4 to 8 A.M. the thermometer ranged from 70° to 76° Fahr. and at 12 M. 80°. Sand flies and mosquitoes by the million. None to report on sick list. Paid Mary, the negro wench on shore, a wash bill of 50/100 doll. Gave Harry ℥ iv. ol. ricini for Old Sampson, who felt rather indisposed and wished a little castor oil to take now and then. 6 P.M., a boat, commanded by Actg. Master Leary, from the *Potomska* arrived en route for St. Simons Sound, there to speak the *Keystone State* so as to make arrangements with Capt. Le Roy [Commander

William E. Le Roy], senior officer present, as regards the mail etc. They remain on board until morning.

April 21, 1863. The weather was rather pleasant today—a cool northeast wind blowing. None on the list. Our caterer gave us a porker roasted for dinner, which did not go down very bad. Nothing of any account transpired today.

April 22, 1863. Mr. Leary arrived from St. Simons this morning and brought a small mail. I received nary thing. Wrote a letter to father and one to the postmaster at Port Royal; also sent a note containing a list of medicines to Dr. S. Smith of the *Potomska* requesting him to obtain said drugs from the *Massachusetts*. Mr. Leary informed us that some of the Rebels had paid the island of St. Simons a visit and destroyed part of the coal wharf located there and committed other depredations.

[A boat crew from the *Potomska* had found the wharf at Gascoigne's Bluff on fire. The blaze was extinguished, but the wharf could not be saved. Fortunately the Federal coal depot there was at the time empty; however, a change in the disposition of coal delivered at the station had to be made. Since the place was deserted, it was supposed that Confederate troops from the mainland had started the fire. There was other evidence of nocturnal visitors to the island.]

Hereafter Capt. Le Roy of the *Keystone State* will make arrangements so that we get our mail without going to St. Simons Sound in small boats, for which we are very thankful.

Paymaster Murray and myself took a walk in the direction of Old Sampson's place. On our visit we gathered blackberries sufficiently to gratify our tastes. There will be any amount of berries in a day or two. The aspect is splendid around the place: the corn is growing beautifully; potatoes will be fit to eat in a week or two; watermelons, from the appearance of the vines, will be plenty in a month; and there is every prospect of a large crop of peaches this season. In short, ere long we will live in clover as regards vegetables providing we remain on this station, which from all appearances is very likely, as I see no prospects of our being relieved for some time to come unless some unforeseen event should transpire of which we know not of. We are expecting the arrival of the U.S. steamer *Madgie* with grub from Port Royal, where she has been ever since

Feby. last, undergoing repairs etc. I reported John Hughes—otalgia and Joseph McShane—furunculus sick in my report to the captain.

April 23, 1863. I forgot to mention in my notes of yesterday that two of our Nimrods—viz., William Scott and John Carey—had returned on board last night with a beef, so that we are living high on fresh meat. They both deserve great credit for their skill as marksmen. May they live a long and happy life, with plenty of fresh beef and fair women at their command! I reported my two patients, Hughes and McShane, improving in my daily report of sick. At 2 P.M. Executive Officer Childs, Paymaster Murray, and myself took a ramble on the island, hunting and eating blackberries, at same time having a sociable chat with Aunt Mary, nee Aunt Lizzie, about the affairs of the country, she having a long rigamorole to say about Darien and vicinity. She appears to be very busy with her washing—so much indeed as to compel her to hire help in the shape of Contraband Billy's wife. I dressed Contraband George's foot today, he having hurt it about a week or so ago and thought that he was doctor enough to cure himself, the consequences being that his foot became so much inflamed as to require my services. I immediately, as soon as he made known his case to me, painted the inflamed surface with tincture iodine and applied cerate resinae. He was in a terrible state of mind, thinking that I was going to amputate his leg, the men having told him as much. Poor fellow— he felt better when I told him to the contrary.

April 24, 1863. The weather all day was as mild and balmy as a day in May. All hands were in the best of humor until 8 P.M., when two colored "pussons" tried their skill at fisticuffing on the berth deck, but to their chagrin the master-at-arms soon heard the noise and politely handcuffed them, at the same time giving them a night's lodging in the brig. I suppose ere morning their hot blood will be somewhat cooler than what it was tonight. Serves them right! So much for fighting in the service.

Reported Hughes on the sick list. Mr. Flood, actg. ensign, started on an excursion in the *Old Greeley*, nee *Old Abe*, in the vicinity of Doboy Island. "All went along as merry as a marriage" for an hour or so, when the first thing that attracted our attention was the flag at half mast and union down—in short, a signal of distress. As soon as our executive saw said signal, so soon did he send the 3rd cutter to ascertain the nature of Flood's distress. It appears that he lost his rudder, so that the *Old Greeley* was at the mercy of the waves. All that he could do was to anchor his craft and make a signal of distress. He said that he felt odd when he found himself without a rudder. His idea of losing the rudder excited considerable merriment among the officers and men of ye staunch old *Fernandina*.

April 25, 1863. Reported in my morning report to the captain the discharge from the sick list of John Hughes and none admitted. Mr. Henderson left the ship in the 1st cutter with an armed boat's crew for Sapelo Sound, Ga., there to communicate with the *Potomska* as regards the mail. The lighthouse signal signalized the U.S.S. *Madgie* in the offing sailing southward. Today 4 intelligent contrabands made their appearance in a dugout, having come all the way from the vicinity of Savannah, having travelled ever since Sunday last, and doing without anything to eat since last Tuesday. They were dressed in rags. All appear to have one idea, and that is that to be "free" is to do nothing and have plenty to eat and drink. From their talk, starvation stares the Rebels in the face. They say that flour was $160 per bbl., salt $50 per bushel, tobacco $10 per lb., peas from $1 to $5 per quart, tea and coffee none to be had, shoes and boots from $25 to $100 per pair, and everything else in proportion.

The smartest one of the party says that this is the second time that he run the picket guard of the Rebels. The first time he was caught and for his trouble was favored with 70 lashes on his bare back, after which he was hired out by his mistress at $15 per month to a man to cut rails, who compelled him to split 1,000 rails a week. Not relishing the business of being a "hewer of wood," receiving no pay and nothing but corn bread to eat, he concluded to try to escape the second time from slavery or die, in which he succeeded. He says that his mistress told him that as soon as he came to the Yankees, so soon would they put a harness, prepared for the purpose, on him and compel him to drag cannons and wagons about like horses, and whenever they found that they could not work them (the slaves) any longer, why, then they would sell them and send them to Cuba. But he says that he knew better all the time and that she was only trying to fool him so that he would not run away. He as well as his companions are "bressing de Lord" for helping them to escape—and "T'ank God, we are *free!*" etc. etc. Poor fellows—they are in high glee, and well they might be if all things are in Dixie as they describe them to be. The whole party will be sent to St. Simons Sound, there to be placed on board of the *Keystone State*, as we have no room for them here. From there I suppose they will be shipped North, where they can earn their daily bread and live like human beings and be treated like their free colored brethren of the North are.

Feeling a little indisposed, I took pil hydrarg no i (grs v) tonight and will take a Seidlitz powder in the morning. Read the "Christian Messenger" [published at Halifax, Nova Scotia, 1837-1884, or at Montpelier, Vermont, 1847-1863?] for the month of January 1863 until 9 P.M., when I noted down the items of this day in this, my journal of events, after which I, like a good disciplinarian, turned in at the early hour of 9.30 P.M. I must not forget to mention that the weather all day was lovely and *Fernandina's* officers and crew all in the best of humor.

April 26, 1863. At 1 A.M. a rocket was reported bearing n.w. of the ship. Expecting Mr. Henderson from Sapelo every moment, and that rocket being in his neighborhood, we immediately answered him with a rocket from the ship. At 2 A.M. Mr. Henderson arrived and reported that the *Madgie* had taken our mail to St. Simons Sound; consequently he was not enabled to bring us any letters etc. He brought a few late dates—viz., 12th, 13th, 16th, and 18th—which Capt. Budd sent to Captain Moses. In them we had an account of the Charleston affair, the sinking of the *Keokuk*, etc. Dr. Smith sent me, per Mr. Henderson, some reading matter in the shape of [Sir William Howard] Russell's "[My] Diary North and South" [Boston: T.O.H.P. Burnham; New York: O.S. Felt, 1863; New York: Harper and Brothers, 1863; London: Bradbury and Evans, 2 vols., 1863; the author was war correspondent for the London *Times*]. I must not forget to mention that Captain Budd sent Capt. Moses a box of ale, of which I had the pleasure of drinking a glass at 2.30 A.M.

At 9 A.M. all hands to muster and divine service. 9.30 A.M., Actg. Master's Mate James B. Henderson started with an armed boat's crew in the 1st cutter for St. Simons Sound, there to speak the *Keystone State* and obtain our mail. May he return with a large and interesting mail. The weather all day was rather cool—thermometer 62° Fahr. Since my sojourn on blockade duty, while rambling about on the deserted plantations on the coast of Georgia and South

Carolina, I often gazed for hours at a time upon the grand avenues of live oak, covered, or rather set off, by a superabundant fall from the overlacing arms and intertwined branches of the tillandsia [usneoides], or Spanish moss [not actually a moss but a flowering plant related to the pineapple; often used as packing material and as stuffing for furniture], a weeping, drooping, plumaceous parasite [not, strictly speaking, a parasite but an epiphyte (taking its substance from the air), growing on any solid support], which does to the tree what its animal type, the yellow fever, does to man—clings to it everlastingly, drying up sap, poisoning blood, killing the principle of life till it dies—thinking to myself how foolish it was for those infatuated landholders of the South to concoct treason against the best government that ever existed. "Truly the way of the transgressor is hard." They are paying dearly for their traitorous deeds. Read Russell's "Diary North and South" until 10 P.M., when I turned in to seek repose in the arms of Morpheus.

April 27, 1863. At 8 A.M. the lighthouse lookout signalized "Boats Inland," at 8.15 A.M. the 1st cutter could be seen from our quarter deck between St. Simons and the ship. At 9 A.M. the 1st cutter, Mr. Henderson in charge, arrived with a mail. I received a letter from father dated April 16th, in which he stated that all were well and in good spirits at home, also that on the 11th of April all our family were assembled in the homestead except myself, brother Michael being home on a furlough. Brother David and his little daughter Annie, from Phila.; brother Jefferson, wife, and children, from Harrisburg; brother Frank and family; and Philip Cutler [husband of the diarist's only sister, Rebecca, referred to as Beckie] and family all sat down to a dinner at father's house. Father says everything passed along lovely, and only one thing remained to complete the happiness of the hour, and that was my presence. But I was no less than 1,000 miles away doing blockade duty on board of this craft; hence my being there was out of the question. Their having a happy time and all being well satisfied me.   . . .

I also received a paper from Dr. T. J. Boyer . . . and a paper from A. G. Myers, clerk in the Navy Department at Washington, D.C. The mail was rather a small affair at best. We all expected a larger one.

None to report on sick list. At 2 P.M. all hands to quarters. The crew were exercising the port guns in target practice and done some fine shooting. Finished "Russell's Diary North and South" and must confess that it is rather interesting. I did not expect him to write as candid an account as he did of this rebellion, judging from his Bull Run letter.

["The Battle of Bull Run" (New York: Rudd and Carleton, 1861), from the London *Times*, August 6, 1861; published also in New York, same year, under the title "Mr. Russell on Bull Run"].

April 28, 1863. I had the pleasure of reporting to the captain that there were none on the sick list in my daily report. The weather was rather pleasant all day. Took a stroll on shore and while there took in a small cargo of clams in the raw state. Harry and Billy, two contrabands on Sapelo Island, came to me for some anodyne mixture, or, as they called it, "belly drops to stop the pain and make you sleep." I prepared each one a bottle consisting of tinct. capsici, tinct. zingiber, tinct. opii, ol mentha pip, and aquae, after which they went on their way rejoicing—"bressing de doctee" and "T'ank God!" etc. etc. When asked what they would take for their medicine which the doctor had given them, they answered that no money would buy it! The whole batch of medicine which I gave them was worth about 6/100 dolls. Taking all in all, those innocent causes of the war are as happy as bugs in a rug.

Our caterer served us a dinner today consisting of roast pig etc., which was not hard to eat, for we all managed to lay in large cargoes of the same; in short, we "done justice to Piggy." Paid my steward $2.00 for making a pair of pantaloons for me. While reading the New York "Tribune" of the 10th of April '63, I had the pleasure of seeing the name of Surgeon P. Treadwell of the str. *Columbia* among the list of released prisoners, for be it remembered that he was captured on the coast of N. Carolina sometime in January last [see entry dated February 19, page 71]. I hope that the doctor will have better luck in the next man-of-war. The steamer *Columbia* was run ashore by the wind; hence all hands had to succumb to the Rebels. I don't think that the doctor had a very pleasant time of it while sojourning in a Secesh prison. I shall write to him as soon as I ascertain his address so as to obtain the particulars of his captivity. The doctor is a prince of good fellows. I spent many a happy day with him on blockade duty in Ossabaw Sound.

April 29, 1863.   . . . . I consider the Copperheads to be as bad enemies of the Union as the Secesh of South Carolina [written after reading in the Syracuse (New York) "Weekly Journal" a public requisition on the State of Illinois of Captain Ira J. Bloomfield, of the 26th Illinois Volunteer Infantry, for 300 copperheads that they might be taken to the front and taught "good old doctrines of equal rights, common sense, and the 'Union' forever"]. At 1 P.M. the lighthouse lookout signalized a steamer inland; at 3 P.M. steamer inland showing signals. She proved to be the U.S. steamer *Madgie.* At 4.15 P.M. she passed by the sound, making a bee line for Sapelo, not doing as much as even to say, or signalize, "How are you?" In my estimation I think the captain not sociable, or else he would of spoke us. Let him and his craft go. Who cares? In order to show him that we were independent of him, we as soon as he passed us, at 4.30 P.M., sent Mr. Henderson, in charge of the 1st cutter, to Sapelo Sound, there to communicate with the *Potomska,* whose captain is a gentleman and an honor to the service, and see whether he can obtain some grub from him.

None to report sick. At 9 A.M. Ensign Flood with a party of five men started on a hunt for beef and returned at 7 P.M. without anything in the shape of fresh beef. Reason—the cattle were all too smart for Flood and his Nimrods. Better luck next time. Wrote a letter to father, in answer to his letter of the 16th inst., which I sent to the *Potomska* per Mr. Henderson today. The weather was lovely all day.

April 30, 1863. Not wishing to be considered poor marksmen, two of yesterday's Nimrods concluded to show all hands that they could draw a bead on a bullock; hence they started early this morning on another hunt. At 9 A.M. Paymaster Murray and myself took a walk in the direction of Old Sampson's place. While talking to the old contraband, Harry came to us and told us that Scott and Rickerts (the two Nimrods) had shot one of the cattle and that he was a going to bring it to the ship in his oxcart. Well done, Scott and companion! None can call you poor shots. We'll eat your healths in some of the juicy beef whenever it is served up.

Murray and I had a pleasant time eating blackberries, killing snakes, and viewing the vegetables in Old Sampson's patch. Some of the cornstalks are 4 feet high, others 2 feet, the average being 2½ feet. In a month or six weeks we will have watermelons, peaches, oranges, potatoes, etc. At 2 P.M. Mr. Henderson returned from Sapelo, having a few provisions on board. He reported all well and hardy on board of the *Potomska,* also that our mail left on the *Hope* this morning for Port Royal, S.C.

Today for the first time since last June I had the pleasure of holding in my hand one of those lovely little bits styled a gold dollar. Oh! how I did gaze on said keepsake. My heart swelled with joy. I longed for to transfer said "yellow boy" from my hand to my purse; but alas! the owner said nay, and with an avaricious smile on his face he very quietly pulled out his purse and deposited said piece of shine therein, after which the purse disappeared amidst the folds of his pantaloon pockets—and I of course was compelled to be satisfied with the state in which Mr. Almighty Dollar was placed in. Such was the fate of the little shiner.

[All metal money disappeared with the outbreak of the war, and gold coins, referred to as shiners, yellow boys, etc., were, except in certain parts of the West, rare even in peacetime. Coinage of the gold dollar was discontinued entirely in September, 1890.]

7.15 a rocket was reported bearing n.w. from the ship, upon which all hands were called to quarters. The strange boat proved to be the U.S. str. *Madgie*. Upon ascertaining who she was, the boatswain's mate piped down. She had some money and a few stores for the paymaster. I understand that Dr. Michel, the former surgeon of the *Madgie*, was transferred to the *Memphis* and that Dr. A.B.C. Sawyer [acting assistant surgeon], formerly of the storeship *Valparaiso*, was transferred to the *Madgie*. I have the pleasure of being acquainted with Dr. Michel, whom I met while at anchor in St. Simons Sound, Ga. I also am slightly acquainted with Dr. Sawyer, whom I met on board of the U.S.S. *Vermont* while at anchor in Port Royal harbor, S.C. Both gentlemen appear to be clever boys and know how to keep a hotel. I hope to become better acquainted with Dr. Sawyer ere long.

Paid a mess bill of $7.16 to Caterer W.H. Thomas. Read until 10 P.M., when I turned in.

May 1, 1863. This day is a general moving day up North, also a gala day for school children, who as a general thing go out Maying. I suppose we poor mortals on blockade duty will have to be contented with knowing how the people of the North spend the day without having the pleasure of participating therein. The weather is beautiful. The *Madgie* left for St. Simons Sound at 5 A.M., having on board the contrabands who made their appearance in our midst some time ago. Today Actg. Ensign Christopher Flood entered upon his duties as caterer of the wardroom mess, ex-Caterer Wm.

H. Thomas having resigned the office last evening after having served faithfully three months and a half and Mr. Flood was then unanimously elected caterer for the term of three months unless sooner discharged for misdemeanor in office or is relieved by sickness or death. Mr. Flood assumed the responsible duties of his office in a cheerful manner, promising us a good table and small mess bills. We all hope that he may fulfill his promise.

Today all hands are airing their bedding, it being the day set apart for that purpose in the Navy. They also holystoned [scrubbed with holystone, a soft sandstone used to clean decks] the berth deck. The executive officer, Mr. C.C. Childs, and myself both laboring under the effects of cephalalgia, I, in order to correct the digestive organs, ordered pil: cath: comp: no. v for Mr. Childs and pil: cath: comp: no. iv for myself at 8 P.M. At 11 P.M. the pills commenced to operate upon me beautifully and continued so to do until 12.30, one-half hour after midnight. At 2 A.M. Mr. Childs heard of his dose and continued being an applicant of the transit house until the next morning. It commenced to rain at 11 P.M. and rained hard the next two hours. I placed Alexander Jackson, a contraband, on the binnacle list for the night, he suffering from the effects of a swollen gum, hence not fit to do duty in the night air. Jackson as a general thing is a good-natured sort of a darky, consequently a favorite with all on board.

May 2, 1863. I will continue Alex. Jackson on the binnacle list today. It continued to rain somewhat until 9.30 A.M., when it cleared up. Mr. Childs was telling me that the dose he took last night was a splendid one.   . . . and that Mr. Headache had cut stick [run away] for parts unknown. The lighthouse lookout signalized the *Massachusetts* in the offing sailing south at 4 P.M. Capt. Moses, Paymaster Murray, and myself took a stroll on Sapelo Island so as to stretch ourselves. We had a pleasant time of it. Wrote a letter to mother, enclosing $5, which I'll send by mail tomorrow, directed in care of M. K. Boyer, Esq. The captain obliged me with a copy of the lighthouse signals. They are as follows, viz.:

1. American Flag—Steamer in sight to the Northd.
2. American Flag over Pennant—Steamer in sight to the Southd.
3. English Flag—Sail in sight to the Northd.
4. English Flag over Pennant—Sail in sight to the Southd.
5. Pennant—Vessel in sight is bound North.
6. Jack—Vessel in sight is bound South.

7. French Flag—Steamer inland to the Southd.
8. Spanish Flag—Steamer inland to the Northd.
9. Spanish Flag over Pennant—Vessel in sight is bound into Sapelo.
10. French Flag over Pennant—Vessel in sight is bound into St. Simons.
11. Jack over Pennant—Vessel in sight is bound into Doboy.
12. Yellow Flag—One of our boats inland.
13. Yellow Flag over Pennant—Strange boats inland.
14. Mexican Flag—Vessel in sight has suspicious appearance.
15. Mexican Flag over Pennant—Vessel in sight looks like the *Hope*.
16. Jack over Yellow Flag—Send a boat on shore.
17. Spanish Flag over Yellow Flag—Send in the Dingy.

May 3, 1863. Another six days' work is done. Another Lord's day has begun. During the reading of divine service this morning at 9 o'clock the captain, officiating chaplain, read . . . [A] Prayer [for the President of the United States and all in Civil Authority] . . . Prayer in Time of War and Tumults . . . Lord's Prayer . . . Benediction.   . . . Besides these there were several more prayers read.

At 4 A.M. Paymaster Murray and Master's Mate Henderson in the 1st cutter started for Sapelo Sound, there to speak the *Potomska* and ascertain whether we have any mail matter and provisions on board left there by the *Massachusetts*. At 5 P.M. Paymaster Murray and party returned, having a mail etc. on board. I received a letter from brother Mike of "ye grand armee," which I answered this evening. Also received one from A. G. Myers. I wrote a letter to father concerning some notes. The doctor of the *Potomska* sent me some medicines.

At 5.15 P.M. the officer of the deck cried out that there was a steamer right astern of the ship. Upon looking, she looked like a ram; at best she was a strange craft. We immediately went to quarters and prepared for a fight. I had tourniquets distributed amongst the men, my instruments etc. all ready for "bloody work." In short, we expected one grand fight. Tobacco warehouses stared us in the face. Secesh life in Dixie was thought of. Everyone felt anxious to hear the result, when lo! and behold! to our astonishment she proved to be a tugboat with provisions on board for us. She was the *Oleander*, commanded by Capt. Dennis [Acting Master John S. Dennis], U.S. Navy. Fifteen minutes after her arrival our decks were filled up with barrels, boxes, and bags. We have provisions enough for the next 90 days, so that I see no hopes of going North in a hurry. I also received some killikinick tobacco by the *Oleander*, which the doctor of the *Potomska* had purchased for me from the *Massachusetts*. The tobacco smokes well and is not very high in price, being only 70/100 dolls per lb. Turned in at 10 P.M. My room is very "bilchy" [having the smell of bilge water] tonight—so much so, indeed, as almost to suffocate a person.

May 4, 1863. John Donnelly, lds., at 1 A.M. was visited by an attack of cholera communis, caused by eating, as he says, a peck of blackberries. I, as soon as I knew the nature of his complaint, ordered for him the following dose—viz., pulv opii et ipecacuanha grs x et creta praeparata grs xx—which had the effect of easing the pain and promoting sleep. I gave him a dose of ol ricini at 9 A.M. to carry off the ingesta. He retained in his stomach said dose until 11 A.M., when it acted as an emetic. I immediately gave him another dose of oil, which had a cathartic effect. He says that he had enough blackberries for this season.

4.30 P.M., lighthouse lookout signalized a steamer inland to the southd., and at 5.15 P.M. the *Oleander*, Capt. Dennis, arrived on his return trip. I gave Captain Dennis $200, which he promised to deposit in Adams Express Office at Hilton Head, S.C. . . . The money is to pay off certain notes held against me by Michael K. Boyer. I hope it may reach its destination O.K. Captain Dennis having burned his hand rather severely with a rocket while signalizing the *Keystone State* in St. Simons Sound, I dressed said member with glycerine, lint, etc.—or rather redressed it, for it had been dressed by the surgeon of the *Keystone State* last night. The captain appears to be a jolly old sea dog.

The *Oleander* left at 6 P.M. for Port Royal via inland passage. Capt. Dennis promised to run as a dispatch—i.e., the *Oleander*—between Port Royal and St. Simons Sound, communicating with the vessels in Warsaw [Wassaw according to Geographic Board decision and in the official navy records of the time; Warsaw in Lippincott's *Gazetteer*], Doboy, St. Catharines, Sapelo, Ossabaw, and St. Simons Sound. If that is the case, why, we'll have splendid facilities as regards the sending of mails. The weather was splendid all day. Read Harry [Henry] Fielding's "[The History of Mr.] Jonathan Wild the Great" [which, like others of Fielding's works, had appeared in a number of different editions] until 10 P.M., when I turned in. Paymaster paid me $200 on account.

May 5, 1863. Having purged John Donnelly completely, thus weakening him somewhat, I concluded to give him a tonic today consisting of quiniae sulphas grs ii, acid sulph aromat gtts v, aquae ℥ i, M̶, Sig. Ter in die. I reported him in my morning report to the captain as improving. Patients as a general thing at present are "like the visits of angels few and far between." But, having plenty of fresh beef and vegetables, which we obtain on Sapelo, the ship's company cannot help being healthy.

I had quite a tramp in company with Paymaster Murray hunting blackberries, which are very plenty. We almost ate ourselves sick on blackberries, so plenty and good they were. The weather was warm and sultry until 7 P.M., when it commenced to rain, and continued until 10 P.M. On account of the bilchiness of my room I concluded to sleep on the captain's lounge tonight. So after reading "Tom Jones," by Harry Fielding [*The History of Tom Jones, a Foundling,* or *Tom Jones: The History of a Foundling*—Fielding's "most elaborate and comprehensive work"], until 10 P.M., I endeavored to seek repose in the arms of Morpheus, being aided by a cool room and a good lounge.

May 6, 1863. Donnelly returned to duty feeling all right again. I hope hereafter he will use a little discretion whenever he eats fruit of any kind. Had my berth taken out and the floor of my stateroom corked, puttied, and painted so as to prevent the bilch from coming into my room, after which I replaced the berth—or at least the carpenter's assistant done so. On account of the disordered condition of my stateroom I will spend the night again in the captain's lounge.

The weather was rather pleasant all day. Between smoking, eating, sleeping, and drinking I managed to kill time and drive dull care away. This blockading is rather a dull affair. We all are anxious to make, or take, a journey up North.

May 7, 1863. The U.S. str. *Madgie* arrived from St. Simons at 10 A.M. and remained here long enough for Capt. Moses and myself to step on board of her, after which she started for Sapelo Sound. While on board of her, Capt. Moses and myself had a pleasant time of it in company with Capt. Meriam [Acting Master Frank B. Meriam], Dr. Sawyer, and [Acting Assistant] Paymaster [Bailey] Hascall, drinking ale and sherry and smoking good cigars, at same time cracking jokes and spinning yarns. We remained on board of

her until we were halfway between this place and the plantation—
a distance of 10 miles—after which we up sail and returned in the
gig at the rate of 5 knots. Surgeon Sawyer had 8 on the sick list,
while I had none. After I dined, I took a tramp on shore in the
direction of Old Sampson, whom I found well and in good spirits.
Being somewhat fatigued, I turned in at an early hour—viz.,
8.30 P.M. I might mention that the carpenter painted my room—at
least, he done so partly.

May 8, 1863. Weather cold—thermometer 54° Fahr. Some of the
boys shot a bullock; so we will have some fresh beef. My room is
all O.K. again. Will try to sleep in my berth tonight. Wrote a letter to B. Frank Boyer concerning some ale. Finished Harry Fielding's "Tom Jones," or "The History of a Foundling," and commenced on his "Joseph Andrews and His Friend Abraham Adams"
[*The History of the Adventures of Joseph Andrews, and His Friend,
Mr. Abraham Adams.* Written in imitation of the manner of
Cervantes . . . (London: F. C. and J. Rivington, 1820)].

May 9, 1863. Slept like a trooper last night. My room smells as
sweet as a rose. Bilch is nowhere! Having shut up all cracks, consequently it is played out. I had the pleasure of extracting a molar
for Mr. Gibson this morning, he having labored under the effects of
a decayed tooth some time until, finding that patience ceased to be
a virtue and nature not willing to ease him of the pain, he submitted to the above procedure. I give him credit for his spunk.

Paymaster Murray and myself had courage enough to pick a gallon of blackberries for dinner today. In fact, the captain was surprised to see that we could manage to gather so many when
knowing all the time that we both had a fall out, when young, with
work. I for my part feel proud and think that we both deserve
praise for our readiness to undergo the miseries of hunting berries
in a place where thorns and snakes are so plenty.

Our caterer served us up a dinner, the principal dish being fresh
beef, which was rich and juicy, today which was fit to set before a
king. Bully for the caterer. I have no doubt but what our pockets
will have to suffer at the end of the month when the mess bills are
handed in. "Live while you do live" is our motto; "Eat, drink, and
be merry" is our watchword; and "Drive dull care away" is our object. "Who would not sell a farm and go to sea?" We are spoiling
for a fight! Our only enemies to contend with at present are

mosquitoes, sand flies, and snakes. The weather is rather cool and pleasant.

Commenced to read Charles Reade's "Hearth and Cloister [The Cloister and the Hearth]; or Maid, Wife, and Widow," the events of which transpired during the fifteenth century and taking place in Holland, in the vicinity of Rotterdam, Amsterdam, etc. I find it rather interesting. The hero is one Gerard and the heroine Margaret by name. Turned in at 10 P.M.

8

More Idle Hours in Doboy Sound: The Burning of Darien

Doboy Sound, Ga., May 10, 1863. This is the day set apart for us poor mortals here below to rest from our daily toils and offer up prayers to the Almighty Creator of Heaven and Earth for his kindness in preserving us from all danger and enabling us to spend another Sabbath day in praising his name etc. In order to show that we are not unmindful of the many blessings bestowed upon us, we all assembled at 9 A.M. to a general muster to hear divine service read by Paymaster Murray, the officiating chaplain. The following prayer, amongst many others, was read, which I consider very appropriate, viz.:

> O Eternal Lord God, who alone spreadest out the heavens and rulest the raging of the Sea; who has compassed the waters with bounds, until day and night come to an end; be pleased to receive into thy Almighty and most gracious protection, the persons of us thy servants, and the Ship on which we serve. Preserve us from the dangers of the Sea, and from the violence of the enemy; that we may be a safeguard unto the United States of America, and a security for such as pass on the Seas upon their lawful occasions; that the inhabitants of our land may in peace and quietness serve thee our God; and that we may return in safety to enjoy the blessings of the land, with the fruits of our labour; and, with a thankful remembrance of

thy mercies, to praise and glorify thy holy Name, through Jesus Christ our Lord. Amen.

After divine service the executive officer read several orders concerning paroling of prisoners, rank of officers, and the distribution of the staterooms amongst the wardroom officers, after which the boatswain's mate piped down. The rest of the day spent in reading, smoking, etc.

May 11, 1863. The sick list sports the name of Lewis Y. Close, laboring under the effects of a furunculus, located on the anterior aspect of the right thigh, which was fit and ready for a lance— hence I applied a lance to said boil, after which my steward applied a warm lini cataplasm. Close says that he has a holy horror of my knives and would rather suffer from the effects of a sore than come to me again and have it cut. Poor d—l —he'll feel better after it's done hurting. Two other tars came to me to have some grinders and molars extracted. As a matter of fact, I done so. They left me rejoicing. I need hardly say that they came to me cursing and damning their teeth.

Having finished the "Hearth and Cloister," I commenced perusing Oliver Wendell Holmes' "[The] Autocrat of the Breakfast Table" ("Every man his own Boswell" [inscription in small type on title page of first edition (Boston: Phillips, Sampson and Company, 1858)]) and must say that as far as I have read, I am pleased very much with the autocrat's quaint and wise sayings. . . . .

The lighthouse lookout signalized a steamer going into St. Simons Sound. From her appearance we make her out to be the dispatch boat *Oleander.* Tomorrow we will look for a mail. I sincerely hope it may be a large one. The weather was rather lovely all day. Took a stroll on the island and had a lively chat with Lizzie; also paid her some wash money.

May 12, 1863. Charles W. Jordan, coxswain of the 3rd cutter, was admitted to the sick list laboring under an attack of intermittens. ℞ hydrarg. chlor mite grs vi et ol ricini ℥ i, to be followed in due time by diaphoretics. Lewis Y. Close still continues on the sick list. ℞ cerate resinae, in place of lini cataplasm, for his furunculus.

11 A.M., the lighthouse lookout signalized a steamer to the southward and at 11.30 A.M. that the steamer was bound into Doboy

Sound, which is our station. Huzza! huzza!! huzza!!! for a mail. The officer of the deck reports her to be the *Oleander*. Bully for that! Now I can ascertain whether my money left Port Royal all right. This is the first time in two months that the above signal was hoisted.

12.30 M. The *Oleander* is alongside. She brings us a small mail, but I did not receive any letters or papers. Capt. Dennis handed me a receipt which he received from Adams Express Company in return for $200 which I sent per him. I handed him $1, the amount which he paid to have the same insured. I now feel perfectly safe as regards the "shino" [money]. Capt. Dennis obliged me with 11 stamped envelopes ($0.35), and his executive officer, Mr. Frost [Acting Ensign Joseph Frost], obliged me with 10 postage stamps ($0.30); so now for the time being I am O.K. as regards stamps etc. Wrote a letter to father regarding the money I sent him, also as regards some postage stamps, and sent it to Port Royal per Captain Dennis. I understand that the *Potomska* left for Port Royal a few days ago. Captain Meriam of the *Madgie* has been transferred to another command, and Captain W. H. Polleys [Acting Master Woodbury H. Polleys], who is a passenger on the *Oleander,* takes his place.

May 13, 1863. I retain Chas. W. Jordan on the sick list and discharge Lewis Y. Close. Jordan is taking diaphoretics and tonics; he feels somewhat better. Close is O.K. as regards his furunculus. The weather was rather warm today. The boys are killing snakes more or less every day. I saw three today that measured 19 feet—two coachwhips and one moccasin. One of our seamen told me the way that a coachwhip inflicts his punishment on man [by wrapping his upper body around a leg of the victim and whipping the unfortunate person to death with his tail!]. . . .

May 14, 1863. At 4.30 A.M. Paymaster Murray and myself went ashore in the *Tiger* and took a bath. We used an inlet of Doboy Sound for a tub. We had rather a pleasant time of it. After remaining in the water a short time, we concluded to rub ourselves down with a coarse towel, dress ourselves, and come on board again. We arrived on board at 6 A.M. feeling refreshed and having an appetite for breakfast. We done our duty at the breakfast table as regards eating grub. 9 A.M., a steamer signalized, sailing into Doboy Sound. Who and what she is is the general talk of all hands.

Some say she is our relief; other say she is the *Keystone State*. I for my part hope that she is our relief. As soon as she was within signalizing distance, we fired a gun in order to make her show her colors, or number. No notice was taken. We fired a second one and showed our numbers, after which we seen a boat leave her side. Mr. Henderson was then sent in the gig to speak her and see who and what she was. She proved to be an Army boat named the *Saxon*, commanded by Capt. Lavender [probably a master in the employ of the company from which the vessel was chartered], with part of the 1st South Carolina Regt. Volunteers (colored regt.) on board. We were all at quarters ready to fight in case she proved to be an enemy. What her object is in coming here I cannot tell, but time will show. I am sorry that it was not our relief.

At 6.15 P.M. our executive officer, Mr. Childs, and myself paid the *Saxon* a visit, I to see the captain and asst. surgeon of the company and Mr. Childs to see and have a chat with the captain of the steamer, who appears to be an old whaler. I found Capt. Randolph [probably Captain William J. Randolph of Company C, who was among those given honorable mention by Colonel Higginson for their conduct during the operations incident to an expedition carried on by the regiment in late January, 1863] to be quite a sociable officer. The doctor, on the contrary, appeared to be somewhat of a "stick in the mud"—in plain language, he was anything else than sociable. The *Saxon* was General Butler's flagship at the taking of New Orleans. She is rather a beautiful-looking craft; her wardroom, or cabin, is commodious and well ventilated. I would like to see her transferred into a naval vessel and I have the honor of being her medical officer. We remained on board almost half an hour, when we concluded to return on board of the *Fernandina*.

I reported Jordan as improving. He is taking tonics. Feeling unwell this afternoon, I in order to relieve nature took a nap from 2 to 4 P.M., after which I felt somewhat better. Finished reading Holmes' "Autocrat of the Breakfast Table" and am well pleased with the same. Hope to have the pleasure of perusing some more of Mr. Holmes' writings. After smoking a pipe of killikinick, reading a paper at same time, I concluded to turn in for the night, which I did at 10 P.M.

May 15, 1863. Coxswain Jordan still continues on the sick list. I took the following dose today—viz., hydrarg chlo mite grs vi, jalapa pulv grs xv, M —which operated no less than 12 or 15 times. The captain also took a purgative, in the shape of a blue pill and a Seidlitz powder. Both the captain and myself have been suffering from the effects of a foul stomach, which had caused us to be suffering with a severe cephalalgia. We hope to feel better in the morning. A brisk gale has been blowing all day. Raining part of the time.

May 16, 1863. I was compelled to leave my couch at 2 A.M. to obey a call of nature, the effects of yesterday's dose. The dose continued to operate at 8, 9, and 10 A.M., after which I felt like a new being. The captain, on the contrary, was compelled to take another dose—viz., pil: cath: comp. no. iii. At 7 P.M. he felt O.K., the dose having done its duty. Actg. Master's Mate Jas. B. Henderson was blessed with a severe attack of cephalalgia today, for which I prescribed pil: cath: comp. no. iv at 7 P.M. I expect to find him all right in the morning. Coxswain Jordan is convalescent. My steward went ashore this afternoon to dress Old George's foot, which is very sore. He lanced and cauterized it, after which he applied a lini cataplasm. I had ordered him so to do. I shall go and see his foot myself tomorrow providing the weather is favorable. It has been blowing and raining all day; consequently it was rather dull and dreary on board of ye *Fernandina*. Our steward killed a porker, which he intends to serve up for dinner tomorrow. I placed Mr. Henderson's name on the binnacle list so as to excuse him from duty tonight.

May 17, 1863. The weather is superb. Divine service at 9 A.M., Actg. Paymaster T. A. Murray officiating as chaplain. All hands attended the service. 9.30 A.M., boatswain's mate piped down. 10 A.M., the starboard watch went ashore, it being their liberty day. I sent my steward, R. D. Adams, along with them so that he could dress Old George's foot and report his condition to me. Nothing of any account (outside of the routine of the ship) transpired today. My patients are the same except Mr. Henderson, who returns to duty.

May 18, 1863. Charles W. Jordan returns to duty. My steward, who was ashore to see George's foot, reports it being somewhat better. The *Saxon* left this harbor, bound for Fernandina, Florida, at 9 A.M. She remained at anchor here since last Thursday. What her object was I am not able to tell, unless it be to kill time. As she was not of much account as regards blockading, I am not sorry that she left. The next time she pays us, or at least this place, a visit, I hope it will be the day after we have left Doboy. . . . .

Today some person or persons had the meanness to steal the pocketbook and its contents, which was upwards of $12, belonging to the colored woman Lizzie on shore. As soon as she reported the loss of her money, Captain Moses subscribed $10, Mr. Childs $10, Paymaster Murray $5, and myself $5—in all $30—as a reward, offering anyone the above amount who would point out the party or parties who stole the purse and its contents or who would give any information as regards said theft. The "reward bill" was written and posted on the mainmast, where all hands had an opportunity of reading said reward. Four persons who are suspected of having something to do with said larceny (who were on shore at the time that she lost her purse and money) were immediately put on the black list, at least so far as regards going ashore, none being allowed to go ashore, or leave the ship, under any circumstances as long as we lay at this anchorage. If they are innocent, the punishment is rather severe. If guilty, it is too mild. At best it will do no harm. I hope the thief or thieves will be found, for he or they deserve to be punished to the full extent of the law. It took the poor wench two weeks' hard work at the washtub to earn the above amount ($12), and she cannot afford to lose it.

Old George's foot appears to be somewhat better. My steward is attending him faithfully and will no doubt ere long cure him, I occasionally giving him a little advice as regards the treatment. Captain Moses, who is complaining of an internal soreness, or irritation, is taking a demulcent, consisting of ulmus pulv ℥ ii et aquae bul. O ii; macerate two hours and drink cold ad libitum.

Messrs. Scott and Callieu, two of our Nimrods, who had started on a hunting tour early in the day, at 5 P.M. sent on board a beef in the shape of a young cow but did not return themselves. I suppose they want something better; hope they will draw a bead on a large bullock.

Read until 10 P.M., when I turned in, "Joan of Arc and Minor Poems" by Robert Southey, which is a splendid work. His "Surgeon's Warning" is rather rich and sarcastic. The whole volume teems with wit and common sense.

May 19, 1863. The U.S.S. *Madgie* arrived at 7 P.M. from Sapelo and brought us a mail. I received a letter from father dated May

3rd, in which he states that all were well and in good spirits at home, and one from A. G. Myers, Esq., clerk in the 4th auditor's office, Washington, D.C., written in his usual style. Both Andy and wife were well; his letter is dated May 4th. I also received a "Navy Register" for 1863, "Rory O'More [: A National Romance]," by Samuel Lover, Esq. [second edition, illustrated by the author, published in London in 1837 by R. Bentley], and a Washington paper of May 5th from Andy, which I shall acknowledge in my answer to his of the 4th inst. While on board the *Madgie,* I had a pleasant and sociable chat with Dr. Sawyer and Paymaster Hascall. The surgeon gave me a small quantity of gentian pulv, of which I intend to make a tonic mixture for Capt. Moses. Took a stroll in the direction of Sampson Hillery's plantation and had a chat with Old Sampson and his lady. Gave them a small quantity of tobacco. It was rather pleasant while strolling through the woods to listen to the barking of the alligator, chirping of birds, hissing of the cowardly black snake, deadly rattle of the rattlesnake, humming, buzzing, and stinging of the mosquitoes, sand flies, and horseflies, and the noise made by the lizard while running through the leaves.

May 20, 1863. The *Madgie* left for St. Simons this morning. I sent the surgeon some reading matter in the shape of "Russell's Diary" and "Marion and His Men" [probably *Marion's Men, A Romance of the Revolution,* by the author of "The Old Loyalist," "The Southern Whig," etc. (Philadelphia: A. J. Rockafeller, 1843)]. Wrote a letter to father in answer to his date of the 3rd inst., also one to A. G. Myers, Esq., in answer to his dated May 4. Reported James Sullivan, sea.—catarrhus in the sick report. Old George's foot is about the same.

May 21, 1863. In my daily report of sick I admitted Michael Heeney, capt. forecastle—catarrhus on the list and discharged James Sullivan. Heeney is taking potassae nitras grs v ter in die, having been purged well last night. Thomas Dowd, lds.—catarrhus —℞ hydrarg chlo. mite grs v, jalapa grs xv, ol mentha pip. gtts ii, M̶, Sig. One dose—also was admitted on the list. At 10 A.M. James Turner, aged 22, Phila., lds., came to me, having cut his thumb. I immediately applied one stitch of the interrupted suture and a few adhesive strips and ordered him to keep the part wet with cold water so as to favor union by the first intention. He also became a member of the sick list. Paid Old George a visit and found his foot in rather an unpleasant state. The slough has the appearance of a phagedeanic [phagedenic] ulcer. I ordered the application of acid nitric, to be followed by a lini cataplasm fomented, or medicated, with laudanum. As soon as the ulcer is cleansed, I shall dress it with a lotion consisting of cupri sulph, tinct opii, et aquae.

May 22, 1863. Paymaster Murray, Master's Mate Henderson, and an armed boat's crew started in the 1st cutter for Sapelo at 9.15 A.M., having the mail. Their object is to remain on board the *Potomska* and speak the *Massachusetts* as she passes by the sound so as to receive our mail matter and grub. We all hope that they may be successful in obtaining a large mail and plenty of the good things of this life.

Messrs. Heeney, Dowd (old case), and Barron, lds., 22, Maine— intermittens were admitted on the sick list and reported as such in my daily report to the captain. James Turner returns to duty, at the same time using his cut thumb very little. Old George's foot appears somewhat better. I ordered my steward to use the following treatment in his case: this morning apply acid nitric, to be followed by lini cataplasm and chloride of lime; at 5 P.M. he removed the poultice and applied a lotion consisting of cupri. sulph. opii et aquae, which he will continue using until morning. Nature appears to be trying to throw off the sloughing mass—hence the above treatment. He also is taking internally tinct. ferri chloridi gtts vii ter in die.

Finished the reading of Samuel Lover's "Rory O'More," which I found to be rather interesting and amusing, but it is not to be compared to his "Handy Andy [: A Tale of Irish Life" (London: F. Lover, 1842)]. The weather has been lovely all day—a cool breeze blowing all the time. At 9.30 P.M. the U.S.S. *Madgie* passed by the upper part of the sound, bound for St. Catharines Sound. She burned her numbers [signaled her identification by means of lights]. We answered by burning our number in return. About the same time Mr. Henderson of the 1st cutter sent up a rocket, which we answered.

11.15 P.M. The Sapelo party have returned without having had any communication with the *Massachusetts,* the sea being too rough outside for a small boat, and Captain West [Acting Volunteer Lieutenant William H. West] was not obliging enough to come into Sapelo Sound; hence the *Potomska, Braziliera, Madgie,* and *Fernandina* will have to wait a long time ere they will have the pleasure of having beef, potatoes, onions, or mail matter. I think it a damn shame that the *Massachusetts* does not supply us.

James Sullivan, a seaman, had an attack of epistaxis so bad at 12 o'clock as to compel me to let him go below. After drinking a glass of sherry with Mr. Henderson and a glass of ale with Capt. Moses, I concluded to turn in for the night, it being 11.45 P.M.

May 23, 1863. All on board being anxious for the mail, which the *Massachusetts* left at St. Simons Sound, the captain, in order to gratify our, as well as his own, curiosity, sent Mr. Henderson in the 1st cutter for said sound. He started at 5.30 A.M.

Dowd and Barron still continue on the sick list. Both are improving. Heeney returned to duty. James Sullivan, whom I sent below last night, being subject to bleeding at the nose (epistaxis), is taking tinct. ferri. chloridi gtts viii ter in die—also keep his hair cut short, head cool, and feet warm. Old George's foot is improving. I'll continue the same treatment as yesterday. He slept last night a good sound sleep, the first time in 6 nights. Poor d—l —he suffered considerable. Our steward—i.e., the wardroom's—brought a half bushel of plums on board, which he gathered on one of the neighboring plantations. They are the wild red and yellow plum, rather juicy and pleasant to take. He says that they are very plenty and in a day or two all will be ripe.

10 P.M. Mr. Henderson has returned, and I have received one solitary paper as my portion of the mail. So much for this day's anxiety.

May 24, 1863. Old Sol was out in all his glory today. "Everything was lovely and the goose hung high." 9.30 A.M. found all hands at muster to attend divine service, Paymaster Murray officiating as chaplain. After the reading of service our executive officer Mr. Childs, read the Rules and Regulations for the Better Government of the Navy, or Articles of War, after which all hands were piped down. . . . .

May 25, 1863. My sick list numbers 3—viz., Messrs. Spain, Kingsley, and Birdsall. The sutler schooner *Jas. W. Lawrence* has arrived in port. Capt. Moses, Paymaster Murray, and myself went on board of her this evening. I invested a small trifle in collars, envelopes, etc. My steward reports that Old George's foot was beginning to granulate finely. I therefore told Adams (my steward) to continue the application of the lotion composed of cupri sulph, opii et aqua. Some of the boys feel lively, having imbibed rather freely while on board of the sutler. The weather was rather pleasant all day. Paymaster paid me $30 on account.

May 26, 1863. From early morn until late at night the cry is Sutler! Sutler!! Sutler!!! All and everyone has something to buy. No sooner has a boat returned from the schooner but what there are others who want something else, and I suppose were he (the sutler) to remain here one week, the same want would still exist—for as long as a greenback can be had, so long will it trouble the possessor, and he will not feel satisfied until it has passed into the hands of the Peter Funk[36] of the schooner.

The wardroom mess has laid in quite a lot of stores. Our mess bills will be somewhat higher than what they were last month. The steerage mess also are going it strong. The buying fever has even effected the contrabands on shore. Old George bought flour, tea, sugar, etc. to the tune of $12; Billy, Harry, and Sampson each invested about $15 in grub. They say they are bound to live, let come what will. I admire their spunk. I will quote a few of the sutler's prices so as to show how he imposes on our good nature at a time when we cannot help ourselves but are compelled to pay him his villainous prices. They are as follows: viz., flour $12 per bbl., sugar $20 per 100 lbs., shoes $5 per pair (worth $2.50), pipes $15, envelopes $1 per hundred, paper $5 per ream, collars $4 per hundred, sherry, Madeira, and port wine $15 per doz., stomachic bitters $18 per doz., ale $3 per doz., tobacco (killikinick) $5 per bale of 5 lbs., potatoes $3.50 per bbl., and everything else in proportion. It is a confounded shame that he charges such prices, and it looks foolish in us for paying him his prices, but "necessity knows no law."

4 P.M. Blowing a moderate gale from the northeast. Some of the boys have "sore heads" today, the effects of ale and wine, which they managed to get of the sutler on board of the schooner *Jas. W. Lawrence*. A sad change of affairs: last night they felt good and talked of their rich relations, but alas! today they feel poor and miserable and think of their poor relations. . . . .

Three of the parties felt so bad as to compel them to come to me to be excused from doing duty tonight. I, having a little mercy for them, excused them by placing their names on the binnacle list.

May 27, 1863. The three patients, or sick boys, who indulged rather freely in ale and wine and whom I excused last night from duty had the pleasure of taking a dose of hydrarg. chlo mite grs vi, jalapa pulv grs xv, ol. mentha pip: gtts. ii, ℳ, which will relieve them of the poison and clear their drowsy heads, although they remonstrated somewhat as regards the dose. But I was determined to give them both a warning and a cleansing out; hence they had to swallow the pill, however bitter and nauseating. Their names grace the binnacle list. I reported sick Michael Spain—intermittens, Jacob Kingsley—cephalalgia, and William Price—hemorrhoids.

The weather all day was rough. Bought a cap and other articles from the sutler today. Paid a mess bill of $19.14 to the caterer. Took a stroll in the direction of Old Sampson's plantation this afternoon in company with Captain Moses and Paymaster Murray. The corn on his plantation is very high and is commencing to tassel. Everything in the vegetable line is coming on finely.

Old George's foot is improving rapidly. I am dressing it with cerate simplex, and he is taking tinct ferri chlo. gtts vii ter in die, his diet to consist of rice, bread, butter, and molasses, with a cup of tea or coffee occasionally.

May 28, 1863. Three "binnacle boys" went to do duty today, so that I only have two to report sick—viz., William Price, who is improving, and John Denny—catarrhus, the effects of a drunken spree. My steward reports Old George's foot as improving. The second cutter's crew, being on shore, while returning to the ship received a complete drenching on account of the high wind and roughness of the sea. One of the crew, a Mynheer Johannas Schmidt, exclaimed, "Got for damnt! dis ist very vet vetter."

Finished Wilkie Collins' "White Woman," or "[The] Woman in White" [published in seven editions and a number of translations within six months after appearing serially in 1860 in *All the Year Round;* followed in 1862 by *The Yellow Mask; or, The Ghost in the Ball Room,* also read by the diarist], which is a splendid affair. His characters are well brought out.   . . .

May 29, 1863. The weather continues stormy. Reported one case sick—viz., Price, who is improving slowly. George's foot is filling up gradually. Commenced writing a copy of my private journal at the request of Capt. Moses, who wishes a copy of the same. It is rather a tedious job.

May 30, 1863. No change in the weather. The sutler schooner left this morning. One of the sutlers was mean enough to take along the gun belonging to Old George—in plain language, stole it. It is almost as bad as stealing the pennies off a dead man's eyes and kick the body because they were not dollars.

Our Irish potatoes are coming on finely. We dug up one today which measured 3 inches one way, 2 inches another, and 1½ inches the other third. Had a lively sail in the captain's gig. Reported Price improving.

May 31, 1863. The str. *Potomska* and schr. *Hope* being signalized by the lighthouse lookout as in the offing, Capt. Moses immediately sent Mr. Henderson in the 1st cutter to speak them. He returned at 3 P.M., after having communicated with both, with a mail. I received a letter from sister Beckie. The mail matter was rather slim. One of "ye intelligent contrabands" from Macon, Ga., arrived on board, having left Secesh two days ago. When asked by Capt. Moses where he was from, he answered, "From the Southern States." "Oh!" says the captain, "I thought you was from Maine." The darky reports hard times in Secesh, people starving for want of the necessaries of life.

[Slaves who escaped from the Confederacy were a frequent source of information, reliable and unreliable, as to conditions and activities in the region. The day after the above diary entry Acting Master Moses relayed to Commander Le Roy of the *Keystone State* a report of two contrabands who had come by way of the Altamaha River that the enemy were "cotton-cladding three steamers near Darien, preparatory to making an attack in this vicinity" and a statement of an escapee from Darien who had come aboard ship the day before "that a company of twenty-five men have been at work near Darien, under charge of Daniel Bishope, a Northern man, making some 90 bushels of salt per day," guarded by three pickets of five men each, who could "easily be surprised."[37]]

The way he walked into beef, bread, and potatoes was not slow. He allowed that it was the only "full meal" that he had since the war broke out. Poor mortal! Weather warm—thermometer 86° Fahr.

June 1, 1863. Reported William Price improving in my morning report. Thermometer 90° Fahr. in shade. Weather sultry. Thermometer 105° Fahr. in the sun. Mr. Henderson left at 8 A.M. for St. Simons Sound and returned at 9 P.M. He communicated with the *Paul Jones* and *Keystone State*. Nothing new from Port Royal. Read "Orley Farm," by Anthony Trollope [published in three volumes (New York: Dodd and Mead, 1861-1862)]. The characters are well sustained. 3 P.M., target practice with heavy guns. One shot penetrated the target; the rest were all line shots. The boys done well. 7 P.M., partial eclipse of the moon.

June 2, 1863. I shall continue Price on the sick list a day longer, he being somewhat debilitated. Mr. Henderson, in charge of 1st cutter, started at 4 A.M. for Sapelo Sound and returned at 3 P.M. At 2 P.M. Captain Budd of the *Potomska* arrived in his gig. Weather warm—thermometer 88° Fahr. 4 or 5 large sharks seen in the vicinity of the ship. The appearance of the *Potomska's* boat, when she first hove in sight, was rather suspicious; hence the captain started the 2nd and 3rd cutters, manned and armed, in charge of Ensigns Thomas and Flood, so as to speak her and in case of being an enemy capture her. But she proving to be a friend, consequently the boys felt disappointed that they could not have a fight. Read Wilkie Collins' "Yellow Mask; or, The Ghost in the Ball Room." It is "short and sweet." A heavy squall prevails at 7 P.M.

June 3, 1863. William Price was discharged from the list at 8 A.M. and became a member again of the list at 9.30 A.M. Cause— vulnus contusum of scalp. We dropped down a short distance from our old anchorage. Thermometer 89° Fahr.

June 4, 1863. The weather was not as warm as yesterday. Thermometer 80° Fahr. Reported Alonzo Townsend, actg. master's mate, 28, Penna.—intermittens and Wm. Price—vul. contu. sick.

June 5, 1863. The thermometer 82° Fahr. Discharged Messrs. Townsend and Price from the list. Harry, one of the contrabands on Sapelo, brought the news of the death of Ceaser, Old Sampson Hillery's grandson. He will be buried this evening. The carpenter at the request of the captain made a rough coffin for the body. Paymaster Murray and Ensign Thomas as well as 4 of our crew went to attend the funeral. Ceaser was a cripple, 20 years old, and ever since his birth as helpless as an infant. Consequently he is better off in his grave than what he was while living. Peace to his ashes. He was buried at 4.30 P.M., Ensign Thomas reading the funeral service. They returned on board at 7 P.M. well drenched. A squall was prevailing while they were coming from shore in the 3rd cutter. They changed their clothing as soon as they arrived on board. Paid a visit to George; found his foot healing finely. Ordered him to continue the lotion during the day and at night to dress it with cerate simplex.

June 6, 1863. The lighthouse lookout signalized no less than 4 steamers or sails in the offing, all sailing south. By means of the captain's telescope I managed to read the name of one of them, which proved to be the Army boat *Nellie Baker.* She also was signalized as going into St. Simons Sound. One of the others was supposed by her appearance to be the Army boat *John Adams.* The dispatch steamer *Oleander,* U.S. Navy, also was signalized as going into St. Simons Sound. The remaining steamer no one recognized, as her built was strange. But I suppose she also was a boat loaded with troops, for some of the others had their decks full of soldiers.

At 6 P.M. the U.S. schooner *Hope* appeared at the outer buoy, where she anchored and set a signal for us to send a boat for letters. Mr. Henderson immediately started for her in the 1st cutter, taking with him a small mail to be left on board the *Hope* for Port Royal. I sent per Mr. Henderson two Northern letters—viz., one to father and one to sister Beckie, in answer to hers which I received on the 31st of May. Paid a barber bill of $5, which pays him until the 1st of August, 1863. Paymaster paid me $15 on account.

At 9.10 P.M. Mr. Henderson returned with the mail. I was the happy recipient of a letter from father, enclosing satisfied notes to the tune of $224. I immediately tore up said notes, after which I felt good and happy. Thus ends the long chapter of note paying, for I have been paying note after note until I am fairly drained of cash. Henceforth I can pocket all I earn and not be compelled to pay interest etc. In plain language, I am now as free as the air. Bully for me! I also received a Reading "Gazette" from father. All were well and hearty at home when father wrote his letter, which was dated May 18th. Read late dates until 12 o'clock, when I turned in.

June 7, 1863. All hands attended divine service at 9 A.M. The weather was rather warm today—thermometer 85° Fahr. in shade at 12 M. and 89° at 3 P.M. Wrote a letter to father in answer to his

last, dated May 18. Reported none sick. 4 P.M., thermometer 90°
Fahr., at sundown or about 7 P.M. the thermometer stood at 86°
Fahr. In short, the day was a remarkable warm and close one.
Nothing of any importance transpired today.

June 8, 1863. The weather today is somewhat cooler than what it
was yesterday. Quite a breeze is blowing. Thermometer 74° Fahr.
The change in the weather has caused one of the greatest torments
that was ever sent to afflict man for his iniquities in this world,
the mosquito, to skedaddle. This tribe of tormentors begin to
swarm with the returning heat of the season in April and continue
their annoyance till they are stiffened and benumbed by the
cold of November. As soon as the evening shades begin to prevail,
the air is thickened with swarming myriads of these venomous in-
sects that arise in clouds from the marshes like volumes of dust in
the deserts of Arabia. Their murmuring, tinkling singing is so
strongly associated in the mind with the disagreeable sensation of
their bite that their noise is rendered far more unpleasant than the
pealing thunder or the rattling storm. Blood is their cry: nothing
but blood will quench their thirst and satisfy their sanguinary ap-
petites. Compared with them, the mosquitoes of the Northern
States are mere gnats. Furnished with a bill like iron, they perforate
the toughest hide and drink the crimson stream of man and
beast. Without a good mosquito bar or screening curtain to defend
yourself from the unremitting intrusion of these active attendants
upon man's sleeping moments, you might as well endeavor to
seek repose upon a bed of thorns.[38]

None to report sick. Wrote a letter to Prof. Rogers, dean of
faculty, University of Penna., Phila., regarding a catalogue of
students for the session of 1862-3. [Robert E. Rogers, M.D., appointed professor of chemistry at the University of Pennsylvania in
1852 and dean of the medical faculty in 1856; in 1863 he became
acting assistant surgeon at the West Philadelphia Military Hospital.]

June 9, 1863. The *Harriet A. Weed,* an Army steamer, made her
appearance in Doboy Sound at 1.30 P.M. Not knowing who and
what she was when first she came in sight, consequently as soon as
we thought she was near enough for all purposes, we fired a blank
cartridge. She not taking notice of said gun, we gave her the contents of a second one right across her bow—i.e., sent a shot right

ahead of her. This brought her to. We then sent the 1st cutter in charge of Ensign Thomas to speak her. As stated above, she proved to be the Army transport *Harriet A. Weed,* with some Army troops on board. From the tenor of their conversation—for a major and captain (Major Corwin and Captain Holden) [Major B. Ryder Corwin and Captain Oliver B. Holden, both of the Thirty-fourth Regiment, United States Colored Troops, organized at Beaufort and Hilton Head, South Carolina, as the Second Regiment, South Carolina Colored Volunteers] came on board to report to Capt. Moses—I think they are bound on an expedition up the Altamaha River. [The regiment was at the time engaged in a series of expeditions along the coast. Two days after this entry it burned the town of Darien. (See entry March 17.)] I might mention that all hands had been called to quarters as soon as we ascertained that she was bound into this place.

I had everything in the sick bay prepared for the reception of patients etc. in case any should present themselves; also had the tourniquets distributed amongst the men. In short, everyone was ready to show fight. But, thanks to fortune, all passed along merrily. So much for the appearance of one of ye Army steamers. They report that the capture of Vicksburg by our troops is confirmed in the papers of the 30th of May. Thus the Rebel stronghold, the Gibraltar of the Mississippi, is taken. Enough victory for one day. The Army and Navy have achieved new laurels. Long may the Federal government live! We are showing the world that the Yankee nation is the best and able to do her own fighting.

The Army steamer left at 6 P.M. for St. Simons. None to report sick. Thermometer 76° Fahr.

June 10, 1863. I reported George Parker, o. sea., sick in my morning report, affected with a severe cephalalgia. I ordered him a dose of calomel and jalap, which will cure him, I think. I also lanced a boil which was located on Lewis Y. Close's thigh. The way he bawled out was not slow; he damned boils, knives, etc. My steward reports George's foot considerable better. Continue the cerate simplex. Weather warm—thermometer 80° Fahr. Ensign Thomas favored us officers with the following airs on the fife—viz., "Home Sweet Home," "Hail Columbia," "Auld Lang Syne," etc. etc. The way he played the fife was not slow. He was leaning back in an armchair with his feet cocked up on a stool. A straw hat surmounted his head, and he was dressed in a naval fatigue suit. I might mention that his daily companion, a pipe, was placed on a stool by his side, ready loaded for a puff after his exercise on the instrument. Truly, verily indeed, Ensign Thomas is a jolly sea dog. Long may he flourish.

8 P.M., some of the boys are having a lively time on deck "tripping on the light fantastic toe." 9.10 P.M., the officer of the deck reported a vessel at the outer buoy shining a light. Upon a careful examination of said light we ascertained that it was a signal of three lights—red, white, and green. We immediately sent up two rockets and placed a red light at our yardarm. Nothing else transpired as regards the vessels. I suppose they intend to lay outside tonight. Large fire seen on the mainland. The Rebels are burning cotton etc., for I have no doubt but what they have an idea of an expedition etc.

June 11, 1863. The Army boats *Harriet A. Weed, Sentinel,* and *John Adams* arrived in Doboy Sound this morning. The U.S. steamer *Paul Jones* arrived at 9 A.M. Capt. Moses went on board of her at 9.15 A.M. The captain returned at 10 A.M., and at 10.30 A.M. the captain and myself left in the gig for the *Paul Jones.* Master's Mates Henderson and Gibson with 10 armed men left in the 1st cutter for said steamer. The Army steamers then left for Darien, after which the *Paul Jones* brought up the rear. The Army boats shelled the various mills etc. as they passed along. Occasionally the *Paul Jones'* guns could be heard. At 2 P.M. all hands were called to quarters. During the time of quarters her bulldogs could be heard every minute or so belching forth their deadly contents.

We remained at quarters until 5.15 P.M. My station during quarters was with Surgeon Hazleton on the berth deck in the sick bay, which was rather a hot station. The doctor and myself managed with the aid of a tomcat to capture a Rebel in the shape of a rat who had the audacity to make a raid into the dispensary. Mr. Rat forfeited his life for this audacity. No one was hurt on board of the *Paul Jones.* At 3 P.M. the Army troops—i.e., Colonel [James] Montgomery's regt. of contrabands set fire to Darien, and in a short time the whole place was one mass of flame. The sight was beautiful. Whether it was proper and pat to burn the place I know not, but I do know that the place was reduced to ashes.

The *Harriet A. Weed* managed to capture a schooner loaded

with cotton which intended to run the blockade tonight. Thus the rose was nipped in the bud. Said schooner was the one that was to run the blockade some time ago, at which time in order to capture her, in case she attempted to run out, we had secret expeditions fitted out every night. We are only sorry that an Army instead of a Navy vessel captured the prize. She is valued at $25,000. Colonel Montgomery landed his troops at Darien and captured about 20 contrabands, after which the place, as stated above, was set on fire. He then marched into the interior, destroying crops etc. etc. We did not ascend the river all the way to Darien on account of our vessel, the *Paul Jones*, being too large a craft. Consequently we have nothing to do with the burning of Darien, being merely spectators.

At 9 P.M. we made tracks for Doboy Sound again. The Army boats returned at 10 and 11 P.M. They succeeded in obtaining contrabands, furniture, cotton, etc. etc. Thus endeth the chapter as regards expeditions being fitted out in the direction of Darien, Ga., it being the 4th expedition in which I took a part and finally ended in the destruction of Darien, Ga. Darien, Ga., is amongst the things that was. Those beautiful mills, houses, and stores are no more. All that remains of a once beautiful town is one mass of smouldering ruins—one of the effects of civil war. I returned on board the *Fernandina* at 10 P.M.

[The Darien episode was one of a series of raids made on the mainland by army and navy forces along the blockaded coast. The regiment referred to was the Second South Carolina Regiment (colored), under Colonel James Montgomery, which had participated in the occupation of Jacksonville and other expeditions earlier in the year and was now engaged in "a system of incursions" in which bridges, crops, and other property were destroyed, portable assets such as cotton and cattle and horses were appropriated, and slaves were carried away for filling up the ranks of colored regiments.

[The question in Dr. Boyer's mind as to whether it was "proper and pat to burn the place" was being asked by many people in relation to destruction by the military. Two days before the Darien incident Major General Hunter, commanding the Department of the South, had written Colonel Montgomery from his headquarters at Hilton Head calling attention to War Department General Order Number 100 "promulgating a system of 'Instructions for the government of armies of the United States in the field,' " and warning him that it was "peculiarly important in view of the questions which have heretofore surrounded the employment of colored troops in the armies of the United States, to give our enemies (foreign and domestic) as little ground as possible for alleging any violation of the laws and usages of civilized warfare as a palliation for these atrocities which are threatened against the men and officers of commands similar to your own"—to put captured white officers leading Negro soldiers to death. ". . . . you will avoid any devastation which does not strike immediately at the resources or material of the armed insurrection which we are now engaged in the task of suppressing."

["All fugitives who come within our lines you will receive, welcome, and protect. Such of them as are able-bodied men you will at once enroll and arm as soldiers. You will take all horses and mules available for transportation to the enemy; also all cattle and other food which can be of service to our forces. As the rebel Government has laid all grain and produce under conscription, to be taken at will for the use of its armed adherents, you will be justified in destroying all stores of this kind which you shall not be able to remove; but the destruction of crops in the ground, which may not be fit for use until the rebellion is over, or which may when ripe be of service to the forces of our Government occupying the enemy's country, you will not engage in without mature consideration. This right of war, though unquestionable in certain extreme cases, is not to be lightly used, and if wantonly used might fall under that part of the instructions which prohibits devastation. All household furniture, libraries, churches, and hospitals you will of course spare.

["That the wickedness and folly of the enemy may soon place us in a position where the immutable laws of self-defense and the stern necessity of retaliation will not only justify but enjoin every conceivable species of injury is only to be too clearly apprehended; but until such a time shall have arrived, and until the proof, not merely of declarations or resolves but of acts, is unmistakable, it will be both right and wise to hold the troops under your command to the very strictest interpretation of the laws and usages of civilized warfare."

[On July 4, 1863, Confederate General P. G. T. Beauregard wrote General Hunter's successor, Brigadier General Quincy A. Gillmore, concerning the burning of Darien and a series of similar acts that they were attributable to the type of person selected to command the expeditions and to "the employment of a merciless, servile race as soldiers."[39]]

June 12, 1863. The three Army boats, having the schooner in tow, left the sound at 6 A.M. The *Paul Jones* left at 9 A.M. Capt. Moses, Paymaster Murray, and Master's Mate Henderson went along with her to the outer buoy, there to communicate with the *Massachusetts.* They returned at 2 P.M. and reported that the

Wamsutta, stationed in Sapelo, had received our mail, fresh beef, potatoes, and onions—consequently we were *non est* as regards mail matter etc. The paymaster, per order, bought me some sherry and porter to the amount of $9. Paymaster paid me $10 on account. The U.S.S. *Wamsutta* arrived from Sapelo Sound, bringing us our mail and fresh provisions. Capt. Moses and myself went on board. We both had a pleasant time. Found all well and hearty; the surgeon was as lively as usual and Executive Officer Bryant the same old sixpence. Capt. Polleys, A. M. Cmdg. U.S.S. *Madgie*, was on board. He accompanied Capt. Moses on board this craft, where he spent the night. Capt. Polleys appears to be a jolly sea dog. I received per today's mail three papers, which father and brother Frank had the kindness to send me—viz., Reading "Gazette and Democrat," May 30, '63; New York "Herald," June 3, '63; and "Frank Leslie's Illustrated Paper" [Newspaper—a weekly begun in New York City in 1855], June 6, '63.

June 13, 1863. Twenty-four years ago a son was born, named Samuel P., unto Michael K. and Rebecca Boyer, the ancient village of Bernville [a post village on the Tulpehocken Creek, thirteen miles northwest of Reading, Pennsylvania], Berks County, Pennsylvania, being the place of the birth of the said Samuel P. Boyer. His parents resided in the said village until the year 1848, when they moved to the city of Reading, Penna.—remained there until 1852, when they left for Jefferson County, Penna.; the young heir of course accompanied them. In 1855 the said S. P. Boyer left home to attend a literary college. After he received his education, he commenced the study of medicine. On the 13th of March 1862 the honorable title of M.D. was conferred on him. On the 21st of June 1862 he received the commission of a. a. surgeon in the U.S.N. On the 6th day of July 1862 he entered upon his duties as surgeon of the U.S.S. *Fernandina*, and he had the pleasure of spending his 24th birthday on board of said man-of-war, which was stationed, and in fact is still stationed, in Doboy Sound, Ga., on the 13th of June 1863—for be it remembered, the writer of these notes is the said Samuel P. Boyer, M.D., a.a. surgeon, U.S. Navy. Therefore in order to celebrate my 24th birthday, I caused the sherry etc. to flow freely. All passed along merrily. All my comrades wished me many such happy birthdays. U.S. str. *Wamsutta* left for Sapelo Sound at 6 A.M.

June 14, 1863. Another Sabbath to spend in Doboy Sound. Divine service at 10 A.M. Weather moderate—thermometer 80° Fahr. Reported Jos. Short—pleurodynia, Augt. Rickard—furunculus, Geo. Thompson—rheumatismus chronica, and James Crusey —contusion sick in my morning, or daily, report. Nothing of any account transpired today.

June 15, 1863. Reported Richard Welsh—rheumatismus, Geo. Thompson—rheumatismus, Jos. Short—pleurodynia, James Crusey —contusion and Augt. Rickard—furunculus sick. The rheumatic cases are taking potassii iodidii grs v ter in die and externally Spanish fly blisters; the case of pleurodynia Spanish fly blister externally and tart antim et potas. gr ⅛ ter in die. The other two patients are treated on general principles. 6 P.M. Messrs. Short and Thompson came to me and reported that they thought the blisters had done their duty. Upon examination I found that they were right. I immediately dressed the blisters a la mode, after which they felt better. Welsh also reported himself. I found that his application had a rebefacient effect. I also treated him *secundum artem.* They all expressed themselves well satisfied with my treatment, admitting that it was rather painful. I answered that "necessity knew no law." Weather splendid—thermometer from 77° to 82° Fahr. Paid Old George a visit. His foot is healing up finely. Read Wilkie Collins' "No Name" [New York: Harpers, 1863] today. . . .

June 16, 1863. My patients—viz., Short, Welsh, Thompson, and Crusey—are coming on finely. Old George is in the best of humor; his foot is improving rapidly. Weather warm—thermometer 83° Fahr. Took a stroll on Sapelo. The carpenter made quite an improvement in my daily companion (pipe) by placing a ferule on the end of the bowl and putting other extra touches on the stem etc.

June 17, 1863. The U.S. tug *Daffodil,* Capt. E. M. Baldwin, a.m. cmdg., arrived at 8 A.M. from Port Royal per inland passage. We received a small mail. I was the recipient of a letter from A. G. Myers, Esq., Washington, D. C. He brings no news from Port Royal. Our paymaster received a small box per express. Amongst other things he received some lemons; I was accommodated with *one.* Murray appears highly elated with his express matter. The *Daffodil* left for St. Simons Sound at 8.30 A.M. Wrote a letter to A. G.

Myers, Esq., in answer to his last, dated June 2, 1863. Also wrote one to Actg. Master James R. Beers, U.S.N., formerly commander of the U.S. schr. *G. W. Blunt.* The one to Capt. Beers was written at the request of Capt. Moses in answer to Beers' last, dated June 3, 1863.

The *Daffodil* arrived into the harbor at 6 P.M. on her return trip. She will remain at anchor here until tomorrow, when she will leave for Port Royal. The weather was warm today—thermometer 83° Fahr. Reported Messrs. Welsh, Short, and Thompson sick—all improving.

Beans, peas, and greens plenty. Had some beans for dinner yesterday; they were not bad to take.

June 18, 1863. The *Fernandina,* I am afraid, will remain at this anchorage the greater part of the summer, for there are no indications to convince us to the contrary. The prospects are rather flattering. Oh! how I long to see a Northern port. The idea of blockading is rather pleasing, but when you are compelled to come down to the reality in the form of doing duty in one place for the term of one year without seeing either friend or foe of any account, you'll find that the prospects are not so pleasing—and after all, "a life on the ocean wave" is not a very pleasant one unless a person is fond of feasting sumptuously every day on salt junk and hard-tack, reading papers a month after they are published, hearing from home once a month, etc. etc. For my part I would prefer the good things of life up North with less pay. I hope that the day is not far distant when I can have the pleasure of stepping upon the wharf at the New York Navy Yard, from there strike a bee line for the foot of Cortlandt Street, step on board one of the Jersey City ferryboats, land in Jersey City, take the cars for Reading, Pa., and take my relations by the hand etc. etc.

3 P.M. I was admiring the blue sky uncheckered by a single cloud, and at 3.15 P.M. I had the pleasure of seeing the heavens overcast and one of those sudden showers not unusual in this latitude prevailing in all its glory. The wind roared, the rain poured down in torrents, the thunder rolled, and the lightning flashed. A beautiful squall was in full blast at 3.15 P.M. Ensign Flood, being out in an open boat, had the whole benefit of said squall and returned on board at 3.45 P.M. as wet as a drowned rat. Mr. Flood, from the tenor of his remarks when he came on board,

rather enjoyed his position. Verily indeed, "there is no accounting for taste."

Mr. Henderson left in the *Old Greeley*, nee *Old Abe*, on a trip up the river towards the plantations at 2 P.M. He has not returned at 10 P.M. Where can he be? Is he a prisoner in the hands of the Rebels? Has he been capsized by the squall and drowned? Or has he run aground and camped out for the night? We all hope for the best.

Reported Messrs. Short, Welsh, and Thompson sick.

June 19, 1863. At 9.20 A.M. Captain Moses sent Mr. Gibson with an armed crew in the 1st cutter on a voyage up the river in search of Mr. Henderson, who has not yet returned. I hope that he will find Mr. Henderson safe and sound. At 3.20 P.M. the 1st cutter returned having the *Greeley* in tow.

It appears that Mr. Henderson and Landsman Pfander, who accompanied him, sailed up the river as far as Sapelo Sound. Whilst going along finely, the squall met them—consequently they had to throw sails etc. overboard and use the seats of the boat as paddles. Poor fellows—night coming on, they were compelled to anchor by running aground; whilst one slept, the other kept watch so as not to be taken by surprise by the Rebels, whom they saw on the mainland, and Mr. Henderson says that they saw him, for they were signalizing to each other on the mainland. They paddled down towards Doboy Sound this morning. Mr. Gibson met them about 5 miles from the ship. They had nothing to eat or drink since yesterday at 8 A.M. Both were compelled to drink salt water so as to cleanse their mouths etc. Their hands were all sore and swollen. Both complained of headache when they came on board. I, in order to clear their heads etc., gave each a "soda cocktail." Mr. Henderson says that it will be a long time ere he goes on a voyage of pleasure again in the *Old Greeley*, nee *Old Abe*—for, says he, "I am not fond of being out in the hot sun all day and then have the pleasure of receiving a ducking at night while camping out in an open boat without anything to eat or drink." "Phanzy his pheelinks!" We were all glad to see Mr. Henderson and company. Hope they have not caught cold.

Reported Messrs. Welsh and Thompson sick. Boy Short returns to duty. Boatswain's Mate Denny and Quartermaster Scott started on a bullock hunt early this morning. May they return with some good, fat, and juicy beef, for I think that all hands can relish some fresh beef after living for some time on salt junk.

Weather moderate—thermometer 76° Fahr. A wind was prevailing all day. 7 P.M. The Nimrods—viz., Scott and Denny—have returned with a beef.

June 20, 1863. My sick list has dwindled down to one case—viz., Welsh—Thompson having returned to duty this morning. A cool breeze blowing all day. Were it not for the breeze, the weather would of been rather close and warm, for the thermometer ranges from 78° to 85° Fahr. in the shade—consequently the breeze is a welcome visitor.

Had some of the fresh beef for dinner. Did not enjoy it. It had rather a greasy and fishy taste. Don't think it will pay to hunt such beef. After all, Northern beef is the best. 3.15 P.M. Looks as though we were a going to have a squall. Squalls are not uncommon in this latitude. 4 P.M. The squall was not of much account. 6 P.M. the breeze has left us—consequently it is very warm and close. 10 P.M. turned in, and by the time that I was falling asleep, a mosquito had the audacity to intrude upon my private quarters and commence his serenading prior to relieving me of some of my crimson fluid. I immediately declared war, commenced battling, and in about 15 minutes I had the satisfaction of knowing and seeing that my enemy, the mosquito, had laid down his guns and bit the dust, after which I again courted sleep; succeeded, and slept soundly until 6 A.M. the next morning.

June 21, 1863. . . . Eleven months and fifteen days have passed away since I reported for duty on board of the U. S. barque *Fernandina* and still remain on said vessel in said capacity of surgeon. How long I'll continue doing duty on this craft remains for the powers that be to tell. I would prefer a steamer to a sailing vessel—therefore I hope that the day is not far distant when I can have the pleasure of sojourning on board of a steamer as the medical officer of her.

Reported Welsh sick in my morning report. Messrs. Crusey, Callieu, and Simmons are binnacle patients. Divine service at 10 A.M., the paymaster reading services. At 1.30 P.M., when the 3rd cutter returned from shore, the coxswain of the boat, Chas. W. Jordan, reported to Captain Moses that two of his crew—viz., Austin Burroughs and John Brown (the former a native of North

Carolina and the latter hailing from New York, both being "gemmun ub culler")—had been bickering all day. The captain, in order to punish them, caused them to march the spar deck in the following manner: after being united together by means of a pair of irons placed on their right wrists by the master-at-arms, thus being back to back, they each shoulder a handspike so as to give them the appearance of soldiers.

The punishment is rather novel but not very pleasant. They don't appear to enjoy themselves very much, although they are playing soldier. It looks rather odd to see one of them march forward while the other one follows him, marching backwards. How long they intend to march I cannot as yet tell. 3 P.M. the captain, thinking them sufficiently punished, having walked 1½ hours, ordered their release. They both appeared to be in good humor when they were released. So much for black squalls.

The weather was rather warm, the thermometer ranging from 78° to 86° Fahr. in shade. From 6 to 8 P.M. we were blessed with a shower, which had the effect of cooling the atmosphere some. My steward reported George's foot in a very good state; he continues cerate simplex.

June 22, 1863. The weather was rather pleasant and cool today, owing to three or four rain showers, the thermometer ranging from 74° to 84° Fahr. on board ship, while on shore it was no less than 98° Fahr. in the shade. Reported none sick. My binnacle cases are Crusey—sore throat and Simmons—furunculus. Dined on chickens, green peas, green beans, potatoes, etc. today. We expect to have roasting ears (fresh corn) in a day or two.

June 23, 1863. The lighthouse lookout signalized a steamer northward, sailing south, at 9 A.M. Capt. Moses, thinking she might be the tug *Daffodil*, sent the 1st cutter to speak her as she passed the outer buoy, but at 9.40 A.M. the lookout reported her to be the *Harriet A. Weed*, an Army boat. The captain then recalled the 1st cutter by firing no. 3 port gun. 12.30 M. lookout signalized the square-rigged vessel to the northward, sailing south, also the *Wamsutta* left Sapelo to speak her. We all judge her to be the barque *Midnight*, come to relieve us. Hope we may be right. Time will tell. 1 P.M. the lighthouse lookout signalized that the *Wamsutta* was towing the barque into Sapelo Sound—consequently she is the *Midnight* without a doubt.

[The *Midnight* was relieving the *Wamsutta* at Sapelo Sound so that the latter vessel might proceed to Doboy Sound to relieve the *Fernandina*, towing her out to sea so that she might go to Port Royal.]

We had several pleasant rain squalls today. Took a stroll on Sapelo. Found it rather hot on shore—thermometer no less than 110° Fahr. in shade on shore.

June 24, 1863. On making my appearance on the spar deck this morning, the first thing that my eyes rested upon was a large marine reptile—a turtle which weighed no less than 300 pounds. It was the largest one that I ever saw. He is a species of turtle called loggerhead (Thalassochelys caouana [now Caretta caretta]), belonging to the order Chelonia, or tortoises, and family Cheloniidae, or sea tortoises. Their feet are formed so as to constitute perfect oars, and thus, though much embarrassed on land, they enjoy great facility of movement in the water. They hardly ever leave the sea except for the purpose of laying their eggs. Their eggs are abundant and also form an excellent article of food. Their flesh is delicious. While on land they are easily captured on account of their slowness in locomotion. The turtle hunter turns them on their back, after which they are powerless as regards travelling. Two of our crew captured this turtle last night on the beach. They also brought between 200 and 500 turtle eggs which they found. Mr. Turtle's back was covered with barnacles and oysters. In short, he is a "beautiful bird." The captain says that he is a "Secesh canary." The captain is going to present the turtle to the admiral. I have no doubt but that it will be acceptable.

2.15 P.M. the *Wamsutta* arrived from Sapelo Sound. She relieves us. We leave this station tomorrow. The executive officer informs us that the *Weehawken* had captured the Rebel ram *Fingal* in Warsaw Sound. *Weehawken's* first shot hit her pilot house; her second struck her bow, after which she surrendered. We captured 160 prisoners.

[The capture of the formidable *Fingal*, or *Atlanta*, watched closely ever since her success in running the Savannah blockade in a dense fog a few days after Port Royal was taken in November, 1861, was an important victory. After receiving a report in early June, 1863, of her presence in the Savannah River to participate in an assault on Fort Pulaski as soon as a new ironclad under construction was ready, du Pont, in order to forestall an attempt to enter Wassaw Sound to attack the blockading vessels there and southward, sent the *Weehawken*, under Captain John Rodgers, from Port Royal and another ironclad, the *Nahant*, under Commander John Downes, from North Edisto to Wassaw Sound, where the inside blockade was being maintained by the *Cimarron*, meanwhile instructed to avoid engagement with the enemy by withdrawing outside the bar.

[Early in the morning of June 17 the *Atlanta*, accompanied by two wooden steamers filled with spectators, was discovered moving down at the mouth of the Wilmington River to capture the two Federal monitors. After an exchange in which the *Atlanta* fired seven shots and the *Weehawken* five, four of which found their mark (it being according to Rodger's report the third and according to that of Confederate Commander W. A. Webb of the *Atlanta* the last, rather than the first, as Dr. Boyer wrote, that struck the pilot house, cutting the top off and severely wounding two pilots and stunning the men at the wheel), the ram, handicapped by being grounded on a sand spit, surrendered, and her officers and crew, numbering one hundred and sixty-five, were taken prisoner.

[As an aftermath of the victory, Commander Downs was soon claiming he should have a share of the commendations heaped on Captain Rodgers. Secretary Welles ruled against him, and later Congress, on the recommendation of President Lincoln, gave Rodgers a vote of thanks.[40]]

Bully for our "cheese box" [vessels of the monitor type devised by John Ericsson]. It is said that the *Fingal* is a formidable craft. She will hereafter be employed in the service of Uncle Sam. Surely the "anaconda" must soon give up the ghost. [It was the North that was playing the part of the anaconda by smothering the South.] All hands in the best of humor. Weather pleasant.

9

Journey to the North

At Sea, June 25, 1863. At 5 A.M. we were under way, the *Wamsutta* having us in tow. 6.45 A.M. outside the harbor under canvas. The *Wamsutta* returned into Doboy Sound. I am not sorry to leave Doboy. Hope we are bound North. We expect to be in Port Royal harbor tomorrow, when we will find where we are bound. We done blockade duty in Doboy Sound ever since the 19th of Feb., 1863, a period of 4 months and 6 days. We spent rather a pleasant time at this station. Let go our starboard anchor at 8.30 P.M. We are anchored between the lightship and the *Wabash*—about 4 miles from the latter.

Port Royal, S. C., June 26, 1863. At 4.30 A.M. we got under way, and at 6.30 A.M. we arrived into the harbor near enough to the *Wabash* to let go our anchor. The captain will report himself to the admiral this morning, when we expect to ascertain whether we are bound North or no. At the captain's return at 10 A.M., he bringing a mail, I was the happy recipient of several letters and papers. One letter was from father date June 8; one was an order from the fleet surgeon.

2 P.M. The tugboat *Daffodil* is alongside; she is a going to tow us in to the beach so as to be able to have our bottom examined by a board of survey. I hope she may prove damaged enough to send her North, for I am anxious to go home on a visit.

7 P.M. We are on the beach. Some of the boys say that some of the copper on her bottom is gone. [Twice aground and with no repairs for two years, destruction of the hull of the *Fernandina* was feared in southern waters if much copper was missing.[41]] I hope the gentlemen will see the same tomorrow. This afternoon Mr. Henderson and myself took a stroll on Bay Point. While there we became acquainted with some of the officers of the 47th Penna. Regt. Vol.[42] Also came across one of ye colored gentry, who sported a gun (which was rather rusty), knapsack, and other articles of dress belonging to a "soger." I asked him, "What regiment do you belong to, and are you on guard?" He answered, "No. Capt. Pocotaligo's company"[43] I remarked, "But what regiment?" He answered as before, "Capt. Pocotaligo," upon which I concluded that he either was d—n ignorant or did not know what my question was. So I left him walking along the beach. I must say that he was a poor specimen of a soldier.

The weather was rather warm today. 8 P.M. I counted no less that 50 lights scattered over the harbor, raised to the mastheads of the merchant vessels, who always set a light in the night. The sight was beautiful—it reminded me of the lamplights (gaslights) in a city up North. All the evening could be heard the drum and fife, the music of which emanated from the camps located on St.

Helena Island [Ninth Maine Regiment; Fifty-fourth Massachusetts, colored; Third New Hampshire; First New York Engineers, Company D; Seventh Connecticut, four companies; Forty-eighth New York, eight companies; Independent New York Battalion, eight companies; Seventy-sixth Pennsylvania, nine companies; Third Rhode Island Heavy Artillery, Company C; and First United States Artillery, Battery B], and I must say that it was rather pleasant. It reminded me of home.

June 27, 1863. A board of survey, consisting of Captains Gardner and Baldwin and Carpenter Boardman [probably Acting Master Arthur S. Gardner, commanding the *Valparaiso;* either Commander Augustus S. Baldwin, commanding the storeship *Vermont,* or Acting Master E.M. Baldwin, commanding the *Daffodil;* and Carpenter Charles Boardman, of the *Wabash*—all of whom were at Port Royal at the time and two of whom (Gardner and Boardman) served on various boards to determine the condition and value of certain prize vessels], held a survey on the condition of our craft. What the result will be I cannot tell, but hope for the best. They talked rather favorable of our cause.

Had a splendid view of some of our monitors, also of the Rebel ram *Atlanta (Fingal),* which the *Weehawken* captured. They all appear as though they were hard to beat. I can't see how they can be disabled to any extent, for they are all under water with the exception of their turrets and smokestacks. Don't think I would like to be attached to any of them. Have an idea that it is rather hot in their wardrooms. I prefer living on board of something above water so that I can see all around. The *Fingal* must of been rather an ugly place to live in, for she is one mass of filth and dirt.

[According to the report of the board appointed by du Pont to inspect the *Atlanta* after her capture, "extreme heat and foul air prevailing in the ship" were such as to preclude more than a slight examination of the ammunition on board. "The ship requires thorough cleaning," wrote the surveyors. "At present she is in great disorder. It is impossible that anyone could remain below the battery deck for any great length of time without serious inconvenience, if not danger, on account of the foul air prevailing there. The officers' apartments, as well as the berth deck, are very imperfectly ventilated, rendering them almost uninhabitable in hot weather; the heat upon the latter is almost insupportable, owing to the

galley being placed there. Before employing this vessel in our own service
we would strongly recommend that measures be taken to provide light
and air below." While the machinery was in general in good condition, a
noticeable feature of the vessel was "the roughness of all the work about
her." "No expense has been incurred for finish or ornament," the board
went on to explain. "The comfort of the crew and its sanitary condition
appear to have been totally disregarded. Efficiency in battle seems to have
been the sole point aimed at." The total valuation of the ship, including
stores and equipment, was $350,829.26.[44]]

4 P.M. The tug *Pettit* towed us off the beach. 4.30 P.M. We are anchored between the *Wabash* and *Vermont*. 6 P.M. Captain Moses
and myself took passage in the steamer *General Hunter* for Beaufort, S.C. While waiting for the arrival of the boat, we happened
to come across [Acting Assistant] Surgeon [A.R.] Holmes of the
Dawn, whom we had not seen since November last. He was on
his return from Beaufort, S.C. He looks well and hearty. We
also met and had a lively chat with Captain Clark of the N.H. 3rd.
We had a pleasant trip—arrived at Beaufort at 8 P.M. Found the
place to be a lively one. In times of peace I think it must of been
one of the finest Southern watering places. The houses are all
large and built in the Southern style—i.e., with plenty of piazzas.
Was introduced to Mr. Ely [no doubt a Northerner, since the
town was abandoned at the time of Federal occupation], a young
merchant of the place. Found him to be a pleasant young man. Engaged a room at the Stevens House. Said room was on the 1st
floor, down the chimney. Turned in at 10 P.M., after using up some
ale and sherry. Attempted to sleep—no use. An insect claiming
the right of possession waged a terrible war on us. The "BBs"
were rather too numerous. Some call them bed bugs, bad bugs, and
big bugs, but I call them bloody bugs. I must admit that we
damned Beaufort and all its connections.

June 28, 1863. At 5 A.M. Captain Moses and myself concluded to
leave our couches and take a stroll on the outskirts of Beaufort.
So after taking a glass of sherry, we started forth. Ere long we
heard the noise of some meeting. In a short time we came across
a hut having no less than 30 contrabands, male and female, inside
of it—and the whole party singing "Glory, hallelujah" like forty.
They felt happy. Saw some of Africa's fair daughters dressed out
in all the colors of the rainbow—calico fair and gaudy. Passed

several camps of soldiers; everything was quiet—only the sentinel could be seen. We also visited St. Luke's Church. It is the oldest Episcopal church in "Dixie."[45] The bell in the belfry had been removed and the organ smashed by some malicious person or persons. Some fine tombstones and monuments mark the last resting place of some of Beaufort's former inhabitants. We remained in the graveyard a short time, after which we returned slowly to the Stevens House. Fine fig, orange, and magnolia trees shade the sidewalks. Apple trees can be seen in the yards of some of the inhabitants, loaded with fruit. The corn is very tall. The population of Beaufort in time of peace was 8000. I need hardly say that sand flies, mosquitoes, and sand are in the ascendency.

We took breakfast at 7.30 A.M. and at 8 A.M. stept on board of the *General Hunter* for passage to Port Royal. While on board I met a friend of mine—viz., Asst. Surgeon [Francis Minot] Weld of the *Nantucket.* Dr. Weld accompanied me on board of the *Fernandina* and took dinner with me, after which the captain took him on board of the *Wabash.* Dr. Weld is very much of a gentleman. After I landed at Hilton Head (where the *Hunter* stops), I had the pleasure of shaking hands with my friend [Acting Assistant] Paymaster [George H.] Andrews of the *Mohawk.* He reports the boys all O.K. on board of their craft. The *Mohawk* is the guard ship of the station at present.

About 25 contrabands (20 females and 5 males) were baptized at Hilton Head today. They marched down to the water's edge singing psalms. They continued singing during the ceremony of "dipping." After they were all baptized, the reverend darky ordered them to sing a Doxology slow metre whilst they marched to the chapel. The whole thing was quite an affair. "Wool" was in the ascendent.

We arrived on board the *Fernandina* at 12 M. From 12 M. to 2 P.M. we had heavy thunder showers. Will turn in early tonight. . . .

June 29, 1863. At 12 M. Captain Moses returned from the flagship *Wabash* (where he had been on business) and ordered the ship to be got ready for sea by 4 P.M., stating at the same time that we were getting ready for a northern port, upon which all hands, even some of my binnacle cases, who are excused from all duty, went to work with a right good will, and in 1½ hours we had the ship ready for sea. I never saw a livelier set of men. All were of one idea, and that was to see who could do the most. Nothing was too much for them to do. "Home, sweet home" is all their talk. I expect to find the greater part of my binnacle cases *non est* in the morning, they having concluded to get well without medicine. We all feel ten years younger. 6 P.M. we are anxiously waiting for a tug to tow us out of the harbor. At 4 P.M. the *Sebago*, having the *Dawn* in tow, left the harbor, bound for New York. They all felt gay and happy. Success to them.

Capt. [Acting Master George R.] Durand of the U.S.S. *Mohawk* paid me a visit. I was happy to see the captain. We had a pleasant chat together. The captain used to be the *Mohawk's* former executive officer. His promotion is well conferred. He reports all my friends on the *Mohawk* well and lively. 7 P.M. The flagship signalized us to set sail for sea. The way the boys manned the windlass to heave up anchor was not slow. I never saw them work with so much enthusiasm before. 7.20 P.M. The tug *Columbine* took us in tow and through the carelessness of her captain run us afoul the *Mohawk*, carrying away our main-topsail yard etc. etc. and carrying away the jib boom of the *Mohawk*. This of course had the effect of delaying us all night until we had sent up another main-topsail yard. Mr. Thomas, actg. ensign, was rather unlucky. When the crash was heard, while the main-topsail yard was being carried away, Mr. Thomas, Paymaster Murray, and myself were on the poop, and in trying to descend Mr. Thomas slipped, fell, and sprained his ankle. Mr. Murray and myself escaped with a slight jarring. I dressed Mr. Thomas' foot with cold water medicated with tinct. opii. I have an idea that he is frightened more than hurt. Upon examination, I could detect no sign of fracture—hence the above treatment. I hope the sprain is a slight one. I can say more about the condition of the injury in the morning. As a matter of course we had to anchor for the night. 12 midnight—the new main-topsail yard is aloft.

At Sea, June 30, 1863. Lat. 32°14′ N., Long. 80°27′ W. Homeward bound at last! We left our anchorage at 4.30 A.M. We are leaving Port Royal to the southward. All that we now want is a fair wind. We are now in every sense of the word "afloat on the fierce rolling tide." Our destined port is Portsmouth, New Hampshire. Hope we may arrive there ere many days.

Reported Mr. Thomas—sprain and Welsh—rheumatismus sick. Mr. Thomas' foot feels somewhat better. The swelling has gone away considerable. Continue aconite lotion and cold-water bandages. Keep part at rest. . . . .

6 P.M. We are going at the rate of 7 knots. Today we have passed by the blockading fleets of St. Helena, Edisto, and off Charleston. A schooner has been keeping us company the greater part of the day. She is off our starboard quarter. 7 P.M. A heavy squall is prevailing. In fact, the weather was rather squally all the afternoon and evening.

Off Cape Romain, July 1, 1863. Lat. 32°44′ N., Long. 79°14′ W. We have been becalmed the greater part of the day; consequently we don't make much headway. Reported Thomas, Welsh, and Holliday sick. Mr. Thomas' sprained ankle is improving slowly. Welsh's rheumatism about the same. I cupped him with wet cups this morning. Holliday is suffering from the effects of ophthalmia. I applied a blister to his right temple and ordered the following collyrium: ℞ plumbi acetas grs ii, zinci sulphas grs ii, tinct opii gtts iii, aqua f ℥ i M; Sig. Apply ter in die.

Made out my 2nd quarterly report for 1863 for the U.S. barque *Fernandina.* During the quarter I admitted 29 cases, discharged 27, and had 2 cases remaining, consisting of the following diseases: viz., intermittens, cholera communis, constipation, haemorrhois, catarrhus, epistaxis, pleurodynia, cephalalgia, furunculus, rheumatismus chronica, synovitis, paronychia, otalgia, vulnus incisum, vulnus contusum, contusio, abrasio. The average no. of ship's company 84, average no. of sick days 80, expenses in medicine $10.47, daily average no. of patients o 80/91, daily average cost per man $0.13 7/80. Taking all into consideration, the health of our ship's company is splendid. I doubt it very much whether I will make out the 3rd quarterly report for the *Fernandina,* as I hope to be ordered to another vessel after we reach a Northern port.

7 P.M. A slight breeze. We are going at the rate of 4 knots. Killed a mosquito; where he came from I cannot say, but I suppose he is the last of his tribe.

At Sea, July 2, 1863. Latitude 33° N., Long. 78° W. Ensign Thomas' sprain is considerably better. Welsh's rheumatism and Holliday's ophthalmia are coming on finely.

Witnessed the signing of the men's accounts. I wrote my name

168 times as a witness, for which I received the thanks of our Nipcheese—a d—m poor pay. The wind all day was dead ahead—consequently we have nothing to do but go about, making little
headway.

July 3, 1863. Lat. 33° N., Long. 78°03′ W. Coxswain Welsh returned to duty. Ensign Thomas and Lds. Holliday are coming on
finely. 12 M. The wind continues dead ahead. I'm afraid it will take
us the better part of this month to reach our destination at the
rate we're travelling at present, unless the wind changes.

Presented Actg. Master's Mate James B. Henderson with one of
Smith and Weston's revolvers, carrying 7 shots.
[The firm Smith and Wesson (often called, especially in rural regions,
Smith and Weston) began in 1855-1856 the manufacture of what are
supposed to have been the first revolvers for metallic cartridges. It held
Rollin White's patent for breech loading, issued in 1855. In 1863 a
"tip-up system" was introduced.]

He received the said gift cheerfully and promised to keep it in
remembrance of me. Hope he may.

Off the coast of N.C., July 4, 1863. Lat. 33°58′ N., Long. 77°45′
W. The U.S. steamer *Mount Vernon* spoke us today at 10.30 A.M.
She does blockade duty off Wilmington, N. Carolina. We recd.
dates up to the 29th ult., from which we ascertain that Gen. Joe
Hooker has been relieved of the command of the Army of the
Potomac and that Major General George Meade succeeds him.
Gen. Meade is said to be a brave and experienced officer. May he
leave his mark. Also that there is no doubt but that Gen. Lee's
whole army is in Pennsylvania and that on the 28th day of June
they were within three miles of the city of Harrisburg—that the
splendid bridge across the Susquehanna at Columbia, a mile and a
quarter long, which cost $1,000,000, was burned by our own troops.

[Lee, on June 22, moving northward after his victory at Chancellorsville
early in May, ordered General Richard S. Ewell, leading the vanguard of
his army, to advance into Pennsylvania toward Harrisburg. Ewell reached
Carlisle, Pennsylvania, five days later and from there sent a division to
capture Wrightsville and York, cross the Susquehanna River at Columbia,
and attack Harrisburg from the rear while Ewell himself made a direct
advance. A retreating regiment of Pennsylvania militia, however, burned
the bridge, and the thwarted Confederates turned to rejoin Ewell, whose

advance troops did come within three miles of the city on June 28. Just as an attack was about to be made, Lee ordered Ewell to abandon the objective and rejoin the main army at Chambersburg for concentration of strength preparatory to the impending battle at Gettysburg.]

The best news are that the gallant Portlanders have captured the *Caleb Cushing* and that the pirate *Tacony* is blown up. Bully for Portland.

[On June 10, 1863, Confederate Lieutenant Charles W. Read, detached from the cruiser *Florida* the previous month to command an expedition of twenty men in the prize brig *Clarence*, captured the bark *Tacony*, bound from Port Royal to Philadelphia. Considering her a much better craft than his own, he transferred his men and equipment to her, burned the ship he had deserted, and cruised on up the coast, burning and bonding enemy vessels. Meanwhile Federal authorities ordered a hunt for the *Tacony*: from Hampton Roads, Philadelphia, and Boston more than twenty vessels, private as well as public, at least fourteen of them steamers, went out to search the seas. Lieutenant Read, fearing capture, once more changed ships. On June 25 he and his crew, now in the small ninety-ton fishing schooner *Archer*, taken as prize off Long Island, left the *Tacony* blazing on the waters off Long Island and sailed up the coast of Maine as a fishing party. The next afternoon they entered the harbor of Portland, passing the forts unchallenged, and at sunset came to anchor. At one-thirty in the morning, shortly after the moon had set, they quietly and efficiently boarded and seized the two-gun revenue cutter *Caleb Cushing*, put into irons the men on watch and the commanding officer, hove up anchor, moved in tow of two boats through the undefended northern passage, and sailed out to sea. The vessel was about five miles away when her loss was discovered.

[The collector of customs at Portsmouth, Jedediah Jewett, secured men and guns from army posts near by, enlisted about fifty citizen volunteers, and chartered vessels in the harbor to pursue the Confederates. Lieutenant Read, seeing that escape was impossible, placed his handcuffed prisoners into one of the cutter's boats, manned the two remaining, and fired the cutter himself, which quickly burst into flames and sank immediately. He and his men were captured and their erstwhile prisoners rescued, and the *Archer*, standing by with provisions and guns, was overhauled. According to a report later made to Richmond by Lieutenant Read, the Confederates' clothing was "distributed as relics to the people of Portland."⁴⁶]

I had the pleasure of taking a glass of sherry with Ensign Flood in honor, as he said, of "Mr. Fourth of July." It was the dullest 4th of July that I ever experienced.

July 5, 1863. Lat. 33°11′ N., Long. 77°03′ W. All hands to divine service at 9 A.M., Paymaster Murray reading the service. We are in the Gulf Stream, and the way the old *Fernandina* rocks, rolls, etc. is not slow. Some of the boys are complaining of "nausea marina." The wind, as usual, is dead ahead. Oh, for a stiff breeze! "When will we reach port?" is the question all around. Reported Mr. Thomas sick. His sprained ankle is improving somewhat.

July 6, 1863. Lat. 34°31′ N., Long. 75°30′ W. At 7.20 P.M. the light on Cape Hatteras hove in sight. It is a flash light. We are slowly approaching our destination. Our speed has been about 4 knots per hour. The ship rocks awfully. Had the pleasure of seeing some of Mother Carey's chickens today. Also saw for the first time two or three schools of flying fish.

July 7, 1863. Lat. 35°25′ N., Long. 75°15′ W. At 6 A.M. a schooner within short distance. Fired two guns across her bow to bring her to. Mr. Henderson boarded her in the 1st cutter. She proved to be the schooner *Zanoni* of Rockport, out from Philadelphia, bound to New Orleans loaded with coal. The schooner's captain thought we were the *Alabama,* but he was agreeably disappointed. He went on his way rejoicing.

11 A.M. We are becalmed. Rather pleasant. Weather warm— thermometer 86° Fahr. in the shade. Ensign Thomas stood a watch today. I advised him not to do so, for I don't consider his sprained ankle in a fit condition to use much. I hope it will do him no harm. Time will show. 3 P.M. signalized the U. S. steamer *Bermuda,* bound north. 4 P.M. a pretty fair wind—speed 4 knots. 8 sails in sight today—some bound north and some south. The coast of N. Carolina is visible. We are leaving the waters of "Dixie" slowly.

5.15 P.M. Schooner of suspicious appearance within sight. Executive Officer Childs with an armed crew in the 3rd cutter boarded her. She has the English ensign flying at her main. She proved to be the British schooner *Arrow,* formely the blockade runner *Major E. Willis,* bound to Nassau, N[ew] P[rovidence], from New York.[47] Her papers etc. proving all right, we left her pass on. I for my part think that she will try to run the blockade if she can; if not, why, then she will go to her destined port. I may be wrong. 7 P.M. a good breeze blowing.

July 8, 1863. Lat. 36°32′ N., Long. 74°43′ W. Wm. H. Thomas again becomes a patient. His exercise yesterday done him more harm than good. I now shall keep him on the list until his ankle is O.K. Apply roller and rub in tinct sapo. camph. and keep at rest.

9 A.M. a good breeze blowing. We are sailing along finely. Passed the steamer *Kennebec*. Exchanged signals with a French schooner. Saw large schools of porpoises.

July 9, 1863. Lat. 38°10′ N., Long. 74°14′ W. 10.30 A.M. a ship within hail. Fired a blank cartridge to bring her to, after which Mr. Henderson in the gig boarded her. She proved to be the *Charles E. Duncan* of Boston, bound to New Orleans. Mr. Henderson received dates up to the 30th of June. Also brought the news that Gen. McClellan had taken the place of Gen. Halleck as commander-in-chief of Uncle Sam's Armies. [The report was incorrect.] Bully for "Mac." The people's favorite has received his reward at last. Long my he flourish.

Mr. Henderson also boarded the ship *Albeit* of Bremen, bound to Baltimore, Md., loaded with passengers. Several sails were reported from the masthead as being in sight. Our average speed was 4 knots. Large amount of porpoises in sight all day. Mr. Thomas' ankle is improving rapidly.

July 10, 1863. Lat. 38°54′ N., Long. 73°45′ W. No less than 20 sails in sight today. At 5 P.M. Mr. Henderson boarded the English brig *Princess Alice* of Honduras (balize), bound to Havana, Captain R. C. Mears, loaded with sugar boilers. He found her papers all O.K. She left New York on the 7th of July. Mr. Henderson obtained dates of the 2nd, 6th, and 7th of July, in which were the items of the Battle of Gettysburg, Pa. The old Keystone State, it appears, is being purged of Lee's Army. Our gallant Meade has shown himself to be the right man, in the right place. Our Army done wonders. The Stars and Stripes are floating triumphantly over every town, village, and city in Penna. Long may it wave! The appointment of McClellan appears not to be confirmed. . . .

July 11, 1863. Lat. 39°06′ N., Long. 73°36′ W. Reported Mr. Thomas—synovitis—improving; Seaman Smith—paronychia on big toe of right foot; and George Parker—sore arm sick today. We were becalmed the greater part of the day. Our speed from ½ to 1½ knots up to 4 P.M., after which we made from 3 to 5 knots —rather slow travelling.

The boys amused themselves today by catching a species of fish called bonito, that are noted for devouring flying fish. They are rather a beautiful-looking fish. Several large schools of them appeared around the ship between 3 and 5 P.M. I also had the pleasure of seeing for the first time a swordfish.

A large amount of sails in sight today.

July 12, 1863. Lat. 40°07′ N., Long. 72°52′ W. Passed an English barque at 7 A.M., and at 8 A.M. Mr. Henderson boarded the English barque *Sailor Prince* from New York for Baltimore, having a Baltimore pilot on board. A large steamer passed us bound south. Many sails in sight all day. Our average speed today was 2 knots. We were becalmed the greater part of the time. A heavy fog set in at 5.30 P.M. and continued all night.

Reported Mr. Thomas—synovitis—who is improving rapidly, John Smith—paronychia—improving, and George Parker—furunculus—improving sick in my morning report to Capt. E. Moses.

I might mention that the *Sailor Prince* had left New York on the 7th inst., 5 days ago. She either was becalmed the greater part of the time or else had light winds. The old adage "Misery loves company" comes very handy. We felt better when we heard the above, knowing thereby that we were not the only craft that done such fine sailing as we have done the last 4 or 5 days.

July 13, 1863. A dense and heavy fog surrounds us. The lunar orb of the heavens is not to be seen—hence we cannot well reckon our altitudes etc., so that I am not able to state the latitude and longitude of the good old ship's position for this day. A heavy wind dead ahead is blowing. Nothing is heard but "Go about," "Tack ship," etc. etc. We are compelled to go over a large space of water to make any headway at all. Our sailing can well be compared to the locomotion of a horse attached to a heavy wagon and going up a steep hill, for the horse will travel from one side of the road to the other so that by the time he reaches the top of the hill, he will have travelled thrice the distance that he would if he had gone in a direct line. We are sailing at the rate of 4½ knots. The fog is not like an ordinary one in the States. It has as much moisture attached to it as a drizzling rain in the spring of the year. To be exposed 10 minutes in it is to be wet to the skin. Besides it being damp, foggy, and windy, it also is raw, cold, and blustering, the thermometer being 65° Fahr. In short, it is a cold, dull, and dreary day. It is the coldest day that I experienced for the last two months—but then I was 'way down in "Dixie" on the coast of Georgia, while today I am on the coast of Connecticut in the vicinity of Long Island.

6 P.M. The captain called me on the poop to see a steamer passing astern of us. She was a large European steamer outward bound. If she had been 5 minutes later, why, the probability would of been that she would of run into us. We are ringing our bell all the time so as to let other vessels know where we are, for we are not able to see the ship's length from us on account of the fog, and we are sailing 7 knots. Our condition is anything but pleasant. We are liable every moment either to run into another vessel or else be run into by some craft. I sincerely hope that the fog will die away ere many hours, for I don't fancy this idea of going it blindly.

7 P.M. The rest of the night we will ring our bell at intervals of 5 minutes. 10 P.M. raining like thunder. 11 P.M. calm. 12 midnight I am sound asleep.

July 14, 1863. 6 A.M. Mr. Henderson boarded a Yankee schooner bound from Maryland to Boston, loaded with timber. She was the *Chronometer.* We had to fire three guns in order to bring him to. The captain of her appeared to be quite a jolly dog. 8 A.M. the man at the masthead reported "Land ho!" on our lee bow. I suppose it is part of Long Island. The wind all morning was rather favorable. The fog has been pretty well scattered by the wind. The sun is beginning to shed its rays once more. Everything appears to have a lovely aspect.

10 A.M. Once more we are enveloped in a fog, thicker than ever. Taking all in all, this has been very changeable weather. We had quite a shower at 2 P.M. Caught a glimpse of the sun at 4 P.M. Fog again at 4½ P.M. Clearing up at 6 P.M. Saw while clear two schooners astern of us. At 7 P.M. it commenced to be foggy again and continued the rest of the night. During the day we fired a gun every half hour. Whether it was to warn vessels of our whereabouts or whether it was a signal for a pilot schooner I am not able to tell. Of all the fogs I ever saw, I never saw such a one as the one prevailing at present. It puts a London fog all in the shade. . . .

This foggy weather causes more coughs and colds amongst the ship's company than is pleasant for "ye sawbones," for he is rather short of expectorants and feels rather lazy, consequently not overanxious to have a large sick list. Thus endeth for today the fog question. Reported Mr. Thomas, Mr. Smith, and Geo. Parker (all improving) sick.

July 15, 1863. We are not only befogged but also becalmed. Thus we are compelled to spend a rather disagreeable day. The idea of being in a fog and no wind blowing is rather [un] pleasant, at the same time thinking of the tune "A Life on the Ocean Wave" [published in New York by Hewitt and Jacques in 1838; words by Epes Sargent, music by Henry Russell]. In my estimation the man who wrote the above tune, or combination of words, is a fool, one who has never been to sea, one who never saw a storm at sea. I am sure that he never could of been caught in a fog while on the briny deep, or else he would of written his song in a different strain. Everything in and about the ship is damp. Clothing, books, papers, instruments, accoutrements, decks, and staterooms are not only damp but beginning to get mouldy. Decayed teeth begin to ache. The chills-and-fever boys are commencing to complain. Some of my old cases of rheumatismus chronica are coming to me for some medicine to drive away, as they say, their "damn pains." In short, all are as grim as bears with sore heads. Nothing tastes good; reading matter not interesting; and none feel like sleeping.

Talking of toothache, I had the pleasure of extracting two molars—at least the remains of two—from the lower jaw of Mr. Childs this afternoon, they having tormented him for the last three days. Prior to the extraction of them my steward had used creosotum and ol. caryophilli, all doing no good—so today he became courageous enough to have them pulled out. Now the only pain that remains is that caused by the lacerated gum, which is nothing compared to his former companions. By tomorrow I expect to find him smiling etc. He says that he has three or four more that I can pull as soon as we have fairer weather. When that will be I cannot tell, for the fog is as thick as ever. Some pretend to say or prophesy a change of weather in a day or two from the fact that the moon changes today at 5.57 P.M., when we will have a new moon. I only hope that they may prove to be in the right, for I am anxious to come to our journey's end.

Our water report today read 500 gallons, which will last us one week at the rate of ¾ of a gallon to each man per diem. Said allowance is ¼ of a gallon less than the regular allowance. We have plenty of hard-tack and salt junk. Our meals consist of salt junk, or "turkey," as the boys call it, one day, and the next day we have salted pork and beans, or "goose a la mode." So I don't think that any of us will suffer with podagra, or gout. Potatoes and onions are played out. Our diet is a regular prison one.

At 7 P.M. I had the satisfaction of seeing several stars, and at 10 P.M., a few minutes after I had retired, the lookout, or watch, cried out, "Light oh!" on the starboard bow—also that he heard a horn—upon which all hands turned out. The captain gave the orders to ring the bell. After waiting patiently 5 minutes to hear the result of said light etc., I concluded to turn in. Ere I done so, I heard the captain give the order to strike, or ring, the bell every 10 minutes. It was very foggy all night.

In vicinity of Block Island, July 16, 1863. Fog all around, as usual. We eat fog, sleep in fog, dream of fog, talk of fog, swear about fog. Everything has the appearance of fog. Our grub has a foggy taste. Our water is tinctured with fog. My medical stores are becoming saturated with fog to such an extent as to ruin some of them. We have had fog to such an extent as to disgust us with the very idea of fog. We have all unanimously voted fog to be a bore.

The long-looked-for event has come at last: the man at the masthead cried out the welcome words "Land oh!" at 1 P.M. (the fog having died away some), and at 1.15 P.M. he announced a sail. By this time the fog had nearly all passed away. In less than no time we all saw from the deck 8 sails, consisting of steamers, ships, barques, brigs, and schooners. We also saw Montauk Lighthouse [at the eastern extremity of Long Island, New York], which is painted white and black. Block Island and Gay Head also could be seen by means of a marine glass. We are once more sure of considering ourselves on our course. We no longer are going it blindly. All and everyone feel fifty per cent better. Never looked the land so beautiful to me as it did at 1.15 P.M. The blue sky appeared bluer by 100 per cent. The sun appeared never to have shone as it did today. In short, everything and everybody is lovely. My rheumatic cases declare themselves O.K.; the ague boys say that they cannot shake and consequently don't want any more physic. Bully for all.

5 P.M. "A cloud comes over the spirit of my dreams" ["A change

came o'er the spirit of my dream"—line 126 (first line of verse V)
of Lord Byron's "The Dream"] in the shape of an old and unwel-
come visitor, "Mr. Fog"—for he is about again in all his glory,
thereby causing stocks to fall again—but, thank fortune, we have
one advantage, and that is, notwithstanding the fog, we know our
whereabouts and course which we have to go. We were becalmed
the greater part of the day. 5.40 P.M. a brig passed us.

8 P.M. The fog is not as thick as it was. The heavens appear
bright and clear. The stars can be seen very distinctly. We have
every indication of a westerly breeze ere morning. Hope we may,
for that will rid us of this fog. Reported Mr. Thomas—sprained
ankle and George Parker—furunculus—improving, and discharged
John Smith—paronychia in my morning report of sick. The bell
was rung every 10 minutes as long as the fog existed. Turned in
early.

July 17, 1863. Lat. 41°35′ N., Long. 70°41′ W. The fog lasted
until 9 A.M., when it cleared up. No less than 15 sails were in sight.
Spoke a New Bedford pilot boat. During the fore part of the day
Captain Moses caught two codfish, which we had for dinner—and
a capital dish they were. I never ate a better fish in my life before
than what they were. Don't think I enjoyed as good a dinner for
the last twelve months. They were a perfect godsend, as it were,
after feasting luxuriously upon salt junk, salt pork, and beans for
the last 16 days. Hope we may catch some more codfish. Passed the
lightship. We are heading for Gay Head, called so from the gay
appearance of the clay during sunset. We had a fair breeze the
greater part of the forenoon. The lightship is called the Sow and
Pigs Lightboat—rather a select name!

3 P.M. Passing through Martha's Vineyard Sound, passed no less
than 50 sail, mostly schooners and brigs loaded with lumber. As
we pass along, we leave Cuttyhunk Island, Nashawena Island,
Quick's Hole, Pasque Island, Robeson's Hole [Robinson Hole],
Naushon Island, and Tarpaulin Cove on our port side, or left-
hand side, and Martha's Vineyard Island and No Man's Island
[No Mans Land] on our starboard side, or right-hand side. I had
the pleasure of seeing some loyal rocks, sand, and clay land once
again, the first time since June 1862. I also saw one of Eve's fairest
daughters in one of the schooners, the *Kate Walker,* as she passed
us on our port quarter. I must admit that my heart went "pittypat,

pittypat"—for a piece of calico, especially a white and beautiful one, is a rare article on the Southern blockade. Hope to have an opportunity of not only seeing some feminines but talking to them ere many days.

The stately and ancient Bowdoin mansion, located on Naushon Island, was to be seen as we passed along. The said owner, or builder, of said mansion, Mr. Bowdoin, was an Englishman. He built said mansion prior to the Revolutionary War, in 1772. When he died, he said that in a certain number of years he would show himself—consequently for a great many years said mansion was deserted because it was said to be haunted. About 20 years ago a merchant prince of Boston, John M. Forbes, bought said place from the English heirs and has since that time occupied said house as a summer residence. He nor his kindred ever saw anything like a ghost—consequently Old Bowdoin, like a sensible being, rested quietly in his grave, notwithstanding he boasted of appearing again after his death. So much for the Bowdoin place.

We are opposite Wood's Hole [Woods Hole (Geographic Board spelling); frequently Wood's Hole or Wood's Holl], a small village, or town, in the township of Falmouth, Barnstable County, State of Massachusetts. It appears to be quite a pleasant place. Our executive officer, Mr. Childs, hails from Wood's Hole. He pointed out to all the officers his house—at least, as much of it as could be seen from the ship, which was the chimney, roof, and upper story of the house. He feels good.

5.30 P.M. a pilot came on board. He took us into Holmes' Hole [or Vineyard Haven; sometimes written Holmes Hole and sometimes Holme's Hole], Martha's Vineyard Island, where we arrived at 6.15 P.M., when we let go our port anchor. At 6.30 P.M. Mr. Childs, Paymaster Murray, and myself went in the gig ashore. We landed at Holmes' wharf. Proceeded to his store; had quite a pleasant time of it. Any amount of natives had congregated at the store. Found them very talkative and hospitable. Bought a box of segars. Drank some good water. Felt good, it being the first time since June 1862 that I set a foot on true Yankee soil. We intend to lay in a small cargo of water, after which we will take a bee line for Portsmouth, N.H., via shoals etc. The pilot, whose name is Smith, is quite a character. He was a privateer in the war of 1812— one of ye genuine stock of Yankees.

Read the papers of the 12th of July up to this date—viz., July

17th—in which the glorious news of the taking of Vicksburg, Port Hudson, etc. are stated. It appears that we bagged in all about 100,000 Secesh soldiers. Bully for Uncle Sam! [General Grant placed the number of prisoners captured at around 37,000.] Also read that the riot in New York was pretty well squashed.

[Antidraft rioting from July 13 to July 16 was brought under control only with the help of troops. Prevalent throughout the Northern states at one time or another, violent demonstrations, with much destruction of property, were particularly serious in the city of New York. Sentiment against the war was fanned by injustices in the draft law, high prices, corruption, and especially by profiteering on the part of the war contractors. Newspapers such as the *World* and the *Journal of Commerce* openly criticized the government, and on July 4 Governor Horatio Seymour publicly charged the administration with violating individual liberty. Many, including the governor, believed conscription unconstitutional.]

The new admiral of the South Atlantic Blockading Squadron has commenced his attack on Charleston, S. C.

[Rear Admiral Dahlgren, who succeeded du Pont on July 6, 1863. The change in command was a direct result of disagreement between the administration and du Pont over Charleston. Secretary Welles, greatly disappointed in the failure of April 7 (see April 13 entry) and even more so in the admiral's unwillingness, after his "constant call for more ironclads" and "all our outlay and great preparations, giving him about all our force and a large portion of the best officers," to make another attempt to take the city, had become increasingly dissatisfied with du Pont's "demoralizing" and "depressing" attitude, smacking of "the old army infirmity of this war, dilatory action." By late May he had decided to replace the able, shrewd, and popular, but, in his opinion, selfish and ambitious man who believed himself "indispensable to the service," who preferred "to occupy his palace ship, the *Wabash*, at Port Royal to roughing it in a smaller vessel off the port," and who found "the modern changes in naval warfare and in naval vessels repugnant," having a "declared aversion" to the much-lauded turret type of ship.

["I do not find . . . in any communication received from you since the 7th of April any proposition for a renewed attack upon Charleston, or suggestions even for active operations against that place," he wrote du Pont on June 3. The government, he went on, was "unwilling to relinquish all further efforts upon a place that has been so conspicuous in this rebellion, and which continues to stimulate treason and resistance . . . and whose reduction is so essential," and since "it appears that your judgment is in opposition to a renewed attack on Charleston, ... with your prolonged continuance on the blockade, the Department has concluded to relieve you of the command of the South Atlantic Blockading Squadron. . . ." The broken-hearted admiral died before the war was over.

[Rear Admiral Andrew H. Foote, selected to succeed du Pont, was prevented by illness from taking his post, and Dahlgren, his recently appointed next in command, who had as early as the previous October expressed an earnest desire to lead the attack on Charleston, was appointed instead. Dahlgren, with army cooperation, immediately began a vigorous campaign, but after two costly failures he reported to Secretary Welles that more land forces were "absolutely required to advance operations." No force the North could muster could quite conquer the defiant city.[48]]

Hope he may be successful. Huzza for the Union! Enough news for one day to read. The Stars and Stripes will ere long float over every house, fort, and arsenal in the Southern States as in days of old. It is an honor to be a citizen of the United States. We are showing to the world how to quell a rebellion and proving to them that a free and republican government can and will succeed, notwithstanding [what] the aristocrats of England say to the contrary. Wrote a letter to father.

This appears to be a splendid harbor for shipping. I counted upward of a hundred sail at anchor and many more coming into the Hole. The greater part of these have been here ever since the fog has set in. When we let go our anchor, we fired two guns.

Holmes' Hole, July 18, 1863. This was a beautiful day. By 11 o'clock we had 400 gals. of water on board. Our caterer, Mr. Flood, was on shore and purchased some fresh veal, new potatoes, eggs, peas, pies, fish, etc., so that we had a splendid dinner today. Mr. Childs paid a visit to his wife, children, and sisters this morning. He returned on board at 11 o'clock. Said he had a pleasant time of it. Found all well and hearty except wife, who had a slight cold. By 12 o'clock we were under way.

4 P.M. In the neighborhood of Cape Cod. Weather cold. The thermometer is between 58° and 65° Fahr. Our old pilot appears not to mind the cold—he is going it in his shirt sleeves. I must not forget to mention that the man who took Mr. Childs to Wood's Hole in his small boat had the audacity to charge him $5. It only being about 3 miles, I don't think that he acted very friendly but have an idea that he is on the "make." Hope he won't have many more such chances to take in men.

5 P.M. We are in 4 fathoms of water. 5.05 P.M. A cold and heavy

fog has set in. A man on the lookout in the forecastle is kept rather busy blowing a foghorn. A schooner on our starboard quarter is blowing his horn, which sounds very much like the bleating of a calf. It caused considerable merriment on board. He was loaded with lumber. His course is to the southward.

5.50 P.M. Cleared Nantucket Shoals. We just passed Pollockrip Light Boat [Pollock Rip Lightship, anchored off Pollock Rip Shoals, two and a half miles east of the south end of Monomoy Island], whose bell sounded much like a church bell. 5.55 P.M. the thermometer is 58° Fahr. We are in a fleet of schooners, some bound northward and the rest southward, all blowing foghorns. Our lookout on the forecastle is tooting his horn every 5 minutes so as to warn other vessels of our whereabouts, for we are not enabled to see any distance on account of the fog.

Off Massachusetts, July 19, 1863. Raining all morning. The fog is very thick. At 9.25 A.M. we passed the Cape Cod Lighthouse [Highland Lighthouse, a sixty-six-foot white tower erected in 1797 on a high clay cliff near a dangerous bar]. Our course now will be for Cape Ann, in the northeastern part of Massachusetts. Our speed is only about 2 knots. We have about 80 miles to go ere we will reach Portsmouth, which distance would be nothing had we any kind of a breeze. We are now afloat on the waters of the Massachusetts Bay, or, as nautical men say, Boston Bay. The sea is very smooth.

11½ A.M. The fog has left us. Many sails in sight. The Highland Lighthouse bears S.E.¼E. at 11.30 A.M. It has ceased raining. Our speed now is about 3½ knots. 5 P.M. hailed a fishing smack. Two of the fisherman came alongside in a small cutter with some fish. They sold them like hot cakes. Our caterer looked out for the interest of the mess. I had quite a time cutting up the heads of some haddock in search of the lucky stones which are lodged in a small cavity alongside the eyes. Tomorrow we expect to dine on "Cape Ann turkeys" (codfish), as the seafaring men call them. Truly, verily indeed they are a palatial dish. Once tasted, they will always be preferred to any other fish. I am now alluding to the fresh codfish and not the dried ones, which in my estimation are a horrible dish. All hands will have fresh fish to eat tomorrow.

7.20 P.M. Fired our 20-pound rifle on the forecastle and our 24-pound howitzer on the poop so as to discharge their shot. At 7.30 P.M. we heard the sunset gun fired on shore, I suppose in the vicinity of Thatcher's [Thatcher; sometimes Thacher] Island. 7.40 P.M. Thatcher's or Cape Ann Lighthouse in sight. 7.40 shorten sail in topmast and lower studding sails. 8 P.M. a heavy fog set in again. It appears that "Mr. Fog" dies hard. He is rather long-lived. The foghorn is being blowed on the forecastle every five minutes. Our old pilot says that they never had such a fog before along this coast, at least in his days—and he is a man of seventy-odd years. So he and his countrymen who live along this coast feel the effects of this fog as well as ourselves, who are strangers here.

25 miles off Portsmouth, N.H., July 20, 1863. The fog lasted until 8 A.M., when it left us; so now all that we want is a good breeze. At 9 A.M. we had to lower the 2nd cutter and tow her bow around; the tide, being stronger than the wind, had drifted her in toward land. 11.15 A.M. a light breeze. We expect to enter the harbor of Portsmouth sometime during the afternoon. The towns of Newburyport, Hampton, and Rye could be seen from the deck as we passed along. At 1.40 P.M. two men in a small boat hailed us and asked whether we wanted a pilot. When asked, "Are you a branch [pilot authorized or commissioned to operate in certain waters] pilot?" he answered, "No, but I can take you in." The captain replied, "I don't want you if you are not a regular pilot." So the would-be pilot pushed off. At 2.30 P.M. a regular branch pilot came alongside, and he was accepted. When asked whether there were any news in Portsmouth, he replied that he had rather bad news to tell the captain—viz., that his father had gone to that bourne from whence no traveller returneth. Poor captain—I sympathize with him, for from all accounts he was a good father. Peace to his ashes.

5.15 P.M. We are opposite Fort Constitution, guarding the entrance to Portsmouth harbor. We were hailed by a man from said fort as follows: "What vessel is that?" The captain answered, "The U.S. barque *Fernandina*." "Where from?" Ans., "Port Royal, S.C."—upon which the soldiers garrisoned there mounted the walls and gave us three cheers and a tiger, at same time dipping their colors, the Stars and Stripes. We mounted the rigging and cheered ship, also dipping our colors. The man on the fort again hailed, saying, "We would fire a salute, but our guns are all shotted." Captain answered, "My guns are all unshotted." Ans., "Aye,

aye, Sir!" We anchored very near the fort. We intend to proceed up the harbor to the Navy Yard in the morning.

The captain left in the gig at 5.30 P.M. for the Navy Yard so as to report our arrival to the commandant of the yard, Captain George F. Pearson. 7 P.M. the gig returned minus the captain. He stays with his family tonight. A bumboat [boat carrying provisions and so forth for sale to vessels in port or off shore] with lobsters came alongside at 5.40 P.M. Some of us officers bought some of them and had them for supper. They tasted well. How we will sleep on them I am not yet able to tell, but hope they will not disturb us.

Two small boys came alongside with papers. We bought them. One was dated July 20, 1863, and the balance were dates of Feb., March, and May. The "sell" was not bad. Several boats with fair damsels passed us after we anchored, whether to see the officers and crew or no I cannot tell. This much I do know: we took a good look at them. Our old and faithful friend the fog made his appearance at 7 P.M. as thick as ever.

Portsmouth, N.H., July 21, 1863. The captain returned from shore at 7.30 A.M. He brought me quite a mail. I recd. letters from father, brother Frank, sister Beckie, Miss Carlisle, and Prof. Rogers, also a note from Mr. Akerman. Provost Marshal Adams sent me his card. The captain also invited me to dine with him today. I understand that several ladies from New York City will be there.

10.15 A.M. Fired a salute of 13 guns. We are slowly sailing up to the Navy Yard.

10

Southern Waters Again

The first cruise of the barque *Fernandina* ended the 24th of July 1863, after which, until the 1st of August 1863, the officers and men of said barque had a leave of absence. As a matter of course, all hands made tracks for their respective homes, families, etc. It were useless for me to state what a happy and jolly time I had while in Old Berks—i.e., state all the particulars—for that would take both time and paper. The only item worth mentioning while home was the making of an Odd Fellow of me by members of the Montgomery Lodge, Reading, Pa., on the 30th day of July 1863. Of course I had to ride the goat and climb the greasy pole. Everything while home passed off lovely, and the goose hung high. On the 1st of August 1863 I left my paternal mansion for Portsmouth, N. H., where I landed on the 2nd of August 1863. Reported myself to Capt. E. Moses, a.m. cmdg., U. S. barque *Fernandina.* On the 5th of August I commenced my duties as medical officer of said barque. Found 8 cases of venereal on hand; next day my sick list sported no less than 28 cases of venereal, both gonorrhoea and syphilis. I was compelled to send 2 cases of syphilis to the hospital, not having room on board. The rest are all well except one or two cases, who still complain of gleet.

I need hardly say that I had a jolly good old time in Portsmouth, for such was the case. The way we boys done the agreeable to the fair sex was not slow. I carried on quite a flirtation with one young damsel; even promised to correspond with her. I am on the fence as regards writing—i.e., have only half a notion of fulfilling my promise. I don't think I shall write any letters to her. So much for carry-on a flirtation in ye city of Portsmouth. On the 27th of August 1863 I had the pleasure of becoming a Master Mason. The St. Andrew's Lodge No. 56 [516], Portsmouth, N. H., claim me as a member. I must say that I consider said order one of the best of societies.

On our arrival in port I had to discharge my steward; consequently I was compelled to appoint a new one. My first one was a young man named Locke, a splendid steward, only too fond of his cup. About two weeks after I appointed him, he broke his right patella, or kneepan, while out riding with a fancy woman, a *nymphe du pave.* Of course he had to be sent to the hospital. I was again compelled to look around for a steward. I, after some trouble, found a landsman, Francis Conefry by name, rather young and inexperienced but always ready and willing to do his duty, whom I appointed surgeon's steward of ye gallant barque *Fernandina.*

Three of our officers, with whom I had the pleasure of spending a very happy time whilst on our first cruise, have left us—viz., Messrs. Henderson, Gibson, and Townsend, all master's mates. The two first have been appointed ensigns, consequently were ordered to do duty on board of steamers; the last named—viz., Townsend —was sick; consequently we had to leave him behind. Instead of the above-named gentlemen we have two master's mates, named Newlin and Wright.

The following is the muster roll of our officers: viz.,

A.M. Commanding	Edward Moses
Acting Master	C. C. Childs
Actg. Asst. Surg.	Samuel P. Boyer
Actg. Asst. Paymaster	Thomas N. Murray
Actg. Ensign	Christopher Flood
Actg. Ensign	William H. Thomas
Actg. Master's Mate	George Newlin
Actg. Master's Mate	John Wright
Surgeon's Steward	Francis Conefry
Paymaster's Steward	Charles Shaw

On the 3rd of September 1863 the Hon. Secretary of the Navy, Gideon Welles, paid the Portsmouth Navy Yard a visit. Early that morning Commodore Pearson, commandant of the yard, issued an order that all naval officers attached to said yard and vessels laying at anchor there would have to appear in full dress, side arms, etc. so as to be in proper trim to receive the Hon. Secy. of the Navy. His Majesty arrived at 2 P.M. and took a look at the yard and officers, after which all hands adjourned to the commodore's house and partook of a lunch.

On the 4th of Sept. 1863 Commodore Pearson paid us a visit, inspected the ship, and pronounced her ready for sea. During said visit all hands were at quarters. Whilst passing by the sick bay, which is my station during quarters, the commodore remarked, "Well, Doctor, I would come in, but I am afraid you'll cut off my leg." "Oh, no, Commodore! Walk in and see our accommodations," says I. "Thank you, Doctor. I'll call again." —and away he goes. So much for inspecting the sick bay.

On the 5th of September 1863 Colonel Jackson of the U.S. Army paid us a visit—at least Captain Moses and myself. I had the pleasure of becoming acquainted with the colonel last November [actually on January 3, 1863; see page 38] while he was encamped at Hilton Head, S.C. He was col. of the 3rd N.H. The colonel spent a happy afternoon on board, after which he left for Portsmouth in company with Captain Moses in the captain's gig. On the 6th of

September 1863 divine services were held on board, Rev. [Theodore
B.] Bartow, chaplain of the Navy, [stationed at Portsmouth Navy
Yard; rank equivalent to that of commander] officiating. Col. Jack-
son and lady; Capt. Moses, his lady, sister, and daughter; Messrs.
Chandler and Bridge of Portsmouth; Mr. Palfrey of Boston; [Acting
Assistant] Paymaster [Henry T.] Mansfield, [Acting Assistant] Sur-
geon [William J.] Gilfillan, Actg. Master [William L.] Churchill,
Ensign Brown [probably Acting Ensign Amos Brown, who resigned
November 11, 1863, there being no Ensign Brown aboard the *Nipsic*
listed in the Navy *Register* January 1, 1864], and [Acting] Ensign
[Albion B.] Prince of the U.S. steamer *Nipsic* [in the last stages of
completion at the yard]; and our officers and men comprised the
congregation. Everything passed off pleasantly.

On the 19th of September 1863 we went to sea, and on the 24th
of September 1863 we let go our starboard anchor in Hampton
Roads, off Fortress Monroe. We lay at anchor here until the morning of the 26th of September, when we put out to sea again [as per
order dated August 4, 1863, to proceed as soon as the *Fernandina*
was ready and report to Rear Admiral Dahlgren], bound for Port
Royal, S. C. We arrived at Port Royal on the evening of the 29th
of September 1863, taking 10 days from the time we left Portsmouth. We stopped 2 days at Fortress Monroe, thus taking us 8
days to make the distance, which is doing some fine sailing. We
had fair winds all the way.

Took a tramp around Hilton Head, S. C., on the 30th of Sept.
Met Captain Polleys, a. m. cmdg., U.S.S. *Madgie,* also Paymaster
Andrews and Sailing Master [Acting Master Alexander] Tillinghast
of the U.S.S. *Mohawk.* All were well and hardy. The two latter
gentlemen are rather anxious to go home. They have been out ever
since July 1862. After we left them, we paid Dr. Walsh a visit
[possibly Dr. John K. Walsh, appointed acting assistant surgeon
September 5, 1863, who was subsequently stationed on the *Mer-
cedita,* in the North Atlantic Blockading Squadron, temporarily at
anchor at Hilton Head in early August]. Found the doctor in the
best of humor. Smoked some of his cigars and drank some of his
sherry. He in return drank some "Navy claret" which we happened
to bring with us [probably "Navy sherry," a term applied to the
grog that had been issued to seamen until September 1, 1862, when
by order of the Secretary of the Navy dated July 17, 1862, the spirit
ration was supplanted by an additional money advance of five cents

a day]. He (the doctor) pronounced it a splendid article. Also met while on shore Old George, a contraband whom we had left on Sapelo Island, Doboy Sound, Ga., last June. He was very glad to see us. Does not like this place as well as he does Doboy. Says he don't make as much money. He receives $10 and one ration per month, doing the work of a fireman at an engine. So much for ye tramp on Hilton Head. . . .

Port Royal, S. C., Oct. 1, 1863. The weather today was lovely. Took a sail in company with Captain Moses in the direction of Hilton Head. While on shore we came across Doctor Walsh, one who knows how to keep a hotel. Also met Aunt Lizzie, Old George's lady. She was dressed up in style but don't appear to fancy this place much. Would rather live in Doboy. The captain and myself returned on board at 3 P.M.

I made out my 3rd quarterly report of sick for 1863 today. During the quarter I had 326 sick days—54 diseases, such as intermittens, dyspepsia, cholera communis, constipation, dysenteria acuta, colica, bronchitis acuta, catarrhus, eczema, furunculus, rheumatismus chronica, synovitis, paronychia, enuresis, gonorrhoea, syphilis primary, syphilis secondary, orchitis, hydrocele, opthalmia, conjunctivitis, vulnus contusum, fractura, contusio, abrasio. The average no. of ship's company was 110. The medical expenses were $23.92. The average daily no. of patients was 3 54/92. The daily cost per man was $0.07 110/326. During the quarter I was compelled to send to the hospital 4 patients as follows: viz., Wm. W. Locke, surgeon's steward—fractura; Michael Heeney, sea.—syphilis secondary; Michael Cunningham, lds.—intermittens; John Brown, lds.—syphilis primary. Today I made out a requisition for medical stores to the amount of $15.20, which I received at 6 P.M. Thus at present I have a good supply of drugs on hand. My report of sick today read, "None on the list." Paymaster Murray and myself played several games of dominoes ere we turned in. . . .

Oct. 2, 1863. The weather was rather pleasant all day. None to report sick. Wrote a letter to father. Nothing of any account transpired today.

Oct. 3, 1863. The U.S. mail steamer *Fulton* fired two guns at 8 A.M. and went to sea. The greater part of our men are engaged in changing shell from one vessel to another per order of the flag officer. Was busy all forenoon making copaiba pills, having one or two trifling cases of gonorrhoea on hand, a disease which some of the boys contracted while on liberty in Portsmouth, N.H. Some of them have an idea that they are paying rather dear for their whistle. In other words, for an hour's pleasure they have to suffer pain and misery for weeks—nay, sometimes for months and very often for years to come.

The captain was on shore today—i.e., Hilton Head. On his return he brought several copies of "The New South" with him. I obtained three copies. One I sent per mail to B.F. Boyer, Reading, Pa.; another to Dr. Boyer, Luthersburg, Pa.; and the third copy I shall retain. From it I shall quote the following articles, which I consider well worthy a place in this, my private journal. In this connection, I might say that "The New South" is a loyal and Federal paper, or sheet, published every Saturday morning in Port Royal, S.C., by Joseph H. Sears, who is both editor and proprietor; price, five cents per copy. The paper [established March 15, 1862] is about the size of a large sheet of foolscap. It has a very large circulation, for all Army and Navy officers are anxious for copies of said paper. Now for the quotations.

"Halleck Improved"

We don't mean General Halleck—he can't be improved—but the poet Halleck.[49]

> At midnight, in his blackguard tent,
> "Old Beau" was dreaming of the hour
> When Gillmore, like a suppliant bent,
> Should tremble at his power.[50]
> In dreams through camp and street he bore
> The trophics of a conqueror.
> In dreams his song of triumph heard,
> He sported Gillmore's gold-laced hat,
> His red-topped boots, his gray cravat,
> As wild his fancy as a bat
> Or "any other bird."
> An hour passed on. "Old Beau" awoke
> Half stifled by a "villainous" smoke,
> Enough the very devil to choke.
> While all around the "stink pots" broke
> And blinded him with sand.
> He cursed the "villainous compound"
> Which stunk like pole-cats far around;

> Then roared with wild, demoniac shriek,
> "Lord, what a smell! the Greek! the Greek!
> Put out the villainous Greek fire,
> Or in the last red ditch expire!
> 'Tis sweet to draw one's dying breath
> For our dear land, as Horace saith,
> But dreadful to be *stunk to death*."

I must consider the above a bully article and the writer of it a damn good boy. Long may he flourish to write more such articles.

[The "stink pots" were incendiary shells. A "liquid fire" that could be thrown from a pump or carried in shells was invented by Alfred Berney of Jersey City, New Jersey, and demonstrated before President Lincoln and the Secretary of War, Edwin M. Stanton, in early 1863. A "Solidified Greek Fire" was devised by Levi Short about the same time. Beginning at one-thirty in the morning of August 22, 1863, both types were tried against Charleston. Though there were several casualties among the Federal troops in firing the new shells, many fires were set. The indiscriminate destruction was condemned both North and South. Robert V. Bruce in his *Lincoln and the Tools of War* (New York-Indianapolis: Bobbs-Merrill, 1956), chap. 17, describes vividly the controversy, sometimes verging on comic opera, that raged around the new means of destruction.

[The author of "Halleck Improved" made Beauregard's protest turn on the noxious aspects of the "fire." Short did propose the addition of noxious elements, but whether that was done is not clear. Obviously the poet either knew of the proposal, or the plan was actually carried out. Bruce quotes (p. 244) the last three lines of the poem, crediting them to the *Nashville Union*.]

Oct. 4, 1863. Today divine service was held on board for the first time since our arrival in the sunny South. Paymaster Murray officiated as chaplain. After services the captain, by order of the New Hampshire Bible Society, distributed Bibles and psalms amongst the crew. I was presented with a German copy of the New Testament, which I am unable to read but hope to do so ere many years —consequently I shall preserve said book until some future period. 10 A.M. Our executive officer, Actg. Master Childs, read the Rules for the Better Government of the Navy of the United States, commonly called the Articles of War.

About 4 P.M. the monitor *Weehawken* went to sea, being towed by a steamer. She looked rather odd, her deck being level with the water. I must say that I don't think I should fancy being attached to her or any other monitor, preferring something more above the water's edge—for instance, the *Fernandina*.

[Although the unfavorable conditions were probably exaggerated at the time, the monitors were considered very uncomfortable vessels on which to serve. In July, 1863, Admiral Dahlgren was cautioned by the Navy Department to relieve officers and men on board them from time to time, and the wages of the crews engaged in attack on the fortifications of Charleston harbor were increased by one-fourth. In addition, ice was supplied for their use and a ship sent for recruiting purposes.[51]]

Reported one case sick this morning—Jos. McShane—otorrhoea. ℞ pil. cath. comp no. iii. Blister behind ear and syringe out ear with tepid water. The weather today had the appearance of a balmy one in spring. Everything appeared lovely and serene. The boys all felt gay and happy. Smiles predominated on their faces. Our decks were as clean and white as the floor of a house amongst the honest old burghers in the days of Peter Stuyvesant used to be after the *jung frau* had scrubbed it. For be it remembered that this day is usually the one to holystone the decks and scrub the cable. The sailor's commandment reads thus: "Six days shalt thou labor and do all that thou art able. On the Sabbath Day holystone the deck and scrub the cable."

[Actually the "GENERAL ORDER RESPECTING THE OBSERVANCE OF THE SABBATH DAY IN THE ARMY AND NAVY" was often read to naval personnel on the blockade. The President on November 15, 1862, copying in part from General Washington's General Order of August 3, 1776, enjoined ". . . the orderly observance of the Sabbath by the officers and men in the military and naval service. The importance for man and beast of the prescribed weekly rest, the sacred rights of Christian soldiers and sailors, a becoming deference to the best sentiment of a Christian people, and a due regard for the divine will demand that Sunday labor in the Army and Navy be reduced to the measure of strict necessity. . . ." Surgeon Boyer copied both the Lincoln and the Washington orders into his diary on May 24, 1863.]

Oct. 5, 1863. Ensign Flood with 35 men left the ship at 8 A.M. to continue the transferring of the shell, commenced on Saturday, the 3rd inst. My case of otorrhoea is improving slowly. I shall continue the tartar emetic in $\frac{1}{10}$-grain doses every two hours, drop glycerine into ear, and dress blister behind ear with cerate simplex.

We received quite a large mail today from the U.S.S. *Vermont*. It being due us last July but having left the squadron for the North, consequently we did not receive it until we arrived in the squadron again. I received a letter from my old friend, the former paymaster of this ship, Andrew G. Myers, . . . dated June 30th, 1863, in which he enclosed three of his *cartes de visite*, to be disposed of by me as follows: viz., one for Captain Moses; one for Jas. B. Henderson, . . . now an acting ensign and attached to the U.S.S. *Nansemond*, of the North Atlantic Blockading Squadron; and one for myself. He gives me particular h—l for the shortness of my letters etc. I shall answer him in a day or two. He also sent me dates of the 3rd and 4th of July, 1863. I received a catalogue of students for the session of 1862 and 3 of the University of Pennsylvania, my alma mater —also several pages from Dr. T. J. Boyer, M. K. Boyer, and Bassler Boyer, attorney-at-law, the former being a brother, the second my father, and the third my nephew.

Wrote a letter to Jas. B. Henderson concerning the *carte de visite* which Mr. Myers sent him per my letter, also about matters and things concerning our sojourn in Portsmouth, New Hampshire.

Oct. 6, 1863. Our orders arrived today from off Charleston, S.C. We are ordered to St. Andrew's Sound, Ga. [St. Andrew according to U. S. Geographic Board ruling dated as early as 1891; St. Andrew's in *O.R.* (Navies).] Said station is south of St. Simons Sound, Ga., which place we blockaded part of last cruise. From all accounts it appears to be an out-of-the-way sort of a place. I have heard that oysters, fish, and game were plenty on the surrounding islands; if so, everything will be O.K. I received a letter dated Sept. 25th, 1863, from Miss A. Carlisle, Trentville, Clearfield Co., Pa.—a young lady of fine talents, good morals, and of a splendid family. . . . I have been corresponding with her for some time. I will answer her letter in a day or two.

Wrote a letter to Sheriff Adams of Portsmouth, N. H., giving him all the particulars of our cruise up to date. Wrote a short one to father announcing our new station. Wrote an answer to Mr. Myers' letter of the 30th of June, 1863 in which I excuse myself for the shortness etc. of my former letter. I also sent the letter along with the above ones that I wrote to Mr. Henderson yesterday. All went on board of the flagship *Vermont* today at 1 P.M.

The captain, Paymaster Murray, Executive Officer Childs, Ensign Flood, and myself invested the sum of five dollars ($5), one year's subscription, for the "[United States] Army and Navy Journal," a weekly journal ["devoted to the interests of the Army and Navy and to the War"; started in New York in August, 1863, under the editorship of Captain W.C. Church; described by Appleton's *Cyclopaedia* for 1863 (page 575), together with the *United States Service Magazine* (a monthly edited by Captain Henry Coppee, a University of Pennsylvania professor, and issued from January, 1864, until its discontinuance in 1866), as being "conducted with ability" and supplying "a want which the war created, but which is likely to be permanent"]. I sent to S. W. Butler, M.D., editor of the "Medical and Surgical Reporter" [a weekly journal that in 1858 superseded a like publication issued in Burlington, New Jersey, and continued in existence until 1898; printed in Philadelphia by King and Baird, 607 Sansom Street], 115 South 7th St., Phila., Pa., the sum of three dollars ($3), one year's subscription for said "Medical and Surgical Reporter." I sincerely hope that we may be successful in getting all the copies of the above journals.

At 2 P.M. we got under way and made sail for sea and at 6.15 P.M. let go our starboard anchor in 7½ fathoms of water. We are about 3 miles from our anchorage. The relief lightship bears s.e. ½s. from us. I had the pleasure of seeing Capt. Durand, sailing master, and Executive Officer Tillinghast and Paymaster Andrews in the distance on board the guard ship *Mohawk* as we passed her. They all appeared gay and happy. Of course we tipped our caps to each other. They are old shipmates of mine. Long may they live in the land of the brave and the free.

Reported McShane—otorrhoea—improving—he continues same treatment; William Halstad, lds.—paronychia on thumb of left hand—lanced it, and apply lini cataplasm; Angus McPhae, sea.— remains of an old gleet—℞ tinct. ferri chloridi gtts vii ter in die, and apply tinct. iodine to part, in my morning report to the captain.

The weather was rather lovely all day. The wind was dead ahead, or else we should have gone to sea instead of letting go our "mudhook" [anchor] where we did. We all hope to have a favorable breeze in the morning so as to be able to get to our station and settle down for the winter campaign.

7 P.M. Having occasion to go to the forward part of the ship, I was pleased to see how the crew enjoyed themselves. In one corner

might be seen a group of them singing "The Star Spangled Banner," another party "Columbia, the Gem of the Ocean," one party
listening to a yarn which a comrade appeared to be spinning, every
now and then bursting out in a laugh. Some of the boys were having
a social game of dominoes, whilst another group were watching
two of their comrades practising the "manly art of self-defense,"
or sparring, with a pair of gloves. I must say that considerable science was displayed by the contending parties. The last party of
them were having a general plantation walk-around. The way they
done up "Old Bob Ridley"[52] was not slow. Their hornpipes were
equal to a Christy, Morris, Sandford, or Mulligan—but the way
they danced juba to the patting upon the knee by a messmate
capped the climax.[53] In short, "joy appears unconfined."

The above sports etc. continued until 8 P.M., when the night
watch was called. Fires and lights all put out on the berth deck,
pumps sounded, batteries secured, and an extra anchor ready to
let go at any moment. From this moment until morning, unless
something extra turns up, everything will be quiet. Nothing is
heard save the steady and regular tread of the officer of the deck as
he walks his lonely watch. Every half hour the tap of the bell announcing the hour of the night can be heard, and occasionally the
quartermaster's voice is heard hailing a boat which may happen to
be coming to the ship or else passing by within hailing distance. In
the cabin and wardroom, on the berth deck as well, everything is as
quiet as the grave.

Several Army transports made their entree into this harbor,
loaded with troops, horses, and provisions. Two or three gunboats
also arrived from off Charleston, one of which was the U.S.S. *Paul
Jones,* commanded by Captain [Commander James M.] Duncan,
formerly of the U.S.S. *Sebago.* The *Paul Jones* had been under the
charge of Captain Steedman . . . for a long time, and while in command of her he was the terror of the Rebels along the Atlantic
coast. On our last cruise we blockaded part of the time in company
with the *Paul Jones* while under the command of Captain Steedman. She is a splendid gunboat. Read old dates until 10 P.M., when
I turned in.

Port Royal Entrance, S. C., Oct. 7, 1863. At 5.30 A.M. we got
under way, and at 6 A.M., a calm setting in, we were compelled to
let go our starboard anchor once more, so that we made very little

headway. Oh, for a stiff breeze! 2 P.M. Upon examination of the horsepipe [hawsepipe] of the port anchor it was seen that it was broke; consequently we were not in a safe condition to go to sea. So at 6 P.M. we made sail for the vicinity of the flagship *Vermont*. When we arrived close enough to her for all purposes, we let go our starboard anchor. I understand that it will take several days for us to obtain a new horsepipe, as a mould has to be made so as to cast a new one. Rather an awkward state of affairs.

Invested the sum of $2 for 4 months' subscription for the Philadelphia "Inquirer," which I shall enclose in a letter directed to the editor, W[illiam] W[hite] Harding . . . [The paper was a leader in the prompt and full publication of war news, and the government sometimes ordered special editions for distribution to the troops.] Reported McShane—improving; Halstead—improving; and William Ryan, boatswain's mate—orchitis— ℞ antimi et potassi tart in ⅟₁₆-grain doses every three hours, apply lead lotion to part, enjoin rest in his hammock, and ℞ Dover's pulv grs xii when he turns in at 8 bells this evening, in my morning report to the captain. Read Charles Lever's "Barrington" [London: Chapman and Hall, 1863], a novel [of middle-class Irish social and domestic life], until 11 P.M. . . .

Port Royal, S. C., Oct. 8, 1863. Admiral Dahlgren . . . made his appearance in the harbor this morning, having left Charleston in the steamer *Philadelphia,* his flagship. What his business is I cannot tell; in fact, I am not interested enough to care or trouble my head about his affairs [he had come to find out about the completion of monitor repairs and to investigate the possibility of devising for the ironclads a defense against torpedoes].

I was compelled to blister and purge boy McShane, who is affected with otorrhoea, again this morning, so as to cure him of said inflamation. McPhae has a lini poultice applied to his perineum. Ryan's orchitis is about the same. Discharged Halstad to duty this morning. McShane, McPhae, and Ryan will continue on the sick list.

One of the bands belonging to the Army stationed at Hilton Head came off and serenaded Admiral Dahlgren between the hours of 8.30 P.M. and 12 midnight. The music sounded beautifully across the water. I have an idea that they must have had a good time on board of the admiral's flagship. The whole cabin etc. was beautifully illuminated. The band left, playing "Way down South in Dixie," about 11.30 P.M.

Bought "Shoulder-Straps, A Novel of New York and the Army, 1862" [Philadelphia: T. B. Peterson and Brothers, 1863], by Henry Morford, editor of the New York "Atlas," and, having read part of it, must say that I am pleased with it. Answered Miss Carlisle's letter of the 24th of September.

Our paymaster plucked up courage enough to go on shore, on Hilton Head side, for the first time since our arrival in the harbor. All hands were astonished, for he as a general thing is tied to his books and safe.

Oct. 9, 1863. There don't appear to be any material change as regards the health and condition of my patients—viz., McShane, McPhae, and Ryan. I dressed McShane's blister and told him to continue his tartar emetic mixture. Painted McPhae's tumor with tinct. iodine and ordered for him ol ricini $\frac{3}{2}$ i. Ryan—℞ ol. ricini $\frac{3}{2}$ i and continued lead lotion. Both Ryan and McPhae have taken up quarters in the sick bay. I shall endeavor to rouse them out of that as quick as I can. 11 A.M., the oil not operating, I ordered a second dose. 3 P.M. I was compelled to order an injection of tepid water, salt, etc., which had the desired effect. I am alluding to Ryan's case.

At 10.30 A.M. the admiral left in his flagship for off Charleston. Our executive officer, Mr. Childs, having been to Hilton Head, returned with a box of Havanas, of which I was the happy recipient of 25/100. The cigars smoke right well. Mr. Childs deserves a vote of thanks for his generosity. May he never be in want of a cigar or short of a pipe of tobacco.

Finished reading "Shoulder-Straps," which is quite a novel, and commenced the perusing of Dumas' "Felina de Chambure; or, the Female Fiend" [paper-bound edition published in New York by H. Long and Brother between 1852 and 1855; another in Philadelphia by T. B. Peterson between 1855 and 1858—each priced at fifty cents], which, like all French tales, is full of love, murder, treachery, and the devil. The story is of such a nature that when once commenced, it is hard to lay it aside until finished. I kept myself busy reading it until 12 midnight, when I finished it. Of course vice was punished and virtue rewarded.

8 P.M. The boys on deck are having a fine time "tripping on the

light fantastic toe" and pummelling each other with boxing gloves, or, in other words, dancing and sparring. Truly they are a jolly set of tars.

Oct. 10, 1863. The *Fernandina* still remains at this anchorage. Little did I think a week ago that we would still be hugging the shores of South Carolina at this date. On the contrary, we all had an idea that we might be blockading one of the many sounds on the coast of Georgia. But such not being the case, on account of our horsepipe being broken, we will no doubt be in St. Andrew's Sound, Ga., next Saturday. Time and tide will tell.

I had the pleasure of discharging to duty this morning boy Mc-Shane; consequently I only had McPhae and Ryan, both improving and coming on as well as can be expected, considering the nature of their cases, to report sick this morning.

I sent several copies of "The New South" North today; at least I enclosed a copy to Dr. Boyer, Clearfield Co., Penna., and one copy to M. P. Boyer, Berks Co., Penna., in letters and mailed them. They leave by tomorrow's mail. Amongst the many good and comic items published in the above interesting sheet—i.e., "New South"—is the following: viz., An enraged parent had jerked his provoking son across his knee, and was operating on the exposed portion of the urchin's person with great vehemence, when the young one dug into his parental leg with his venomous little teeth. "Blazes! what are you biting me for?" "Well, who beginned this 'ere war?" Bully for the young idea!

Wrote quite a long and interesting letter to one of my medical friends, Dr. [Hiland Hall] Banks, who is attending the medical lectures at the Jefferson Medical College, Phila., Penna. [registered in 1862 and 1863; not graduated]. Dr. Banks is a citizen of Reading, Berks County, Pa. He is a gem of the first water. Long may his phiz be seen here below.

Oct. 11, 1863. At 10.15 the mail steamer *Arago* left this harbor with the mail of the Navy and Army forces for the North. May she have a successful voyage and return ere long with a large mail, the *Fernandina,* of course, coming in for a lion's share. All hands were called at 9.30 A.M. to muster to attend divine service. A. A. Paymaster T. N. Murray officiated as chaplain. Not feeling very bright, I got our worthy and efficient executive officer to excuse me from attending service.   . . . . Reported McPhae and Ryan sick in my daily report. The weather was lovely all day.

Oct. 12, 1863. Thirty-five of our crew are busy unloading a steamer loaded with lumber. They are in charge of Ensign Thomas and Master's Mate Wright.

This morning I introduced a lancet into McPhae's tumor, after which I caused a lini cataplasm to be applied. He is to have a sol. antim. et potass. tart gr i to aqua ℥ ii; M̶; Sig. Teaspoonful every two hours. I am keeping warm fomentations applied to Ryan's scrotum—℞ antim. et potass. tart grs i ss, morphiae sulphas gr ss, magnesiae sulph. ℥ i, sach. albi ℥ ii, aquae ℥ vi; M̶; Sig. Table-spoonful every three hours.

The supply steamer *Union* leaves today bound north. She will take a mail with her.

Captain Moses and myself paid Dr. Walsh of Hilton Head a visit. We found the doctor in his usual good humor. While chatting with the doctor in his "sanctum sanctorum; imbibing occasionally of that which cheers but not inebriates, a neighbor of his, Mr. Steele, jeweller and watchmaker, dropped in. Mr. Steele appears to be one of Nature's noblemen. In a short time Mr. Steele sent to his establishment [for] a box, or case, of Burgundy wine. Of course all hands done justice to the fluid. We spoiled that box ere many minutes. The beauty of the affair was [that] we all belonged to the Masonic order. Ere the captain and myself left for the ship, Dr. Walsh gave each of us a cigar tube [holder] and Mr. Steele pre-sented us with a case of his Burgundy. We arrived on board be-tween 8 and 9 P.M., rather fatigued. Met Capt. Durand of the *Mohawk* and Surgeon Sawyer of the *Seneca*. Both were well and hardy. The *Seneca's* station is Doboy Sound, Ga. The *Mohawk* is guard ship at the entrance to Port Royal.

Oct. 13, 1863. Upon turning out this morning, I found myself rather indisposed. My limbs ached me; head felt full and dull. In short, I caught a severe cold last night. I shall confine myself to my room.

[Acting Assistant] Surgeons [Ezra] Pray and [S. N.] Fisk paid me a visit. Dr. Pray used to be the medical officer of this craft. He is a tall, robust-looking fellow with a large red beard and a very good talker—full of jokes etc. He was attached to the *Dinsmore* but, like a good Samaritan, gave up his place to Dr. Fisk, who, by the by, is a married man, and has been away from his wife for 14 months. The reason for the exchange is that the *Dinsmore* is ordered North, which gives Dr. Fisk an opportunity to go home. . . . Dr. Fisk used to be attached to the barque *Braziliera,* stationed at St. Andrew's Sound, Ga. The doctor is apparently a young man, say 25 years, a good companion; knows how to appreciate a glass of sherry, claret, and "Navy claret"; also can smoke a good cigar. They remained on board about one hour, when they left. We had a good and jolly time together. As soon as they left, I turned in and took a nap. The captain also caught a cold last night. 2 P.M. He is taking a nap. 6 P.M. He feels better. 7 P.M. Both the captain and myself turned in.

Reported Ryan and McPhae sick in my daily report of sick to the captain. Both are improving slowly. Nothing else of importance transpired today.

11

On Duty in Sapelo Sound

[*Sapelo Sound, Ga.*] Oct. *14, 1863.* At 8.30 A.M. we got under way, and at 6 P.M. we let go our starboard anchor—and where? Why, in Sapelo Sound, Ga., instead of St. Andrew's Sound, Ga., as our former orders read—for be it remembered that ere we sailed, we received orders to relieve the barque *Midnight* in Sapelo Sound instead of the barque *Braziliera* in St. Andrew's Sound. Not having been here heretofore, of course I am not able to tell which is the best station, but from what some of the officers of the *Midnight* say who have been eleven months at St. Andrew's Sound, this station—viz., Sapelo Sound—is the better station of the two.

As soon as we had anchored, Executive Officer Mr. Coffin, Paymaster Miller, and [Acting Assistant] Surgeon [J. M.] Garner of the *Midnight* came on board. I had met the first two gentlemen before; the latter was a stranger, but it did not take me long to become acquainted with Dr. Garner. They are all trumps. We had a jolly old time together. It were idle and misspent time for me to devote in writing to state that the claret flowed freely and that our cigars (mine) were duly appreciated. They are in the best of humor because they are going North, and we were in good humor because we were ordered to this station. So when both parties are pleased, then comes the fun, or, as the Dutch have it, "When Dutch meet Dutch, then comes the lager beer." ...

Reported Ryan and McPhae, who are improving, and John Daly, o. sea.—furunculus, which I lanced and poulticed, sick today.

Sapelo Sound, Ga., Oct. 15, 1863. Mr. Childs and myself returned the visit paid us by the officers of the *Midnight* this morning. We had quite a delightful time. I purchased three medical works from the doctor—viz., Wood's "Practice," 2 vols., [George B. Wood, *A Treatise on the Practice of Medicine,* the first edition of which was published in Philadelphia in 1847 by Grigg, Elliot and Company] $7, and Bumstead's work on venereal [Freeman J. Bumstead, *The Pathology and Treatment of Venereal Diseases: including the results of recent investigations upon the subject,* the first edition of which was published in Philadelphia in 1861 by Blanchard and Lea], $3.75. The doctor and rest of the officers gave me about 10 or 20 novels, so that I have quite a lump of reading matter. The paymaster made me a present of a bound edition of Thackeray's "Philip" [*The Adventures of Philip on his Way through the World: shewing who robbed him, who helped him, and who passed him by,* published in three volumes in London by Smith, Elder and Company in 1862, a Tauchnitz edition appearing the same year].

The *Midnight* got under way at 2 P.M., upon which we fired a salute and dipped our colors. They all feel gay and happy, for they are homeward bound. Won't they walk into the good things of life? Crinoline will be plenty where they go. Hard-tack, salt horse [salted beef], pork and beans will be at a discount when they come North. Soft bread, fresh beef, and fresh vegetables will be all the go. In short, they expect to have and no doubt they will have a good and happy old time.

By some mistake or other the *Midnight* got aground, consequently can not leave the harbor today. It is really too bad. Captain Kirby made Captain Moses a present of a third cutter, a dingy, and the *Old Greeley,* which he received at Doboy Sound. The presents were duly appreciated by Captain Moses.

I lanced McPhae's abscess and evacuated about $\tilde{3}$ i of pus. I shall continue lini cataplasm. Ryan is improving. Daly's cheek looks better.

Oct. 16, 1863. A boat in charge of a master's mate with a pilot and paymaster on board coming from St. Catharine's Sound, Ga., belonging to the *Mahaska* arrived at 8 A.M. Their object is to remain here until the *Massachusetts,* our supply steamer, arrives. She is due today, tomorrow, or next day. The [acting assistant] paymaster, whose name is [Charles] Fairchild, appears to be a very nice sort of a person. The pilot is a jolly old sea dog all the way from Cape Cod. The *Midnight* went to sea this morning.

The caterer of our mess and some others went after fish etc. They returned with some splendid ones. We had some of them for tea. The weather was splendid all day. Reported Ryan, McPhae, and Mowatt sick and discharged to duty Daly.

Oct. 17, 1863. The famous little sand fly, one of the greatest pests extant, has made its appearance this morning in our midst. Won't we have to take it!

The *Massachusetts* has been here and left again in about twenty minutes. We obtained some stores, fresh beef, ice, etc. I am in for $3 worth of sherry. Received a letter and some newspapers from father; the letter was dated Oct. 4, 1863. The mess bought some shot etc. We received dates up to the 10th inst. The *Mahaska's* party recd. their cargo and left. Mr. Wright, in charge of one of our boats, went along with them so as to enable the paymaster to take all his stores with him. I hope they may have a happy time together whilst on their journey.

Oct. 18, 1863. All hands were called to attend divine service at 9 A.M., Paymaster Murray officiated as chaplain. Our 3rd cutter returned from St. Catharine's Sound this morning. The boys say they had a pleasant time of it. The weather was splendid all day. Our paymaster went on shore today, and upon his return he declared that it was an awful place and that he was fairly disgusted with the aspect of things on shore. Reported McPhae sick.

Oct. 19, 1863. The crew are busy watering ship and overhauling the rigging. The captain with a party started out on a voyage of discovery. He returned with a lot of green oranges—i.e., branches of the tree with its fruit attached. I was the happy recipient of several clusters, with which I decorated my small stateroom. For the last two or three days we have been living sumptuously on fresh beef, fish, and clams—something unusual for seafaring people. McPhae is improving. Weather warm and pleasant.

Oct. 20, 1863. The gallant tars attached to the U.S. ship *Fernandina* have been busy all day watering the ship and making boarding nettings. The captain took another one of his sails of discovery and upon his return presented me with a sweet orange, which was splendid. Scott, one of our quartermasters, started out on a hunt. When he will return I cannot tell. Read the greater part of the day Dumas' "Memoirs of a Physician" [a two-volume English translation (London: Simms and M'Intyre) of which appeared in 1847 and an American edition (Philadelphia: T.B. Peterson) about three years later], which I consider one of his masterpieces, equalled only by his "Three Guardsmen" [a paper-bound translation of which, published at fifty cents in 1850 by Long and Brother, New York, was followed between 1852 and 1855 by another, published at seventy-five cents].

The weather has been rather warm for this season of the year.

Upon asking the captain his opinion of this station, after he returned today from his sail etc., he replied, "It is the damnedest hole we been in yet"—rather an unfavorable sort of an answer! Everyone appears to say that it is an awful place. Well, well! We'll have to grin and bear it. I think I shall confine myself to the ship and go on shore as little as possible, for I see nothing to attract me ashore.

Reported McPhae sick. He will return to duty in a day or two.

7 P.M. Scott has returned. He reports the prospects as regards hunting good. He saw two deer, killed a snake, and got caught in a bush, when he concluded to return. He talks of starting out some day in earnest, for, says he, "I only went this time to see how the land lay."

Oct. 21, 1863. Spent a very pleasant morning, or forenoon, in my sick bay making pills for Mr. Childs, who appears to need an aperient. Said prescription read: R rhei pulv aloe pulv āā ℥ i, ipecac grs x, saponis Ɔi, aqua q.s. to form a mass; M; pilulae no lx (60); Sig. One every night. Upon presenting said box of pills to Mr. Childs, he commenced to thank me to such an extent as to compel me to request him to stop his blarney etc., telling him that I done no more than my duty. I hope they may have the desired effect. My patient McPhae, who has been suffering for some time from the effect of an abscess in the perineum (perineal abscess), is convalescent. I order him tonics and gentle exercise.

The little *Paul Jones, Jr.,* a small steamer, made her appearance this afternoon. She was in search of a landsman who had deserted from the U.S.S. *Seneca,* Doboy Sound. She left for St. Catharine's Sound after she had made known to us her business. The *Paul Jones, Jr.,* is used for the purpose of carrying mails etc. from one end of the station to the other. She was built by the *Paul Jones* while she lay at anchor in St. Simons Sound. Formerly she was one of her launches. She is quite a snug little affair.   . . .

Oct. 22, 1863. Ensign Flood with an armed boat's crew started in the 3rd cutter for St. Catharine's Sound, there to communicate with the U.S. steamer *Mahaska,* at 9 A.M. He returned at 7 P.M. having some lima beans and sweet oranges, which he purchased from some contrabands living in the vicinity of St. Catharine's Sound. Mr. Flood was kind enough to leave me have twenty-five of said oranges, for which he charged thirty cents, the same that he paid the darkies. He also made arrangements as regards washing etc.

Madison Scarlet, a colored gentleman rope hauler, came to me at 8 A.M. with his left cheek all swollen. Upon examination I found that the cause of said swelling was nothing more or less than a decayed molar tooth. As a matter of fact, I very quietly hauled out my extracting instruments, cut the gum, and applied a piece of cold iron to said offending member in the shape of a pair of forceps, the finale being the extraction of the tooth, a pleasant smile on said darky's countenance, and his admission on the binnacle list with face tied up for this day. Contraband had no objection; consequently all parties were satisfied.

On account of there being little extra work to be done today, two of the boys—viz., Collins and Powers—thought fit to play sick. I ordered each of them a double dose of castor oil, which did not appear to suit them; but down the dose went. I have no doubt but what they will feel rather weak in the morning. McPhae is coming along finely. Thermometer ranged between 74° to 78° Fahr. today.

Oct. 23, 1863. Paymaster Murray and Ensign Thomas started this morning at 8 A.M. for Doboy Sound. They take the land route —i.e., after being landed on Sapelo Island, they commenced to walk. They expect to return tonight. The distance is 6 miles—12 miles going and coming. I hope they may have a good time.

7 P.M. Messrs. Murray and Thomas have returned, and they appear well pleased with their tramp. They found Old Man Sampson

and his wife, Aunt Margaret, as lively as bugs in a rug. Allie and his little wife were in the best of humor. Billy and his "honey," as he calls his wife, almost bursted with joy, so happy were they to see them—for, be it remembered, while the *Fernandina* blockaded Doboy Sound, they (the darkies) had a pleasant time of it, for we supplied them with a great many of the necessaries of life and treated them like human beings; consequently they were all sorry to see us leave.

Old Sampson reports that all their crops were splendid—corn by the hundred bushels, pumpkins by the cartload, and potatoes (sweet) plenty to supply nearly all creation. He says that they had a very large crop of peaches, figs, and watermelons when they were in season. In short, they appear to have all that man could desire in the way of food; consequently they cannot but help being happy as bees. They served up a dinner for the gentlemen consisting of fresh beef, potatoes, corn bread, and eggs. They both acknowledged that it was as good a meal as they had eaten for some time, even if they had to eat it out of pans instead of off chinaware with the aid of silver knives and forks. They remained there about two hours. Upon their return they both felt somewhat fatigued, and the way they dug into their supper was not slow. In short, they felt both hungry and tired. They say that they saw any amount of cattle on Sapelo Island within three miles of the ship and that they appeared to be very tame.

The captain talks of sending some of our Nimrods out tomorrow in search of some of "kine species." Paymaster Murray says that the distance is more than 6 miles; he has an idea that it is in the neighborhood of 9 miles. Well, who has a right to know better? Has he not walked the route, and is he therefore not able to tell? Certainly he ought to be able to judge the distance. So hereafter I shall consider it 9 miles inland from Sapelo Sound to the plantation inhabited by King Sampson in the vicinity of Doboy Sound. I hope ere long to have the pleasure of walking said distance myself so as to be certain as regards the distance. The captain says that I am too "damn lazy" to walk to Doboy Sound and says that in case I happen to pluck up courage to try the experiment, he is ready to accompany me and take back the above remark. I think I shall show him ere many days that I am not as lazy as he thinks for. But enough of this blarney.

John Smith, sea.—catarrhus and McPhae—abscess were reported

on the sick list this morning. The former took ol ricini ℥ i et hydrarg chlorid mite gr vi and the latter tinct ferri chloridi gtts vii ter in die. . . .

In order to kill time and drive away dull care, I read Dumas' "Memoirs of a Physician." Nothing of any account transpired today on board, the boys having little or nothing to do. Thermometer 76° Fahr.

Oct. 24, 1863. Acting Master's Mate John Wright and Quartermaster Scott went not like Marryat's Japhet in search of a father but in search of a bullock. My wish is that they may be successful and return with some rich and juicy beef. The hunting ground is on Sapelo Island.

It has been raining nearly all day. The weather is quite cool. The boys are busy mending their clothing, this being the day set apart in the service for that purpose. Such an overhauling of bags etc. is not often seen. I devoted the greater part of this day in reading. While glancing at the Olean "Advertiser," a paper published in one of the rural districts of New York, I happened to see the following poetical effusion, which I consider not bad:

" 'Tis the Last Silver Dollar"

'Tis the last silver dollar,
Left shining alone,
All its laughing companions
Have melted and gone;
Not a coin of its kindred,
No specie is nigh,
To echo back softly
Its silvery sigh.

You must leave me, bright dollar,
The last of my few,
Since thy mates have departed,
Skedaddle then too.
Thus kindly I send thee,
To wander afar—
In the sky of shinplasters
A glimmering star.

So soon may I follow,
When thou art no more,

> And I wreck of starvation
> On shinplaster shore,
> When the purse never jingles,
> And shiners have flown,
> Oh! who can feel wealthy
> On pictures alone?

So much for "ye poetry" as it flowed from ye ancient town of Olean, Cattaraugus County, New York. I ought of said flowed from the pen of the poet editor of the Olean "Advertiser," but as I have given the above-named journal credit for the same, I don't think it makes much difference. Olean is the birthplace and home of our illustrious, good, efficient, and patriotic paymaster, Thomas N. Murray . . . Paymaster Murray says that it is a right smart place —plenty of fine ladies but d—n bad whiskey.

Angus McPhae returns to duty, and John Smith—catarrhus continues on the sick list. The binnacle list sports the following names: John Collins and Miles Powers, both having an idea that they are indisposed and not fit for duty. I shall order them the fluid extract senna in ℥ i doses. They both will have the pleasure of skedaddling from the list and go to duty in the morning. Messrs. Murray, Flood, and myself spent a happy evening playing dominoes, each one for himself, or, as it is called, the cutthroat game.

Oct. 25, 1863. A cold blusterly wind is blowing. There is every indication of a bad spell of weather. Thermometer 62° Fahr. in the shade. At 9 A.M. all hands attended divine service. As usual, our paymaster officiated as chaplain. 9.30 A.M. piped down.

While perusing the columns of a Philadelphia daily sheet, I came across an article, which, as a medical man, interested me. . . . .

[The article appeared in many papers. It concerned "a new disease called 'Febris Crustacea,' or shell fever," that had broken out in Charleston since General Gillmore's batteries and the cannon of the gunboats had been pounding the city. The effect of the disease was "a sort of 'Chorea,'" or "sudden jerking of the muscles of the lower limbs, causing a tendency to locomotion, the disposition being not to move about from one place to another, but rather more to exercise in a straight line to some distant point. . . . ."]

Comments on said article are not necessary, for it speaks for itself. The only remedy is the withdrawing of Uncle Sam's many and powerful gunboats, which is an event not likely to happen for some time to come; at least they will remain along the Southern coast harassing the inhabitants so long as the Rebellion lasts —consequently I am afraid that the people of Charleston etc. will have to put up with the "shell fever" and do the best they can under the circumstances. Such are some of the fruits of treason.

Mr. Wright and Scott have returned from their hunt, having two fine buck in their possession, so that now we shall have plenty of venison to eat for the time being. Both parties were somewhat fatigued. They report plenty of deer, turkeys, and bullock on Sapelo Island.

John Smith—improving—was reported sick. 8 P.M. Coxswain Price complains of colica. ℞ Dover's powder grs xv, creta prep grs xx; M̶. 11 P.M. ℞ tinct. opii gtts xxx, tinct zingiber gtts x, ol. menthae pip gtts i, magnesia ʒ i; M̶.

Oct. 26, 1863. At 2 A.M. the messenger boy announced, or rather reported, to me that Coxswain Price wanted to see me—that he suffered considerably. I told him to tell my steward to give Price pil. cath. comp no iv, also tell him to keep quiet and not disturb me until morning. Upon receiving said pills and the verbal order, he (Price) turned over and went to sleep. At 8 A.M. I ordered him ol. ricini ʒ i. While prescribing for him, I was called upon by John Galleghar, lds., who had a large furunculus on his neck. I lanced said boil; ordered lini cataplasm to be applied and ℞ ol. ricini ʒ i. My patient John Smith is taking quinine in grs v doses three times a day. Thus my sick list sports three names. Was busy the greater part of the day dissecting the skulls, or heads, of the bucks that were shot yesterday. One is intended for Captain Moses; the other I shall keep myself.

Two of our tars—Rickards and Carey—started this morning on a hunt on the island of Blackbeard [a small heavily wooded island across Barn Creek from the northern end of Sapelo Island; named for an English pirate, William Teach, thought to have made his headquarters and buried his treasure on the island, who terrorizing the region, wore his bushy black beard tied in small tails, sometimes looped behind his ears; used from 1840 to 1910 as a government quarantine station and subsequently as a game preserve].

They consider themselves as good hunters as Wright and Scott. Hope they may be successful and return well laden with game. Our caterer, Ensign Flood, went ashore on St. Catharine's Island and there communicated with some contrabands who live at the upper end of the island. He returned with some beans, chickens, eggs, honey, etc.

The weather continues cold and blusterly. Thermometer 56° Fahr. in the shade. Read until 11 P.M. [Irish novelist William Hamilton] Maxwell's "Brian O'Linn; or, Luck is Everything" [three volumes, published in London in 1848; a two-act farce entitled *Brian O'Linn* (New York: Samuel French), appearing about 1850, attributed to Samuel D. Johnson], when I turned in.

Oct. 27, 1863. After I had attended to my morning sick call, Captain Moses called me into his cabin and informed me that it was his birthday; consequently I had to take a glass of sherry with him in honor of said event, which I done with the greatest pleasure. May he live to enjoy many more birthdays.

I had myself landed on St. Catharine's Island at 9 A.M., where I remained until 3 P.M., busily engaged in the dissection of the heads of two deer. The two Nimrods—viz., Rickards and Carey—returned on board at 1 P.M. having in their possession 4 deer. Well done, old boys; they deserve the champion belt. Venison therefore flows, as it were, spontaneously. We have at present 6 deer aboard. We had some chops for breakfast, a fine roast for dinner, and cold sliced venison for tea, so that we really lived on venison today. At 2 P.M. Ensign Thomas and Landsmen Gray and Headley started in search of game on St. Catharine's Island. They returned at 6 P.M. with three live pigs, which we intend to fatten for barbecues. Some of the boys went in search of oysters and returned with quite a nice lot of them. Taking all in all, I think we have no right to complain as regards the condition of our larder, which is well supplied with the necessaries of life at present. From all indications there appears to be plenty of game on the neighboring islands, and I think we will endeavor to profit by the same.

Rickards, one of the hunters who was out all last night in the woods, came to me at 6 P.M. complaining sick, having caught cold. I ordered him pil. cath. comp no iv and told him to stay in his hammock all night. My sick list sports the names of Price, who is improving; Galleghar, also improving; and Joseph Short, boy—

abscess—lini cataplasm and ol ricini ℥ i—in all, three names. John Smith returns to duty.

The captain and paymaster between the hours of 2 and 3 P.M. enjoyed themselves setting fire to the tall grass on St. Catharine's Island. Their reasons for so doing are that they want to make the snakes skedaddle or else perish in the flames, also to clear the ground so as to make it pleasanter travelling. The weather continues windy.

Oct. 28, 1863. The weather has been cloudy and stormy all day. Some of the boys are on shore, trying to capture porkers. My sick call sports the names of Price, Short, Rickards, and Galleghar. The crew are variously employed, doing little or nothing. Wrote a letter to brother Michael and one to sister Beckie. Commenced on Ferguson's "Practical Surgery" [Sir William Ferguson, *A System of Practical Surgery*, of which the first American edition (Philadelphia: Lea and Blanchard) appeared in 1843, the second in 1845, and the third in 1848]. My intentions are to read medical works this winter so as to keep myself from getting rusty.

Oct. 29, 1863. No change in the state of the weather. On the contrary, it appears to blow as hard as ever. Our nautical part of the officers—i.e., old salts—say that it is blowing a stiff gale, compelling a vessel to sail with close-reefed topsails. Thanks are due to the powers that be, for they sent us to a hole where nothing like a gale unless it be a hurricane can affect us.

Part of the crew are employed scraping the gun carriages, whilst the rest are lounging about the berth deck. I caused Coxswain Price and Landsman Rickards to skedaddle from off the sick list and go to duty, while I left Landsman Galleghar and boy Short remain on the list—hence their names can be seen on the binnacle list as well as in my morning report of sick to the captain. The furunculus of Galleghar's is improving. I lanced it again this morning and reapplied lini cataplasm. Boy Short still continues to poultice his cheek with a flaxseed poultice.

Some of our crew were on shore today in search of young porkers, and after running over one-half of the island, they managed to capture two small ones the size of a large rat. The stocks as regards pig hunting are down in the market. Large fires are burning on St. Catharine's Island, caused by the application of a match in the hands of some of the crew to the dry underbrush. The sight is magnificent. The snakes will have to travel.

Oct. 30, 1863. Old Boreas has concluded at last to leave us and make room for Old Sol, who made his appearance today in all his glory, much to the gratification of all hands. We all were anxious to see the good and pleasant countenance of Old Sol—hence when he showed himself this morning, you can well imagine how welcome he was. May he continue in shining forth in all his glory.

Two more venisons were added to our well-stocked larder, thus making 8 deer in all that we have shot since our arrival into this sound. Everyone appears anxious to volunteer his services as a hunter. I must say that I never had an idea that we had so many Nimrods. The captain generally sends out two at a time; they manage to stay a day or two in the woods ere they return with any game.

My sick list has dwindled down to one name—viz., Joseph Short—and he is improving so rapidly that in a day or two he will leave the list. I will not be sorry, for I am not overanxious for patients, and my stock of medicines is getting rather low, at least as regards castor oil, salts, and cathartic pills.

Our piggery contains 8 pigs in all, some of which will be fit to kill by the 1st of December next.

I am busily engaged perusing Ferguson's "Practical Surgery." . . . His ideas are very good. Some of the operations are performed in the old style, yet the majority are modernized, so that it is a splendid textbook.

Oct. 31, 1863. Since the first of May, '63 Ensign Flood has performed the honorable duties of caterer of the wardroom mess. . . . He always managed to keep the table well supplied and our bills high. Finally, after serving faithfully 6 months, he with his own free will and accord offers up the books, papers, etc. to a successor, whomsoever he may be. He is magnanimous enough to yield up the sceptre to any enterprising individual who is anxious to perform the duties of caterer. He is willing to abdicate, providing the members of said right and honorable mess will consent. In the best possible humor he offers to give up the head of the table to anyone whom the mess will choose to succeed so illustrious a predecessor. Mr. Flood upon entering on the duties as caterer of this glorious, peaceable, and worthy mess found an empty larder, but to the contrary he leaves a full larder for his successor to work upon. Well done, good and faithful servant. You retire to the humble position of member with a brow encircled with laurels.

Alas! Alas!! We ne'er shall see your like again. "Who will succeed Ensign Flood?" is the cry.

6 P.M. At a meeting of the members of the wardroom mess it was unanimously resolved that Ensign Thomas, ex-caterer, who had performed the arduous duties of caterer heretofore, be elected caterer of this mess from this time forth; he enters upon his duties as caterer tomorrow, the first of November, '63. May he have a happy time. May our table be well laden with the good things of life. May our mess bills be small. May he never be tired of serving as caterer of this sociable mess. Amen. The present caterer, Ensign Flood, presented a small bill of $11.23, this making the third bill since the 10th of August, 1863. The first bill amounted to $53.13, the second to $5.64—in all, $70. Rather a salty dose to swallow; nevertheless, it is so.

Josiah Pettingill, lds., aet. 30, England, came to me this morning complaining of a rawness in neighborhood of scrotum. Upon examination I found it to be eczema. I ordered magnesii sulphas ℥ i internally and apply externally a lotion of sodae bicarbonas. Boy Short still continues on the list. His sore is suppurating finely. Continue tinct iodine and lini cataplasm.

The crew are busy mending their clothing and overhauling their bags and diddy boxes [ditty-boxes—small boxes for thread, needles, tape, and so forth], it being the day [Saturday] allowed them in the service for that purpose. The spar deck presents more the appearance of a secondhand clothing store than the deck of a man-of-war, the way the pants, shirts, coats, hats, socks, etc. are scattered and hung about the deck. In one part of the ship can be seen the ship's barber, Landsman Pfander, busy shaving the boys as well as cutting the hair of some of them. He has 50 customers at the rate of $0.12 per month or three cents a shave, they finding razor, soap, brush, towel, and strap. Pfander shaves the officers at the rate of $0.50 per month, they also finding their own traps [personal belongings].

I read medicine until 9 P.M., when I turned in. A schooner was reported in the offing all day. Who and what she is we are not able to tell.

Nov. 1, 1863. All hands were mustered at 9 A.M. to attend divine service. Our acting assistant nipcheese officiated as chaplain.

Our new caterer, W.H. Thomas, entered upon the duties of his office today. His first breakfast consisted of ham and eggs, fried fresh fish, vension balls, potatoes, and salt beef—rather a sumptuous meal. We all hope that he may cater to our taste in that style throughout the whole term of his service as caterer.

I shall continue Landsman Pettingill and boy Short on the sick list.

The schooner that was seen in the offing yesterday entered the harbor today. She proved to be the U.S. mortar schooner *Dan Smith*. The captain of her [Acting Master Benjamin C. Dean] is ordered to report to the senior officer present, who proves to be the captain of the *Mahaska* [Commander J. Blakely Creighton], stationed at St. Catharine's Sound. The *Dan Smith's* station will be the Altamaha River, in vicinity of Doboy Sound. Her officers are an acting master, ensign, master's mates, and paymaster's and surgeon's stewards. The intentions of Captain Dean are to remain here at anchor and communicate with the senior officer by means of one of his cutters.

Two contrabands from Sapelo Island—viz., Old Billy and Uncle Allie—made their appearance at 4 P.M. in a dugout, having sweet potatoes, pumpkins, etc. to sell. Their goods met with a ready sale. All hands were pleased to see the two old darkies. They had a long yarn to spin about their place since we left them last June. They report all hands well except a young wench who appears to be in a rather delicate situation, every moment expecting to give birth to a small responsibility.

Nov. 2, 1863. The two intelligent contrabands who visited us yesterday left this morning in the best of humor, carrying along with them quite a boatload of grub. They promise to call again ere long.

The captain of the mortar schooner, with Mr. Wright of our ship as pilot, started in his cutter for St. Catharine's Sound by the inland passage early this morning. The port watch are on St. Catharine's Island scrubbing their hammocks; the starboard watch scrubbed theirs last Wednesday. Part of the starboard watch are busy scraping the gun carriages, whilst another party of them have left in one of the cutters, Ensign Flood in charge, for the upper end of St. Catharine's Island, there to communicate with some contrabands who live on said island so as to purchase vegetables etc. and at same time receive the washed clothing which they received dirty on the 26th of Oct.

At 4 P.M. Mr. Flood returned, having the washing and some

peanuts in his possession. The washed clothing looked as though they had not been washed at all. In fact, the officers have concluded not to send any more washing to them. The peanuts were quite a treat. Mr. Flood paid them 5/100 doll. per qt. I relieved him of six quarts, he having sixteen quarts in all. Everyone was anxious to purchase some.

The captain of the mortar schooner *Dan Smith* returned from St. Catharine's Sound at 4.30 P.M., he having communicated etc. with the senior officer. He reports nothing new as regards the *Mahaska*. All were well and anxious for a mail. He has an idea that he would like this station because there is so good a site for game. Don't blame him, for the Altamaha station will be anything but lovely.

Two of our Nimrods—viz., Scott and Rickards—having been out after game, returned at 4 P.M. with a fine buck and about 1,000 oranges. The oranges were the sweet kind. Our captain divided the whole lot of them equally amongst the crew. Such a scrambling I never saw before on board of this craft. Each and every one was anxious to be served first. I must not forget to mention that Rickards gave me a fine pomegranate which he picked off the tree while out hunting. I have the same suspended by means of a string in my stateroom.

5 P.M. All hands are busy munching their oranges. 7 P.M. Singing and dancing takes the lead at present amongst the crew. 8 P.M. All is quiet as the grave. Hammocks being piped; consequently all hands except the watch have turned in below.

Nov. 3, 1863. James Hall, sea., aet. 23, Buenos Aires—erysipelas was admitted on the sick list this morning. I ordered him a dose of calomel and jalap and painted his face with tinct. iodine. Some of the boys say he looks like an American Indian. Boy Short left the list this morning. The weather was lovely all day. The surgeon's steward of the mortar schooner *Dan Smith* paid me a visit. He was in need of some iodine and whiskey, which I supplied him with. In return he sent me some alcohol and tinct ferri chloridi.

My steward was on shore today; he had quite a tramp. I sent him at 8 A.M. with the head of a buck so as to boil it. As soon as he landed, he built a fire, placed the head in a kettle over the fire, and left, thinking, no doubt, that the water would boil and not evaporate. He returned to his kettle at 3 P.M., six hours after he

lit the fire. As a matter of fact, he found his head burnt to a crisp
—consequently all ruined. As soon as he came on board, the captain asked him, "Where is the head?" Ans.: "Shure, while I was
up the beach after this tooth (the sword of a swordfish, which he
had in his hand), it burned all up!" Poor ignorant Irishman—he
was all sunburnt and felt rather bad. I am often reminded of
Samuel Lover's "Handy Andy; or, More Blunders than One."
[The subtitle of the London: F. Lover, 1842 edition of *Handy Andy*
is *A Tale of Irish Life*.] My Pat generally commits a blunder
regular every day. I am in hopes that I will be able to tame him
ere long, for at present he is a "rale wild Irishman."

The captain does not feel well today. He is suffering from a
severe attack of influenza. Sage teas etc. are in great demand.

Nov. 4, 1863. The captain feels somewhat better this morning.
The mortar schooner *Dan Smith* left the sound this morning. My
patient James Hall feels somewhat better this morning. I shall
continue the application of the tinct iodine, also order him anti-
monials internally in the following form, viz.: ℞ antim. et potas.
tart. grs i ss., magnesiae sulph. ℥ i, morphiae sulph. gr ss.l, sach.
albi. ℨ ii, aquae ℥ vi; M. Sig. Tablespoonful three times a day.

The weather rather pleasant all day. Nothing else of any account
transpired today worthy of note.

Nov. 5, 1863. The captain is improving gradually; his cold is
"breaking up," as he says. James Hall is about the same; his face
is rather swollen more than yesterday. Shall continue tinct. iodine
externally and the antimonial and saline mixture internally.

The weather is rather close and warm today; thermometer 78°
Fahr. Wrote a letter to B. Frank Boyer . . . , giving him a description of my steward and his antics as regards the buck's head on the
3rd inst. Scott and Rickards were landed on Sapelo Island this
morning to go in search of game.

Nov. 6, 1863. Captain Creighton, Paymaster Fairchild, Pilot
Baker (an ensign), and the paymaster's clerk and two boats' crew,
all of the *Mahaska,* arrived on board at 8 A.M., having left St.
Catharine's Sound at 4 A.M. They intend to remain here until tomorrow so as to communicate with the *Massachusetts;* she is due on
the 7th, which will be tomorrow. 10 A.M. A gunboat appeared off
the harbor. At first we took her to be the *Massachusetts.* We hoisted
our signals, or numbers, and fired a gun. 10.30 A.M., she is not the

Massachusetts. 6 P.M. A steamer reported coming into the harbor. Upon signalizing by means of Coston signals [burning lights of different colors, each vessel being distinguished by certain ones, designated by number—so named for their inventor], we made her out to be the *Tennessee.* [The *Tennessee*, a vessel in the West Gulf Blockading Squadron, was not in the Atlantic. She returned to New Orleans on October 15, 1863, from a reconnaissance cruise down the coast of Texas, and less than a month later she was reported in port at New Orleans undergoing repairs.] A heavy fog setting in obscured her. Some say she is the *Massachusetts.* Nothing more was seen or heard of her this night. Wrote a letter to brother Frank in regard to some ale.

Nov. 7, 1863. The strange craft last night proves to be the *Massachusetts.* All hands are in the best of humor. We received a large mail and Northern papers as late as the 31st of October. My mail consisted of five letters, twenty papers, and one dime novel. The papers were sent by M. K. and M. P. Boyer; the letters were written by father, dates Sept. 28 and Oct. 27; brother Michael, Oct. 19; brother Jefferson, Sept. 22; and the editor of the "Medical and Surgical Reporter," Phila., dated Oct. 20. Father's letters were full of good and cheering news about home; brother Michael's letter teemed with politics, war, law, and wit; brother Jefferson's letter enclosed a *carte de visite* of the doctor himself, for which I am thankful—the tenor of said letter was decidedly political. The dime novel, the title of which is "The Scout" [a ninety-six-page novelette, "A Story of Early New-England," by Warren St. John; published in New York by Beadle and Company about 1863], was mailed by M. P. Boyer, ex-lieutenant of U.S. Army. The story is a wishy-washy affair—considerable love, blood, and soft soap and very little sound sense. What his ideas were in sending me said pamphlet I cannot divine, but I don't suppose that he thought it was what it really is—not worth a cobbler's curse. I shall write to him and torment him about the same, but I will have to acknowledge him to be a trump, for he is never slow in sending me reading matter in the shape of newspapers.

As usual, we got a good supply of fresh beef, ice, and vegetables from the *Massachusetts.* The *Mahaska* received her supplies, and at 1 P.M. Captain Creighton and all hands left for St. Catharine's Sound. Ensign Flood accompanied them with one of our cutters.

The staunch Union men of Pennsylvania, Ohio, and Iowa have been giving the Copperheads h—l. Traitor Vallandigham was defeated by a majority of 100,000 votes—rather an unkind cut. Ohio done her duty as becomes a loyal State.

[Clement L. Vallandigham, prominent Ohio radical Democrat, had been arrested by the military and charged with treason after a speech at Mount Vernon, Ohio, on May 1, 1863. He was sentenced to close confinement for the duration of the war, but Lincoln instead banished him to the South. Fleeing through the blockade to Canada, he launched a campaign for the governorship of Ohio. His opponent won by a majority of a hundred thousand votes, yet under adverse conditions he obtained an unprecedented Democratic ballot.]

The Keystone State is right side up with care. Iowa was not slow in showing her devotion to the Union.

[In Pennsylvania, where disturbing factors such as the Emancipation Proclamation, draft legislation, military reverses, and arbitrary arrest of individuals suspected of disloyalty had combined in 1862 to make for the election of a full Democratic slate, the political tide was turned by victory at Gettysburg, and Andrew G. Curtin was in 1863 reelected governor by a vote of 269,506 to 254,171 for his Democratic opponent. In Iowa, where trouble brewed, where the Knights of the Golden Circle flourished, and where paid Confederate agents were reported to be stirring up trouble, a wounded veteran, Colonel William M. Stone, defeated the Democratic candidate by thirty thousand votes.]

Nov. 8, 1863. The usual morning routine having been performed all around, all hands were called at 9.30 A.M. to muster to attend divine service.

Josiah Pettingill came to me complaining of having two furunculus, one located on the neck and one in small of back, also of an eruption extending from his breast to his scapula on the right side. Upon examination I find it to be a case of herpes zoster (shingles). I shall order him pil. cath. camp no iv this morning and pulv opii et ipecac. grs x tonight so as to ease the pain in his chest and promote sleep. Externally I shall order a lotion of soda bicarb for his eruption and dress his boils with resin cerate, having lanced them first. My case of erysipelas—James Hall—is improving rapidly. Shall continue the tinct iodine externally and the antimonial and saline mixture internally. . . . .

Nov. 9, 1863. A cold wind is blowing. Thermometer 53° Fahr. The ship is rolling like an old washtub. Pettingill is about the same; order the antimonial and saline mixture for him. Hall returns to duty.

Cold! Cold!! Cold!!! Old Boreas is about once again. Nothing worthy of note transpired today.

Nov. 10, 1863. Stern winter has come at last. Old Boreas is in all his glory. He has marshalled his hosts in battle array to such an extent as to cause Old Sol to make rather a hasty retreat. Thermometer 42° Fahr. at 7 A.M. A regular gale is prevailing. The old *Fernandina* is rolling beautifully.

Josiah Pettingill is somewhat better. His boils are improving; dress them with cerate simplex, apply glycerine to the herpetic eruption, continue the antimonial and saline mixture, which consists of tartar emetic, morphine, salts, sugar, and water, and order him sol. morphiae sulphas ʒ ii when he turns in at 8 bells. The eruption is beginning to scab; pain in chest not so severe. Not feeling well myself, I thought it proper and pat to take a dose of magnesiae sulphas—say ʒ ss. In about 1½ hours I was compelled to make tracks for the transit house and so continue doing nearly all day, the result being a thorough cleaning out but rather weakening me. The captain called me "Salts" all day.

The captain concluded at 9 A.M. that it was cold enough to have a stove put up in the cabin so as to take off the chill of the place. So to work goes his boy, and in less than no time he has the stove rigged and a blazing fire in full headway. Everyone attached to the cabin and wardroom appreciate said stove. We are now able to laugh at Old Boreas. The boys on deck are promenading fore and aft on the spar deck laughing, chattering, and singing so as to keep warm. Our contrabands don't seem to fancy the cold weather; they would rather have a broiling hot sun to shine upon them. Poor D—s —the way they roll their eyes is not slow.

Nov. 11, 1863. The weather today is cold and clear but not as cold as it was yesterday. My case of herpes zoster and furunculus combined is improving. His boils are almost well. Continue simple cerate. Pain in chest considerably easier. Continue glycerine to the eruption and ℞ hydrarg. chloridi mitis grs vi, jalapa pulv. grs xv, ol. mentha pip. gtts i; M; continue using the antimonial and saline mixture. The object of my giving him the purgative is to relieve his bowels, which are costive.

Boy Allen came to me complaining of aches and pains all over his body. Says he has had the pains for over a week. Being as he is not able to localize the pains, I shall order him a dose of calomel and jalap x by x, or "Rush's thunderbolt," as it used to be called, now going by the name of "a devil of a dose" amongst some. [The enormous dose of ten grains each of calomel and jalap, called "ten-and-ten" in Revolutionary War days, was greatly increased by Dr. Benjamin Rush during the plague in Philadelphia in the summer of 1793.] I think that will ease him of all pains and aches.

At 1 A.M. the thermometer stood at 47° Fahr., at 8 A.M. 50° Fahr., and at 12 M. 55° Fahr., so that by noon it was quite pleasant.

10 P.M. I was blessed with a fit of vomiting followed by purging so that by 11 P.M. I was pretty well cleaned out and felt rather languid. I am suffering with a severe catarrhal affection of my bladder or chronic cystitis, caused either by eating or drinking some irritative substance, for which complaint I took some copaiba and spts ether nitric, which caused me to vomit and be purged. At same time it had a beneficial effect on the bladder. Rather a severe mode of treatment.

6 P.M. Wright, Scott, and Headley returned from a hunt with two bullock, one deer, and one turkey. Bully for them!

Nov. 12, 1863. I feel rather weak this morning—the effects of the severe vomiting and purging last night. Nothing daunted, I took a dose of the same drug this morning. Up to the time of writing these notes—11 A.M.—it has not nauseated me. I hope that I may be enabled to retain said medicine in my stomach so as to cure the irritability of my bladder.

The U.S. tug *Oleander,* Captain Dennis in command, made her appearance in this sound at 8 A.M. via inland passage. He is on his way to St. Catharine's Sound and intends to return tomorrow so as to take our mail along with him to Port Royal. His idea in stopping here this morning was to see how we were, shake hands with us, and take a drink of sherry. Captain Moses sent per him to Capt. Creighton half of the venison that the boys shot yesterday. He (our captain) also intends sending Capt. [Commander William] Reynolds of the U.S.S. *Vermont* a saddle of venison per Captain Dennis when he returns in the morning to Port Royal. Capt. Dennis received some of the beef, also a lot of oranges, so that all were supplied. 8.30 A.M. The *Oleander* left for St. Catharine's Sound.

Wrote a letter to father in answer to his dates of Sept. 28 and

Oct. 29, one to brother Michael in answer to his date of Oct. 19, and one to the editor and proprietor of the "Med. and Surg. Reporter," enclosing him twenty cents, one year's postage on the medical journal, for which I am a subscriber. Also wrote an answer to brother Jefferson's date of the 22nd of Sept. thanking him for the *carte de visite etc.* and giving him my views of the existing state of affairs, which are contrary to his views, I being an administration man and he a Copperhead. I admire his courage, yet I think he is altogether too radical in his ideas. I also congratulated him on his late success in the late campaign. I am alluding to his election to the state legislature of Pennsylvania.

My patient Pettingill is improving. He continues the external treatment, also internally the antimonial and saline mixture. His boils are healed up; the eruption is dispersing. Boy Allen continues on the binnacle list. He is taking the antimonial and saline mixture.

4.45 P.M. The *Oleander* has returned from St. Catharine's Sound, having [Third Assistant] Engineer [Elisha] Harsen of the *Mahaska*, who is detached from said steamer and ordered to the *Wabash*, on board. There is also a hospital patient affected with scurvy on board whom the surgeon of the *Mahaska* sends to Port Royal for treatment. Scurvy appears to be quite prevalent on board of the *Mahaska*. I hope our crew will not become affected with said complaint. I shall keep a bright lookout that the men have plenty of vegetables and fresh beef.

My bowels have been rather open today; other ways I think I am somewhat better. The smarting, shooting, or darting pains in the perineum, along the urethra, and at the neck of the bladder are not so severe. I have passed very little if any blood during micturation today. I am in hopes ere long to be able to eat and drink like of old—i.e., plenty of animal food and as much ale and wine as I choose. At present I lose all the rich and juicy beef, venison, and turkeys. But never mind—all will be right in due time. "Every dog has his day," and I suppose I am having my worst days at present. I shall be careful what I eat or drink next time.

Captains Dennis and Moses, Paymaster Murray, and myself spent a pleasant evening together playing several games of dominoes. The weather has been pleasant all day. Thermometer 57° Fahr. at 8 A.M. and 62° at 12 M.

Nov. 13, 1863. The U.S. tugboat *Oleander* left the harbor at 6:30 A.M. Captain Dennis had quite a large mail in his charge which the *Fernandina* sends North. Landsman Pettingill and boy Allen are both improving. Isaac McKenzie, a gentleman of color, or, as some call them, Americans of African descent, came to me complaining of influenza. I ordered him a large dose of ol. ricini with grs vi of calomel.

I feel quite smart this morning. Ate with quite a relish some fried fresh fish, a few potatoes, and a piece of bread for breakfast this morning. Hope I have not overloaded my stomach. I shall commence to drink coffee again as a beverage ere long. I have deprived myself of said exhilarating fluid for some time on account of its stimulating properties, but since a change has shown itself in my case, I have strong hopes ere another week to be able to call myself a well man again. . . . 5.30 P.M., not feeling any ill effects from the eating of the fish for breakfast this morning, I concluded to eat some for tea tonight.

The weather today was warm and pleasant. Thermometer at 8 A.M. was 60° Fahr. and at 4 P.M. 68° Fahr.

10 P.M. signalized the U.S.S. *E. B. Hale* by means of Coston signals, coming up from Doboy Sound inland. All hands had been called to quarters. She is from St. Johns River, Florida, on her way to Port Royal, having been ordered there for repairs. She brought us a small mail. We received Philadelphia dates as late as the 4th of Nov., 1863, from which we learn that New York, New Jersey, Massachusetts, and Wisconsin had gone Union by large majorities and that the Copperheads were routed horse, foot, and dragoons.

[Whereas the 1862 congressional elections had gone heavily against the Republicans (the Democrats winning in New York, Pennsylvania, Ohio, Indiana, and Illinois; splitting Wisconsin evenly; increasing their lead in New Jersey; and greatly reducing the opposition majority in Maine, New Hampshire, Massachusetts, and Michigan), the 1863 elections ran strongly against the Copperhead element despite dissatisfaction with the conduct of the war.]

Huzza! Huzza!! Huzza!!! for that. Enough glory for one day.

Nov. 14, 1863. The U.S.S. *E. B. Hale* left early this morning, bound north.

B. F. Headley, lds., having been out hunting had the misfortune to run several points of palmetto into his left knee, lacerating the skin to such an extent as to cause considerable inflammation of an erysipelas character. He came to me this morning with his knee all swollen, painful, red, and hot. I painted the parts with tinct iodine and apply a lini cataplasm. His bowels being in good order, I ordered for him internally the antimonial and saline mixture, which consists of tartar emetic, salts, morphine, sugar, and water. At same time he is to keep the part at rest in a horizontal position. Pettingill is coming along as well as can be expected. ℞ tinct. ferri chloridi gtts x three times a day. He showed me another boil located on left natis. I lanced it and applied cerate resinae. Boy Allen was discharged to duty this morning.

The weather was rather changeable today—sunshine and warm at 8 A.M.; rain, cool, and windy at 12 M.; sunshine and wind at 1.15 P.M.; 4 P.M. cloudy with slight symptoms of rain. Our efficient caterer, Ensign Thomas, served us up the following dinner, which I don't think can well be beat on board of a man-of-war: viz., first course—beef soup and toast; second course—roast turkey with dressing, mashed, boiled, and roasted potatoes, boiled cold ham, etc.; third course—mince pie; fourth course—oranges and apples. By George! by the time we ate the above, we were completely satisfied as regards our inner man. I am afraid that I ate altogether too hardy [hearty] for an invalid, but the viands looked so tempting that I dug into the good things without thinking of "Mr. Bladder." I'll hope for the best.

The thermometer was 68° Fahr. at 12 o'clock today, 66° at 5 P.M. Some of the crew who had been in search of oysters returned with quite a load of them at 7 P.M.

Nov. 15, 1863. This, the third Sabbath of the month, set in with a cool breeze, the sun at same time shedding its rays. Thermometer at 8 A.M. stood 65° Fahr. Charles Burns, sea., aet. 22, Ireland— odontalgia—applied ulmus cataplasm and ℞ pil. cath. comp no iii— was added to my list this morning. The two patients Headley and Pettingill are coming on as well as can be expected. Shall continue the same treatment in both cases as heretofore.

I enjoyed a good night's rest last night. The sumptuous feasting yesterday did not do me any harm, it appears. Made a breakfast on oyster soup and fried oysters—i.e., ate nothing else for breakfast except it be a piece of bread and drank a weak cup of coffee.

Divine service at 9.30 A.M., Paymaster Murray officiating. Obtained the jawbone of a large fish which was found on shore. Some call it a cowfish, some blackfish, and some a porpoise. The fish was 11 feet long and weighed about 500 pounds.

Nov. 16, 1863. A landsman, Robert Hall by name, aet. 29, a native of New York, came to me complaining of a large furunculus located on the wrist of the right arm. I lanced it freely and applied tinct. iodine and a lini cataplasm; also ℞ pil. cath. comp no iv. The gumboil of Burns burst last night—continue a poultice of flaxseed. Pettingill is improving slowly—continue same treatment. The inflammation of Headley's knee is somewhat reduced—continue lini cataplasm and internal medicine. George Thompson, sca., a native of Chile, came to the sick bay complaining of some complaint, or, as he said, "I am sick!" "Where are you sick?" "I donna know! I ish not well at all." "Steward, give him a dose of calomel and jalap, which will cleanse his stomach and clear his head, after which I have no doubt but that he can localize his aches and pains." He takes the dose. 1 P.M. The report is that Thompson is on the go! 4 P.M. He localizes the pain; it is in his chest. I tell him that he must grin and bear it until morning. Seaman Thompson very indignant! 8 P.M. rouses out my steward and tells him that he feels bad. Steward comes to me and reports accordingly. I order him to keep quiet until morning, as I don't consider myself justifiable in giving him any other medicine so soon after being purged. 8.30 P.M. Thompson turns in, growling like a bear with a sore head.

Boy Hoyt also thought that he was sick. ℞ calomel and jalap. It purged him severely. 8 P.M. He turns in, in the best of humor. Boatswain's Mate Mowatt complains of pain in stomach. ℞ argenti nitras grs ¼, opii grs ¼ three times a day. Medicine don't taste good; concludes that two doses are enough. 8 P.M. reports himself all right again. Will go to duty in the morning.

Landsman Reilly, a son of the Emerald Isle, was unlucky enough at 8 P.M. to fall from the spar to the berth deck and bruise himself about his left thigh and hip. Ordered an aconite liniment to be well rubbed in, also turn in and not keep watch. Irishman leaves the sick bay in rather good spirits. . . .

Nov. 17, 1863. The following patients reported themselves to me for treatment this morning: viz., Hall, whose boil appears to be of a carbuncular nature—I lanced it freely, applied a lini poultice,

and cauterized it with argenti nitras—℞ tinct. ferri chloridi gtts
vii three times a day in an ounce of water; Burns—his cheek is
somewhat swollen still—shall order him tinct. ferri chloridi gtts vii
three times a day and apply an ulmus cataplasm to his cheek;
Headley—the abrasions are suppurating finely—the swelling, heat,
pain, and redness are considerably reduced—continue the application of lini cataplasm—℞ tinct. ferri. chloridi gtts vii three times
a day; Pettingill—his boils are all healed up—he still continues to
be laboring under the effects of the herpetic eruption, which appears to be very obstinate—shall order him the following lotion—
viz., ammonae carbonas, plumbi acetas āā ℨ i, Aquae f. ℥ viii;
Thompson—still in a bad humor—says he wants a dose of castor oil
—shall order him a large dose—1 P.M. order him magnesiae sulphas
℥ i ℳ; Reilly—feels quite easy—slight ecchymosis of the muscles of
thigh and hip—continue the use of an arnica liniment; Mowatt and
Hoyt—both return to duty.

The weather was quite cool this morning. The thermometer
stood 48° Fahr. at 6 A.M. and 54° Fahr. at 8 A.M. Took a sail in
company with Capt. Moses in his gig between the hours of 8 and
11 A.M. Landed on St. Catharine's Island, where we remained an
hour or two. This was my first sail since the 27th of October. Our
live stock on shore (viz., 6 hogs) is coming along finely. Acting
Master's Mate John Wright and Quartermaster George Briggs, who
have been out on a hunt, have returned at 3 P.M. with a large
bullock which they shot this morning. Our judges of beef on board
pronounce it splendid, rich, and juicy. Hope they may be correct.
Acting Ensign Christopher Flood communicated with the contrabands who live on St. Catharine's Island and obtained from them
some hominy, also sending along with them a haunch of venison intended for Capt. Creighton of the *Mahaska* with Captain Moses'
compliments. The venison will be acceptable, I have no doubt.

I am beginning to feel quite gay and happy again. I shall continue taking medicine a few days longer so as to make all things
doubly sure. My appetite is improving. I still abstain from eating
salt meats, pickles, and spices and drinking strong coffee and malt
liquors.

Nov. 18, 1863. The weather has been rather cool all morning.
Thermometer at 6 A.M. 46° Fahr. My patients—viz., Burns, Hall,
Pettingill, Headley, and Thompson—are improving. Reilly re-

turns to duty. The yeoman Danl. B. Reilly came to me suffering under the effects of a sty or hordeolum. Applied an ulmus cataplasm. The boys caught a young raccoon in a trap this morning. They are having quite a gay time with him on deck. 1 P.M. The weather is quite pleasant. Thermometer 71° Fahr. Nothing of any account transpired today.

Nov. 19, 1863. George Thompson has worked himself into a nice fever. His bowels being opened, I ordered him quiniae sulphas as follows: 5 pulvs., grs i, ii, iii, iv, and grs v, to be taken 5 times, the last one one hour before the expected chill comes on. Hall—on account of the slough coming away, he has quite a good-sized ulcer, or abscess, left on his wrist—continue the application of warm poultices and ℞ tinct ferri chloridi gtts vii ter in die. Headley—will be able to return to duty in a day or two—continue the application of tinct. iodine. Pettingill—improving slowly but surely—continue the application of the ammoniae and lead lotion; ℞ tinct. ferri chloridi gtts vii three times a day. Burns—returns to duty. Daniel B. Reilly's hordeolum burst last night; came to me this morning and reported himself all O.K. Scott, the wardroom cook, came to me last night complaining of angina pectoris, or neuralgia of the heart; I ordered him grs x of quiniae sulphas and this morning pil. cath. comp. no. iv.

Weather moderate. Thermometer 54° Fahr. at 6 A.M., 55° Fahr. at 8 A.M., and 66° Fahr. at 12 meridian. 3.30 P.M. The *Mahaska* and *Huron* signalizing each other off the harbor. We hauled up our number so as to make known our character. 3.50 P.M. Captain Moses sent Ensign Thomas in the first cutter to speak the *Huron,* who is at anchor at the outer buoy. Hope he may return with a mail. 4.05 P.M. Signalized, or rather recalled, the 1st cutter. 4.25 P.M. The 1st cutter has returned. The *Huron* got under way at 4 P.M. and sailed southward. The *Mahaska* is coming into the harbor. 5 P.M. She has anchored.

The *Mahaska* comes to relieve us, and we are ordered to St. Catharine's Sound, her former station. We leave this place in the morning, providing the wind is favorable. She brings no news. Captain Creighton paid Captain Moses a visit after his vessel came to anchor. They appeared to have a lively chat together.

Some of the crew have been after some oysters. They returned with quite a large cargo. The wardroom as well as all hands had plenty of oysters. Our caterer promises us a splendid and rich soup prepared of some of said bivalves in the morning at breakfast.

7 P.M. The wardroom cook, Scott by name, came complaining of his heartache. I ordered the application of two wet cups and ℞ sol. morphiae sulphas ℥ ii when he turns in. Thompson says he feels better; the sulphate of quinine prescribed this morning cut the disease short—i.e., prevented the chill at the regular hour; in fact, he has had no chill today at all. Headley says that he has an idea of going to duty in the morning, so that I need not look for him at 8 A.M. in the sick bay. Hall feels like a new man tonight, he says. His sore arm looks quite healthy this 7 P.M. Promised to let him go to duty ere long. Pettingill reports himself at 7 P.M. feeling quite lively, his pain in chest of very little moment and the herpetic eruption scabbing beautifully. I expect to discharge the above patients in a day or two.   . . .

Nov. 20, 1863. The wardroom cook, Edward J. Scott, 28, Delaware, comes again complaining. Upon careful examination I pronounce his case pleurisy and not anginose in its character, as heretofore stated. Shall continue counterirritation and order tartar emetic grs ⅟₁₆ every two hours. Thompson takes the following: magnesiae sulphas ℥ ii, mint water ℥ x, tinct. colchici semi. ℥ i, magnesiae ℈ viii; M; Sig. Tablespoonful every two hours until he has four or five evacuations. Hall coming on finely. Continue tinct. ferri chloridi in gtts vii doses three times a day and apply externally cerate resinae. Pettingill—improving slowly—continue same treatment. Headley—returns to duty this morning.

8 A.M. Signalized a steamer in the offing. She is anchored at the outer buoy. The *Mahaska* gets under way at 8.15 A.M. to speak her. 9.30 A.M. They are communicating together. 11.20 A.M. The barque-rigged steamer came to anchor within two ships' length of us. The *Mahaska* steamed to the north from the outer buoy. 11.40 A.M. Captain Moses went on board the steamer. We make her out to be the *Lodona* by her signals. 1 P.M. The captain returned and reported that the *Mahaska* had been ordered off Charleston and that the *Lodona* came to relieve her. The captain sent Ensign Flood via inland passage to Doboy Sound to solicit a pilot from the senior officer who is stationed there to pilot us to our station. The *Lodona* draws too much water to pilot us to St. Catharine's Sound by the inland passage, and she knows nothing as regards the channel from the sea—hence our sending to the senior officer for assistance.

The *Lodona* brought no mail. She had Philadelphia "Inquirers" as late as the 10th ultimo [instant?]. The *Lodona* is a propeller, 7 guns, 850 tonnage; rate—third class.

The crew have been busy getting the ship ready for sea, sending yards aloft, bending [fastening] on sails, overhauling the rigging, fastening the guns, watering ship, and bringing our live stock on board. Some of the boys who were out hunting returned with one solitary turkey, which our caterer intends serving up for dinner tomorrow. They say that they never had such bad luck before.

7.30 P.M. Scott and Thompson both reported themselves. Scott says that his medicine nauseates him, just what I intended it to do —℞ pulv opii et ipecac grs x when he turns in. Thompson feels better—℞ pulv. opii et ipecac grs x when he retires to his hammock tonight. Hall—his arm is healing finely—order him to continue the resin cerate. Pettingill—complained of a slight headache tonight—℞ pil. cath. comp no vi. The weather was pleasant all day.

Nov. 21, 1863. My patients are about the same as they were yesterday. I made no change in their treatment. Billie and Allie, two contrabands from Doboy Sound, made their appearance at 7 A.M. in a dugout, having a cargo of sweet potatoes, pumpkins, turnips, corn, and honey for sale. They disposed of their cargo in a short time. Everyone was anxious to purchase.

The weather was quite stormy all day. 5 P.M. the U.S.S. *Seneca* arrived via inland passage from Doboy Sound with Ensign Flood on board. She will tow us to our station, St. Catharine's Sound, in the morning. The surgeon, paymaster, and an ensign attached to the *Seneca* made us a call between the hours of 5.30 and 8 P.M. We entertained them according to Gunter. I took them to my stateroom, where we all enjoyed a glass of sherry, port, and claret, after which we sat down to tea, ending with good tobacco and brierroot pipes. The captain of the *Seneca* paid our captain a visit. They appeared to have a jolly old time together, judging from the noise they made. Wrote a letter to father.

7 P.M. My patients all expressed themselves as feeling better. I very politely requested them to continue feeling better until they felt all well again.

Nov. 22, 1863. The sick are improving slowly. Scott—℞ antimonial and saline mixture. Thompson—℞ quiniae sulphas grs xvi, acid sulph. aromat. ʒ i, wine (sherry) ℥ iv, aquae ℥ iv; M; Sig. ℥ i three times a day. Hall—℞ cerate simplex. Pettingill—℞ ammonia carbonas, plumbi acetas āā ℨ i, aquae ℥ viii; ℳ; fiat lotion.

The boys captured another live raccoon, making two in all. They have tamed the first one, and they intend to tame the second one so as to have two pets.

The *Seneca* took us in tow at 1.10 P.M. 2 P.M. we are passing the Waldburg mansion [on St. Catherines Island]. By the by, I must not forget to mention that we are taking the inland passage. We all took a last look at Sapelo, Blackbeard, and St. Catharine's Islands ere we left.

I intend laying aside my pipes and tobacco and stop smoking the narcotic weed. I sold my pipes to Ensign Flood for $3.25. 5.30 P.M. we let go our port anchor in St. Catharine's Sound. The *Seneca* left at 6 P.M. for Ossabaw Sound.

12

"*Milk and Honey*" in
St. Catherines Sound

St. *Catharine's Sound, Ga., Nov. 23, 1863.* A cool, blusterly day. A stiff gale blowing. The atmosphere is very damp. Raining at times.

My patients with the exception of Thompson all report themselves feeling better. Scott—continue the same treatment. Hall—the ulcer looks well—continue cerate simplex. Pettingill—cauterize eruption with argenti. natras. and apply cerate simplex. Thompson —℞ tonic mixture; order the cook of his mess to make him a flaxseed tea.

Messrs. Thomas, Childs, Murray, and Wright at 1 P.M. left the ship and landed on the beach with the intention of going to Smart's plantation [the Waldburg plantation, occupied at the time by a group of former slaves headed by one named Smart], which is one mile from our anchorage. All passed along merrily, when all of a sudden Mr. Thomas who weighs between 200 and 300 pounds, called out for help. Mr. Wright, answering the call of distress, found Mr. Thomas fast and sound up to his groins in the mud. He, thinking it solid ground, had stept into a marshy plot—hence the above accident. Mr. Wright pulled him out of the mire—and such a sight was seldom to be seen, said Mr. Murray, one of the excursionists. Mr. Thomas was one mass of mud; he was swearing and sweating like a trooper. I have no doubt that he weighs ten pounds less on account of his perspiring so freely. This put a damper on their spirits, and all hands made tracks for the ship. Their expedition proved unsuccessful. Mr. Thomas presented a laughable appearance when he arrived on board. He says that he has had enough of that kind of pleasure. Should not wonder if he has. Upon reading the above remarks to Mr. Thomas, he requested me to state that after Mr. Wright had pulled him out of the mire, he had to retaliate by pulling him out. Thus it appears that both Mr. Wright and Mr. Thomas were muddy subjects for the time being. Both Wright and Thomas acknowledge the accuracy of the above notes.

I finished the deer heads which I commenced to operate upon on the 26th of October, 1863. The captain has one of them, and I keep the other as my property. They both require some bleaching yet to make them perfectly white. I shall expose mine to the weather by suspending it on the limb of a tree on St. Catharine's Island.

The captain paid the plantation occupied by Old Smart and clique a visit. He reports twenty contrabands, mostly superannuated darkies, both male and female. One of the contrabands is 115 years old and is perfectly helpless. They appear to have plenty of fowls, dogs, pumpkins, corn, and potatoes. He (the captain) says that it is a splendid plantation.

From all indications I rather like this anchorage; at least, I think it preferable to Sapelo Sound. There are plenty of fish, oysters, and clams to be had here. The darkies say that raccoons are very plenty on this end of the island; so all that is required is a good trap and plenty of apples to bait said trap. We also can get our washing done here by the wenches, who seem to be very anxious to wash for us, at five cents a piece, we finding the soap. Cheap enough at that, I think.

The plantation—in fact, the whole island of St. Catharine's—was owned by a wealthy Southern planter named Waldburg, who left with 800 head of darkies on the 25th of Dec., 1861—so say the contrabands, or former slaves of Mr. Waldburg, who are left behind simply because they were not fit for much labor. Rather a rough procedure. Old Smart says that his "massa" took all his children and grandchildren along with him except one. There's humanity for you. The weather not very pleasant.

Nov. 24, 1863. Fog! Fog!! Fog!!! The fog is rather watery. Everything in and around the ship is damp. Made a requisition on the paymaster for the following articles for the medical department of the U.S. barque *Fernandina:* rice, lbs. 5—$0.30; sugar, lbs. 5—$0.80. The rice was intended for my patient Thompson, who, by the by, is rather poorly—continue tonics and stimulants. The sugar is to be used for cough syrups. The remaining patients: viz., Hall—is improving rapidly—continue cerate simplex—cut down false granulations by means of argenti nitras; Pettingill—considerable improvement in his case—continue application of cerate simplex; Scott—returns to duty. . . . .

Our caterer, W. H. Thomas, having been ashore on a visit to the plantation, returned on board at 12 o'clock meridian with eggs, chickens, tomatoes, and one quarter of fresh beef, which he obtained from the contrabands. The eggs are worth 25/100 dolls. per doz., chickens 25/100 dolls. per pair; as for the rest, I know not the current prices. We all consider Mr. Thomas a good caterer. He is in every sense of the word a caterer, the right man in the right place.

1 P.M. The fog has cleared away; Old Sol is shedding his rays sparingly. 1.10 P.M. Actg. Master's Mate Wright with a boat's crew started on an expedition in search of oysters. Hope he may return with a good cargo of bivalves.

The captain reports that little insect y-clept [called] sand fly as being on shore by the myriads. We all expect to see them ere long on board of the ship. If they do make their appearance, won't we have a happy time of it! It'll be scratch! scratch!! scratch!!! from morning until night and from night again until morning; in short, it'll be scratch all around, nothing else but scratching to be done.

4.30 P.M. Mr. Wright and party have returned with a splendid lot of single oysters, enough for one mess all around. Bully for that! How are you, oysters? 6 P.M. Mr. Wright and Quartermaster Scott, having left the ship at 4.50 P.M., have returned with a bullock, which they shot within hailing distance of the ship. Truly, verily indeed we are living in a land that flows with milk and honey. All hands feel good at the idea of fresh beef and oysters being so plenty at this anchorage as they are. At 5 P.M. that pleasant and agreeable varmint y-clept sand fly made his appearance on board of the famous barque *Fernandina,* much to the chagrin of all hands. The thermometer ranged from 62° to 65° Fahr. today. It rained nearly all night. Nothing of note transpired during the night.

Nov. 25, 1863. The fog has partly left us. The sand flies have been rather plenty all morning. My patient Thompson is rather poorly this morning—has no appetite (at least, he refuses to eat)—order him to have some oyster soup prepared by the wardroom steward, also make for him as a drink flaxseed tea—℞ quiniai sulphas grs. ii, acid. sulph. aromat gtts v, whiskey ℥ i, aquae ℥ i; M; three times a day—apply two small blisters, one behind each ear. Hall's wrist looks well—reduce false granulations by means of argenti nitras—continue the application of simple cerate. Pettingill about the same—continue the simple cerate dressing.

4 P.M. The blisters have drawn finely on Thompson—dress them with cerate simplex. He has eaten some today. I begin to have some hopes for him. The weather has been rather wet and close all day. Thermometer 66° Fahr. Not a breath of wind stirring—a perfect calm prevailing all day. Mr. Wright has again been after some bivalves and returned with some rich luscious ones. The captain and myself had quite a lunch at 11 A.M. on oysters. The pill was not bad to take—at least not hard to swallow.

Wrote a long and interesting letter, of 16 pages of letter paper, to brother Michael P. Boyer, late lieutenant of the Army of the Potomac, in which I gave him a rich and racy description of the gallant officers of the U.S. barque *Fernandina* etc, etc. The officers all acknowledged the accuracy of my pen-and-ink sketch of them etc. etc. after I read the same to them.

It appears that Mr. Waldburg, the former owner of the Waldburg plantation on St. Catharine's Island, was married to a lady of Trenton, New Jersey, whom he met at boarding school. She was very wealthy and wanted him to emancipate his slaves during the Harrison campaign, 1840, but Mr. Waldburg did not consider it feasible. The slaves say that both massa and mistress were very kind and allowed them only three days between Christmas and New Year as a holiday. They were all sorry to see massa leave—yet they say that they never lived as well as they do now. The plantation must have been in its palmy days a perfect paradise. The mansion, or "big house," as the slaves call their massa's house, was a splendid affair; large cotton houses, sugar refinery, fine houses for the slaves. In short, it was at one time a pleasant place, no doubt.

The contrabands have sent word that they want to see the doctor. I understand that there are two sick ones amongst them. One, an old nigger, had himself badly bruised by an enraged bull whom he had shot, merely wounding him slightly; the other one is an old wench with misery all over. I shall send one a dose of salts and the other a little liniment, which will satisfy both.

Our caterer served us up the following dishes for tea: viz., fried fish, cold sliced roast beef, cold sliced corned beef, boiled sweet potatoes, fried Irish potatoes, toasted bread, soft-tack [leavened bread], cold sliced beef tongue, and tea. I don't think that the above can well be beaten by any other caterer. Our caterer knows how to set a table. I suppose he will have quite a smart row of figures at the end of the month to charge us with—i.e., present us with a large mess bill. 7 P.M. The atmosphere quite clear.

Thanksgiving Day, Nov. 26, 1863. This, the last Thursday of the month, was set apart by President Abraham Lincoln as a day to be devoted to general prayer, thanksgiving, and feasting for the many blessings bestowed upon us by the Almighty.   . . . [President Lincoln's proclamation as copied by the diarist is omitted.] In accordance with this proclamation, Captain Moses caused all hands to assemble on the spar deck of the U.S. barque *Fernandina* to attend the reading of divine service by our paymaster, Thomas N. Murray; also caused all work to be suspended as though it were the Lord's Day—Sabbath, or Sunday. In other words, it was a general holiday.

It generally is the custom up North to spend this day—i.e., Thanksgiving Day—in feasting instead of fasting. The roast turkeys, pumpkin pies, etc. flow in abundance on such occasions. In some parts the day ends in a general dance all around, and joy appears to be unconfined. In other parts, again, people can be seen assembled together in the House of God devoting the last hours of the day in prayer and praise. In others the salvos of artillery can be heard heralding the approach of and the departure of the day, whilst on board of a blockading vessel the last hours of the day are either ended in reading old letters, answering some, writing to new parties, reading old dates, or talking about the happy times that the "old folks at home" are having.

I do not consider it out of place to mention what kind of a Thanksgiving dinner our caterer obliged us with today. The following dishes were served up *à la mode:* viz., 1st course—beef soup and toast; 2nd course—roast chickens, chicken potpie, roast beef, stewed and raw tomatoes, boiled and roasted sweet potatoes, mashed and roasted Irish potatoes, hominy, soft-tack, fried oysters, pickled onions, and cucumbers; 3rd course—plum pudding and sauce; 4th course—mince pie; 5th and last course—apples and oranges, after which those who had sherry and claret indulged in said fluids in their staterooms. Some of the officers, and in fact all, remarked that you could hardly rake up a better dinner up North, where everything is plenty.

In the afternoon I, in company with Paymaster Murray and Ensign Thomas, paid the Waldburg plantation a visit. It being my first visit to the place, consequently I had quite a pleasant time of it. I counted 60 houses in all besides the residence of the planter. The slave houses are all built of oyster shells and mud, whitewashed, or painted with lime. They look rather comfortable. There are twenty contrabands living on the place at present. The following are some of their names: viz., Smart and his wife; Young Cudgel, his wife, and grandson Mike (Young Cudgel is, as he says, 50 years old, and his grandson Mike is 4 years old and as tricky as the "Old Boy" [the devil]); Old Cudgel, a widower; Old John, a carpenter, who is a grass widower, if I may use the term, and considerable of a sharper for a nigger; Old Bob, an old widower, full of fun and the devil, a general favorite; Old Man Willie, who the darkies say is 110 years old (truly a decrepit old man in his dotage, "sans teeth, sans eyes, sans taste, sans everything," if I may quote the language of Jaques in Shakespeare's "As You Like It"); Aunt Estrella, sister to Smart's wife, quite an intelligent old wench (our paymaster has taken quite a fancy to her on account of her sparkling eye); Aunt Nabbie, the youngest wench on the place, and rather good-looking (she is, I believe, the principal washwoman); and Aunt Mollie, the best-natured wench, one who has a smart answer for everything that you say to her. She [Aunt Mollie] has a name for every one of us. Our paymaster is fairly in love with her—has an idea that she is the brightest nigger wench in existence. "So mote it be." Besides the above-named parties there are about a half a dozen or so old wenches whose names I do not remember.

I gave Old Smart a dose of magnesiae sulphas and a small vial of sapo. camph. tinct., Old Cudgel a dose of salts, and Aunt Estrella a dose of magnesiae sulphas, all three complaining of "misery all over." Old Smart and wife, Old Cudgel, Aunt Estrella, Aunt Nabbie, Old Uncle Willie, and two old wenches all received some tobacco from me as a present. It was "T'ankee, Massa! T'ankee, Massa!" "God bless you, Doctor!" etc. all the time that I remained with them after I gave them the tobacco. We remained on the island until 4.15 P.M., when we pushed off from the wharf and proceeded on board. We landed on deck at 4.50 P.M., well satisfied with our tramp.

I had the pleasure of reporting my patient Thompson as improving in my morning report to the captain. I ordered him to continue his tonics and stimulants. He complained of aphtha—℞ potassae chloras grs xii, aqua ℥ i; ℳ; gargle 4 or 5 times a day—diet him on food sent from the wardroom mess. Hall is improving rapidly—continue the application of argenti nitras and cerate simplex to his sore wrist. Pettingill is improving slowly—continue the cerate simplex.

The weather was quite cool all day. The thermometer at 7 A.M. was 46° Fahr., and at 12 o'clock meridian it was 48° Fahr. At 4 P.M. the officer of the deck logged the weather on the log slate [a folding slate on which to note events and progress before entering them into the log book] 57° Fahr., so that the average temperature today was 50° Fahr.

The boys are collecting money, or rather making up a purse, for the purpose of laying in a cargo of the good things of life so as to have a general feast on Christmas. They very politely sent into the cabin and wardroom for a little assistance. The captain handed them two dollars, and the rest of the officers (viz., Messrs. Childs, Murray, Flood, Thomas, and myself) gave them the sum of five dollars—in all a purse of seven dollars. They appeared well satisfied at our generosity. I hope they may have a happy time of it. They intend to purchase their stores from the U.S. supply steamer *Massachusetts.*

Nov. 27, 1863. At 8 A.M. the weather was rather cloudy and cold; 10 A.M., strong symptoms of rain.

My fever patient, George Thompson, does not feel quite as well as yesterday—order him as a drink a solution of citric acid, sugar, and water—continue his tonic mixture—diet, light. Pettingill—considerable improvement in his case—continue the cerate simplex

—shall discharge him to duty ere long. Hall—his wrist is not quite well—still I, at his request, discharged him to duty—order him to continue the application of simple cerate. Our paymaster came to me last evening and complained that he had passed vermes of the species Ascaris lumbricoides. I ordered him hydrarg. chlorid. mitis grs vi, sach. alba grs xx; M, and this morning he swallowed ol. ricini ℥ i suspended in a cup of tea. He swallowed said dose without making a wry face. The way he will travel a certain route will not be slow. The captain is rather under the weather this morning. I ordered him pil. cath. comp. no. iv so as to relieve the congestion of his liver.

Acting Assistant Paymaster Thomas N. Murray, one of nature's noblemen, handed me not a "What is it?" but an American quarter of a dollar of the year 1856—i.e., it was coined in 1856. The Goddess of Liberty, having the staff of Liberty surmounted by the cap of Liberty in her left hand, holding on to an American shield with her right hand, the word "Liberty" engraved on said shield—said goddess appears to be seated on the rock of ages, and thirteen stars with the figure 1856 surrounding her, for the front portion of said quarter dollar, whilst on the reverse the American eagle, having three arrows in one claw and the olive branch in the other; surrounding said emblem, or American eagle, are the words "United States of America" and "Quar. Dol." Thus I have endeavored to describe a coin which at one time was the principal currency of the United States. But since the advent of "greenbacks" and "postage currency" that kind of currency—i.e., silver and gold—has passed away and can be reckoned amongst the things that were. I shall treasure up said piece of bullion—i.e., the twenty-five-cent piece of silver which our illustrious paymaster handed me—so as to show the rising generation what used to be the currency of Uncle Sam's dominions during the good "auld days of lang syne."

At 12.30 M.—i.e., half past twelve o'clock today—Paymaster Murray and Ensign Flood with twenty-two armed men left in the first cutter and the launch for Sapelo Sound, there to communicate with the U.S.S. Lodona so as to be enabled to communicate with the U.S. supply steamer Massachusetts. They expect to return tomorrow afternoon. . . . . Both the cutter and launch had their canvas spread when they left the ship; the wind was fair, but the tide was against them—still they are able to stem the tide with the present wind. I hope they will be successful and return with a good cargo of stores and a heavy mail.

A light fog made its appearance at 8.30 A.M. and continued all day. The thermometer at 8 A.M. was 59° Fahr. 12 M. No change in the appearance of the weather. 2 P.M. Commenced to rain. 5 P.M. Still continues to rain, and there is every prospect that it will continue all night. 12 o'clock midnight, still rains. Took a quiet nap between the hours of 1 and 4 P.M. At 4.30 P.M. Messrs. Childs, Thomas, and myself had each a glass of claret punch, I finding the claret and oranges (we had no lemons—hence our using oranges) and the caterer, Mr. Thomas, finding the sugar and water. 6 P.M. the officer of the deck reported a fire on the mainland looking as though it were a signal fire of the Rebels.

I forgot to mention in my notes of yesterday the plucking of pink roses from rosebushes in front of the Waldburg mansion by Paymaster Murray and myself. We also found a small watermelon in what used to be a watermelon patch. It was the last one of the season, left all alone. We cut it open and merely tasted it so as to be able to say that we tasted of a watermelon in the month of November.

Nov. 28, 1863. At 4 A.M. Mr. Wright, the officer of the deck, reported said light on the main [land] as flashing. 8 A.M. a white flag reported on the mainland at same place where the fire was seen last night. Also three persons can be seen walking up and down the beach. At 8.30 A.M. Captain Moses sent Actg. Master's Mate John Wright with an armed crew in the third cutter to ascertain the meaning of said flag of truce. 9 A.M. The 3rd cutter is returning with three strange parties in her; whether white or black remains to be seen.

9.30 A.M. The 3rd cutter has returned with Mr. Wright and three refugees on her. The flash of light seen at 4 A.M. was caused by them; they threw a handful of powder on the fire so as to attract our attention. They are three hardy-looking men, having escaped from Savannah in a dugout. They were employed in the business of salt making.   . . . They report hard times. Salt was worth $20 per bushel, shoes from $80 to $200, and everything else in proportion. They say that Savannah is well fortified—embankments thirty feet thick encircle the city. Every man is forced into the ranks except those employed in the manuacturing of salt. They were dressed tolerably well. One of them lost his shoes yesterday that had cost him $100—rather tough. They bring very little news. Their names: F.G. Turner, ——Turner, and Richard Benz. They had the "Daily Morning News" for Wednesday morning, November 25, 1863, published at Savannah, Ga., by Theodore Blois, W.T. Thompson editor. . . . .

One of the refugees, the said Richard Benz, is a young Kentuckian, aged 23, who left Louisville on the 15th of April, 1861, as a private in a company that left the sacred soil of Kentucky to fight for the South. He says that at that time all were sanguine of success; that their hot blood was up; that they had an idea that they could flog Uncle Sam, the devil, etc. But they all found to their chagrin that they had rather a bitter pill to swallow. He, not fancying the idea of living on hard grub, hard work, and poor pay, concluded to skedaddle to Uncle Sam and seek repose in the arms of a "mudsill" [a term applied opprobriously to Northerners]—says that now he can feel like an honest man again. He damns the Southern cause high and low; says that Jeff Davis is looked upon as a god. The poorer and middle class believe all that the stump speakers tell them. So much for his affairs.

I shall now note down some copies of passes etc. that were granted to one of the refugees—viz., F. G. Turner—who appears to have had some friends amongst the Rebels. [There were two passes to Savannah and one to go "any" where in Georgia]. He is a native of Connecticut and came South some six years ago. One of his brothers is in the Confederate Navy. He himself was conscripted several times, but he always managed to get free because he belonged to the Ordinance Department, also because he had salt works. . . . .

The following, which is a copy of the original in his possession, he considered the most valuable of all his papers, being it exempted him from doing military duty, a business which he was determined not to follow, for, says he, "I would of died ere I'd lifted up an arm to fight against the North!"

Georgia   I have enrolled
   Richmond County   F.G. Turner

as a conscript, but I hereby certify that he is exempt from military service in the Confederate Army so long as he shall remain in the service or employ of "Lofbourne and Tommers Foundry." Whenever he leaves said service or employ he is hereby ordered to report to Major John Dunwoody, at Camp Randolph, or to the Commander of the Military District of Georgia, under penalty of being published as a deserter.

V.M. Barnes
Augusta, Aug. 2, 1862.   Sub-Enrolling Officer

_____ " _____

It appears that F. G. Turner was considerable of a sport, the way he dug into the good things of life; the following hotel bill speaks for itself.

Savannah, Nov. 17, 1863

All Bills Payable Weekly.

Mr. F.G. Turner

  To *Pulaski House,* Dr.

W.H. Wiltberger and Co.

Nov. 10—Segars 2.00, Segars 2.00, Whiskey 15.00	$19.00
" 11—Whiskey 15.00, Claret 10.00, Segars 1.00, Segars 1.00	27.00
" 14—Whiskey 15.00, Segars 1.00, Segars 1.00	17.00
" 16—Segars 1.00, Segars 1.00	2.00
" 17—Bill for W. Willing	22.50
Board for one week	70.00
	$157.50

Received Payment.

The cigars were 25/100 per piece, whiskey $15 per pint, claret $10 per pint.

1 P.M. The 1st cutter and launch have returned with all hands safe and sound. The *Massachusetts* had called at Sapelo Sound and left our mail and provisions on board the *Lodona* for us, so that Ensign Flood and Paymaster Murray left Sapelo Sound at 10 A.M. I received a letter from brother Frank dated Nov. 16 in answer to mine of Nov. 6; he stated that he had sent the ale that day—i.e., he enclosed the express receipt. The ale came along today in the 1st cutter. It cost $4.00, the cask $2.75, expressage $0.75; total, $7.50. He informs me of the birth of another daughter Nov. 7, making three in all. I received quite an interesting epistle from my friend A. G. Myers. He appears to be in the oil business up in Pennsylvania. Brother Michael sent me a Philadelphia paper. The "Medical and Surgical Reporter" for Oct. 31 and Nov. 7 made their appearance—the first copies that I have received since I subscribed

for said periodical. Acting Asst. Surgeon [Thomas W.] Meckley of
the *Lodona* sent me three Lehigh County papers per Paymaster
Murray. I will thank him for the same per letter the next time the
boat leaves for Sapelo Sound.

The weather was quite stormy all day. 6 P.M. a heavy thunder
shower, sharp lightning. Thermometer 70° Fahr.   . . .

Nov. 29, 1863. Rained all last night. Continues to rain at 8 A.M.
Thermometer 67° Fahr. at 7 A.M. My case of fever, George Thompson, is coming along finely—appetite improving, temper better, etc.
—℞ pil. cath. comp. no iv—diet consists of soup and tapioca—acidulated drinks to act as diaphoretics. Pettingill is improving nicely—
order him to use the ammonia and lead lotion. Michael Quinn,
landsman, complains of glossitis—℞ ol. ricini ℥ i, and order the
following gargle: potassae chloras grs xxiv, aquae ℥ ii; M; Sig. Use
4 or 5 times a day.

Dull! Dull!! Dull!!! Nothing but rain all day. We fairly *eat* rain.
Everything in and around the ship is saturated. We are compelled
to keep between decks etc. so as to keep dry. We kill time and
drive dull care away by reading late dates.   . . . .

Ceased raining at 6 P.M. 10.30 P.M. a storm prevailing. Let go
the starboard anchor; the ship drifted some. A light reported on
the mainland.

Nov. 30, 1863. Cold and stormy. Thermometer at 5 A.M. 30°
Fahr., at 7 A.M. 32° Fahr. Heavy woolen goods in great demand. 12
M. 41° Fahr.

Josiah Pettingill returns to duty this morning after a long stay
of 22 days on the sick list. Ellis Scarlet, 3rd-class boy, aet. 18,
Georgia—urticaria—℞ magnesiae sulphas ℥ i—externally ablutions with soap and water, after which use the following lotion:
amoniae carbonas, plumbi acetas āā ℈ ss, aquae ℥ iv; M—was admitted on the list. Quinn—improving—continue gargle of potassae
chloras grs xxiv, aquae ℥ ii; M. Thompson—about the same as
yesterday—continue same treatment, omitting the cathartic.

Paid Caterer Wm. H. Thomas a mess bill of fifteen dollars and
twenty-six cents. One of the refugees, F. G. Turner, showed me
the following order so that I might see how near he came being
sent to the Confederate camp. I thought proper to obtain a copy
of it.

Ordinance Depot
Savannah, 12th Nov. 1863

F.G. Turner,
   Savah.
       Sir—
          You are hereby ordered to report for duty at the shops without delay, otherwise your detail will be revoked, and you will be turned over to the conscript officer.

                              I am
                            Respt.
                A.T. Cunningham
           1st Lt. Arty. and Ord.

Dec. 1, 1863. Cold and clear. Thermometer 32° Fahr. at 8 A.M., 34° Fahr. at 10 A.M. Quartermaster Scott shot three bullock last night. Their carcasses were brought on board this morning. The beef looks rather palatable.

Thompson says he feels somewhat better—℞ ol. ricini ℥ i. Scarlet—improving—continue the ammonia and lead lotion. Quinn—improving—order a gargle consisting of vinegar, water, tinct. capsicum and salt.

Commenced to board the three refugees this morning—i.e., allow them their meals in the wardroom. Wrote a letter to Mrs. M. K. Boyer, enclosing her five dollars as a Christmas gift from her youngest son. Wrote a letter to Mrs. P. J. Cutler, my only sister, enclosing her five dollars as a Christmas present from her youngest brother. Paymaster Murray paid me twenty dollars on account.

4 P.M. The weather somewhat warmer. Thermometer 52° Fahr. In order to kill time and drive dull care away, I read Charles Lever's "Tom Burke of Ours," a military novel [published in various editions (the first of which appeared in 1844), including one by G. Routledge and Sons the preface of which is dated 1857].

My steward reported that Thompson complained of having rather a small portion of grub served out to him. He appears to have found his appetite again. Shall order him fresh beef tomorrow, as well as a few potatoes. Scott, Wm., complained of pyrosis at 6 P.M. I ordered him a dose of pil. cath. comp., say no iv. Turned in rather early.

Dec. 2, 1863. Weather moderate—thermometer 45° Fahr. at 8.30 A.M. Old Sol is showing himself. My patients—Thompson, Quinn, and Scarlet—are all improving. The first has quite an appetite again; his bowels are regular; little or no fever. Ordered him his tonic mixture. The second continues his capsicum mixture. The third does not scratch as much as he did—continue the ammonia and lead solution. Wrote a letter to brother Frank thanking him for the ale etc.

The U.S. barque *"Fernandina's"* Mousquetaires, a corps composed of 40 of her crew, had quite a happy time at 3 P.M. drilling on the beach, Quarter Gunner Richard Costar being the drilling master, and 1st-Class boy Short served in the capacity of drummer boy. They kept step to the music like veterans of the Army of the Potomac. All felt highly elated, and everything passed off lovely.

Captain Moses and myself took a tramp to the plantation. While there I served out some resin cerate to Young Cudgel and an anodyne to Aunt Estrella, promising Aunt Estrella some pills the next time I came on shore. I also gave some tobacco to the following parties: viz., Aunts Estrella, Nabbie, Cudgel, Grunty, Jennie. I plucked a beautiful bunch, or cluster, of oranges, which I brought off with me, and hung it in my stateroom, it adding very much to the appearance of said room. The captain was busy superintending the cleansing out of wells, preparatory to watering ship.

I came across the resting place, or last home, of quite an old darky named Toney Walburgh, aet. over 100 years, who died in 1850. His resting place was marked by a beautiful white head and foot board bearing the following inscription:

> Sacred to the Memory of Toney Walburgh,
> Who died Sept. 4th, 1850. Aged over 100 years.
> A bright and shining light is gone out of Israel.
> Blessed are the dead who die in the Lord.

The grave is shaded by large fine live-oak timber. Peace to Toney's ashes.

The male portion of the contrabands of the island were out in the fields digging sweet potatoes, hauling them home, and housing them for the winter. They say that they have a very poor potato crop this season. Their corn crop turned out well; consequently they have plenty of the slave's "staff of life" (corn) to live upon during the winter. The old wenches were busy washing clothing for the ship's company. Some of them were sunning themselves and smoking their pipes. Our executive officer, C. C. Childs, an actg. master in the service, while on shore today plucked a white rose, which he presented to me.

Dec. 3, 1863. At four A.M. all hands were roused up by the springing of a rattle in the hands of the executive officer. In two minutes by the watch all were at their quarters, the gunners ready for the word "Fire!" so as to be able to discharge the contents of their guns and land said shot, shell, or shrapnel in amongst the enemy and the decks cleared for a fight, when lo and behold! the order to pipe down was given—so we all turned in again. The officers all felt anxious to see how promptly the crew would respond to said call to quarters, and their anxiety was gratified by the above result. Let me assure the outsider that to be awakened, turn out, draw on your pantaloons, boots, etc., rush on deck, and clear the guns ready for action in two minutes is no lazy job.

In my morning visit to the sick bay I found the following parties waiting there for the arrival of "Physic" so as to get some medicine: Thompson, who does not feel quite so well, has rather more fever —continue same treatment with slight alteration in the proportions of said tonic mixture; Quinn—improving rapidly—continue same treatment; Scarlet—discharged to duty; William Brophy, ordinary seaman—complaining of indigestion or constipation—ordered him a strong and good dose of magnesiae sulphas, say ℥ i; William Scott, quartermaster, complaining of sickness and acidity of stomach—order him the following: ℞ magnesiae ℥ ii, spts ammon. aromat f. ℨ ii, aquae f. ℥ vi; ℳ; Sig. Tablespoonful every half hour until he feels relieved.

The weather was rather pleasant all day. Thermometer 45° Fahr. at 8 A.M., 60° at 12 M., 53° at 6 P.M.—mean, 53°. The boys were busy watering ship. The water is brought from the Waldburg plantation. Sent Aunt Estrella, one of ye intelligent wenches, who holds forth on St. Catharine's Island, about 60 laxative pills, she being in want of an aperient. Took a tramp on St. Catharine's Island in company with the captain. We had quite a pleasant time burning the tall grass and underbrush so as to be able to travel about said island without tearing one's clothing or treading unaware upon a snake. The fire burned beautifully. The captain is having a road cut through the brush from this side of the island to the other, also cutting a road to the plantation.

Laboring under the effects of constipation, I thought I would take four pills, composed of the following medicines, when I turned in tonight. The following is the formulary: ℞ rhei pulv aloe pulv āā ʒ i, ipecac pulv grs x, saponis Ɔ i, aquae q.s. to form a mass; pillulae no. lx. Sig. One every night as a laxative, and whenever a purgative is required, from 4 to 6 pills. 9 P.M. I took four of the above pills.

Dec. 4, 1863. William Donaldson, seaman, came to me last night complaining of dysentery. I then ordered him ol. ricini ʒ i et tinct. opii gtts vi, which caused him three or four fine evacuations. This morning I ordered the following mixture: argenti nitras grs iii, opii pulv grs iii ss, aquae f. ʒ ii, M. Sig. Teaspoonful three times a day. Michael Quinn, who is affected with stomatitis, is improving. He continues to use the vinegar gargle, which consists of ℞ acetum f. ʒ iv, tinct. capsici f. ʒ i, sodium chloridi ʒ i, aqua fontana f. ʒ iv; M; Sig. Use as a gargle six times a day. George Thompson continues the same treatment. Scott and Brophy did not report themselves.

The weather was pleasant all day. The thermometer was 47° Fahr. at 8 A.M., 60° at 12 M., and 52° at 6 P.M.—mean, 53°. Ensign Flood, with the 1st cutter and crew, was busy sounding, or rather surveying, the harbors. The crew busy watering ship; we have upwards of 2000 gallons of water on board. . . .

Dec. 5, 1863. I had the pleasure of reporting but one patient in my daily report of sick to the captain this morning, and that one is George Thompson—intermittent fever, who is improving slowly but feels somewhat debilitated. He continues using the tonic mixture, which, as heretofore stated, consists of the following ingredients: viz., ℞ quiniae sulphas grs xxxii, acid. sulph. aromat f. ʒ i, tinct zingiber f. ʒ ss., whiskey ii f. ʒ ii, aquae f. ʒ vi; M; Sig. Tablespoonful three times a day. Michael Quinn and William Donaldson were discharged to duty. . . . .

We have finished watering ship. The executive officer informs me that we have at present 4700 gallons on board.

The captain, being stricken with Izaak Waltonism, went and caught about 30 fish today. I had the pleasure of eating one of them with him at noon. Paid Aunt Sallie a small wash bill, amounting to forty-five cents.

The weather has been quite cool all day—thermometer 50° **Fahr.**

at 8 A.M., 55° at 12 M., and 60° at 4 P.M.—mean, 55° This has been rather a dull day for me. Nothing to read except it be medicine, and that is rather dry reading, after having thumbed said books for the last 4 or 5 years. We are all anxiously waiting for a mail. Our paymaster expects some provisions from Port Royal next week, when we all expect to receive mail matter. The regular mail boat, the *Massachusetts*, will not be due until the 17th of this month—so that, unless sooner relieved, we will have to wait until that time.

Read Charles Lever's "Davenport Dunn, A Man of Our Day" [London: Chapman and Hall, 1859] until 9 P.M., when I concluded to lay it aside, turn in, and court Nature's sweet restorer, balmy sleep.

Dec. 6, 1863. A slight breeze prevails at 8 A.M. 11 A.M. It blows like the Old Harry. 9 A.M. all hands called to muster to attend divine service, Paymaster Murray officiating as chaplain.

George Thompson improving—continue tonic treatment. His name was the only one that graced the sick report and binnacle list today. The weather was rather cool as well as it was windy all day. Thermometer 52° Fahr. at 8 A.M., 56° at 12 M., and 58° at 4 P.M.—mean, 55°.

The quartermaster reported a large fire bearing N½W (north half west by compass). The fire was reported at 7 P.M. 8 P.M. It is blowing a regular snorting gale of wind. The *Fernandina* is rolling some.

Dec. 7, 1863. Still blowing quite smartly. Reported George Thompson improving in my report of sick. He continues to take the tonic mixture. His appetite has improved. Ensign Thomas was busy all day superintending the digging of a well ashore so as to have fresh water handy for our live stock—viz., six pigs—that we are fattening for Christmas. Weather rather cool all day. Thermometer 42° Fahr. at 8 A.M., 48° at 12 M., and 50° at 4 P.M.—mean, 47°.

Dec. 8, 1863. Weather squally; slight symptoms of foggy spell. Thomas O'Neil, lds., was admitted on the sick list this morning suffering with a bad cough. I ordered him an expectorant mixture as follows: viz., ℞ ext. glycyrrhizae ℨ ii, syr scillae f. ℥ i, sach. alba ℥ i, sol. morphiae sulphas f. ℥ ii, aquae f. ℥ xii; M̶; Sig. Tablespoonful three times a day. Thompson—improving—continue same plan of treatment.

The weather was rather cold, wet, and disagreeable all day. Thermometer 46° Fahr. at 8 A.M., 49° at 12 M., and 51° at 4 P.M.— mean, 49°. . . .

Our caterer, Ensign Thomas, purchased some fowls and 2 hogs from the contrabands on the island. The fowls are old breeding hens, and the caterer has an idea that he can raise some chicks next spring. Hope he may realize said pleasure. The hogs are to be added to our litter of pigs on shore, making our "pile" amounting to 11 pigs—quite a family of the porcine species of the animal kingdom. . . .

Dec. 9, 1863. One of the intelligent contrabands on board named Austin Burroughs, having, I suppose, the Heenan and King affair in his head, took a notion into his black skull to pitch into a seaman named Alex Kenny, and the way he used his maulers was not slow. The said Kenny's face was all bloody; the crimson flowed like claret. Of course Kenny came aft and reported his case to the captain. Both Kenny and Burroughs were then placed in the brig, heavily ironed, until after breakfast, when both parties were heard, after which witnesses were examined. The result of said trial was that the plaintiff, Alex Kenny, was acquitted and the defendant, Austin Burroughs, sent back into said brig, double-ironed, and fed on bread and water. All hands were pleased with the verdict and hope it may have a beneficial effect on said parties. Thus ends the great fight on board.

James Johnson, quartermaster, aet. 54, Sweden, came to me with rather a sore hand—abrasio accompanied by erysipelas—paint part with sol argenti nitras of the following strength: ℞ argenti nitras ℨ i, aquae ℥ i; ℳ—also apply a lini cataplasm. O'Neil is about the same—continue the same treatment. Thompson—continues to improve—cont. same treat.

The weather was cool all day—thermometer 55° Fahr. at 8 A.M., 58° at 12 M., and 57° at 4 P.M.—mean, 57°.

At 8.40 A.M. Charles Burns, a seaman, was placed in double irons and confined in the brig for refusing to do duty. His diet is to consist of hard-tack and cold water. Serves Burns right; he ought to respect the laws and obey his superior officer. Hope it may have a beneficial effect on the rest of the crew. The discipline of the ship must be upheld, or else the service will go to the devil. I am in favor of punishing all criminals to the full extent of the Rules and

Regulations for the Government of the Navy, for I consider one good punishment worth more than a dozen of trifling ones such as light extra duty etc. There is nothing so good for cooling a man's temper as a diet on bread and water seasoned with solitary confinement. The remedy appears to work as a charm. It is seldom that a second dose is required. I have known men in less than two days after being thus confined send word to the executive officer that they would like to see him; and after he came to them, they with tears running down their cheeks would beg and pray to be let off, promising to do better in the future etc. etc. During the rest of the cruise those very men would prove themselves to be the best-behaved fellows on board, whereas I have seen men who were placed on the black list do their extra duty with smiling countenances, laughing in their sleeves at the idea of calling that punishment and looking as though they did not care a damn for such work. Those men are always eyesores, as it were, during the whole cruise—hence the utility and advantage of punishing a man at once to the full extent of the law whenever such punishment is called for.

Quarter Gunner Richard Costar had the boys on the beach this afternoon drilling them with small arms—and nobly was it done; the boys appear well versed in drilling. But after all, you cannot make a soldier out of a sailor. A sailor loves a soldier about as well as he does a snake. The following saying is one of their maxims: "A messmate before a shipmate; a shipmate before a stranger; a stranger before a dog; and a dog before a bloody soldier."

. . . Made my steward a present of a flannel coat that had been worn some by me last cruise so that he could keep his best one free from dirt and drugs in the sick bay. He thanked me very kindly.

Dec. 10, 1863. The weather today has more the appearance of a balmy day in May than a usually stern cold day of December. The sun has marshalled his hosts in the heavens in all their glory and is bringing his whole force to bear upon us. We all feel in the best of humor this morning; even the prisoners in the brig feel delighted at the idea of having beautiful weather. We all are anxious for a continuation of this kind of weather.

This morning between the hours of 8 and 9 o'clock as Ordinary Seaman Powers and Landsman Gray were paddling themselves ashore in a small dugout, or canoe, one of them happened to make a misstep and capsized the boat, the result being rather a wet reception in the arms of Mother Ocean. The captain immediately lowered a boat and made for them; but ere he reached them, they had swum ashore safe and sound. One of them remarked that he had no idea that the water was so wet and cold—also that he did not fancy swimming in salt water at this time of the year. I need hardly state that both were as wet as drowned rats and somewhat frightened. They were at the time of the accident pulling ashore with some fodder, or slop, for the hogs on shore.

My three patients—viz., Thompson, O'Neil, and Johnson—are improving. They all continue their respective remedies prescribed for them yesterday, or when last reported. Thompson and O'Neil are unfit for duty—consequently they were reported in my daily report of sick also had their names placed on the binnacle list; whilst Johnson, notwithstanding his having a very sore hand indeed, being fit to do his duty, which merely consists of keeping a quartermaster's watch, had not his name reported to the captain or placed upon the binnacle list. In fact, Johnson requested me not to report him sick as he could do his duty. Well done, Old Man Johnson; you don't fancy the idea of seeing your name on the binnacle list.

Took a run on shore this afternoon; had quite a pleasant time strolling along the beach. Whilst walking along, I found quite a coil of rattling stuff underneath a tree—also one or two small relics. The captain and Mr. Thomas had rather a lively time burning the underbrush. Mr. Thomas has quite an extensive well on shore. He says that he can draw 100 gallons of water out of it at a time. The captain caused a chicken house of the following dimensions to be built on shore—viz., 12 feet long, 8 feet broad, and 6 feet high—almost large enough for a dwelling house. The only thing wanting are the chickens. He hopes to have some ere long to put therein.

Some of the crew have been after oysters. They returned with a good cargo of bivalves. One of the porkers purchased by our caterer on the 8th instant has "kicked the bucket," or, as some have it, "pegged out," leaving our family of porkers to consist of only ten head. The rest are all in good order. He (the caterer) promises to give us a fine barbecue ere long.

The weather, notwithstanding the warm influence of the sun, don't appear to change the mercury in the thermometer much. The scale reads as follows: viz., 56° Fahr. at 8 A.M., 57° at 12 M., and 57° at 4 P.M.—mean, 57°. The officer of the deck reports a large fire on Ossabaw Island.

7 P.M. A slight gale of wind. 8 P.M. The officer of the deck reports everything O.K. on and about the gallant barque *Fernandina*.

13

Christmas Feast in St. Catherines Sound

St. Catharine's Sound, Ga., Dec. 11, 1863. The seaman named Alexander Kenny, who was unlucky enough to have the darky Burroughs pitch into him roughshod on the 9th inst., came to me this morning with a very sore hand. Upon examination I found said sore to consist of a contused wound, caused by the said Burroughs' teeth on the day of the fight. The wound had commenced to suppurate to such an extent as to compel me to cauterize said sore rather freely with argenti nitras so as to cut down the false granulations and cause said wound to take on a healthier action, after which I applied a lini cataplasm and ordered him to take pil. laxative no iv. Kenny therefore becomes a member of the sick list for the time being. The said Kenny is 22 years old, born in Scotland, an able seaman, and his disease goes under the head of vulnus contusum.

Thomas O'Neil, the case of bronchitis acuta, is coming on finely. He says he coughs easier, sleeps better, feels better, and, in short, is better. James Johnson, the case of abrasio accompanied with erysipelas, is improving rapidly—continue the application of lini cataplasm. George Thompson, the old case of intermittens, is also improving rapidly—continue his tonic mixture. Besides the above cases I had 4 or 5 minor cases requiring either a dose of ol. ricini, magnesiae sulphas or pil. cath. comp.

Some of the crew have an idea that unless they take a dose of physic once per month, they will get sick and require a cargo of doctor's stuff—hence they come as regular as clockwork once per month for their dose of oil, salts, or pills. Of course I ordered my steward to gratify their whim. They take the dose and leave the sick bay in the best of humor, thinking, I suppose, themselves safe and sound from all aches and pains for the next four weeks to come. I must confess that as a general thing those very same persons never lose a day as regards doing duty; in other words, their names are never seen on the binnacle list. Then again there are others who delight in playing sick and swallow medicine. We are often compelled to use harsh remedies in order to drive said "sogers" to duty, such as internal doses of tinct. guaiac., arom. jalapa, etc. and Spanish fly blisters and dry and wet cupping externally.

Mr. Childs, the executive officer, left the ship armed with ten pounds of salt pork with the intention of purchasing some hens from the contrabands on St. Catharine's Island. He remained absent above four hours, when he returned on board with one small insignificant barnyard pullet, for which he paid about 80/100 dolls. His reasons for paying so large a price were simply these: ere he left the ship, he made a bet of one dollar that he would return with four old hens. Well, after he had landed at the plantation, talked to the niggers, and displayed his cargo of salt pork, he found much to his chagrin that his four old hens were nowhar!—and, not wishing to return without at least an apology for a hen, he gave all his pork for the above said pullet. He has an idea that the stocks are rather low in the market as regards the "old hen business." I am afraid that he will have to take it for some time to come. Ever since his return he has remained quiet as regards the "old hen trade."

In order to add to the punishment of the fighting Austin Burroughs and show him the beauties of a peaceable nature, the wardroom mess from this day forth consider him no longer worthy of holding the situation of wardroom boy, an honor of no mean import, to said mess; consequently as soon as he is relieved from confinement, he goes on deck again instead of coming into the wardroom, and Andrew or Alexander Jackson, a contraband aged 19, comes in his place. He (the said Jackson) enters upon the duties of wardroom boy today, his principal duty being to keep the room of the executive officer and that of the doctor's (mine) clean. From all indications I think that the interests of the mess are advanced by the change. Jackson is a quiet sort of a darky, whereas the said Burroughs always was rather fond of travelling on his muscle. "Truly the way of the transgressor is hard."

Commenced to rain at 1 P.M. The weather was rather foggy all day. Thermometer 56° Fahr. at 8 A.M., 58° at 12 M., and 54° at 4 P.M.—mean, 56°. 6 P.M. Continues to rain; the prospects ahead are a wet and foggy night—rather disagreeable for the poor men on watch. I should not fancy keeping the watch of the officer of the deck tonight. Still when duty calls, we are bound to obey; so all that the watch officers can do is grin and bear it. 9 P.M. rains as hard as ever; no signs of its ceasing.

Dec. 12, 1863. Continues to rain. One of the 1st-class boys, George Allen, aet. 17, New York, with a sore finger, came to me at 8 A.M. for treatment. Upon examination I found it to be a case of paronychia. I lanced it well and then applied a lini cataplasm. Kenny—his hand looks better—dress the sore with cerate resinae— ℞ magnesiae sulphas ℥ i. Thompson—had a slight chill last night —does not feel so well this morning—his bowels are in good order— I ordered him liq. potassae arsenitis gtts v in aquae ℥ i three times a day. O'Neil—is improving slowly—continue the expectorants. Johnson—his abrasio looks well—dress it with cerate resinae. Antonio De Cruiz, ship's cook—constipation—℞ pil. laxative no. iv, to be followed in three hours by ol. ricini. John Collins, lds., aet. 25, New York, complains of blennorrhoea—he has had it for some time—℞ tinct. ferri chloridi gtts x three times a day and inject with the following solution three times a day: ℞ zinci sulphas grs iii, aquae f. ℥ ii, M.

11 A.M. This has been rather a dull forenoon. Nothing to read, too lazy to sleep, and plenty of rain. It has been drip! drip!! drip!!! all the time. Everything in and about the ship is fairly saturated with rain. We are compelled to *see* rain; *eat* rain; *drink* rain; *laugh* in the rain; *talk* about rain; *sing* amidst the rain; *sleep* in the rain; and, in short, it is *rain* here and *rain* there, until we all are fairly disgusted with wet weather. Some of the officers attempt to weather the crisis by reading old dates, some by yawning, some by writing letters, and others by playing dominoes, draughts [checkers], or backgammon. The captain and myself have tried to drive dull care away by playing several games of dominoes, and we have partly succeeded. We stuck to the game until 10.55 A.M., when we concluded to stop. We recontinued playing at 6 P.M. and played 6 games by 7 P.M., when we both felt tired of the game.

The weather was rather warm notwithstanding the rain. The following is the range of the mercury today: 60° Fahr. at 8 A.M., 63°

at 12 M., and 62° at 4 P.M.—mean, 62°. 7.45 P.M. the stars are out in all their glory. A heavy wind blowing. Every prospect of a clearing up.

After sporting a moustache for one year, I plucked up courage enough to sacrifice said hirsute appendage of the face. It caused considerable change in my personal appearance—some say for the better, whilst others will have it that I was very foolish to shave it off. I rather think the want of hair on my upper lip is an improvement and not a fault; consequently I shall shave said part of my face and only allow a goatee to grow. I can say that I have quite an extensive crop of hair on my chin. I feel rather proud of my dozen spears, as the captain calls my chin beard.

At 8.30 P.M. Quartermaster Scott and Landsman Hall, who had left the ship on the 4th of this month for Sapelo Island in search of wild turkeys etc., returned, having in their possession one dead turkey, one dead deer, and twenty-one live chickens. The turkey and chickens belong to the wardroom mess, and the deer they (the hunters) shared between them. The chickens cost the mess three dollars. They (Scott and Hall) were completely fagged out. They report the contrabands on Sapelo Island all well.

Dec. 13, 1863. Divine service at 9 A.M. Reading of the Articles of War by Executive Officer Childs at 9.30 A.M.

One of the messenger boys, S. H. Hoyt by name, came to me at 8 A.M. complaining of sickness. Knowing full well his complaint, I ordered him the following pleasant dose—viz., ℞ antim. et potassae tartras gr i, ipecacuanha pulvis grs xx; M; to be washed down his throat by means of a tumbler of warm water. Ten minutes after the administration of said dose he heard from it in the form of emesis and catharsis. The way he vomited and was purged was not slow. I don't think that he will complain of bile in his stomach again for some time to come. Kenny's hand is improving—dress it this morning with a flaxseed poultice. Allen's finger looks better—it is suppurating finely—continue the lini cataplasm. O'Neil—he is coming on slowly—continue expectorants. Thompson—feels considerably better—continue same treatment. Johnson's hand looks well—dress with cerate simplex. De Cruiz—says that he feels right smart again and is ready to do all the cooking in the ship. Collins—is to continue the iron internally and use the injection three times a day; he is fit for duty.

11.10 A.M. We dropped out toward sea about half a mile from our anchorage. 11.30 A.M. Quartermaster Scott and Landsman Headley left in the dingy for Sapelo Sound, there to communicate with the *Lodona*. They took the mail with them. I sent the letters that I had written on the 1st of December, 1863, to mother and sister Beckie along with Scott so as to leave them on board of the *Lodona,* from whence they will leave for their destination by the first opportunity which presents itself. I also sent the letter that I had written to A. G. Myers, Esq., on the 8th inst. along with the rest of the mail. I hope they will reach their destination safely—also that Scott and party may return with a good mail.

The weather was rather cloudy and somewhat inclined to be rainy all forenoon. 1 P.M. It has cleared up beautifully. The sails are all loosened so as to get dry in the sun, which is out in full blast. The thermometer ranges as follows: 63° Fahr. at 8 A.M., 64° at 12 M., and 65° at 4 P.M.—mean, 64°.

Our caterer served us up for dinner today the turkey that the hunters shot and brought with them last night, and I must say that roast turkey is not a bad pill to swallow. None of the members of the wardroom mess refused any of said dish when offered to them by the carver. . . .

At 7 P.M. I found boy Hoyt, to whom I had administered an emetic this morning so as to cleanse his stomach and intestines, rather weak but admitting that the dose done him some good, for, says he, "I don't have such a bad headache." I advised him to turn in for the night and told him that he would feel better in the morning. He says that he does not fancy that style of physic (meaning medicine) but prefers either castor oil, salts, or pills. I am not surprised at all at his remark, for who does fancy an emetic? Still it is a quick way of relieving a foul stomach of its mass of indigestible matter.

Dec. 14, 1863. Boy Hoyt reported himself at 8 A.M. as feeling somewhat better. I shall order him a tonic mixture today—also allow him to lounge about the berth deck. The tonic consists of the following ingredients: viz., ℞ quiniai sulphas grs ii, acid sulph. aromat gtts v, aquae f. ℥ ss; ℳ; Sig. Three times a day. George Thompson—feels better this morning—℞ quiniae sulphas grs ii, acid sulph aromat. gtt x, aquae f. ℥ ss; ℳ; Sig. Three times a day. Alexander Kenny—his hand is healing finely—dress the same with resin cerate. Boy Allen—returns to duty this morning. Thomas O'Neil—returns to duty but still continues his expectorant mixture, which consists of the following ingredients, consequently somewhat demulcent: ℞ ext glycyrrhizae ʒ ii, syr. scillae f. ʒ i, sach. alba. ʒ i, sol. morphiae sulphas f. ʒ ii, aquae f. ʒ xii; M; Sig. Tablespoonful three times a day. James Johnson did not report himself. I therefore take it for granted that his hand is well again; hence I make no further entry of his case in my medical journal of practice.

At 1.30 P.M. Scott and Headley returned from Sapelo Sound having a small mail in their possession. I was the happy recipient of a long and interesting epistle from my only sister, Beckie P. Cutler, in answer to mine of Oct.—,1863, two papers which father sent me, and the "Medical and Surgical Reporter" for Nov. 14.

Paymaster Murray plucked a beautiful red rose on shore today from a rosebush in front of the Waldburg mansion. He intends sending it home to his friends as an index (if I may use the term) to the climate on this coast. The weather was rather stormy all day. Thermometer 67° at 8 A.M., 67° at 12 M., and 64° at 4 P.M.— mean, 66°. 7 P.M. The weather has moderated some. Wrote a long letter to father concerning our station etc. 10 P.M. it is a beautiful starlight night. Read late dates until 10.15 P.M.

Dec. 15, 1863. My fever patient, Thompson, allowed this morning that he was "commencing to lay in ballast so as to equalize his craft," by which he means to imply that he is improving finely with a hearty appetite. I ordered him to continue his tonic mixture. Boy Hoyt will be fit for duty in the morning. He continues the quinine mixture, or, as he calls it, "damn bitter stuff," in same doses as last report.

Whilst perusing Northern papers, I came across the account of the ceremonies at the dedication of the great national soldiers' cemetery at Gettysburg, Pa., on the 16th [19th] of November, 1863, on which occasion a dedication speech by the President of the U.S., an oration by the Hon. Edward Everett, and a presentation of a standard and speech by Gov. [Horatio] Seymour of New York were delivered. . . . . [The President's speech was quoted in full.]

The weather was pleasant all day—thermometer 49° Fahr. at 8 A.M., 68° at 12 M., and 64° at 4 P.M.—mean, 60°. Had a lovely run on shore in company with Paymaster Murray. Our caterer was on shore superintending the butchering of a porker, which he intends to serve us up for dinner tomorrow. Wrote a long letter to sister Beckie P. Cutler in answer to hers of the 17th of November.

Dec. 16, 1863. The fighting contraband, or at least he who used to be a slave, Austin Burroughs, was released from confinement this morning. So also was the seaman who had refused to obey orders on the 9th inst., Charles Burns.

George Thompson—is improving rapidly—continue tonic mixture. Alexander Kenny's hand—looks splendid this morning—dress the sore with resin cerate. Boy Hoyt—complained of headache this morning—order him ol. ricini ℥ i.

Wrote a short note to [First] Lieut. William Cornelius of the U.S. Army. His station is Washington, D. C., being attached to the Invalid Corps.

[The Invalid Corps (renamed Veteran Reserve Corps in March, 1864), consisting of personnel no longer fit for active field duty, was organized by authorization of General Orders 105, dated April 28, 1863. General Orders 212, dated July 9, 1863, stipulated two classes or battalions, the members of the first doing guard duty and of the second serving as cooks, nurses, clerks, orderlies, and so forth and as guards at hospitals, offices, storehouses, supply depots, and other public buildings. Rank, pay, and allowances corresponded to those in the Infantry. By the end of October 17,764 enlisted men and 491 officers were enrolled.]

Finished the letter to brother Frank that I commenced on the 2nd inst., enclosing fifteen dollars to pay for the ale that he sent me, which cost $7.50, and for another ½ bbl. of ale at same price, $7.50, or, as stated, $15 in all. I hope he may receive it all correct. I also sent the cask to his address, requesting B. Frank Boyer, Esq., to collect the price of the cask from the brewer and give me credit for the same, providing the cask arrives safe by express.

I forgot to note down Lieutenant Cornelius' address; . . . it is Lieut. William H. Cornelius, Headquarters 75th Company, 2nd Battalion, Invalid Corps, United States General Hospital Desmarres [corner of Fourteenth Street and Massachusetts Avenue], Washington, District of Columbia.   . . .

1 P.M. Commences to rain. Our caterer had a splendid barbecue served up for dinner today. All hands in the mess done justice to said porker. The thermometer at 8 A.M. was 58° Fahr., at 12 M. 60°, and at 4 P.M. 57°—mean, 58°.

Dec. 17, 1863. At 11.30 A.M. Captain Moses and Paymaster Murray with an armed boat's crew . . . in the gig and Master's Mate

Wright and the three refugees (viz., Frank G. Turner, John Turner, and Richard Benz) with an armed boat's crew . . . in the first cutter left for Sapelo Sound to communicate with the *Lodona* and remain on board of her until the arrival of the U.S. supply steamer *Massachusetts*. Said supply steamer is due tomorrow, the 18th inst. The captain had the mail in charge. I sent per mail the following letters: viz., one to B. F. Boyer, . . . enclosing the sum of $15; one to father; one to sister Beckie; and one to Surgeon Meckley of the *Lodona*, enclosing requisition and two blank receipts on Dr. Hutchins of the *Massachusetts* for medical stores. I also sent Dr. Meckley some reading matter of a light nature.

The following patients reported themselves at 8 A.M.: George Gray, a gentleman rope hauler of color, reported himself sick, complaining of "misery all over"—I ordered him antimonii et potassae tartras gr. i, ipecacuanha pulveris grs xx; M, as an emetic so as to empty his stomach; George Thompson, who is to continue his tonic mixture; Alexander Kenny, whose hand required the application of cerate simplex. Boy Hoyt returns to duty this morning.

There has been quite a stiff breeze blowing all day. The thermometer was 65° Fahr. at 8 A.M., and 68° at 4 P.M.—average 68°. Strong symptoms of rain. Weather rather hazy. Rather lonesome all day. We miss the captain and paymaster. Messrs. Childs, Flood, and myself had several games of dominoes this evening.

Dec. 18, 1863. A stiff northwestern blowing—cold as Christmas. All hands on deck are sailing around in fine style so as to keep warm. Slow crafts are played out!

We are living sumptuously on salt horse and hard-tack. Will live better when the boats return from Sapelo Sound with stores. Also expect to have plenty of reading matter by that time.

Landsman Gray—took a dose of oleum ricini, say ℥ i—also to have an expectorant mixture this afternoon—says he feels better—shouldn't wonder. Thompson—is hurrying along finely. Kenny—continue the cerate simplex—his hand looks well. Does not want to come in contact with any darky's teeth again; says he "has enough of said sport." . . .

3 P.M. Continues to blow, and blows hard at that. The thermometer was 45° Fahr. at 8 A.M., 50° at 12 M., and 50° at 4 P.M.— average, 48°. The above mercurial scale shows quite a change in the weather since yesterday. A difference of 20° Fahr. is quite an item. I don't fancy this cold spell—would prefer warmer weather. Think

I should like to live in a warm country; don't care about going North as long as the cold weather lasts. Have an idea that the powers that be will cause the old *Fernandina* to remain at this anchorage for some time to come. Am tired of this craft; would prefer a steamer.

3 P.M. All hands to quarters. 3.10 P.M. The guns' crews are exercising the heavy guns—in short, are having a mock action. They were exercising at the broadside guns. Messrs. Childs, Flood, and the doctor played several games of muggins.

Dec. 19, 1863. Weather not quite as stormy as yesterday but somewhat colder. My case of influenza, Gray, is improving—continue using an expectorant mixture. George Thompson, who is recovering from a severe attack of fever, is coming on finely—he is taking the following mixture: $\textrm{R}$ quiniae sulphas grs viii, acid sulph. aromat. gtts xl, tinct zingiber gtts xl, aquae f. ʒ viii; M; Sig. Tablespoonful three times a day as a tonic. Kenny's hand looks nicely this morning—continue the cerate simplex application. Michael Spain, berth deck cook, complained of a stiff neck—$\textrm{R}$ ol. ricini ʒ i, and apply volatile liniment to the muscles of his neck—able to do duty. Boatswain's Mate William Ryan complained of aches and pains—$\textrm{R}$ ol. ricini ʒ i and plenty of exercise. Landsman Holliday, a colored gentleman rope hauler, complained of having a sore finger—lanced and apply cerate resinae—able to do duty. Quartermaster James Johnson, blessed with another sore hand—lanced and applied lini cataplasm—able to do duty. I also ordered him pil. cath. comp. no iv, his bowels being somewhat constipated. Ellis Scarlet, 3rd-class boy, who was discharged from the sick list on the 3rd inst. after having been treated for what I then considered urticaria, comes to me again, complaining of said disease in a more aggravated form. I am now better able to form a diagnosis. I consider it, from the appearance of said eruption, a severe case of psora for the simple reasons that it is located in the vicinity of the wrists, upon the back of the hands, and between the fingers; that the vesicles are as a general thing distinct, acuminate, and filled with a transparent viscid liquid; and the itching properties of said eruption at night, when the parts are heated by the warmth of the bed clothing. I ordered him pil. cath. comp. no iv so as to open his bowels, forbid him animal food, restrict him to a farinaceous diet; external ablutions by means of soap and water, and apply today a lotion consisting of the following ingredients: viz., ℞ ammoniae carbonas, plumbi acetas āā ℨ ss., aquae f. ℥iv; M; Sig. A cloth saturated with said lotion to be kept applied to the parts so as to cleanse it thoroughly. I will order him sulphur ointment in the morning; at least I think I shall. I had quite a corps of sick to attend to today; will cause some of them to skedaddle on Monday morning next.

4 P.M. Weather not quite as cold as this morning. The thermometer was 38° Fahr. at 8 A.M., 49° at 12 M., and 45° at 4 P.M.—average, 44°. Dined on stewed chickens today; had bread pudding as a dessert—quite a change since yesterday, for then we dined on salt horse and beans, with no dessert. Don't fancy the salt junk and hard-tack diet; would prefer fresh beef and vegetables. . . .

Dec. 20, 1863. Cold! Cold!! Cold!!! Regular winter weather! Overcoats, heavy boots, and scarfs are in great demand. My case of psora, Ellis Scarlet, is about the same—order him the following ointment: viz., ℞ sulphur ℨ i, potassae nitras grs xx, adeps ℥ i; M. George Gray—influenza—is improving—continue same treatment. Alexander Kenny—continue application of cerate simplex to his hand—will return to duty in a day or two. Thompson—says he is happy—will go to duty in the morning. Johnson's sore hand turns out to be a case of furunculus—apply lini cataplasm—still keeps his quartermaster's watch. Spain's neck not as stiff as last reported—continue external application—not on the list. Holliday did not report himself for treatment this morning. I understand he does not fancy my pocket case of instruments, especially the thumb lancets.

Boatswain's Mate Ryan reported himself as follows: "Good morning, Doctor." "Good morning, Ryan. How are you this morning?" "Well, Sir, it affords me great pleasure to be able to report myself in the best possible condition, Sir." "I am glad to hear that you feel well again." "Thanks are due you, Doctor, for your skill in curing me so quickly of my aches and pains. Hoping you may live a long and happy life, I'll bid you good morning and proceed on deck so as to be able for active service whenever called upon." Here Ryan leaves for the deck. Said Ryan is rather fond of hearing himself use high-flowing language.

Huzza! Huzza!! Huzza!!! The long-looked-for steamer *Massachusetts* is reported in the offing. All hands in good humor. 2.15 P.M. *Fernandina's* launch called away. . . . At 2.30 P.M. the launch left the side of the ship . . . bound for Sapelo Sound, there to communicate with the U.S. steamer *Lodona* per orders etc. Weather not quite as cold as this morning. The thermometer was 31° Fahr. at 4 A.M., 32° at 8 A.M., 40° at 12 M., and 45° at 4 P.M.— average, 37°. 3 P.M. the *Massachusetts* and the blockading vessel stationed in Ossabaw Sound are communicating by means of small boats off Ossabaw Buoy. . . .

7 P.M. It is a beautiful moonlight night. At 3 o'clock this morning a light was reported in the offing. Upon examination it proved to be the morning star. So much for an optical delusion [illusion]. One of our master's mates was guilty of the following pun: viz., "At 3 A.M. a light was seen out to sea. Called the head sailor, who pronounced it to be the supply steamer *Venus.*" Not bad for a tar!

Dec. 21, 1863. Hip! hip!! hip!!! hurrah!!!! Give three cheers with a will all around! Let joy be unconfined, and on with the dance! Another mail has come. The launch and first cutter have returned with stores and a mail. I received quite a budget of mail matter. I received a letter from father, dated November 30, in which he informed me that all were well and in good spirits at home, also announcing the birth of a daughter in brother Frank's family, at same time telling me of his reappointment for another three years. Received a long and sarcastic letter from brother T. J. . . . , dated Nov. 27, in answer to mine dated Nov. 12, and a short but sweet letter from Miss Carlisle, dated Nov. 30, in answer to mine dated Oct. 8. Father sent me the Reading "Gazette," date 28th, and the Philadelphia "[Sunday] Transcript" [a weekly, begun in 1856], dated Nov. 29th. The following numbers of the "Medical and Surgical Reporter" came to hand today: viz., Oct. 3, 10, 17, 24, 31; Nov. 7, 14, 21, 28. We received late dates up to the 12th inst., in which we saw the President's annual message and the reports of the cabinet officers. The one of most interest to us was the Hon. Secretary of the Navy's report. His ideas as regards the Volunteer Corps meets with our hearty co-operation, applause, or sanction; the increase of our wages 25 per cent is a very essential necessity; so also is the offer of bounties to seamen. In short, Old Gideon has done his duty well and acquitted himself nobly. Long may he live to sport his grey head and heavy spectacles. I hope Congress may vote favorably on said propositions. By so doing, Jack will give an extra hitch to his trousers, roll his tobacco quid from one cheek to another or take a new quid, and go to work in right good earnest and with a hearty will for his Uncle Sam.

[In his report dated December 7, 1863, Secretary Welles mentioned "the important service rendered by volunteer officers, and the courage and skill displayed by them, as also their adaptation to the profession" and suggested promotion of "those who have served long and faithfully, and by their conduct, zeal and ability merit it"; proposed that since "the enhanced prices in every department of business, and even in the necessaries of life, operate with peculiar hardship on many who are in the government service," Congress consider an advance in pay of twenty-five per cent, to continue a year after the close of the war; and brought up the question of unsettled bounties for the destruction of enemy vessels (to be divided among officers and crew in the same way as prize money, as provided by Act of Congress dated July 17, 1862), asking for provision for payment.]

At 3 P.M. the captain and paymaster returned in the gig, both rather cold, tired, and hungry. The paymaster handed me a receipt of medical stores that the surgeon of the *Massachusetts* sent me per requisition dated Dec. 16. I received medical stores to the amount of $12.71 today, consisting as follows: acid. citric., acid. sulph. arom., acid. tartaric., aether. nitric spts., alcohol, ammoniae liq., capsici tinct., ferri chlo. tinct., magnesii sulphas, ol. menthae pip., ol. ricini, pil. cath. comp., potassae bitart., soda bicarb., whiskey, paper cap, paper letter. Asst. Surgeon [Thomas N.] Penrose appears to be the surgeon of the *Massachusetts* instead of Hutchins, the former surgeon [resigned June 24, 1863].

We received news today that the U.S.S. *Huron*, stationed at Doboy Sound (our old station last cruise), had captured a Rebel prize, loaded with 300 odd bales of cotton, a few days ago. Rather pleasant for the *Huron* boys.

[The Confederate steamer *Chatham*, an old Savannah River boat, bound from Darien, Georgia, for Nassau, New Providence, with a cargo of "299 bales of cotton and a quantity of tobacco and resin," was discovered attempting to run the blockade off Doboy Sound in the very early morning of December 16. After a chase, in the course of which ten shots were fired at her, she was boarded and taken possession of by the captain of the *Huron*, Lieutenant Commander George A. Stevens. She was subsequently turned over for service in the South Atlantic Blockading Squadron.]

Ensign Flood with an armed boat's crew left the ship at 7 P.M. in the 2nd cutter for the purpose of keeping picket watch between us and Ossabaw Island in vicinity of the Florida passage. Our idea is to try and capture a schooner loaded with cotton that has been making preparations for some time and that intends to run the blockade. Our informants were three refugees—viz., Messrs. Turners and Benz. I hope we may be lucky enough to capture said prize. It is rather a cold business to do picket duty in an open boat at night, but such being the fortunes of war, we have no right to complain. The crew were in the best of humor when they left the side of the ship. I sincerely hope they may have a happy night of it.

The weather today was not as cold as yesterday. The thermometer was 40° Fahr. at 8 A.M., 49° at 12 M., and 49° at 4 P.M.—average, 46°.

In my report of sick for Dec. 21, 1863, I reported the following cases: viz., Ellis Scarlet—psora—about the same—order ablutions with soap and warm water—apply sulphur ointment—confine him to sick bay; Alexander Kenny—continue the simple cerate application; George Thompson, who had quite a long spell of sickness, was discharged today, in the best of humor, to duty; George Gray was discharged to duty; Johnson—dress his boil with resin cerate —continues to do duty as quartermaster.

Bo't some killikinick from Ensign Flood, 2½ lbs. at 60/100 dolls. per lb., I having come to the conclusion to take up my pipe again.

Dec. 22, 1863. The weather was "a kinder cold" this morning. Ensign Flood and party returned on board, both cold and sleepy, at 7 A.M. Of course they were allowed their hammocks, and in less than no time they were fast asleep.

I found my case of scabies rather sore. He has scratched his skin all raw to such an extent as to cause me to remit the sulphur ointment and apply, after performing ablutions per means of soap and warm water, oleum olivae—℞ sulphur ℥ ss. three times a day. Alexander Kenny—continue the same treatment. Two outdoor patients—viz., Johnson, who has a large boil on his wrist—is improving —continue resin cerate; and Richard Costar, quarter gunner, who has a sore tongue and mouth—is taking the following: ℞ ferri chloridi tinct. gtts vii, aquae f. ℥ i; M; Sig. Three times day, and use the following gargle four or five times a day: ℞ potassae chloras grs xxiv; aquae f. ℥ ii; M; Sig. Use as directed.

The weather becoming warmer. The thermometer was 47° Fahr.

at 8 A.M., 56° at 12 M., and 59° at 4 P.M. average, 54°. 5 P.M. dressed
boy Scarlet's arms and hands with an emollient poultice of slippery
elm so as to remove the scabs, dirt, etc., intending using an alkaline
treatment in the morning. He appears to be suffering some; does
not fancy his complaint. Was told by some of the boys that he had
the seven years' itch. Poor d—l —he believed them; consequently
felt rather bad, but felt easier after I told him to the contrary. At
same time told him to cheer up and take it patiently.

The picket boat is under the control of Act. Master's Mate
George Newlin. They left the ship at 8 P.M. May they have a
pleasant night of it.

William Scott at 8 P.M. complained of nausea etc. In order to relieve his stomach, I ordered him an emetic consisting of tartar
emetic gr i and ipecac grs xx, which had the desired effect.

Dec. 23, 1863. The day set in beautifully—every prospect of a
splendid day. All hands in good spirits. Mr. Newlin and party, who
were on picket duty last night, returned at 7 A.M., all tired and
sleepy. Their hammocks were allowed them, and they were not
slow to enter them.

Alexander Kenny, who had been on the list since the 11th inst.
suffering from the effects of a wound caused by the teeth of our
fighting darky, Austin Burroughs, on the 9th inst., or the day that
he (Burroughs) pitched roughshod into the said Kenny, was discharged to duty this morning. He still continues the application of
cerate simplex to his hand. Boy Scarlet, who is the only one reported sick today in my daily report of sick, appears to be somewhat better. There is a slight improvement in his case. Shall
continue the application of oleum olivae; at same time keep the
parts clean with soap and water.

Wrote a long letter to Miss Carrie Carlisle, enclosing a small
note to her sister Amanda. The weather was lovely all day. The
thermometer was 45° Fahr. at 8 A.M., 60° at 12 M., and 57° at 4 P.M.
—average, 54°. Quarter Gunner Richard Costar is drilling the boys
on the beach. They have the drum and a set of colors. The way
they handle the small arms is not slow. The picket boat is under the
control of Acting Master's Mate John Wright. They (the party)
left the ship at 7 P.M. 9 P.M. blowing quite a gale.

Dec. 24, 1863. Cold! Stormy! and Windy! Mr. Wright and party,
who have had rather a rough night of it, returned at 7 A.M. blue,

cold, and shivering. Brave boys—they were entitled to their hammocks and received them.

Scarlet—there is no change in his case—continue ablutions and oleum olivae externally and sulphur and potassae bitartras internally. The boys are busy preparing for a grand Christmas dinner tomorrow, which, from all accounts, is going to be a splendid affair. I hope they may have a big time, for they, the sons of Mars and Neptune, deserve it.   . . .

This has been a cold, blusterly day. Thermometer was 38° Fahr. at 8 A.M., 44° at 12 M., and 43° at 4 P.M.; average—42°. At 7 P.M. a light was reported by the officer of the deck, bearing W.N.W. (west northwest). The picket boat was under the command of Acting Ensign William H. Thomas. They (the party) left the ship at 7 P.M. The boys will spend rather a cold Christmas Eve and night. At same time they will be engaged in a good cause.

The president and vice president of the *Fernandina* Social Club sent Captain Moses and the following members of the wardroom— viz., C. C. Childs, S. P. Boyer, T. N. Murray, Christ. Flood, and Wm. H. Thomas—written invitations to the Christmas dinner given by the *Fernandina* Social Club on the 25th of Dec. The following is the copy of the invitation sent to the wardroom members: viz.,

> U.S. Barque *Fernandina*
> St. Catharine's Sound

Gents—

The pleasure of your company is respectfully solicited to participate in the "Christmas dinner" given by the *Fernandina* Social Club tomorrow, Dec. 25, 1863, at 2 o'clock P.M.

> Respectfully Your
> Obdt. Servts.
> Thos. O'Neil, President
> R. W. Costar, Vice President

To C. C. Childs, S. P. Boyer, T. N. Murray,
Christ. Flood, Wm. H. Thomas.

The following is a copy of my letter of acceptance:

> U.S. Barque *Fernandina*
> St. Catharine's Sound, Ga.
> Wardroom, Dec. 24, 1863.

Gents:—

In times like these, that try men's souls, it behooves every good lover of liberty to participate in all social gatherings whose purposes are to sustain the righteous cause of freedom; therefore I accept with the greatest of pleasure your kind invitation inviting me to be present at the Christmas dinner given by *Fernandina's* Social Club. That you all may have a happy and social time is the wish of

Yours truly etc.

Samuel P. Boyer,

A.A. Surgeon, U.S.N.

To Messrs. O'Neil and Costar,
   President and Vice President
   Fernandina Social Club.

Christmas Day, Dec. 25, 1863. The day from all prospects is going to be a splendid one, only a little cool. Divine service at 9 A.M., Paymaster Murray officiating as chaplain. All hands were present except the picket guard, who returned at 7 A.M. rather cold and stiff.

Scarlet, my psora patient, is about the same—continue treatment. The diagnosis in this case was erroneous. It is a beautiful case of impetigo.

A Peep on the Berth Deck, Christmas Day, 1863:

Sancho Panza, Don Quixote's squire, was said to have exclaimed, "Blessed is the man that invented good Christmas dinners!" Now, they who are surrounded with all the luxuries of life, with whom a good dinner is of daily occurrence, who were never known to sit down to a Christmas, Thanksgiving, New Year's, or Easter dinner without feasting on roast turkeys etc. and topping off with a glass of sherry, port, or claret, may think it rather a foolish expression of mine; but were they compelled to leave their cosy firesides and enter either the Merchant Marine or naval service of their country, where salt junk and hard-tack prevail to a greater extent than fresh beef, soft-tack, etc., where good dinners are of rare occurrence (at same time I am ready to acknowledge that Uncle Sam's sailors are the best-fed seamen on the globe), where roast turkey does not grow on every bush or is to be had by a mere nod of the head, where such beverages as sherry, port, or claret are only known as things that were —then, and only then, would they see the force of my exclamation. But enough of this, or else the landlubbers will begin to think that my object is to give vent to my spleen against the powers that be, whereas, on the contrary, I have the greatest respect for them and would be the last man to complain of my lot when, as in this case, uncalled for.

Were they (the landsmen) enabled to have had themselves transported on board of the gallant and saucy man-of-war U. S. barque *Fernandina* on Christmas Day, 1863, they would of seen a sight which would of reminded them of auld lang syne. I mean the sumptuous feast to which the hardy and brave crew of this craft sat down.

Ere I enter into a description of the contents of said table etc., I deem it proper and pat to state how the gallant rope haulers of this craft got up said Christmas dinner. The first step was the posting up of a notice on the berth deck announcing a meeting of all hands to assemble in the vicinity of the yeoman's headquarters, which are in the forward part of the ship on said berth deck, as matters of interest were going to be discussed. The meeting was held and attended by the whole crew. They appeared to have had a lively time of it. The result of said meeting was the posting up of a second notice on the bulletin board of the berth deck, announcing a Christmas dinner (the permission to have said dinner having been asked and granted by our worthy and obliging captain), inviting all those who wished to participate therein to step up to the yeoman's office, sign their names to a list, and deposit a certain sum of money in the hands of said yeoman. In a short time they (the boys) netted the snug sum of two hundred and fifteen dollars. As soon as said sum was raised, a third notice was posted on the bulletin board of the berth deck, calling a meeting of all hands to assemble in the vicinity of the gunner's headquarters on said berth deck for the purpose of electing officers etc. Said meeting was held, attended by all the crew, when the following officers were unanimously elected: viz., president—Thomas O'Neil; vice president— Richard W. Costar; secretary—Daniel B. Reilly; treasurer—Francis Mc-Guire; committee of arrangements—William Price (chairman), Michael Spain, John Carey, James Barron, Jeremiah Riordan, Mathew Motta, William Pfander. They were going to elect a toastmaster, but, having nothing stronger than coffee and orangeade to drink, they concluded that it were a waste of time to elect one.

On the 20th inst. the committee of arrangements, assisted by our worthy and well-beloved "ten-per-cent" [paymaster], communicated with the U. S. steamer *Massachusetts* and purchased the necessary articles of food for said feast. To the credit of said committee, aided and assisted by our paymaster, be it said that their purchases suited the interested parties to such an extent that an extra meeting was called for the purpose of passing a vote of thanks thanking said committee etc. etc.

The boys were busy two or three days prior to the 25th preparing for said banquet, our obliging executive officer having granted them time and permission so to do. A table 40 feet long and 3 feet wide had to be constructed; benches prepared; wreaths of orange, live oak, pine, cedar, boxwood, and hemlock branches; tablecloth sewed and finished off; swinging mottoes painted on canvas; the best frocks, pantaloons, neckties, tarpaulins, boots, and shoes put in shipshape order; one party sent in search of fish and another after a cargo of bivalves. The ship's cook (for we boast of but one good cook, and Antonio De Cruiz is his name; we consider the rest of our cooks a sample of the quaint saying amongst shell-backs [old sailors] referred to when they make use of the expression "The Lord sends victuals, and the devil sends cooks") was busy preparing the pastry, the turkeys, and the vegetables. In short, nothing was seen, heard, or talked of except the preparation for, of, and about the Christmas dinner for the last three days.

Thus, having given a short account of how said banquet was got under way, I'll now descend the after hatchway and commence my peeping. I find said hatchway beautifully decorated with cedar and boxwood branches. After landing on the berth deck and facing the starboard side, I saw a curtain formed of the American ensign, looped up in the centre, over which was placed the following in large letters: "Sailors' Rights." Upon drawing said curtain aside, I was astonished to find myself confronted by a gallant son of Neptune with a drawn cutlass in his hand, the point of which was presented toward my breast, as if to say, "Enter if you dare." I need hardly say that I threw back my body, shuddering like an aspen leaf, and did not attempt to make another effort to enter until called upon by some of the obliging, polite, and enterprising managers of said festival, who assured me that there was neither goat to ride or greasy pole to climb (for I have heard of fellows being taken in by those secret societies and frightened half to death, and I am not fool enough to try to see the elephant). So as a matter of course I very politely accepted their kind verbal invitation and entered the antechamber where the fellow with the confounded sword stood, and therein I saw muskets stacked with drum and fife underneath, cutlasses displayed in all manner of style. In short, all the paraphernalia of war was displayed in said antechamber.

Well! after taking a good look at the room and an extra one at the saucy imp who had the audacity to frighten me fairly out of my senses, so as to know him in case I should happen to meet Mr. Swordman in some other part of the "consarn," I left said room and entered the banquet hall. Time—2 o'clock P.M. And lights burning? Aye, verily indeed! For, in the language of some of the boys, "Do you think we intend doing things half? Nary time! We're bound to have our dinner *a la* Astor House!"

Now let me assure the reader that what I saw on said berth deck would of put some of our Northern banquets quite in the shade. The first thing my eyes landed upon, of course, was the table, groaning underneath the good things of life, for, notwithstanding the hard times, we poor mortals here below are slaves to our stomachs and really think more of the *inner* than of the *outer* man. Oh, ye Gods! what a feast! How juicy that old gobbler does look, surrounded by fifteen other smaller turkeys, in the centre of the table! The fried, baked, and boiled fish look delicious. The stewed, fried, broiled, and raw bivalves look rather tempting! Those stewed tomatoes alongside the turkeys remind me of the days of the "Merry Monarch." How nicely the sweet and Irish potatoes are prepared —the fried, mashed, boiled, and baked ones fairly made my mouth water. Tempting baskets of oranges here and there placed on the table. The pastry, consisting of fresh- and dried-apple pies; sweet-potato tarts; pumpkin pies and custards; cakes, fruit and plain; plum, apple, and orange puddings, was splendid. Almonds, raisins, peanuts, and shellbarks were to be seen by the pounds on various parts of the table. In short, there was no end to the many good things of life. It was just such a feast as Jack Falstaff would of fancied, only lacking his favorite beverage, sack.

After having taken a good long and earnest look at the table and contents, my eyes lit upon the following mottoes etc., posted along the starboard side of said deck: viz., "God and our Country," "We honor our name," "Sailors' Rights," "F.S.C." [*Fernandina's* Social Club]—entwined with garlands of evergreen. The Stars and Stripes were displayed beautifully. The Union Jack appeared surrounding the beautifully constructed bayonet chandelier, which was suspended over the centre of the table. Twenty-eight bayonets; ribbons red, white, and blue; tissue paper; cedar, orange, and boxwood branches; and three finely carved hoops were required to prepare said chandelier, and it was done in such a style as none but sailors could divine its nature. Fine wreaths and orange branches full of fruit, besides any amount of tasty ornaments, decorated the ceiling and sides of the berth deck. I must not forget to mention that the Russian ensign and American eagle were placed in close fellowship at the head of the table—i.e., the American eagle soaring alongside the Russian flag, with the following words underneath: "God and our Country" (the boys all having a peculiar inkling after the Russian bear). I was hardly in the room ere I was met by the polite chairman of the committee of arrangements, offered a seat, and handed the following bill of fare:

Bill of Fare

Roast Beef	Fried Oysters	Fried Fish	Sweet Potatoes
Roast Turkey	Raw Oysters	Baked Fish	Irish Potatoes
Boiled Ham	Stewed Oysters	Boiled Fish	Tomatoes

Broiled Chicken	Broiled Curlew	Roast Pig
Stewed Chicken	Broiled Ducks	Roast Raccoon
Roast Chicken	Broiled Sand Pedes	Roast Rabbits

Green Corn

Plum Pudding	Apple Pie	Plain Cake
Apple Pudding	Mince Pie	Fruit Cake
Orange Pudding	Pumpkin Pie	Sponge Cake

Pineapple Cheese

Coffee	and	Orangeade
Apples	Peanuts	Raisins	Oranges
Almonds	Shellbarks	Currants	Dates

I read it and reread it—pinched myself so as to be certain that I was not dreaming, for I could hardly believe my own eyes that what I really saw was the naked truth. Nevertheless, it was so, and, being an invited guest, I had no cause to complain. (By the by, don't some of my fellow reporters envy my position?)

"Halloo! What's all the fuss about?" "What next is coming?" By George, there goes the drum and fife, and here comes the "sawbones," "nipcheese," and in fact all the officers except the captain (who sent a letter stating why and wherefore he could not be present), and there they sit down at the head of the table. The martial music ceases, and the honorable president, Thomas O'Neil, rises in his seat at the head of the table and delivers the "inaugural speech," which on account of its length and this lengthy article I will have to omit; therefore suffice it to say that it was rich, spicy, and appropriate for the occasion. Three cheers and the tiger for the hon. president were given with a will, after which all hands went to work to satisfy the inner man—and the way Jack ate was not slow. The cloth being removed, toasts, sentiments, etc. followed next. I will here quote a few of the many toasts that were drank, using water and coffee as the beverages:

1—"The President of the United States." Surgeon Boyer responded to said toast in a short but pithy speech.

2—"The Secretaries of the Army and Navy." Responded to by Francis McGuire, singing "Columbia, the Gem of the Ocean."

3—"Rear Admiral John A. Dahlgren." Paymaster Murray responded in a neat speech.

4—"Rear Admiral Samuel F. du Pont, one of Nature's noblemen." Responded to by Dr. Boyer, making a few appropriate remarks.

5—"Our obliging and worthy captain." Thomas O'Neil responded by singing "The Red, White and Blue."

6—"Here's to our vessel, a jolly little barque,
Whose guns are well shotted and always true to the mark."
Daniel B. Reilly responded in a spicy speech to said toast.

7—"Here's to the flag we sail under—
The glorious Stars and Stripes.
Victorious in many a naval fight,
God grant that it may long wave on high,
For the emblem it is taken from is torn from the sky."

All hands responded to said toast by singing "The Star-Spangled Banner."

8—"The day we celebrate." Responded to by a short speech from the executive officer, C. C. Childs.

9—"Here's to the fair sex, the guiding stars of our destinies." All hands responded by singing "The Girl I Left Behind Me."

"Paddy's Wedding" and a host of other witty songs were sung by the best-natured, best-humored, and greatest joker in the ship, one Jeremiah Riordan by name. Our quarter gunner, Richard W. Costar, sang *"Vive la America"* in fine style. The following-named parties sang several very appropriate songs: viz., Messrs. Thomas and Wright; Seamen Donaldson, Price, Ryan, Hughes, Spain, Close, and a host of others whose names have slipped my memory. In short, joy appeared unconfined. To have seen Jack after the feast laying back with pipe in his mouth and express his feelings requires an abler pen than mine to do the subject justice.

In conclusion I must say that the only thing wanted to make said festival a banquet of the good old style was the presence of the fair daughters of America. At same time I doubt whether any ship's company in the whole naval service spent a happier or a Merrier Christmas Day.

"Sigma"

Samuel P. Boyer

I intend sending said account to the editors and proprietors of the New York "Sunday Mercury" [noted for its fiction, humor, and illustrations], requesting them to publish it as a special favor.

The members of the wardroom mess had roast pig etc. for dinner, but all having invitations to the Christmas dinner given by the *Fernandina* Social Club, they did not appear to appreciate the caterer's dinner.

The picket boat was in charge of Ensign Flood and left the ship at 7 P.M. The thermometer was 40° Fahr. at 8 A.M., 50° at 12 M., and 49° at 4 P.M.—average, 46°. Wrote a letter to father in answer to his dated Nov. 30, 1863.

Dec. 26, 1863. The weather little warmer than yesterday. The thermometer was 48° Fahr. at 8 A.M., 53° at 12 M., and 53° at 4 P.M. —average 51°. Scott and Headley left at 8 A.M. in the dingy for Sapelo Sound.

Boy Scarlet's arm one mass of pus—keep clean by means of a weak solution of plumbi acetas.

Paid Caterer Wm. H. Thomas a mess bill of thirteen dollars and twenty-six cents. Credit ten dollars on account of refugees.

Mr. Newlin was in charge of picket boat tonight.

Dec. 27, 1863. Every prospect of a pleasant day. At 7 A.M. the picket party under the command of Actg. Master's Mate George Newlin returned on board. It took but a few moments to encase themselves in their blankets and hammocks. At 9.30 A.M. all hands to muster to attend divine service. After the reading of the services by Paymaster Murray our executive officer, C. C. Childs, read several naval orders. After all hands were piped down, the captain, paymaster, and Ensign Thomas went ashore to the plantation to attend the contrabands' church. Our paymaster read the Episcopal service for this day to them, which pleased them very much, it having been a long, long, long day since they had heard the Word of God read to them, and hoped to have the pleasure of hearing the same every Sabbath Day. The three officers were well pleased with their visit and intend to pay them other visits; in fact, all the officers hereafter will pay them visits to attend their prayer meetings.

Boy Scarlet—large quantities of pus and greenish-yellow scabs were washed from his arm this morning—I ordered the following lotion; ℞ plumbi acetas grs xvi, aquae O i; ℳ; Sig. Apply to the arms by means of perfectly saturated rags—℞ Fowler's solution gtts vi three times a day. The boy appears to be in better humor; says it does not pain him so much; slept well last night.

The thermometer was 58° Fahr. at 8 A.M., 66° at 12 M., and 62° at 4 P.M.—average, 62°.

The picket party tonight is in charge of Actg. Master's Mate John Wright. They left the ship at 6 P.M. At 11.55 P.M. all hands were called to quarters by the springing of the rattle in the hands of the executive officer, C. C. Childs, and at 11.58 P.M. all were reported ready for action, thus taking three minutes to answer the call. At 12 o'clock midnight all hands were piped down. 1 o'clock A.M. Commences to rain.

Dec. 28, 1863. Still continues raining. Boy Scarlet—the pustules are beginning to evacuate their contents and undergoing the scabbing process, whilst other scabs are falling off—continue the lead lotion.

At 8.30 A.M. Mr. Wright in charge of picket party returned on board. They (the boys) had rather a wet night of it.

Upon looking over my cash account, I find myself short one

50/100 dolls. I suppose it went for tobacco etc. The thermometer
was 60° Fahr. at 8 A.M. 60° at 12 M., and 60° at 4 P.M.—average,
60°. The picket boat left the ship at 6 P.M. in charge of Acting
Ensign William H. Thomas.

Three of the boys took it into their heads that it were sport to
play "old soger." I ordered ol ricini to one, sulphate magnesia to
the second; and the third had the pleasure of applying cold-water
rags to his knee all day. None of them appeared to relish their
prescriptions.

Dec. 29, 1863. A lovely morning. The sun is out in all his glory.
A sail reported out at sea, bound to the southward.

Boy Scarlet coming on finely—continue the plumbi acetas lotion
and ℞ Fowler's solution gtts iii three times a day. Thomas Mocklar,
landsman, had the misfortune to land on the berth deck on his
knee instead of his feet while descending the forward hatchway,
thereby causing a slight contusion—dress with arnica tinct and
cold water. George Parker, ordinary seaman, complaining of indigestion etc.—℞ pil. cath. comp no iv last night, and this morning
℞ antim. et potas. tart gr i, ipecacuanha pulv grs xx; M—it cleansed
his alimentary canal completely.

The thermometer was 50° Fahr. at 8 A.M., 53° at 12 M., and
60° at 4 P.M.—average, 54°. The Rebel pickets could be seen on the
mainland from our quarter deck by means of the marine glasses.
The picket boat under the command of Ensign Thomas arrived
at 7 A.M. on board. The picket party that left the ship at 6 P.M.
was under the command of Ensign Flood. I hope they may have a
pleasant time of it. Nothing of any importance worthy of note
transpired today. Read "Asmodeus; or, the D—l on Two Sticks"
[by Alain René Le Sage, translated by Joseph Thomas; London: J.
Thomas, 1841] today. It is quite an instructive book, showing the
ups and downs of life.

Dec. 30, 1863. Ensign Flood and his hardy crew, who were on
picket duty last night, returned on board 7 o'clock this morning, safe and sound.

Boy Scarlet—the pustules are scabbing and falling off gradually
—continue the lead lotion, and ℞ Fowler's solution gtts iv three
times a day. Mocklar—improving—apply tinct. sapon. camphorata.
Parker—ol tiglii to chest so as to cause pustulation, hence irritation, and order the following: ℞ antim. et potas. tart. grs ii, mor-

phiae sulphas grs i, sach. alba. 3 iv, magnesiae sulphas ʒ ii, aquae
f. ʒ xvi; M; Sig. Tablespoonful three times a day.

The weather rather pleasant. The thermometer was 55° Fahr. at
8 A.M., 55° at 12 M., and 55° at 4 P.M.—average, 55°.

At 8 A.M. a flag of truce was seen towards the mainland, looking
as though it was waved from a canoe. Acting Ensign William H.
Thomas was immediately sent with an armed boat's crew in the 2nd
cutter to ascertain the nature of said signal. At 9 A.M. we could, per
means of marine glasses, distinguish the character of said party, and
at 9.30 A.M. we sent the 1st cutter to the assistance of the 2nd
cutter, which appeared to be towing the canoe and its occupants.
At 10 A.M. the 1st and 2nd cutters, with the canoe in tow, arrived
alongside of the ship. Said canoe had a cargo of 13 Americans of
African descent on board. The captain and myself went to the
plantation in his gig. Whilst there I was called upon by the whole
village to prescribe for their aches and pains. Not having any
medication with me, I promised to bring them some in the afternoon, which satisfied them, after which I commenced to quiz the
newly arrived contrabands. The whole party were under the control of Cain, an escaped slave formerly belonging to William King
of McIntosh County, Ga. The following are the names, ages, and
former masters of said party.

William King's former slaves
Cain—aet. 27 yrs.—stout and robust-looking darky
Bella—aet. 22 yrs.—fat and lively nigger wench
Romeo—aet. 6 yrs.—Bella's child—fair complexion
Lizzie—aet. 25 yrs.—rather a homely-looking wench
Joseph— aet. 12 yrs.)
Sam— " 4 ")
Eve— " 2 ") children of Lizzie
Martha— " 5 months)
Widow Harris' former slaves
Sallie—aet. 32 yrs.—tall, strapping-looking wench
Fannie— aet. 11 yrs.)
Joseph— " 7 ")
Emma— " 2 ") children of Sallie
Ben— " 7 months)

Bella had a very sore thumb—a severe case of paronychia, which
I dressed by washing it carefully, cauterizing the false granulations,

and applying cerate simplex. I promised to visit her every day or two and dress her finger. I might here mention that it was in the afternoon when I dressed her finger, having at same time in my pockets the medicine that I promised the former, or old, citizens of the village, which consisted of ol. ricini for the old women and a solution of chloride of lime for one of Smart's children, who is suffering from the effects of ozaena.

The picket party was under the command of Acting Master's Mate George Newlin and left the ship at 6 P.M. They will have quite a pleasant time of it, at least as regards the temperature of the weather.

Dec. 31, 1863. The picket party last night had rather a wet night of it. It commenced to rain at 12 o'clock and continued for some time. They returned on board at 7 A.M.

I dispatched my steward off to the plantation this morning, there to apply a Spanish fly blister to the lumbar region of Smart's back, dress Bella's sore finger, and deliver to Old Cudgel's wife a bottle of the following mixture: ℞ quiniae sulphas grs xvi, acid tannic. grs. iii, antim. et. potas. tart. grs iii, morphiae sulphas grs i, sach. alba. ℨ ii, magnes. sulphas ℥ ii, aquae f. ℥ xii; ℳ; Sig. Tablespoonful three times a day. Boy Scarlet—improving—continue application of lead lotion—℞ liq. potassae et. arsenitis gtts v three times a day. Mocklar—the sprain and contusion caused by his falling from the spar to the berth deck caused slight synovitis of the knee joint—apply a Spanish fly blister to side of knee joint—℞ antim. et potas. tart grs 1 ss., morphiae sulphas gr ss., sach. alba. ℨ i, magnesae sulphas ℥ i, aquae f. ℥ vi; ℳ; Sig. Tablespoonful three times a day.

The weather was lovely all day. The thermometer was 59° Fahr. at 8 A.M., 68° at 12 M., and 64° at 4 P.M.—average, 64°. The picket party tonight is under the command of Actg. Master's Mate John Wright. The party left the ship at 6 P.M. We were blessed with quite a squall at 7.30 P.M. Commenced to rain at 8 P.M.

Ere many hours Old Eighteen Hundred and Sixty-Three will be numbered amongst the things that were; another year will then have passed by. One year ago tonight the good old ship *Fernandina* lay at anchor in the harbor of Port Royal, S. C. Little did I think at that time that I would be the medical officer of the said man-of-war one year from that time. I sincerely hope that one year hence I

may be on board of another man-of-war, for I am sick and tired of
this old craft. I have an idea that she ought to be laid on the shelf
—in other words, go out of commission—and all hands be transferred to a steamer.

Scott and Headley returned at 1 P.M., having several bushels of
sweet potatoes and a small quantity of game in their possession.
Commenced the dissection of several duck heads. Nothing else
worthy of note transpired today. Adieu, Old Eighteen Hundred and
Sixty-Three! And welcome, Eighteen Hundred and Sixty-Four!

14

"A Prize at Last!"

St. Catharine's Sound, Ga., Jan. 1, 1864. . . . . There is
rather a stiff breeze blowing all day. The weather is rather cool.
The thermometer was 48° Fahr. at 8 A.M., 42° at 12 M., and 40° at
4 P.M.—average, 43°.

Ellis Scarlet—impetigo—continues to improve—order him the
following lotion: ℞ ammonae carb. plumbi acetas āā ʒ ss., aquae
f. ʒ xvi; M; Sig. Use as directed, and ℞ Fowler's solution gtts vi
three times a day. Thomas Mocklar—synovitis—the blister drew
finely—dress surface with cerate simplex, and continue the antimonial and saline mixture. George Gray, lds., N. C.—abrasio on
the right ankle—said abrasion having commenced suppurating ere
he applied for treatment, I was therefore compelled to apply lini
cataplasm. George Parker, ord. sea., aet. 22, France—bronchitis
acuta—cause friction and counterirritation by means of ol. tiglii,
and order expectorant mixture.

Wrote to the Hon. Secretary of the Navy, applying for examination as assistant surgeon in the United States Navy. Wrote a
letter to the chief of the Bureau of Medicine and Surgery concerning my application for the position of assistant surgeon in the
U.S. Navy, asking him to present my application to the Hon.
Secretary of the Navy. Wrote to the Hon. S[ydenham] E[lnathan]
Ancona, [Democratic] member of Congress from Berks County,

Penna. [1861-1867], asking him to hand my application . . . and my letter . . . to Surgeon William Whelan . . . at same time endorsing said application.

The members of the wardroom mess furnished, or rather served up, a sumptuous feast for the contrabands on the Waldburg plantation, numbering 35 head, our caterer, William H. Thomas, officiating as host. They had a good old time and appeared to enjoy their New Year's dinner. The head members of the *Fernandina* Social Club favored the officers and all hands with a minstrel performance between the hours of 6 and 8 P.M. Taking all in all, they done right well. Our caterer served us up a good dinner today, consisting of roast pig etc., topping off with a glass of sherry and claret.

I made out my 4th quarterly report of sick for 1863. During the quarter I had 196 sick days, 32 diseases, medical expenses $29.06, daily average no. of patients 2 12/92, daily average cost per man $0.14 162/196. The following were the diseases: viz., intermittens—1; erysipelas—1; urticaria—1; stomatitis—1; dyspepsia—1; constipation—2; dysenteria acuta—1; bronchitis acuta—1; catarrhus—1; influenza—2; pleuritis—1; impetigo—1; herpes—1; eczema—1; furunculus—3; abscessus—1; odontalgia—2; synovitis—1; paronychia—2; gonorrhoea—1; orchitis—1; scrofula—1; otorrhoea—1; vulnus contusum—1; abrasio—1. Also made a return of property on hand, receipts and expenditures for medicines, etc.—in other words, made out my yearly return (form C) for January 1, 1864. I enclosed my 4th quarterly report of sick with duplicate copies of requisitions, receipts, and vouchers for medical stores during said quarter, also my yearly return of medicines (form C), with a letter in an envelope directed to Fleet Surgeon William Johnson [who had replaced Surgeon Clymer in August, 1863], South Atlantic Blockading Squadron, off Charleston, S.C.

The picket party tonight is under the command of Acting Ensign William H. Thomas. They will have rather a stormy night of it.

I commence the New Year with a credit on the paymaster's books of four hundred and odd dollars and have but a debt of twenty-five dollars—i.e., a note of that amount, with interest—to pay in order to see me out of debt. Not a bad beginning. I entered the service in 1862 with a debt of seven hundred and odd dollars on my shoulders, which I have paid with the exception of the above note for twenty-five dollars and interest.

A Happy New Year to all.

Jan. 2, 1864. This really is a cold day. The picket party had rather a cool night of it. They returned on board at 6 A.M. On account of the cold weather we omitted the washing of decks this morning. The thermometer was 24° Fahr. at 8 A.M., 36° at 12 M., and 40° at 4 P.M.—average, 33°. Paid my colored patients at the plantation a visit and found them all improving. Aunt Sukie, Young Cudgel's wife, is getting rid of her chills and fever slowly. Bella's finger looks well; a large slough came away today—continue applying nitrate of silver to cut down the false granulations and dress with cerate simplex. Old Smart's blister drew finely; he feels better. Boy Scarlet is coming along finely—continued the lotion and ℞ Fowler's solution gtts. vii three times a day. Parker—improving—continue expectorant mixture. Mocklar's knee feels better—continue cerate simplex, and continue taking the antimonial and saline mixture. Gray's ankle is about the same—apply tinct. iodine and a lini cataplasm.

Paid Billy, the barber, a barber bill of one dollar and a half, which settles my account up to the 1st of January, 1864. The picket party tonight is under the command of Acting Ensign Christopher Flood. They'll have rather a cold night of it.

Jan. 3, 1864. Boy Scarlet—continue the lotion of ammonia carb. and plumbi acetas—℞ liq. potassae et arsenitis gtts viii three times a day. Lds. Mocklar—continue same plan of treatment. Ord. Sea., Parker—continue same plan of treatment. Lds. Gray—dress ankle with cerate resinae. Weather not quite as cold as yesterday. The thermometer was 36° Fahr. at 8 A.M., 44° at 12 M., and 49° at 4 P.M.—average, 43°.

All hands to muster and attended divine service at 9 A.M., Paymaster Murray officiating as chaplain. Paymaster Murray and Executive Officer Childs attended the colored prayer meeting on shore after our services were over. Francis Conefry, my steward, went ashore this morning and dressed Bella's thumb. I ordered him to apply the following by means of a rag: viz., ℞ acid tannic grs xxxii, cupri sulphas grs iii, opii tinct. f. ℥ iv, aquae f. ℥ xvi; M; Sig. Use as directed.

1 P.M. A sail reported in the offing, headed to the northward. 1.15 P.M. Quartermaster Scott and Landsman Headley left in the dingy for Sapelo Sound, there to communicate with the *Lodona*. I sent a short epistle to the doctor begging for some muslin, being very much in need of said article.

The picket party under the command of Ensign Flood returned on board at 6 A.M. Ensign Flood reported firing of heavy guns last night at 10 o'clock in the direction of Sapelo Sound—also that it was rather cool last night in an open boat. The picket party tonight is under the command of Actg. Master's Mate George Newlin. May they have a pleasant night of it and accomplish the object of said picket duty.

Dined on duck, curlew, and sand pedes today. At 3.30 P.M. a steamer reported going into Ossabaw Sound. Hope it may be a mail steamer. Commenced to rain at 8 P.M. and continued doing so all the night. This was rather a dull day—nothing to do, see, or read. I understand that we have but three days' more bread on hand; so unless we receive supplies soon, we will be compelled to live on half rations, which will be rather tough.

Jan. 4, 1864. Still continues to rain. James Allen, carpenter's mate, aet. 23, New York, came to me this morning for treatment. He has a large furunculus on left wrist and two abrasions on left hand—apply lini cataplasm. Scarlet—continue lotion— ℞ liq. potassae et arsenitis gtts vii three times a day. Mocklar—improving— continue the antimonial and saline mixture. Parker—improving— continue expectorants. Gray—continue resin cerate.

Scott and Headley returned from Sapelo Sound at 3 P.M. Surgeon Meckley sent me a yard of muslin—also answered my epistle dated the 3rd inst. . . . Wrote a letter to Hon. Charles R[ollin] Buckalew, United States senator [Democratic, from Bloomsburg, Pennsylvania, 1863-1869] . . . , asking him to advocate my claims for the Regular Navy.

The weather was cloudy all day. The thermometer was 46° Fahr. at 8 A.M., 50° at 12 M., and 52° at 4 P.M.—average, 49°. The picket party tonight is under the command of Mr. Wright. Rainy all night.

Jan. 5, 1864. It has been rather foggy this morning. Ordinary Seaman Parker was discharged this morning to duty. William Pfander, lds.—vulnus incisum—apply two stiches, dress with cerate simplex, and keep part at rest—said wound is in the palm of left hand. Mocklar—improving—continue same treatment. Allen— about the same—continue lini cataplasm. Gray's ankle looks better —continue resin cerate. Scarlet—improving rapidly—continue lotion— ℞ Fowler's solution gtts vi three times a day. My steward

went on shore to superintend the medical affairs there. Returned at
5 P.M.

At 2 P.M. a boat from the U.S.S. *Lodona* arrived in charge of
Acting Ensign Le Grand B. Brigham, having [Coast] Pilot [Rufus
B. K.] Murphy and his (Murphy's) wife and mother-in-law on
board. Mr. Brigham left the feminines on St. Catharine's Island, at
the Waldburg plantation, there to remain until we will be enabled
to send Murphy and them off to Ossabaw Sound on board of the
U.S.S. *Water Witch*. Mr. Brigham intends returning to Sapelo
Sound in the morning. He appears to be a nice sort of a young sea
dog.

The weather continued rather foggy and rainy all day. The thermometer was 51° Fahr. at 8 A.M., 55° at 12 M., and 56° at 4 P.M.—
average, 54°. Acting Ensign Wm. H. Thomas was in charge of the
picket party tonight. I am afraid that they will have rather a wet
night of it.

Jan. 6, 1864. There still continues to be a fog pervading the
atmosphere. Would not be sorry to see it clear up. At 9 A.M. the
Lodona's cutter left in charge of Acting Ensign Le Grand B. Brigham, having Ordinary Seaman Edward Worcester on board, his
time having expired consequently he intends going North in the
Massachusetts. I sent along with Mr. Brigham to Dr. Meckley
"Memoirs of a Physician," by Dumas. We also sent our mail matter
so that if by accident any steamer should happen to call at Sapelo
Sound it would have a chance of going North. I sent per him my 4th
quarterly report of sick for 1863, with duplicate and vouchers for
medical stores, my annual return (form C), and requisition for
medical stores with two blank receipts, directed to Fleet Surgeon,
South Atlantic Blockading Squadron—also the following letters:
Hon. Gideon Welles, . . . Surgeon Wm. Whelan, . . . Honorable
Chas. R. Buckalew, . . . Hon. S. E. Ancona, . . . Hon. T. J. Boyer,
. . . Messrs. Cauldwell and Whitney (New York), Michael K. Boyer,
and Miss Carrie Carlisle.

My sick—viz., Pfander, Allen, Mocklar, Scarlet, and Gray—are
all improving. Ordered them to continue the same treatment as
last reported, except Scarlet, who is to take only five drops of
Fowler's solution three times a day instead of six drops.

We had a splendid mess of fish (sea bass) for breakfast today.
Boatswain's Mate Mowatt caught them yesterday. He also brought

quite a cargo of oysters with him. Bought a pair of blankets from the paymaster's stores at five dollars and forty cents per pair; also a pair of new merino undershirts from Ensign Flood for two dollars. Wrote a letter to father as regards some cologne, bay rum, cigars, etc. that I want him to purchase and send me per the *Massachusetts.*

The weather was foggy and rainy all day. The thermometer was 52° Fahr. at 8 A.M., 55° at 12 M., and 52° at 4 P.M.—average, 53°. Acting Ensign Christopher Flood has charge of the picket party tonight. Rather a wet night for them. Acting Master's Mate John Wright and Gunner's Mate Francis McGuire left the ship at 8 A.M. on a hunting excursion on St. Catharine's Island. They returned at 7 P.M. having a noble bullock in their possession.

Jan. 7, 1864. It has been raining all last night and still continues to rain hard this morning. Gray—apply lini cataplasm to thumb. Scarlet—℞ Fowler's solution gtts iv three times a day. Allen—apply resin cerate. Pfander—continue simple cerate. Mocklar—apply volatile liniment, and ℞ tartar emetic grain ½, morphine grain ½, sugar drachm 2, salts ounces 2, water ounces 16; ℳ; Dose—a tablespoonful three times a day. Richard W. Costar, quarter gunner, aet. 25, N.Y.—sore and inflamed tongue, glossitis of long standing—keep bowels regular and apply the following per means of a camel's-hair pencil night and morning to tongue: ℞ sodae boras ʒ ii, mel f. ℥ ii; ℳ; Sig. As directed.

At 11.15 Cain and Sam, two contrabands who made their appearance on board of this craft some time ago, came alongside in a canoe and reported that they had left nine colored brethren and sisters on the first hammock (sand bank) from the ship. At 11.30 A.M. our captain sent the 1st cutter after them to bring them on board. I might here mention that Cain and Sam left the ship in a canoe a few days ago for the purpose of rescuing their relatives etc. from bondage; hence, the expedition proving successful, they arrived on board as stated above. The following is the name, age, sex, etc. of the newly arrived contrabands, as well as their former master's or mistress' name. (The 1st cutter returned with said darkies at 12 M.)

Bank Jones' "Nigs," or Ex-Slaves
from Laurel View, near Sunbury, Ga.[54]

Grace, aet. 45
Children of Grace—Judy, Elizabeth, Phoebe, Victoria, James

Grace's grandchildren—Arphee, Virginia, Clarissa, Edward
Grace's son-in-law—Charley

As soon as they landed on the spar deck of this craft, they each received a hot cup of coffee etc., after which they were sent up to the plantation so as to have an opportunity of warming themselves, drying their clothing, and prepare their quarters.

Nothing but rain! rain!! rain!!! to be seen, except it be a slight fog. The thermometer at 8 A.M. was 42° Fahr., at 12 M. 43°, and at 4 P.M. 44°—average, 43°. Commenced to read [Henry] Gray's "Anatomy, Descriptive and Surgical" [London, 1858, and subsequent editions, both English and American]. I intend to spend an hour or so daily in reading medical works so as to refresh my memory and keep myself from becoming rusty. In fact, I have nothing else to read, being entirely out of light literature. We all expect to receive plenty of mail matter upon the arrival of the *Massachusetts,* she being due the 10th instant.

Acting Master's Mate George Newlin is in charge of the picket party tonight. Poor fellows—they'll have both a wet and cold night of it.

Jan. 8, 1864. Ceased raining. Weather rather cool. Pfander—wound healing up slowly—continue simple cerate dressing. Allen—boil looks better, swelling reduced—apply tinct. iodine and dress with cerate resinae. Mocklar—swelling reduced, joint less painful, stiffness partially gone—continue same treatment. Scarlet—the scabs have nearly all fallen off—skin beginning to assume its natural appearance—itching all gone—sleeps well—appetite good —continue ammoniae and plumbi lotion, and ℞ liq. potassae arsenitis gtts iii three times a day. Gray—dress thumb with lini cataplasm—looks better. Mowatt—continue flaxseed poultice (not on list). Costar—his tongue appears to look better this morning—continue same treatment. William Donaldson, sea.—furunculus on wrist—apply lini cataplasm. Geo. Thompson—complains of rheumatic pains in his inferior extremities—order ol. terebinthinae externally and guaiac. tinct. aromat., f ℥ i, three times a day internally.

Wrote a letter to Surgeon Meckley of the *Lodona* in answer to his date of the 3rd ultimo [inst]. At 1 P.M. vessel reported in the offing sailing southward. Said to look like the *Oleander.* Hope it may prove to be the *Oleander* with mail and grub for us.

Weather has been cold, windy, and cloudy all day. The thermometer was 40° Fahr. at 8 A.M., 41° at 12 M., and 42° at 4 P.M.—average, 41°. The picket party tonight is under the command of Acting Master's Mate John Wright.

Jan. 9, 1864. Cold and windy. At 8 A.M. Captain Moses and Paymaster Murray left in the captain's gig for Sapelo Sound, there to communicate with the *Lodona* and remain on board of her until the U.S.S. *Massachusetts* comes, she being due on the 10th inst., and obtain our mail and stores.

Pfander—continue the same treatment. Gray—continue application of flaxseed poultice. Mowatt—place him on list today—continue warm application. Donaldson—lanced boil and apply resin cerate. Thompson—says he feels better—continue same treatment. Mocklar—improving slowly—same treatment. Headley, B.F.—paronychia—lanced and applied lini cataplasm. Allen—two more boils made their appearance on left arm and wrist—continue flaxseed poultice—℞ pil. cath. comp. no iv. Scarlet—is in a fair way of being relieved entirely of his loathsome disease—continue external application—℞ liq. potassae arsenitis gtts ii three times a day.

The thermometer was 34° Fahr. at 8 A.M., 38° at 12 M., and 36° at 4 P.M.—average, 36°. At 8 P.M. a rocket sent up by the U.S.S. *Lodona* was seen to explode in the air by us. We immediately sent one up in return. The object was to see whether or no the two ships could communicate together by means of rockets in case either one wished to telegraph the arrival of a mail etc. I must say that both worked admirably. The vessels in Ossabaw and Doboy won't know what in thunder was up. The picket party tonight is under the command of Acting Ensign Wm. Thomas. It is a beautiful starlight evening, only rather cool.

Jan. 10, 1864. A cold but beautiful Sabbath morning. My sick list is increasing daily. I reported the following this morning: George Briggs—complains of a sore throat—apply cold-water rag to throat and cover with a dry cloth—℞ vinegar, water, salt, and cayenne pepper gargle—order him to use it four or five times a day; Pfander—hand healing up slowly—continue same treatment; Mowatt—lanced finger and reapplied lini cataplasm; Allen—lanced boils and reapplied tinct iodine and lini cataplasm; Thompson—continues to improve—same plan of treatment; Headley—finger looks better—℞ cerate resinae; Mocklar—continue treatment; Scarlet—℞ liq. potassae arsenitis gtt i three times a day; Gray—discharged to duty.

All hands were called to muster at 9 A.M. Roll called and then piped down. The thermometer was 35° Fahr. at 8 A.M., 42° at 12 M., and 44° at 4 P.M.—average, 40°. My steward went on shore today in order to dress the sore back of Old Smart and Bella's finger. He returned at 1 P.M. and reported both improving. At same time told me that a little colored child had one of its legs burned, or burnt, severely. Not having any limewater prepared, I sent him on shore again at 2 P.M. with some ol. ricini and muslin, which he is to apply until tomorrow, when I intend to send an ointment composed of creta prep., ol. lini, and suet. The principal object aimed at in those cases of burns is to exclude the external irritation caused by the air, thereby promoting the healing process.

The members of the wardroom mess dined sumptuously on roast pig today. Not a bad dose to swallow. The picket party tonight is under the command of Acting Ensign Christopher Flood. I hope they may have the pleasure of capturing a prize. There is no doubt but that they all will catch a cold, even if nothing else. We are all anxiously awaiting the arrival of the captain and party from Sapelo Sound with the mail so that we can hear from the dear ones at home. After all, there is no place like "Home, Sweet Home."

4.30 P.M. Slight sprinkling of hail. . . . 6.30 P.M. More hail. Every prospect of a bad, damp night. The officer of the deck, Mr. Wright, reports a light N.W. by W.

Read part of Sterne's "Sentimental Journey through France and Italy." I consider his "Tristram Shandy" splendid. His "Koran" is not bad. In short, I am a great admirer of Sterne's writings.

[The collected works of Laurence Sterne were available in a number of editions, including one in five volumes printed in 1804-1805 by John Wyeth in Harrisburg, volumes one and two containing *The Life and Opinions of Tristram Shandy, Gentleman,* and volume four *A Sentimental Journey through France and Italy* and *The Koran: or, The Life, Character and Sentiments of Tria Juncta in Uno. A Political Romance.*]

Jan. 11, 1864. Weather rather pleasant. Not very cold. My sick list not as large as last reported. I have discharged to duty boy Scarlet and Landsmen Headley and Mocklar and admitted the following patients: Joseph McShane, 1st-class boy, aet. 17, N.Y.—

paronychia—lanced and applied lini cataplasm; Briggs—feels better—continue same plan of treatment; Pfander—improving slowly—continue same treatment; Thompson—improving slowly—continue same treatment; Allen—improving slowly—continue same treatment; Mowatt—finger feels easier—continue lini cataplasm. The thermometer was 42° Fahr. at 8 A.M., 41° at 12 M., and 40° at 4 P.M.—average, 41°. 7.15 P.M. commences to rain.

Took a nap this afternoon of three hours. Upon turning out, found our steward, who had been after oysters, had a splendid cargo of bivalves, of which I ordered a dozen or so and had quite a hearty lunch. The picket party tonight is under the command of Acting Master's Mate George Newlin. May the Lord of Lords and King of Kings guide, bless, and protect not only the picket party but the whole ship's company.

It rained more or less all night. At same time the weather became warmer. Read until 11.30 P.M. Gray's "Anatomy." The "sawbones" of this craft turned in for the night at 12 o'clock midnight.

Jan. 12, 1864. Weather cloudy—slight symptoms of rain. The following cases reported themselves for treatment: Chas. Mowatt—dress finger with flaxseed poultice; Jas. Allen—coming along finely—apply lini cataplasm; Wm. Pfander—continues to improve—same treatment; Geo. Briggs—improving slowly—same treatment continued; Jos. McShane—℞ lini cataplasm; Geo. Thompson—continue tinct guaiac. arom. ℥ i three times a day—apply externally ol. terebinthinae.

At 1 P.M. the gig with Paymaster Murray returned from Sapelo Sound, having in charge plenty of nothing besides a few books which Captain Moses sent along and "The Diary of a Physician," by Dr. Warren [*Passages from the Diary of a Late Physician,* by Samuel Warren, D.C.L., F.R.S.; published serially in *Blackwood's Magazine* 1830-1837; initial separate publication made in two volumes in 1832, followed by a number of editions, including one by William Blackwood and Sons, Edinburgh and London, preface dated 1858], which Dr. Meckley had the kindness to send me. Capt. Moses sent me a short note, which I will answer. The gig returns to Sapelo tomorrow. The thermometer was 52° Fahr. at 8 A.M., 52° at 12 M., and 52° at 4 P.M.—average, 52°.

Purchased a silk necktie and three skeins of silk from the paymaster's department for the sum of one dollar and twenty-two cents. Sent my steward up to the plantation to attend to the sick patients. He reports all in a fair way of recovery. Raining more or less all night. Placed Seaman James Simmons on the binnacle list tonight on account of a sore throat. Ordered him ipecacuanha et opii pulvs grs x internally and a turpentine rag externally.

The picket party tonight was under the command of Acting Master's Mate John Wright.

Jan. 13, 1864. Rain! Rain!! Rain!!! This will be a nasty, dirty, wet day. All hands have concluded to keep within doors today. I admitted James Simmons on the sick list today, affected with laryngitis. Order him a gargle composed of vinegar, salt, cayenne pepper, and water, and apply externally volatile liniment. The rest of my patients—viz., Briggs, McShane, Pfander, Thompson, Allen, and Mowatt—are all improving and will continue same treatment.

4 P.M. There is no apparent change in the weather—nothing but rain and fog to be seen all day. The thermometer was 51° Fahr. at 8 A.M., 51° at 12 M., and 51° at 4 P.M.—average, 51°. The picket party tonight will be in charge of Acting Ensign William H. Thomas.

Jan. 14, 1864. Weather foggy. Admitted Francis Grimes—boil, on sick list and discharged to duty George Briggs. The rest are all improving. The gig left for Sapelo Sound at 9 A.M. The thermometer was 53° Fahr. at 8 A.M., 60° at 12 M., and 64° at 4 P.M.—average, 59°. Wrote a letter to father regarding postage stamps. At 10 A.M. the fog left us and the sun came out in all his glory.

10.15 A.M. a steamer reported in the offing sailing southward, looking as though she were bound into Sapelo Sound. Hope she will communicate with the *Lodona* and leave a heavy mail and grub for all hands. We are all anxiously awaiting the arrival of the U.S. supply steamer *Massachusetts*. She certainly is due. We are becoming rather short on grub. Truly, verily indeed, this must be one of the jumping-off places. Here we have been for seven weeks without receiving news from home. Rather rough, I think.

8.30 P.M. This is a lovely moonlight and starlight night. Oh, how I would love to be promenading with some fair daughter of Eve by my side tonight in one of our Northern cities! It would be enough to make one feel as though he were transplanted to one of the seven heavens, with an angel pouring "lasses" (molasses) down one's throat. The picket party tonight is under the command of Acting Ensign Christopher Flood. They (the boys) have rather a pleasant night for their duty. Hope they may enjoy themselves.

I laid Gray's "Anatomy" aside today and commenced the perusing of "The Diary of a Physician," by Dr. Warren. Said diary is a splendid work, full of interesting, heart-rending, and instructive cases. The doctor was a great advocate of bloodletting. He opened a vein in almost every case. I hardly think that the eclectic school of practitioners would sanction his mode of treatment, for they are opposed to venesection, calomel, and tartar emetic, whereas we allopathics, like sensible physicians, use all three remedies. In short, everyone has his own peculiar ideas as regards the practice of medicine.

My steward was on shore this afternoon. He reports all the colored patients improving under their respective treatments.

Jan. 15, 1864. Weather lovely at 8 A.M. The following parties left the sick list this morning: viz., Thompson, McShane, Allen, and Pfander, consequently leaving but three names to adorn the binnacle list: viz., Grimes, Mowatt, and Simmons. The reasons for discharging McShane to duty, although his finger is far from being healed up, are that him and Austin Burroughs (our fighting contraband) pitched into each other roughshod this morning at 7 A.M.; consequently I concluded that a man who is well enough to fight is certainly able to do duty. Our executive officer placed both combatants on the black list, causing them to do extra duty. Thus ends the fight. Hope both may profit by their punishment.

1 P.M. Symptoms of an approaching storm. Weather cloudy and growing gradually colder. 1.30 P.M. A sail reported in the offing, Hope she may prove to be the *Massachusetts*. Time will tell. 2.30 P.M. She proves to be a monitor and is bound into Ossabaw Sound.

The thermometer was 59° Fahr. at 8 A.M., 63° at 12 M., and 56° at 4 P.M.—average, 59°. The picket party tonight will be commanded by Acting Master's Mate George Newlin. Joy be with them. At 4 P.M. it commenced raining. The picket party tonight will have rather a wet and cold night of it. 9 P.M. Continues to rain and growing colder. 10.30 P.M. Cleared up beautifully. The moon and stars are shining brightly.

Jan. 16, 1864. A cold but splendid day. Reported two cases sick this morning—viz., Mowatt and Simmons, both improving—and discharged to duty Grimes.

At 1 P.M. a sloop was discovered inland bearing by compass west northwest from the ship. Mr. Childs, the executive officer, immediately dispatched the following boats etc. to attempt either to capture or destroy her. The 1st cutter was manned by the following armed men: William Smith, coxswain; William Ryan, boatswain's mate; William Scott, quarter master; Richard W. Costar, quarter gunner; James Sullivan, seaman; Charles Burns, seaman; Miles Powers, ordinary seaman; Jeremiah Riordan, ordinary seaman; Augustus Rickards, seaman; Thomas Dowd, ordinary seaman; Mathew Motta, ordinary seaman; John Burns, landsman; Joseph Short, boy—13 men in all, commanded by Acting Ensign Christopher Flood. The 2nd cutter was manned by the following armed crew: John Carey, coxswain; Francis Grimes, landsman; John Lahey, ordinary seaman; Michael Spain, landsman; Cocheran, landsman; Alexander Kenny, seaman; Sheldon H. Hoyt, 1st class boy—7 men in all, commanded by Acting Master's Mate George Newlin. At 2.15 P.M. the Rebels run the sloop ashore. Our boats boarded her and took possession of her by hoisting to her main the glorious Stars and Stripes at 2.49 P.M., upon which the ship's company gave three hearty cheers. 3 P.M. Our boats have her in tow heading for the ship. 4 P.M. Mr. Wright and crew in 3rd cutter went to assist the other boats. 6 P.M. Mr. Wright has returned and reports that said sloop was loaded with 38 bales of cotton, 20 barrels of ol. turpentine [according to official records twenty-five barrels of spirits of turpentine], and 45 boxes of tobacco. Huzza! Huzza!! Huzza!!!

The *Fernandina* has captured a prize at last! She is worth about $40,000. 6.30 P.M. Mr. Newlin returned in the 2nd cutter with 4 men who were captured in said sloop. They say (that is, 2 of them) that they were passengers, having paid a passage (money) of $200 in gold. The other 2 men were the crew employed by the captain and pilot to run the vessel. The captain and pilot left last night in a boat for the mainland, after having her run aground by mistake, for fear that if they remained on board, they might be taken prisoner. Their object was to run out last night. As soon as the 4 remaining men saw our cutter approach, they let go their anchor and run up a white flag. They appear to be pleased at the idea of getting out of "Secessia." The captain, when he left, took the compass, papers, etc. with him.

The Rebel pickets stationed on the mainland ordered the sloop to make tracks for Sunbury, Ga., where the pickets could be ready to protect her in case we might try to capture her. As soon as she made sail, we discovered her—hence her capture. Bully for us! The *Fernandina* stock is up. The cargo was owned by a stock company in Savannah, her destination being Nassau, where she arrived (over the left) ["over the left shoulder," signifying that the reverse of what is said is meant]. Uncle Sam's bluejackets were rather too smart for them.

The prisoners' names are as follows: J. G. Cohen, John Feely (the two passengers) and George King and Charles Norman (the two crew of said sloop). Her captain's name was Doyle; pilot's name, Harding. The sloop's name was Anna [*Annie Thompson*]. . . . .

I need hardly mention that no picket party leaves the ship tonight, for we have caged the bird at last. All hands are in the best of humor. Well they might, for we all have done a good day's work. We'll receive in the course of time quite a snug sum of prize money. By George! I feel good. Hope we may capture another prize ere long. Ensign Flood remains, with an armed crew, on board of our prize as prize master. She is anchored under our guns. The prisoners say that each bale of cotton contained on an average 350 pounds, each box of tobacco 100 pounds. In short, the cargo is worth between $30,000 and $40,000. The craft herself is not of much account. The cotton is upland cotton, worth about 85 cents per pound. Turpentine is worth up North between $2 and $3 per gallon. Tobacco will bring about $0.70 or $0.80 per pound. So much for our first prize. . . . [The gross proceeds from the capture of the vessel were $14,847.96; costs and expenses, $1,639.50; amount left for distribution, $13,208.46.] . . .

11 P.M. A fine cool moonlight night. All hands turned in except the watch. Our prisoners are on the berth deck, fast asleep. Our gunner's mate and master-at-arms are acting as sentinels so as to be sure in case said prisoners should prove to be up to mischief. There's nothing like being cautious. Since we're right, we'll keep our eyes open.

Wrote a letter to father announcing to him the capturing of the *Anna* [*Annie*] *Thompson*.   . . . At 8 P.M. the officer of the deck reported a large fire on the mainland bearing by compass north from the ship. I suppose it was a signal fire of the Rebels. . . .

15

Last Days Among the Golden Isles of Guale

St. Catharine's Sound, Ga., Jan. 17, 1864. Every appearance of a splendid day. Discharged my two sick men from the sick list this morning—viz., Mowatt and Simmons. At 8.30 A.M. Paymaster Murray and Ensign Thomas with an armed crew left on the launch for Sapelo Sound, having in charge the prisoners, whom they intend to land on board the *Lodona.* From there I suppose they'll go North in the U.S.S. *Massachusetts* whenever she'll make her appearance, which I hope she will ere many hours.

At 9 A.M. a cutter from the *Water Witch,* stationed at Ossabaw Sound, Ga., in charge of Acting Master [William B.] Stoddard, having Pilot Murphy on board, arrived. They came after Murphy's family. Mr. Stoddard reports that some refugees who had escaped from Savannah came on board of the *Water Witch* having late Savannah papers in their possession in which was stated that Gillmore was shelling Charleston in right good earnest—that upwards of one hundred shell had been thrown into the heart of the "infernal hotbed of treason"; in short, that Charleston was about played out.

[Charleston, at the time under steady bombardment, withstood not only this siege but subsequent ones as well. On February 8, 1864, the Confederate congress thanked General Beauregard and his officers and men "for their gallant and successful defense" during "an attack scarcely paralleled in warfare."]

Hurrah for Uncle Sam's "Swamp Angels" [eight-inch two-hundred-pound Parrott guns mounted in a swamp by Union men during the siege].

The vessel that entered Ossabaw Sound on the 15th inst., which we thought was a monitor, appears to have been the tugboat *Oleander,* loaded with stores for all hands; hence we will receive our supplies in a short time.

5.45 P.M. The gig with the captain, paymaster, and our four

prisoners returned from Sapelo Sound. The launch, in charge of Mr. Thomas, returned shortly after. They had neither mail or grub on board, the *Massachusetts* having not as yet arrived—why and wherefore I cannot tell; some seem to think she is frozen up in the Delaware River.

At 1 P.M. all hands were called to muster. The weather was somewhat warmer than yesterday. The thermometer was 50° Fahr. at 8 A.M., 53° at 12 M., and 53° at 4 P.M.—average, 52°.

Jan. 18, 1864. Rain and fog. Commenced to rain at 1 A.M. Still continues so to do at 9 A.M. 1 P.M. Ceases to rain. 1.30 P.M. Heard a gun fired in the offing. 1.40 P.M. A steamer reported sailing into Ossabaw Sound; said to be the *Massachusetts.* At 1.50 P.M. the captain and paymaster left in the gig for Sapelo Sound. The thermometer was 58° Fahr. at 8 A.M., 51° at 12 M., and 56° at 4 P.M.—average, 55°.

At 9 A.M. Mr. Childs, our executive officer, and myself, per orders, caused our prisoners to open their carpetbags and clothes bags in our presence so as to see whether or no they had any documents etc., contraband goods of war, concealed in them. Nothing of any account was to be seen except tobacco and dirty clothing. 3.30 P.M. The *Massachusetts* left Ossabaw Sound. We fired one of our broadside guns so as to notify the *Lodona* of her arrival. 8 P.M. We sent up a rocket. George Briggs' and Jean Berghens' names were placed on binnacle list.

Jan. 19, 1864. Weather cold and stormy. 1.30 P.M. Mr. Wright left in the 1st cutter for Sapelo Sound. 2 P.M. A large three-masted steamer reported in the offing sailing to the northward. We are all anxiously looking for the return of the captain and paymaster from Sapelo Sound. The thermometer was 41° Fahr. at 8 A.M., 48° at 12 M., and 45° at 4 P.M.—average, 45°.

I had the misfortune to break my gold pen today, thereby depriving me of my daily companion; hence I am compelled, much to my chagrin, to take hold of a substitute in the form of a steel pen, after all not a bad substitute after one becomes accustomed to its use. I shall purchase a new gold pen as soon as I can, for I do not fancy either a quill or steel pen.

At 3 P.M. the captain and paymaster returned from Sapelo Sound. The *Massachusetts* has come at last. She bought rather a small mail. I received the "Raftsman's Journal" [a weekly paper (established in 1854) devoted to news and politics, published at Clearfield, Pennsylvania] and the "Berks County Press" [a weekly published at Reading, Pennsylvania, 1835-1865]. Miss Carlisle sent me the former, and brother Mike sent me the latter. I received by the *Massachusetts* a barrel of ale that brother Frank sent me per letter dated Dec. 16, 1863. The wardroom officers of this craft have sent in a petition, or letter, to the Hon. Secretary of the Navy showing why and wherefore the U.S.S. *Lodona* is not entitled to share in our prize captured the 16th inst., we understanding that they have sent in their claim. The captain, paymaster, and myself were busy until after 12 o'clock tonight preparing the documents etc. for said prize.

Jan. 20, 1864. The prize sloop *Annie Thompson* left this morning for Port Royal in charge of Acting Ensign Christopher Flood as prize master, the crew consisting of Austin Burroughs, Edward Worcester, and Ellis Scarlet. I hope she will arrive safe in the harbor of Port Royal.

Bought Ensign Flood's right, title, and interest in a box of sherry for the sum of five dollars and sixty cents. Lieut. William Cornelius, Invalid Corps, Washington, D.C., answered my letter dated Dec. 16, 1863. His letter was dated Jan. 7, 1864. I shall answer the same in a day or two. The weather was rather cool all day. The thermometer was 42° Fahr. at 8 A.M., 53° at 12 M., and 52° at 4 P.M. average, 49°.

Jan. 21, 1864. Weather pleasant. Reported the following cases sick this morning: Jean Berghens, sea.—erysipelas of face—℞ pil. cath. comp. no iii, and apply sol. argenti nitras to parts; John Collins, Michael Quinn, Wm. Donaldson, John Lahey, and Mathew Motta—influenza—℞ ol. ricini ℥ i, calomel grs vi; M; Miles Powers, o. sea.—furunculus—lanced and apply resin cerate; Wm. Halstad, lds., 25, England—ophthalmia—apply blister to temple— use the following collyrium: ℞ plumbi acetas, zinci sulphas āā grs ii, aquae f. ℥ i; M; Sig. Apply by means of a soft rag—order him some cathartic—keep in a dark room.

At 4.30 A.M. Mr. Wright left with an armed crew in the 1st cutter for Sapelo Sound in order to bring paymaster's stores to this ship which were left by the *Massachusetts* on board of the *Lodona.* Heavy guns were heard this forenoon in the direction of Ossabaw Sound. The weather continued pleasant all day. The thermometer was 45° Fahr. at 8 A.M., 55° at 12 M., and 55° at 4 P.M.,—average, 51°. At 5 P.M. Mr. Wright arrived with some stores from Sapelo Sound.

Jan. 22, 1864. My sick are all improving. Order Berghens tinct ferri chloridi gtts vii three times a day and the rest of the patients the antimonial and saline mixture. Discharged to duty Powers.

At 12.30 P.M. the *Oleander* made her appearance in the harbor, bringing us stores and a heavy mail. I received a letter from father dated Jan. 3rd in answer to mine of the 14th of Dec., '63, one dated Dec. 13 in answer to mine dated Nov. 23, one from brother Michael dated Jan. 5 in answer to mine dated Nov. 25, one from sister Beckie, enclosing a note from Aunt Lucy L. Boyer [Lucy Ludwig Boyer, wife of Jacob K. Boyer, brother of the diarist's father, residing in Oley, Pennsylvania], dated Jan. 4 in answer to my two last, and one from my nephew Alonzo H. Boyer [son of the diarist's brother David], a medical student attending lectures at the Jeff. Med. College, Phila., dated Nov. 30. The fleet surgeon sent me a circular regarding instructions etc. for medical officers of the U.S. Navy. Father sent me quite a budget of newspapers, for which he has my thanks. Brother Michael also favored me with late dates. Miss Kate Carlisle favored me with a note and several Clearfield County papers.

Our former executive officer, C. C. Childs, has received his detachment from this craft and is ordered to report for duty on board the U.S.S. *Marblehead*. [The *Marblehead* was sent North for repairs the same month as this entry. Acting Master Childs was given command of the *Acacia*, on the outer blockade, but was relieved from this command in April because of negligence in allowing a Confederate schooner to escape.] Acting Master [Richard B.] Arrants, formerly of the *Norwich*, comes to relieve him. Acting Master's Mate George Newlin received orders to report to Port Royal for examination as to his qualifications for the position of acting ensign in the Navy. My sincere wish is that he may succeed, for he is a damn fine fellow.

Bought a box of segars (cigars) from the wardroom steward of the *Oleander* for the sum of five dollars. The weather was lovely all day. The thermometer was 48° Fahr. at 8 A.M., 60° at 12 M., and 57° at 4 P.M.—average, 55°. Wrote a letter to sister Beckie in answer to her date of Jan. 4. Wrote a short letter to father in answer to his dates of Dec. 13 and Jan. 3. Wrote a letter to brother Michael in answer to his date of Jan. 5. Nothing else of any account transpired today.

6 P.M. Lewis Y. Close—colica—ordered him an emetic etc.

Jan. 23, 1864. The *Oleander* left this morning. Mr. Childs and Mr. Newlin are passengers on her. Thus one by one my fellow officers leave this ship for better vessels. Whose turn will come next remains yet to be seen. We are all anxious for a change. My sick are about the same. Discharged Lahey to duty. The weather was beautiful today. The thermometer was 49° Fahr. at 8 A.M., 57° at 12 M., and 60° at 4 P.M.—average, 55°. The two prisoners named Cohen and Feely who were taken prisoner, or captured, in the sloop *Annie Thompson* left in the *Oleander* for Port Royal.

Jan. 24, 1864. A beautiful Sabbath morning. My sick are improving. Discharged to duty Collins, Motta, Donaldson, and Quinn. 9 A.M. All hands attended divine service. Ensign Thomas read several orders after services. The weather continued pleasant all day. The thermometer was 52° Fahr. at 8 A.M., 59° at 12 M., and 67° at 4 P.M.—average, 59°. Wrote a letter to my nephew Alonzo H. Boyer in answer to his date of Nov. 30. At 12 o'clock midnight one of the *Lodona's* cutters, in charge of [Acting] Ensign [Nathan W.] Rathburn, arrived, having been out at sea, to speak the U.S.S. *Memphis,* said steamer being anchored at Ossabaw Bay, having relieved the U.S.S. *Water Witch.* All hands were called to quarters upon the approach of said *Lodona's* boat.

Jan. 25, 1864. The crew are busy watering ship. The *Lodona's* boat left at 8.30 A.M. for Sapelo Sound. Reported Halstad and Berghens sick—both improving. Discharged Close to duty. Heard several guns in the direction of Ossabaw Sound at 8 A.M.

[Suspected enemy activity as reported by picket boats led Commander Thomas H. Stevens of the ironclad *Patapsco,* stationed at Wassaw Sound, to make "an extended reconnoisance" up the Wilmington River. On January 26 the party routed out a number of Confederate Sharpshooters and captured a "very good boat." Four days later a cutter was sent to Ossabaw to investigate gunfire heard and a strange vessel seen. It was believed that the "mysterious movements" might be connected with possible erection by the enemy of new batteries along the Savannah and Wilmington Rivers. A combined naval and military movement against Savannah was at the time under consideration.[55]]

The weather was lovely. The thermometer was 50° Fahr. at 8 A.M., 61° at 12 M., and 67° at 4 P.M.—average, 59°. Bought a gold pen, no. 10, and holder for the snug sum of five dollars. Boatswain's Mate Chas. Mowatt and Landsman Benj. Headley, having left this morning in search of fish, returned at 7.30 P.M. with a large cargo of the finny tribe, enough for a "mess" for all hands, both fore and aft. They are both great disciples of the famous Izaak Walton. They have the thanks of the whole ship's company.

Nothing of any importance transpired during the night. Read Gray's anatomy of the arm and forearm—i.e., that part relating to the muscles and their action in cases of fracture of the bone.

Jan. 26, 1864. The crew still busy bringing water on board. My two patients—viz., Halstad and Berghens—are coming on finely; continue same plan of treatment. The weather today was more like a balmy day in May than a usually cold winter's day. The thermometer was 58° Fahr. at 8 A.M., 62° at 12 M., and 69° at 4 P.M. —average, 63°.

The captain, paymaster, and myself took quite a stroll on St. Catharine's Island today. Old Bob was our pilot or guide. We travelled across the island to what is called the East End, a distance of three miles. We had quite a pleasant time of it. Old Bob's dog caught a wild sow, which tickled Old Bob almost to death. In short, we had considerable sport and exercise.

Our fishermen—viz., Mowatt and party—returned at 6 P.M. with a splendid cargo of very large fish. The way all hands intend walking into fried, baked, and boiled fish will not be slow.

Jan. 27, 1864. Weather continues pleasant. The thermometer was 60° Fahrenheit at 8 A.M., 67° at 12 M., and 76° at 4 P.M.— average, 67°. My sick are improving rapidly. Nothing going on today, except it be that the boys are watering ship.

Jan. 28, 1864. Boys still watering ship. Reported Berghens, who is improving rapidly, and Jos. McShane—furunculus sick today. Discharged to duty Halstad. The weather was rather pleasant. The thermometer was 62° Fahr. at 8 A.M., 70° at 12 M., and 67° at 4 P.M.—average, 66°. Exchanged my trunk, which was too small for my purpose, for another one belonging to Mr. Arrants, giving him six dollars to boot. My trunk cost me in Portsmouth, N.H., between five and six dollars, and Mr. Arrants paid twelve dollars for his trunk in Philadelphia, Pa.—hence my paying him six dollars. We are both satisfied with our respective bargains. Mr. Arrants says that he knows whole families who are always satisfied.

Wrote a letter to Mr. Alfred Moses of Portsmouth, N.H. Mr. Moses is a brother of Captain Moses, a.m. commanding, U.S. barque *Fernandina.* 1.14 P.M. Heard the report of several guns S.S.E. from the ship. Some say they heard 8 guns, and other 12 guns. Some were louder than others. Very likely the shots were fired by the *Lodona* chasing a prize. If so, why, being in gunshot distance, we'll share in the prize. 7.30 P.M. A light reported in the offing. 7.40 P.M. Heard the singing of frogs on shore. The people up North say that the singing of frogs is the sign of the approach of spring, or warm weather. Hope it may prove so, for I am partial to warm weather.

Jan. 29, 1864. Boys busy supplying the ship with wood.   . . .

At 2.30 P.M. a boat from the *Lodona* in charge of Henry G. McKenna [McKennee], acting ensign, arrived via island passage. His object was to ascertain whether we had captured a prize, having seen the light in the offing last night that we saw, also heard the report of several heavy guns this morning. We heard the same guns, but they appeared to have been fired north from us. Poor fellows—they have their trouble for their pains. Said boat left again at 3 P.M. Better luck next time.

3.30 P.M. Ensign Thomas arrived on board. He left the ship at 9 A.M. on a hunt after ducks. When he left the side of the ship, he talked as though he was a going to bag all the game on St. Catharine's Island, but lo and behold! upon his return he had nothing but one insignificant blackbird in his bag. Whether he intends to eat it or not I cannot tell. Poor boy—he feels rather bad about it. Hope he may meet with better success next time.

James Cochran, lds., was placed on the black list for 8 days for insolence to his superior officer. My sick are improving. 8.30 P.M. heard the report of some heavy guns in the direction of Ossabaw. Shortly afterwards saw a light in same direction. What can it mean?

Jan. 30, 1864. At 1.30 A.M. the approach of a boat was announced by the crying out by the quartermaster of "Boat ahoy! What boat is that?"—answer being given that it was the *Lodona's* boat. It appears that upon the return of Mr. McKenna and party at 8.30 P.M. last night they (the officers of the *Lodona*) heard the report of two guns, also seen a rocket (the same, I suppose, that we heard and saw at 8.30 P.M. last night). Taking it for granted that we had a mail (a new term for the capturing of a prize), the captain of the *Lodona* dispatched another boat at 9.30 P.M. in charge of Acting Ensign [R.C.] McKenzie to ascertain the cause of the firing. I need hardly say that they had their labor for their pains. The boat left again for the *Lodona* at 8.30 A.M. Mr. McKenzie brought the captain dates of Jan. 23rd and 24th.

The *Lodona* boarded an Army steamer yesterday; obtained late dates—also ascertained the nature of the firing yesterday morning. It appears that the firing was at Hilton Head, S.C.

Discharged to duty Jean Berghens, and continue Jos. McShane upon the sick list. He is improving slowly. Wrote a letter to Mrs. Lucy L. Boyer in answer to her note enclosed in sister Beckie's last letter. Wrote a second answer to sister Beckie's letter of Jan. 4. Wrote a letter to father. The weather mild and springlike. The thermometer today was 60° at 8 A.M., 68° at 12 M., 68° at 4 P.M. Paid Caterer Ensign Thomas a mess bill of twenty-four dollars and thirty-one cents; credit seventeen dollars and sixty cents on account of refugees, prisoners, etc.

Jan. 31, 1864. This was a beautiful Sabbath Day. The thermometer was 67° Fahr.: 60° at 8 A.M., 73° at 12 M., and 68° at 4 P.M. All hands attended divine service at 9.30 A.M. After dinner at 1 P.M. the executive officer (Mr. Arrants), Paymaster Murray, and myself had ourselves landed on the beach at Squeedunk, or Pigtown, after which we started for the beach on the eastern part of the island via inland route. It took us no less than three hours to walk a distance of three miles. Our route lay through swamps, briars, palmettos, ditches, etc. After reaching the beach we walked along said beach about a mile, when we took a splendid road for the Waldburg plantation, where we arrived shortly afterwards. Found all the contrabands, with the exception of Aunt Nabbie, who is sick with influenza, in the best of humor. We remained there a short time, when we left again for the ship, taking a new route.

Old Cudgel told us to cut across a large cotton field, when we would strike a fence, where a large poplar tree would be seen, at which tree we would come into a fine road, which would lead us to the beach opposite the ship. We left in good spirits, thinking to reach the ship in a short time. We passed through the field to the fence, but nary poplar tree was to be seen. Still, seeing a road in the woods, we travelled on, when lo and behold! we run afoul of a large swamp; consequently we had to go about and make sail for the cotton field again. We travelled inside of the fence until we saw a large road. This road certainly must be the right one. We travelled on for about one-half hour, when we run afoul of another snag in the shape of a swamp. Another blunder—so we were compelled to travel through briars, palmettos, and over logs, tearing our clothing, scratching our hands and faces, and doing some tall ——. Every small path that we saw we certainly thought must be the right one; so on we go, or went, until we as a natural consequence (for the paths were nothing more or less than pig paths leading to water) run afoul of swamps and we had to retrace our steps and make other attempts.

Finally, after crossing one of the numerous swamps for which this island is noted, we reached the beach, about two miles from the ship. If ever three mortal beings felt good and relieved, we three did when we landed on said beach. We now made all sail for the ship, where we arrived at 5.45 P.M. fatigued, hungry, wet feet, and our clothing rather the worse for wear. After changing, or shifting, our clothes, we sat down to and ate a hearty supper. Our fellow officers laughed themselves nearly out of their senses when we related to them our cruise. Thus ends the great expedition of Messrs. Arrants, Murray, and Boyer. Taking all in all, we walked no less than 10 miles and had considerable sport after all.

I reported my sick case—viz., McShane—as improving this morning. The U.S.S. *Memphis* was plainly in sight today from our decks as she lay at her anchorage in the vicinity of Ossabaw Bay.

Feby. 1, 1864. Reported Joseph McShane—improving rapidly. Wrote a letter to Lieut. Cornelius, U.S. Army, in answer to his date of January 7. Sent some medicine to Aunt Nabbie and Ellsie and Old Joe, all contrabands living on the Waldburg plantation. Thermometer 66° Fahr.

Feby. 2, 1864. At 8 A.M. sent a boat, in charge of Ensign Thomas, out to speak the *Memphis*. We all sent our mail matter along so that in case the *Memphis* should happen to speak a passing vessel, the letters will leave for the North sooner than what they would were they to lay on board of this craft. 3 P.M. Mr. Thomas has returned. It appears that the *Memphis* had been relieved by the *Sonoma* and that the *Acacia* had relieved the *Sonoma;* hence Mr.

Thomas communicated with the latter vessel—i.e., the vessel at present blockading Ossabaw Sound, which is the *Acacia*. He obtained neither grub, news, nor mail.

Old Cudgel and Smart came on board today in search of grub. Poor Old Cudgel got seasick, upon which the captain told him that the cause of the vessel rolling was the men walking about the deck; hence the old contraband told the boys not to walk around, as though they would obey his orders. He said that he never would come on board again. Reported McShane sick. The thermometer was 60° Fahr. Weather rather pleasant.

Feby. 3, 1864. Quite a gale prevailing. Reported McShane sick. Bought 9 yards of blue flannel, $0.75 per yd., from the paymaster, paying him six 75/100 dollars for the same. Thermometer 60° Fahr.

Feby. 4, 1864. Weather pleasant. Thermometer 52° Fahr. Reported McShane sick. Large fires on mainland. Took a stroll on St. Catharine's Island. . . .

Feby. 6, 1864. Reported McShane fit to return to duty in the morning. Today he continues on the list—℞ resin cerate. Sent a pint bottle of antimonial and saline mixture to Old Aunt Sukie and one ounce of ol. ricini to Old Aunt Maria, both parties being sick, one complaining of a febrile affection and the other of constipation. Hope the medicine may do them some good. Think it will. Have considerable trouble with the contrabands. They are continually asking for medicine of some kind: one wants salts, another oil, and the third either pills, liniment, or camphor. ("Camfire" is what they call the last.)

The weather was rather lovely, the thermometer averaging 61° Fahr. in the shade.

Feby. 7, 1864. Cold Sabbath morning. Thermometer 43° Fahr. at 8 A.M., averaging 48° during the day. All hands attended the reading of divine services by Captain E. Moses. . . . Discharged to duty McShane—i.e., dropped his name from the sick list, still retaining him as an outdoor patient. 1.30 P.M. A sail reported in the offing heading southward. . . .

Feby. 9, 1864. Weather springlike. Thermometer 56° Fahr. Paid a visit to the Waldburg plantation. Supplied Aunts Nabbie and Sallie with some aperient medicine. Gave Aunt Sukie, Aunt Maria, Aunt Judy, Aunt Nabbie, and all the other aunts, whose names have slipt my memory, some tobacco, upon the receipt of which they all commenced to thank me etc. to such an extent as to cause me to skedaddle. In short, I made them feel good and happy.

The captain, Mr. Thomas, and Paymaster Murray with a crew of men are busy preparing ground for a garden. The season for planting is near at hand: the trees are commencing to bud, the green grass is shooting forth from the earth, and the very birds are chirping, heralding, as it were, the approach of warm weather. Whilst coming from shore in a boat this morning, we saw a large alligator in the water. From all accounts this is a great place for that kind of varmints. None to report sick.

Feby. 10, 1864. At 7 A.M. a skiff with three white men was discovered between us and the sea. The 1st cutter was immediately lowered, placed in charge of Ensign Thomas, and sent to the aid of said skiff. They proved to be refugees from Savannah, Ga., named as follows: viz., Peter Meyer, aet. 27, native of Germany, former occupation head clerk in a rum mill in Savannah, lived 4 years in Savannah and 2 years in New York City; John Rudolph Meyer, aet. 32, native of Germany, former occupation clerk in a clothing store—i.e., Jew slopshop [store carrying cheap ready-made clothes]—in Savannah, lived 10 years in Savannah and a few years in New York City; Thomas Hanson, aet. 28, native of Norway, occupation ship carpenter, lived in Savannah 4 years, New York City 6 years. He was employed by the Confederate Government to work at the building of the rams etc. On account of him being in the employ of said Government he was furnished the following pass, viz.:

Savh Feby 8th, 1864.

Pass Mr. Hanson to No. 1 1/2 Way Station A. & G. R.R. and return. Mr. Hanson is in our employment on Government work.

Kranson & Hawks

per G. F. Palm[56]

The said Hanson took advantage of said pass and made his escape out of the Confederacy, "Bully for him." The whole party appears to be glad that they have escaped. They are full of plenty of yarns as regards the condition of the Confederacy. Starvation etc. seems to be the order of the day. They are rather well clad. I obtained some Secesh money from them, also a marine, or opera, glass, or, as some style them, a "lorginette." Of course I paid them for the same; I paid five dollars for the glass, a thumb lancet, Secesh money, etc. They remain on board until a steamer arrives, when we will send them to Port Royal. I sold the glass afterwards for the sum of $5.50.

The weather was quite cool all day—thermometer 52° Fahr. in the shade. Paymaster Murray and myself made an attempt this afternoon to find an inland passage from Squeedunk (i.e., Pigtown) to the plantation. We finally succeeded after travelling through briars, palmettoes, and swamps and climbing over logs. As soon as we landed on the outer limits of the plantation, we found that we had but time enough to reach the ship by way of the beach; so on we started for the eastern beach, where we arrived in a short time. On our way I found a skull of a Secesh pig, which I brought along with me on board. We arrived on board at 6 P.M., tired and hungry, with wet feet and torn clothing. So much for our sport. The captain, who was at the Waldburg plantation this morning, reports the peach trees in blossom. Rather early, I think.

Our fishermen, Mowatt and Headley, have returned on board with a large cargo of fish, some of which will weigh 8 or 10 pounds. Large fires burning on the south end of St. Catharine's Island. Cause of said fire not known. None to report sick.

Feby. 11, 1864. Quite a cool breeze blowing. Thermometer 52° Fahr. Our new and efficient executive officer, R.B. Arrants, . . . issued the following "Weekly Routine" of duty for the crew: viz.,

Weekly Routine
Sunday
Morning—Wash decks, clean bright work, square yards, haul taut gear fore and aft. At 9 A.M. General muster. 7.30 P.M. Quarters for muster and clear battery.

Monday
Morning—Wash clothes, scrub decks, clean bright work, square yards, haul taut gear fore and aft. At 9.30 A.M. Exercise at general quarters. 7.30 P.M. Quarters for muster and clear battery.

Tuesday
Morning—Wash decks, clean bright work, square yards, haul taut gear fore and aft, general overhauling ship's riggin. 7.30 P.M. Quarters for muster and clear battery.

Wednesday
Morning—Wash decks, clean bright work, square yards, general drill with small arms and single sticks. 7:30 P.M. Muster and clear battery.

Thursday

Morning—Wash decks, clean bright work, square yards, haul taut gear fore and aft. 9 A.M. Fire quarters. 7.30 P.M. Quarters for muster and clear battery.

Friday

Morning—Wash clothes, clean decks, clean bright work, square yards, haul taut gear. 8 A.M. Holystone berth deck. 7:30 P.M. Quarters for muster and clear battery.

Saturday

Morning—Holystone spar deck thoroughly, clean bright work, square yards, haul taut gear. Afternoon—Make, mend, and mark clothes. 7.30 P.M. Quarters for muster and clear battery.

Ten minutes allowed to get up and stow all hammocks. The men can have their bags at all meal hours and at no other time without permission from officer of the deck.

Feby. 12, 1864. Weather cloudy at 8 A.M., pleasant at 1 P.M. Thermometer 57° Fahr. Reported Henry Boland, sea.,—intermittens sick this morning in my report. Ordered him pil. cath. comp no iii last night and magnesiae sulphas ℥ i this morning. Thomas O'Neil has another attack of bronchitis. After opening his bowels, I ordered him the following: ol. tiglii externally to chest to cause counterirritation; ℞ acetum ℥ viii, aquae ℥ viii, molasses ℥ viii, antim. et potas. tart grs iii, opii tinct. ℨ ii; M; Sig. Tablespoonful three times a day, and opii et ipecac. pulv grs x when he turns in tonight. Place him on the binnacle list—i.e., his name—so as to excuse him from all duty.

Feby. 13, 1864. Weather pleasant. Thermometer 58° Fahr. Boland feels somewhat better—order him antimonial and saline mixture and apply two blisters, one behind each ear. O'Neil—continue expectorant. Took a short stroll on St. Catharine's Island in company with the paymaster this afternoon.

Feby. 14, 1864. Weather lovely. Thermometer 62° Fahr. 9 A.M. All hands to muster. Ensign Thomas read the Articles of War. 10 A.M. Mr. Arrants and myself went on shore and remained there, walking around, until 3 P.M., when we arrived on board, somewhat fatigued and hungry. While on shore we had a lunch consisting of roasted sweet potatoes, boiled eggs, and peanuts. Reported Boland and O'Neil, my two patients, improving. Both continue same treatment as last reported.

Feby. 15, 1864. Weather windy. Wind S.S.W. Thermometer 65° Fahr. Reported same sick as yesterday. 9 A.M. All hands were called to general quarters so as to exercise the crew at the broadside guns. Went on shore in company with the captain. Having considerable of a breeze, we shot through the water like an arrow. The gig is not a bad boat. Found the darkies all busy, the male portion preparing the ground for spring crops and the female portion washing clothes. The captain and myself returned on board at 12.15 P.M. Wrote a letter to father today. Hope we may receive a mail ere long.

Feby. 16, 1864. Weather cool but still pleasant—somewhat inclined to be windy. 8 A.M. Paymaster Murray left in the 1st cutter for Ossabaw Sound, there to communicate with the U.S.S. *Acacia.* I sent my steward along with him with orders to try to obtain muslin, quinine, etc. They returned at 4 P.M. My steward obtained a small quantity of quinine and two yards of muslin. 3 P.M. a sail in tow of a steamer reported in the offing. Discharged Boland to duty. Thermometer 58° Fahr. Thomas O'Neil, who is suffering from an attack of bronchitis, is improving slowly. Besides his usual expectorants I have ordered him the following counterirritation on his throat—viz., apply a wet cloth to his throat, over which place a dry necktie, to be left there until tomorrow morning, I having only applied the rag at 8 P.M.

One Peter Farrel feeling somewhat out of shipshape, this morning I had ordered him pil. cath. comp. no iii. Not operating by 2 P.M., I ordered him a second cathartic in the shape of ol. ricini ℥ i, and that having no effect, I concluded to give him the following emetic: tartar emetic gr i, ipecacuanha pulvis grs xx, which I have no doubt will not only cause him to vomit but also start the purgatives to work. 8.30 P.M. the emetic has done its duty.

Acting Master's Mate Jno. Wright, who was on shore today, returned on board with a letter for Captain Moses from Captain [Acting Lieutenant Edgar] Brodhead of the *Lodona* in which he states that the *Massachusetts* had been at Sapelo Sound and left, that our stores and mail were left on board of the *Lodona,* that the *Oleander* was expected daily, and that he would send us our stores and mail by the *Oleander*—so that we are compelled to wait for our mail etc. until the *Oleander* arrives. Now, I consider this damn mean and hard. Why in thunder could not Captain Brodhead send us our mail via inland instead of keeping us waiting for it?

When we were stationed in that sound, we always made it a point to forward all matter, whether mails or stores, to other vessels as soon as received, and we done nothing more or less than our duty. But "self" appears to be the order of the day. I hope we may receive our mail tomorrow or next day. Words cannot express my feelings that I experienced when I heard of the detention of our things on board of the *Lodona*.

Feby. 17, 1864. Weather rather cool this morning—thermometer 31° Fahr. at 5 A.M., 33° at 8 A.M., and 46° at 3 P.M. A sailing vessel reported in the offing sailing southward. . . . .

Reported the following cases sick this morning: viz., Peter Farrel, to whom I had administered the cathartics and emetic yesterday and last night—the emetic operated, but the purgatives had no effect—so I ordered him magnesiae sulphas ʒ i this morning, which had the desired effect; Jeremiah Riordan, ord. sea. and captain of the afterguards, aged 24, New York—conjunctivitis—apply small blister behind left ear—use a collyrium of plumbi acetas grs iii to aquae ʒ i, and ℞ pil. cath. comp. no iii internally; Thomas O'Neil—improving slowly—continue same treatment.

Feby. 18, 1864. Not quite as cold as yesterday—thermometer 35° Fahr. at 7 A.M. 8 A.M. Paymaster Murray left the ship in the 1st cutter for Sapelo Sound, there to communicate with the *Lodona*, obtain our mail, etc., and return this afternoon. Hope he may return with a large mail. 6 P.M. the *Oleander* [arrived] having Murray on board, also a large mail. I received my detachment, which reads as follows: viz.,

Navy Department
Washington 9th January 1864

Sir:

You are hereby detached from the *Fernandina* and you have permission to return North and report to Surgeon Greene at the Naval Asylum, Philadelphia, for examination as to your qualifications for the position of Assistant Surgeon in the U.S. Navy.

Very Resp'y
Gideon Welles
Secretary of the Navy

Acting Asst. Surgeon
  Samuel P. Boyer
    U.S.S. Fernandina
      S. Atlc. Block'g. Squad'n.
R.H. Dahlgren

I need hardly say that I felt rejoiced, for such very naturally would be the case. I immediately commenced packing my trunk, and by 11 P.M. I was ready, my trunk sent on board the *Oleander*.

Feby. 19, 1864. Rather a cold morning—thermometer 32° Fahr. Bid all hands adieu by shaking hands. Stept on board the *Oleander* at 9 A.M. 9.15 A.M. the *Oleander* left. All hands on board the *Fernandina* mounted the rigging and cheered ship for me—an honor of no mean import. I felt pleased to see how well I was loved by the officers and crew of my former ship. Remained all afternoon and night in Sapelo Sound. Dined with Surgeon Meckley of the *Lodona*. Sold him my sword for $16.

Feby. 20, 1864. Entered Warsaw Sound, Ga., there to speak the ironclad *Patapsco*. Saw a college chum, Dr. Peltz, U.S.N. [Assistant Surgeon Samuel H. Peltz of Philadelphia, stationed on the *Patapsco*]. The doctor gave me money to subscribe for the "Med. and Surg. Reporter," Phila. Feby. 21 arrived at Port Royal. Reported to Commander [William] Reynolds [commanding the naval depot at Port Royal] for passage North. Feby. 22 wrote to Capt. Moses. Feby. 23 paid mess bill (*Oleander*), $3.25. Feby. 24 arrived on board *Fulton*. Feby. 27 arrived in New York. Left for home same day. Feby. 29 left home for Philadelphia. March 1 reported for examination. March 9 examination over. Left Philadelphia for Reading. March 10 wrote to Surgeon Whelan for leave of absence. March 12 received an answer granting me 15 days leave of absence. Acknowledged receipt of said letter.   . . .

Reading, Pa., March 12, 1864. Wrote letter to Capt. Moses.   . . . Wrote letter to Frank Leslie, Esq., enclosing three dollars for one year's subscription to his "Lady's Magazine" for sister Beckie [*Frank Leslie's Lady's Magazine,* a popular monthly featuring pictures, serials, and humor; started in New York in 1854, the name had changed periodically]. Received letters from Dr. T. J. Boyer . . . Jas. B. Henderson . . . Mr. Hoyt (Connecticut), Miss Carrie Carlisle, and B. Boyer, Esq. Sister Beckie made me a present of a pair of slippers, Mrs. M. K. Boyer a wrapper, Mrs. B. F. Boyer a smoking cap, Miss Nettie Clauser a pair of sleevelets, or, as some call them, pulse warmers. Presented sister Beckie with a very fine veil, costing seven dollars. Bought from Brooks Brothers, clothers, New York City, the following bill of goods: viz., overcoat and cape, Navy blue—$60; undress suit, Navy blue cloth, consisting of coat, vest, and pants—$58; jacket, Navy blue cloth—$28.50; one pair blue flannel pants—$8. Bought from Lange, Phila., a Navy cap—$5.50. Bought from Mr. Stoner 5 galls. domestic wine and keg—$8. Bought from Jameson and Co. 1 box collars—$4. Bought from Jas. C. Brown, Reading, Pa., 2 negligee shirts—$8; and 2 pair drawers —$5. Bought pair kid gloves (lined) from Eshelman, Phila.—$2.50. Thus ends my purchases etc. for this date. Took tea at sister Maggie's.

March 13, 1864. Dined with brother Frank. March 14 dined with Aunt Lucy. March 22 dined with Messrs. [Jacob] Conrad and [Samuel] Summons, steward and clerk at the Berks County almshouse [three miles out of Reading, on a farm once owned by Thomas Mifflin and acquired by the county in 1824]. March 23 my nephew, B. Boyer, . . . left, having paid me a short visit. March 25 took a few dancing lessons with Prof. Frank Stouch, Reading. Recd. a letter from B. Boyer, Esq., announcing the death of his wife's grandfather on the maternal side, one Mr. Uhland by name. Am waiting patiently for orders from Washington, D. C. Recd. Miss Clauser's and Miss Millie Boyer's *cartes de visite.* Promised mine in return; also promised Miss Regina Conrad one, she having given me one of hers.

[With the exception of the duplicate entry for March 12, diary entries from April 20 to March 25 were obviously hurriedly done, and none at all were made between March 25 and April 12. The doctor's rank still remained acting assistant surgeon.]

PART THREE

NORTH ATLANTIC BLOCK-
ADING SQUADRON: THE
U.S.S. *MATTABESETT*

16

Action in Albemarle Sound

U.S.S. Mattabesett, *Navy Yard, New York, April 12, 1864.*
Ere I note down the events today, I think it well to mention that
on the 8th of the month I received orders to report for duty on
board of the [double-ender] *Mattabesett* and that I reported for
duty on the 9th. The vessel is commanded by Commander J[ohn]
C. Febiger. My messmates are all young and lively men. In the
course of time I will note down the officers of this ship. The *Mattabesett* went into commission on the 7th of April, 1864. I reported
[Acting] Ensign Albert F. Dill, aet. 22, Mass.—intermittens sick
today. His treatment today has been calomel grs vi, followed by
castor oil ℥ i.

Brooklyn Navy Yard, April 13, 1864. Quite a large binnacle list.
Mr. Dill improving slightly—℞ antimonial and saline mixture. My
Steward, J. H. M. Karsner, reported for duty. Appointed boy Cor-
win as my nurse.

At Sea, April 19, 1864. The *Mattabesett* left the Navy Yard this
morning bound for Fortress Monroe. We are to convoy the ironclad
Onondaga.

[The *Mattabesett* was on her way to join the North Atlantic Blockading
Squadron, under the command of Acting Rear Admiral S. P. Lee. She
was accompanying the *Onondaga* for the purpose of giving aid if necessary; the ironclads, not being seaworthy vessels, required convoys when
taken from one port to another.]

5 P.M. at anchor off Sandy Hook. The following were reported sick
this morning: John Bogus, sea.—erysipelas; G. T. Smith, lds.—
laryngitis; Jos. W. Barns, lds.—sore foot; Jacob Nixson, boy—
bronchitis; besides quite a large binnacle list.

April 21, 1864. At 5 A.M. we got under way, having the ironclad
Onondaga in tow. The tug *Rose* also comprises part of the fleet.
The weather is altogether lovely. The pilot and Prof. Fry [possibly

William W. Fay, assistant professor of ethics and English studies, attached to the U.S. Naval Academy] left at 10 A.M. in pilot boat no. 10 for New York, taking the mail along with them. Our present speed is 7 knots. We are leaving the highlands behind us, and by sunset we expect to be out of sight of land. Passed an English mail steamer bound for New York this morning. Dipped colors. The Englishmen appeared astonished at the sight of our ironclad— and well they might, for she is rather a dangerous customer in a fight. Reported the following cases sick: A[lfred] M. Beck, [acting] master's mate—colica; Thos. Martin, —— —hypochondriasis; John Martin, sea.—catarrhus; John Bogus, sea.—erysipelas; E. Nunes, lds.—colica; G. T. Smith, lds.—laryngitis; Jacob Nixson, boy—bronchitis; Rich. Lee, o. sea.—rheumatism; Jos. W. Barns, lds.—sore foot—all improving except the case of hypochondriasis.

8 P.M. Absecon Light [at Atlantic City, New Jersey, near the mouth of Absecon Inlet] in sight. Our average speed today has been 8½ knots; hence alone we will be able to travel from 15 to 18 knots.

On the 19th of April I forwarded a check for $600 to B. Frank Boyer. . . . .

Fortress Monroe, Va., April 23, 1864. We arrived here safe and sound this morning. Thus far we have had the best of luck. I sincerely hope and pray that it may thus continue. As regards our station, all that I know is that we are bound somewhere on the coast of North Carolina. May we have plenty of prizes. Wrote letters to father, Wm. S. Dumm (Reading), Capt. Moses . . . , and Ensign Jas. B. Henderson. The weather has been rather lovely all day. Have no inclination to write any notes—hence the brevity of this day's log.

At Sea, April 24, 1864. We are on our way to Albemarle Sound, N. C., there to fight a Rebel ram. We expect rather hot work. Capt. [Melancton] Smith of the *Onondaga* accompanies us and is the senior officer in command.

[Captain Smith was "to assume command in the sounds of North Carolina for the purpose of attacking, at all hazards, the rebel ram there in the best manner to insure its destruction by running it down with the double enders, or in any other manner." On the basis of his success in vanquishing the "old ram" *Manassas,* sunk in single combat below New Orleans two years previously by the *Mississippi* under his command, he was expected to "make short work of that young ram." The recently completed *Albemarle* was a powerful flat-bottomed iron-prowed ironclad screw sloop armed with two 100-pounder rifles (a Brooke and a Whitworth) that could pivot on either side or ahead and astern. It had come down the Roanoke River the morning of April 19 during a Confederate attack on Plymouth, North Carolina, strongly fortified key to the river, struck and sunk the Federal gunboat *Southfield* and crippled the *Miami* (killing Lieut. Commander C. W. Flusser), and made the fall of Plymouth inevitable by cutting off any possibility of getting re-enforcement.[1]]

He uses our ship as the flagship. Lieutenant Foster [Acting Volunteer Lieutenant Amos P. Foster, commanding the *Commodore Perry*, then under repair at Baltimore] also volunteered his services, so that we have a damn good crowd and expect to do some gay fighting. I am going to put the medical department in ship shape. We all expect to come out cock of the walk.

Off Hatteras, April 25, 1864. We have been cruising about all day. 9.30 P.M. My messmates are having a gay and festive time dancing, singing and playing on musical instruments. The brimming cup of wine passes around freely. In short, "joy appears unconfined." Truly we are a gay set of sailor boys.

Hatteras Inlet, N. C., off Fort Clark, April 26, 1864. We arrived here this morning. Captain Smith and Lieutenant Commander [Walter W.] Queen [commanding the *Wyalusing*] came on board, when we made tracks for Newbern, the tug *Goliah* having us in tow.

[New Bern, "City of Five Flags" and "Athens of North Carolina," second oldest town in North Carolina (settled by Swiss and German colonists in 1710 and incorporated in 1723); provincial capital and first capital of the state. The name is spelled in various ways: New Berne in both army and navy official records; Newbern in Appleton's *Cyclopedia* for 1864; and Newberne on a map in Appleton's. Within less than a year (September 7, 1865-August 16, 1866) a local paper carried in connection with its name, the *Daily Times*, three different forms—New Berne to March 13, New Bern to April 28, and Newbern to August 16. Lippincott's *Gazetteer* and *Hammond's World Atlas* give Newbern, and the sixth report of the Geographic Board (1932) gives New Bern (not Newbern), a reversal of a decision published in 1892. A recently published guidebook (Gertrude S. Carraway, *Historic New Bern*, tenth edition, 1954) has New Bern. Dr. Boyer usually wrote Newbern; sometimes New Berne.]

. . . Ere long we found ourselves aground hard and fast, the tide falling—consequently we were compelled to remain here. Up to the time of writing these notes—i.e., 8 P.M.—we were still aground. Still the pilot says that by 11 o'clock we will be afloat. If so, why, by morning we expect to reach Newbern, after which I suppose we will go into action. In the meantime all hands will take it coolly.

I reported the following cases sick this morning: viz., John Bogus, sea.—erysipelas—improving; Edward Nunes, lds.—rheumatism— slight improvement; Jacob Nixson, boy—bronchitis—slight improvement; Robt. Moore, o. sea—phthisis—very sick indeed.

April 27, 1864. Still hard and fast aground. Made several attempts to get afloat. No doubt but that ere long we will be afloat and on our way to Newbern. The *Mattabesett* has quite a goodly number of officers on board at present. The following are their names etc.: Captain Smith, commander ironclad *Onondaga;* Commander Febiger, commander U.S.S. *Mattabesett;* Lieut. Commander Queen, commander U.S.S. *Wyalusing;* Vol. Lieutenant Foster, commander U.S.S. *Commodore Perry;* Lieutenant [Archibald N.] Mitchell, executive officer U.S.S. *Mattabesett;* Actg. Master [James L.] Plunkett, Actg. Asst. Paymaster [Henry C.] Meade, Actg. Asst. Surgeon Boyer, Actg. Ensign [Francis H.] Brown, Actg. Ensign Dill, and Actg. Ensign [John] Greenhalgh, doing duty on *Mattabesett;* 2nd Asst. Engineer and Chief [John T.] Hawkins, 2nd Asst. Engineer [Augustine] Sackett, 2nd Asst. Engineer [Charles J.] McConnel, 3rd Asst. Engineer [Isaiah] Paxson, 3rd Asst. Engineer [Alexander B.] Bates, 3rd Asst. Engineer [Wm. A.] Mintzer, Actg. Master's Mate [Isaac A.] Peirce, Actg. Master's Mate Beck, Actg. Master's Mate [Charles F.] Fisher, Captain's Clerk Taylor, Paymaster's Steward Richardson, Surgeon's Steward Karsner, and Gunner Soule, attached to *Mattabesett,* besides any amount of petty officers.

Reported the following sick: John Bogus—erysipelas—coming on finely; Edward Nunes—rheumatism—somewhat better; Robt. Moore—phthisis—no better. Today I made out three hospital tickets for the following cases, whom I will send to the hospital as soon as an opportunity presents itself: Robt. Moore, o. sea.— phthisis pulmonalis; Thos. Martin, sea.—hypochondriasis; Saml. Hutchinson, Lds.—dementia. The first case came on board sick; the

2nd and 3rd are either "old sogers" or else objects of pity—hence my sending them to the hospital.

Pamlico Sound, N. C., April 29, 1864. Yesterday we managed to get afloat again, and today we are steaming up the sound on our way to Newbern. 1 P.M. On our way up the Neuse River. 2 P.M. Let go our starboard anchor in the Neuse River at the city of Newbern. Shortly after, E[manuel] Mellach, actg. asst. paymaster [pay officer in charge of the naval depot at New Bern], came on board. Paymaster Mellach is very much of a gentleman indeed. At 5.30 P.M. Paymaster Mellach and Meade and myself went ashore to Newbern, and while there we had quite a gay time seeing the sights and drinking good liquor. Paymaster Meade and myself invested $6 apiece in pipes etc. Newbern is quite a fine city. Ere the war the population was 13,000. There are some very fine buildings. The Gaston House, Governor's Mansion etc. are buildings of no mean appearance.[2] Our paymaster and myself returned on board at 7 P.M., well pleased with our visit and Paymaster Mellach's hospitality.

Newbern, N. C., April 30, 1864. Weather lovely, only rather warm. Took a stroll on shore. Met Actg. Asst. Surgeon Lucian Kendall, U.S.N. He is in charge of a hospital on shore [a small temporary naval hospital, not listed in the Navy *Register*] and at the same time is attached to the *Commodore Hull*. Dr. Kendall is a college chum of mine. A fine boy he is—knows how to keep a hotel. Also became acquainted with [Acting Assistant] Surgeon [George] Hopkins of the *Tacony*. Consulted with him as regards the captain of the *Tacony*, who is suffering from the effects of gout. Saw [First Assistant] Engineer [Thomas M.] Dukehart of the *Tacony*. Took a drink of b— with him. He is a townsman of mine.

May 1, 1864. Sent three patients to the naval hospital on shore with hospital tickets addressed to Surgeon Solomon Sharp, in charge of the Norfolk Naval Hospital, named Robert Moore, Samuel Hutchinson, and Thomas Martin, affected with phthisis pulmonalis, dementia, and hypochondriasis.

[The naval hospital at Norfolk, Virginia, established in 1827—one of the first two permanent hospitals built from the marine hospital fund—was, like other naval property there, taken over by the military authorities occupying the town in May, 1862, who relinquished it to naval authorities only "after much trouble," during which temporary quarters had to be pressed into service. Surgeon Sharp, on duty at the naval station, was placed in charge of the hospital, retaining the post for three years. Although temporary bases set up in North Carolina at New Bern, Washington, and Plymouth were "amply supplied with hospital accommodations" and arrangements had been made for care of naval personnel at the army hospital at Beaufort, many cases were handled at Norfolk.[3]

Paymaster Meade, Engineer Hawkins, Ensigns Brown and Greenhalgh, Captain Foster, and myself went to Newbern this afternoon. We had quite a pleasant time of it. Met [Assistant] Surgeon [William H.] Campbell of the 58th Regt. Penna. Volunteers [stationed at Washington, North Carolina, in the subdistrict of the Pamlico], a college chum of mine. Were happy to see each other; paid the Gaston House a visit and took a social drink. He is on his way to Fortress Monroe. During our rambles this afternoon we dropped in at the naval clubrooms; had a lunch of sardines etc. and indulged rather freely in ale etc. Also called on Dr. Kendall. In short, we had a bully old time.

Roanoke Island, N. C., May 3, 1864. Here we are at last on our way to meet the Rebel ram and have a pop at Plymouth. [The *Mattabesett* had been "detained at New Berne for the want of a pilot, coal, and indispensable repairs on her machinery."] From morning till night and from night till morning we have been busy practising all hands at the guns, for we expect to have quite a stormy time. The *Mattabesett* is the flagship of the expedition, consisting of six or seven other gunboats. . . .

Albemarle Sound, N. C., May 4, 1864. 7 P.M. Still no ram in sight. Captain Foster of the *Commodore Perry* left today for Fortress Monroe. We were all sorry to see him go, for he was very good company. Captain Smith's secretary arrived on board today; he is a wardroom officer. Captain [Acting Ensign Jacob L.] Hayes of the *Seymour* sent me 5 patients today. After prescribing for them, I went with them on board of the *Seymour* and told Captain Hayes what to give them, I finding the medicine. Met several obliging officers on board the *Seymour*. Took a drink of Navy sherry with one of them. Received a small mail today; but I was one of the unlucky ones, not receiving any letters. We have dates up to the 1st of March. My sick list is rather small at present. I have quite a lot of outdoor patients. Most of the officers and men have a slight diarrhoea; cause—bad water. I have had quite a sorry time of it myself. Hope to feel better in the morning.

Wrote a short letter to Brother Michael. . . . Reported the following cases sick: Edward Nunes, lds.—rheumatism—improving —liniment externally and ℞ potassii iodidii grs v three times a day; and Carrol Emory, lds.—pleuritis—brown mixture ℥ ss. three times a day for his cough, and antimonial and saline mixture for his inflammation—counterirritation externally.

Naval Fight. May 5, 1864. Today we had quite a stormy naval fight with the Rebel ram and two other Secesh gunboats. We captured one gunboat; the other skedaddled, and the ram fought us all day until dark, when she skedaddled and we concluded to stop the fight on account of various damages etc. done the vessel. Our fleet consisted of the *Mattabesett* (flagship), *Sassacus, Wyalusing, Miami,* and two or three small gunboats. Shot and shell came fast like hail. I had to report 2 killed and 4 [6] wounded. The ram is something like the *Atlanta.* Whether she sustained any injury I cannot say. We expect to have another fight either tonight or morning.

[At two o'clock in the afternoon of May 5 the *Albemarle,* accompanied by two other steamers—the *Cotton Plant,* carrying troops, and the *Bomb-shell,* carrying provisions and coal—was discovered emerging from the Roanoke River by the *Miami,* the *Commodore Hull,* and the *Ceres* and the army steamer *Trumpeter,* on picket duty at the mouth of the river. The navy gunboats, following previous instructions, retreated slowly about ten miles down the sound, decoying the *Albemarle* and the *Bomb-shell* (the *Cotton Plant* having turned back) toward the rest of the fleet, while the army steamer went on ahead to report to Captain Smith. Shortly after three o'clock the *Mattabesett* (leading the right column), the *Wya-lusing,* the *Whitehead,* and the *Sassacus* got under way and proceeded to meet the enemy, the *Miami* leading the left column into supporting position. The battle, reported later by Rear Admiral Lee as a "remarkable action, which adds a brilliant page to the exploits of the Navy," was begun at four-forty.

[The *Albemarle* opened fire on the *Mattabessett,* destroying her launch and wounding six men, all belonging to the forward rifle gun. Five minutes later the *Bombshell* surrendered. In accordance with a prior suggestion from the Navy Department that ramming be tried, the *Sassacus* struck the *Albemarle's* stern, remaining in contact about ten minutes before disengaging herself (her starboard boiler burst by a hundred-pounder rifle shot from the ram) and retiring from action, taking the *Bombshell* in charge. In the confusion the smaller ships got out of line and by their rapid firing made it dangerous for the larger ones to follow up the advantage. The *Albemarle's* colors came down, giving a temporary impression of surrender. The fight continued, however, until about seven-thirty, when the *Commodore Hull* and the *Ceres* were sent to follow the ram to the mouth of the Roanoke River and there remain on picket duty, the *Mattabesett,* the *Miami,* the *Wyalusing,* and the *Whitehead* coming to anchor in the sound two and a half miles below. Captain Smith, while he felt prepared to resume the engagement if the ram reappeared in the sound, believed that an attempt to attack in the river would be disastrous to his forces.

[It was near the end of the engagement that the *Mattabesett,* finding the line was gradually edging off, passed ahead of the *Albemarle* and attempted to foul her propellers by laying a seine in her course. The attempt failed, and in rounding to port so her port guns could be used she received a six-inch rifle shot that fatally wounded two men and did considerable damage to the vessel.[4]]

The following are the names of the killed and wounded:

Killed—2

Ralph E. Lake, 1st-class fireman—Left thigh carried away.

William H. Demilt, 1st-class boy—Right thigh carried away and compound fracture of left thigh, lacerated wound of right wrist, and contused wound of left eyebrow and lid.

    Both the above patients died shortly after receiving their injuries. I done all that lay in my power to make them as comfortable as possible under the circumstances.

Wounded—6

James L. Plunkett, acting master—Contusion of right thigh. He fought his gun during the whole engagement and did not report himself to me until after the fight.

John B. Jewett, lds., 22. Kentucky—Punctured wound of right forearm. He did not report himself until after the fight and then not until I sent for him. He has proved himself a hero in every sense of the word. Dressed his wound etc. Continues doing duty.

Greenberry T. Smith, lds., 31, Tennessee—Contused wound of left shoulder—rather a severe contusion. Dressed with cold-water lotion, medicated; also administered whiskey etc.

James Mulvehill, ord. sea., 21, New York—Contused wound of back and left elbow. Treated upon general principles—viz., cold-water dressings etc.

Daniel Lamon, capt. forecastle, 42, Scotland—Lacerated wound of scalp in vicinity of right ear; pinna of right ear also wounded. Treated upon general principles—cold-water dressings etc.

Charles F. Moeller, 1st-class boy, 17, Germany—Contusion of right knee [and] ankle, and ecchymosis of left eybrow and lid. Apply cold-water dressings.

The *Mattabesett* done noble work. The *Sassacus* run head on to the ram, dismounted some of the ram's guns—so supposed—and received herself a shot in her boiler, scalding quite a number of her ship's company. The *Wyalusing* had one man killed [John A. Oliver, landsman, struck by a fragment of iron]. The *Miami* came off Scotch free—none wounded and none killed. Whether or not the small gunboats had any casualties I cannot say. [The *Whitehead,* the *Ceres,* and the *Commodore Hull* as well as the *Miami* had no casualties. By far the greatest damage not only to ship but also to men was suffered by the *Sassacus,* whose commander, Lieutenant Commander F.A. Roe (subsequently advanced five numbers in grade "for distinguished conduct in battle" in his attempt to run down the *Albemarle*) reported twenty casualties, including the chief engineer and sixteen of his men, badly scalded, of whom five died.] We received several hard shots—one through our water waste [waterways—heavy planking or timbering running the length of the vessel at the junction of deck with sides, forming channels to the scuppers], which caused the death of Messrs, Lake and Demilt. ["When nearly abeam of the enemy," reported Commander Febiger after the engagement, "we received a 6-inch rifle shot which entered on the port side below wheelhouse guards and abaft wheel, passing through waterways, coamings of engine-room hatch, wounding a first-class fireman and boy so severely that they died soon afterwards, and bringing up in small-arms locker.] Poor fellows—peace to their ashes. One shot put a hole through our launch and made the splinters fly, which caused Messrs. Plunkett, Jewett, and the rest to be wounded, besides any amount of damage done to our rigging. Still, notwithstanding, taking all in all, we done credit to ourselves. During the engagement and two hours afterwards I was as busy as a bee attending the killed and wounded, covered with blood from head to foot. I will here give a pen-and-ink sketch of said ram.

So much for the ram fight. Don't fancy such kind of fighting;

would prefer wooden gunboats. Was busy until after midnight making out reports of casualties etc. Turned in shortly afterwards, but on account of the excitement did not rest well. Ere the fight I wrote a letter to B. Frank . . . giving him an idea that we expected to fight a ram. Sure enough we did fight her—and caused her to make tracks for inland. Wonder when next she will make her appearance.

May 6, 1864. The killed were buried today on Roanoke Island. The wounded are coming on as well as can be expected. Made out certificates of death for Lake and Demilt, which I shall send to the fleet surgeon by the first opportunity.

May 7, 1864. The weather has been rather warm today—thermometer 92° Fahr. The wounded men are—with one exception, and that is Lamon—coming along finely. The Rebels sent a flag-of-truce boat to us—i.e., communicated with us—object being to ascertain the condition of the prisoners [thirty-three in number] captured in the Confederate gunboat *Bombshell,* also to ask permission to send money and letters to said prisoners. My private opinion is that they wished to ascertain our condition. All they heard was rather favorable to us. Some of their crew are said to have said that they—i.e., the ram—was used up rather badly.

[After the battle the commander of the *Albemarle* reported to his superior officer that his vessel's tiller had given way and her smokestack had been riddled to the extent of becoming useless; unable to get up enough steam to maneuver the ship advantageously, he had had at last to burn the bulkheads and all bacon, lard, and other combustible items on board in order to make his way back to the river.]

They also say that they intend soon to give us another call—in other words, pay us a visit. They were very careful in what they said.

One of the engineers—i.e., one of our officers—had the kindness to loan me a straw hat to wear until I am able to purchase one. I think he acted the part of a kind and good Samaritan. Wrote a letter to father giving him an account of the fight of the 5th inst.

May 8, 1864. The weather was unusually hot today. Some ice came on board today for the officers and sick—quite a luxury. My wounded patients are coming on finely. [Acting Assistant] Paymaster [Frank W.] Hackett and [Assistant] Surgeon [William B.] Mann of the *Miami* paid us a visit today. We had quite a social chat, smoking good cigars etc. The *Commodore Barney* arrived today, another addition to our fleet. She has a battery of 2 100-pdrs. and 5 9-inch guns.

May 9, 1864. Reported 10 cases sick today: viz., Jas. L. Plunkett, master—diarrhoea; Augustine Sackett, engineer—diarrhoea; Danl. Lamon—lacerated wound, G. T. Smith—contused wound, and Jas. Mulvehill—contused wound (injuries received during the ram fight May 5, '64); Ed. Nunes—rheumatism; Carrol Emory—pleuritis; Thos. P. Swilling—bronchitis; Frank Reilly—bronchitis; John Martin—debility. Also attended to three of the *Seymour's* men: viz., Edmonston—chills and fever—℞ tonics etc.; Garrett—colica —℞ ol. ricini ℥ ss.; Felton—odontalgia—extracted tooth. Expended 1½ lbs. sugar, white, for expectorants. Made one pint of tinct. gentian for the benefit of Messrs. Hawkins and Plunkett, the former being slightly dyspeptic and the latter debilitated.

May 10, 1864. Today John R. Sherwood, actg. 3rd asst. engineer, of the U.S.S. *Ceres,* called upon me for medical advice. I found him afflicted with double inguinal hernia, caused by a gunshot wound recd. in the fight at Plymouth sometime in April [April 17, when a battery of six guns on the port side of the Roanoke River opened fire on the *Ceres,* on her way to the *Whitehead* with dispatches]. I wrote a request to Captain Smith, senior officer, for a medical survey. He immediately ordered a board of survey, consisting of Asst. Surgeon Wm. B. Mann of the U.S.S. *Miami,* Actg. Asst. Surgeon Chas. W. Sartori of the U.S.S. *Wyalusing,* and Actg. Asst. Surgeon Samuel P. Boyer of the U.S.S. *Mattabesett.* Said board recommended his discharge—also that a certificate of disability for pension be made out for him and assert that his disease originated in the line of duty. Master Jas. L. Plunkett returns to duty today, and the rest continue under treatment.

The weather was somewhat cooler today. Had my coat and pantaloons washed today—that is, had the blood received on them from the killed and wounded during the ram fight removed per means of soap and water. The ship's corporal [master-at-arms] had the kindness to renovate said articles of dress.

May 11, 1864. We ascertain today that the ram was alongside the landing at Plymouth without a smokestack etc. Nothing of any account worthy of note transpired today.

May 12, 1864. The medical board of survey reassembled today at the suggestion of Captain Smith . . . to reconsider Mr. Sherwood's case. We finally concluded to send him to the Portsmouth Naval Hospital, there to be disposed of as the authorities saw fit. I made out a hospital ticket for him. Expended all my fresh beef today; reason—unfit for use. Wrote a letter to Jerome L. Boyer, Esq. [son of Jacob K. Boyer, uncle of the diarist], Reading, Berks County, Pa. Reported 8 cases sick in my morning report to Capt. J. C. Febiger. . . .

Off mouth Roanoke River, May 13, 1864. Weather somewhat cloudy; raining at times. Reported 7 sick patients. During quarters today one of the landsmen, named Capps, was foolish enough to hit himself across the right eyebrow by means of a handspike, thereby causing a lacerated wound. I was compelled to introduce two stitches of the interrupted suture, also a small piece of isinglass plaster. Wrote a lengthy letter to Miss Carrie Carlisle . . . in answer to hers dated Feby. 1, which I received on the 12th of March. The Army transport *Massasoit* arrived this evening with a small mail, also fresh beef and vegetables. I was unfortunate enough not to receive any letters. Wrote a letter to father tonight.

May 14, 1864. Expended magnesiae sulphas lb. ½ and quiniae sulphas grs xx for the benefit of the *Seymour's* men. Reported 5 cases sick and binnacled 13 names. Paid Surgeon Sartori . . . a visit this morning; had quite a pleasant time. Wrote a letter to Capt. Edward Moses. . . . I understand that Captain Moses has been very unwell indeed of late. Hope he may receive my letter. Nothing of any account transpired today worthy of note.

May 15, 1864. At 10 A.M. all hands called to attend divine service. Commander Febiger read services. Reported the following cases sick this morning: viz., Chas. Fisher, master's mate—diarrhoea—order him a pill consisting of argenti nitras, opii pulv āā gr ¼, take three pills a day; John Drinkhouse, master-at-arms—diarrhoea—took a dose of castor oil last night—order him today nitrate of silver and opium; Francis Van Winkle, lds.—diarrhoea—℞ argenti nitras, opii pulv āā gr ¼, pil. no i, Sig. 3 pills a day; Edward Nunes—rheumatism—℞ potassii iodidii grs v three times a day, and lini cataplasm to leg; Thomas P. Swilling—bronchitis—cough mixture, Dover's powder gr x at night, and tartar-emetic ointment to chest; Frank Reilly—bronchitis—continue expectorant; John Martin—hydrops—feels easier—order him tinct ferri chloridi gtts x three times a day, also 3 i potassae bitartras three times a day. I also ordered medicine for some of the U.S.S. *Seymour's* men.

We received a New York "Herald" of the 11th of May, which had quite a true account of our fight with the Rebel ram *Albemarle* on the 5th inst.   . . . Also read quite a budget of news concerning Grant's army [General Grant, recently promoted and transferred from the West to the East, had on May 4 crossed the Rapidan with his Army of the Potomac and begun his bloody Wilderness campaign]—victory all around.

May 16, 1864. Reported 8 cases sick—same as yesterday with the addition of Richard P. Steel—furunculus—lanced and applied lini cataplasm. Ordered medicines to be administered to 5 men of the U.S.S. *Ceres.* [Acting Assistant] Surgeon [George C.] Webber and [Acting Assistant] Paymaster [Thomas] Jernegan of the *Commodore Barney* paid us a visit and dined with us as guests of Paymaster Meade and myself. The men practiced target shooting with small arms.

May 17, 1864. The double-ender U.S.S. *Tacony* arrived today. At 10 A.M. I left the ship with an order of a medical survey upon Capt. Queen of the U.S.S. *Wyalusing* and proceeded on board the *Tacony;* there called for Dr. Kendall of the *Commodore Hull* and Dr. Hopkins of the *Tacony.* We all three then repaired on board the *Wyalusing,* held a strict and careful survey upon Lieutenant Commander W. W. Queen, and upon examination found him afflicted with both chronic hepatitis and chronic rheumatism, also that the disease originated in the line of duty. We therefore recommended that he be sent North for further treatment, where he can obtain aid necessarily denied him on board of a man-of-war. Said decision was approved by the senior officer in Sounds of North Carolina, Capt. M. Smith.   . . .

May 18, 1864. Early this morning three contrabands made their appearance on board, having escaped from Secesh—two males and one female.

May 19, 1864. One month ago we left the Brooklyn Navy Yard, and two weeks ago we had a fight with the Rebel ram *Albemarle.* Where will we be one month hence—aye, two weeks hence?

Slight rain showers today. Reported 6 cases sick. Have a slight diarrhoea myself; hope it will wear away without medicine. Target practice with broadside and pivot guns. The men did some fine shooting. Wrote a letter to sister Beckie. Did not send it.

At 9 P.M. the U.S.S. *Whitehead* arrived from Newbern with a large mail; also brought our pilot back again. I received a letter from brother Frank dated April 19 regarding some ale; one from father dated May 11—all well at home; one from Miss Sue E. Yeager, Reading, Pa., enclosing one of her *cartes de visite;* one from my former surgeon's steward, R. D. Adams, Brooklyn, N.Y., requesting a certificate etc.; one from Sheldon H. Hoyt, lds., U.S.S. *Fernandina,* dated April 15. Also received the following numbers of the "Medical and Surgical Reporter": March 5, 12, 19, 26; April 2, 9, 16. Miss Yeager sent me an express package containing a beautiful cigar case with 4 cigars as a present, seal ring, and *carte de visite* of mine, also those of Miss Hampshire, Mr. Underkofer, and Dr. Kaufman. In short, I had quite a budget of news.

May 20, 1864. Weather rather pleasant. We are coaling ship. Wrote the following letters: one to father . . . one to brother Frank . . . one to Miss Sue E. Yeager . . . one to R.D. Adams . . . one to Adams Express Company regarding an express package which is retained in their office at Fortress Monroe. Wrote a letter to Capt. Edward Moses, . . . who is home on sick leave. His home is in Portsmouth, New Hampshire.

May 21, 1864. Sent today two patients to the U.S. naval hospital at Newbern, named John Martin, sea., 40, Maine, affected with general debility causing anasarca—disease did not originate in line of duty, and Edward Nunes, lds, 22, Jamaica—rheumatismus chronic.—disease did not originate in line of duty. They leave in the U.S.S. *Ceres* today. The *Ceres* also takes our mail matter intending North. Reported the following cases sick: Charles Fisher—diarrhoea—convalescent—order him ℞ aquae camphor. f. ℥ iii, tinct opii f ℨ ss, spts lavend. comp, ether sulph. āā f. ℥ ss., tinct capsici f. ℨ ss., sach. albi. ℨ ii, alumina ℨ ss., M, Sig. Tablespoonful after each evacuation; John Drinkhouse—diarrhoea— same treatment as Fisher; Geo. Stamp—bronchitis—℞ cough mixture consisting of tartar emetic, morphine, copaiba, molasses, and water; Thos. P. Swilling—bronchitis and aphonia—counterirritation to chest by means of mustard poultice, and internally cough mixture. . . .

All hands busy cleaning ship fore and aft. The way they handle the holystones is not slow.

Saturday night and at anchor in Albemarle Sound. Although we may every moment be called to quarters to fight the enemy, still we are in the best of spirits, for at this very moment the members of this (the wardroom) mess are having a gay and festive time. Our worthy and efficient executive officer, Lieut. Mitchell, is perched on one of the wardroom chairs playing on the guitar; our gay and happy engineer, Mr. Hawkins, is killing time and driving dull care away by playing on the violin; our gallant and obliging paymaster, Mr. Meade, is accompanying the rest of the musicians by giving us agreeable tunes on the flute; our sailing master, Ensign Brown, is up to all kinds of fun, whether on the light fantastic toe or bones; whilst the rest of the members are either singing patriotic airs or else attempting so to do. I might here say that the doctor is only sorry that he is no musician—still he manages to give an occasional grunt. Thus we endeavor to enjoy ourselves and keep the blue devils away. Oh! who would not sell a farm to enter the Navy? If we had plenty of wine and the presence of the fair sex, why, I think we would be the happiest mortals in existence. We emphatically coincide with Luther when he says,

> He who loves not wine, woman, or song
> Is a fool his long life long.[5]

Why, therefore, in the name of common sense are we not entitled to have a gay and happy cruise?

May 22, 1864. Divine service at 11 A.M. 4 P.M. the *Rockland* arrived from Newburn and brought us quite a small mail. I received three letters from the North—one from father dated May 1, in which he states that he had just recovered from a very severe cold and sore throat, also that brother Frank had attended to some ale which I had ordered from home to send to New York; one from sister Beckie P. Cutler dated May 11, enclosing *cartes de visite* of herself and husband; one from Miss Sue E. Yeager dated May 2, in which she expressed great anxiety regarding the express package which I received on the 19th inst. and which she thought had been missent. Of course I immediately answered the above three letters. The one to father was short and to the point; the one to Sue was rather long but interesting; the one to Beckie will be rather a welcome one, for in it I enclose her a check for twenty dollars, which she is to spend as she sees fit. Expect to receive quite a lengthy answer from her in return.

May 24, 1864. The Rebel ram *Albemarle* was signalized by the *Whitehead* within sight. It appears she came to the mouth of the river, when the contents of the *Whitehead's* one-hundred-pounder in the shape of a shell caused her to go up the river again out of sight.

[This was the *Albemarle's* first appearance since the May 5 engagement. The vessel was accompanied by a rowboat, apparently dragging for torpedoes. Immediately after the *Whitehead's* shot, which exploded near her stern, she steamed up the river. Confederate officials disagreed as to whether to go out into the sound to attack the Federal fleet; some felt that capture, of which there was great danger, would probably mean loss of the entire area recently retaken. A Federal expedition up the river on May 25 to destroy the ram failed.]

Thus we may expect her at any moment. 3.30 P.M. slight thunder shower. The weather was rather hot today—thermometer 96° Fahr. in the shade.

Reported the following cases sick today: Francis McLaughlin, ord. sea.—diarrhoea—℞ tannic acid grs x, morphiae sulphas grs ii, spts ammoniae aromat ℥ ss., tinct capsici ℥ ss., aquae camphor. ℥ iv, ℳ, Sig. Teaspoonful every hour until relieved; Jacob Nixson, boy—diarrhoea—same treatment as McLaughlin; James Smith, lds.—bronchitis—℞ expectorants; Wm. C. Johnson, carpt. mate—chills and fever—order him quiniae sulph grs ii, acid. sulph aromat, gtts x, aquae ℥ ss., three times a day; David Hall, sea.—chills and fever—same treatment as Johnson; Samuel Clayton, 1st-class fireman—chills and fever—℞ pil. hydrarg. no. ii, to be followed in 2 hours by a Seidlitz powder; Thos. P. Swilling, lds.—bronchitis chronic, also affected with aphonia—order him expectorants, counterirritation to chest, and ol. morrhuae ʒ i three times a day; George Stamp, lds.—bronchitis—order him an expectorant mixture consisting of tartar emetic, morphine, bals. copaiba, molasses, and water, also counterirritation to chest; John Drinkhouse, master-at-arms—diarrhoea chronic—order him ipecacuanha grs iii every 4 hours, also a drachm of slippery elm and water, ℥ i to O i, boiled down to O ss.; Wm. Smith, ship's cor-

poral—fever—an emetic, blisters behind ear, and acidulated drinks
—at 7 P.M. pil. cath. comp no iii.

May 25, 1864. Seven men made their appearance on board this
morning—three soldiers and the rest citizens from Plymouth, they
having escaped during the fight on the 17th of April, having been
in the woods ever since. They all felt happy when they landed on
board. The three soldiers belonged to the 1st North Carolina Cavalry.

Reported the same cases sick as yesterday. The diarrhoea patients
are taking the oleaginous mixture, consisting of ol ricini ℥ ii, acacia
℥ ii, sach Alba ℥ ii, aquae mentha pip. ℥ iv, M, Sig. Teaspoonful
every hour. Wm. Smith, ship's corporal, who is affected with a bilious remittent fever, is rather low today. I order him iced acidulated drinks, body sponged with cold water; also let him have a
bottle of ale a day. Tonight I shall give him pil hydrarg no i (grs v).
The rest of the patients will continue the same course of treatment
as yesterday.

May 26, 1864. The Rebel ram *Albemarle* made her appearance at
the mouth of the Roanoke River today. The *Commodore Barney*
sent a few shells at her. She left again for Plymouth. She was
dragging by means of small boats for torpedoes. The *Rockland*
arrived and left again today. She brought us fresh beef and vegetables. Wrote a letter today to father and sent it by her. 5.15 P.M.
Quite a brisk squall. Wm. Smith—bilious fever—is better today.
The rest of the patients are coming along finely. I have any amount
of diarrhoea cases on hand at present.

May 27, 1864. The weather was rather lovely all day. We changed
our anchorage today and anchored off Edenton [Chowan County
seat; one of the oldest communities in North Carolina], about half
a mile from our former anchorage. Reported 7 cases sick today; still
plenty of diarrhoea cases on hand. Up to this time, 9 P.M., nothing
of any account worthy of note has transpired. 11.30 P.M. The
Massasoit arrived. No Mail.

May 29, 1864. Divine service at 10.30 A.M. Reported 4 cases sick
today. Wrote a letter to B. Boyer. . . . Weather quite pleasant.
1.30 P.M. No signs of the Rebel ram; wonder when she will come
and show fight again. 6 P.M. Four Rebel deserters arrived on board.

They formerly belonged to the ram. Report the ram ready to come out again. She does not appear to have been damaged much. Carries 2 100-pounders; manned by 70 men; Captain Cooke, C.S.N., in charge.

[Confederate Captain James W. Cooke, who had superintended the completion of the *Albemarle*, was commander of the vessel until June, 1864, when he was relieved at his own request. His successor, Commander John N. Maffitt, was detached from the command the following September.]

May 30, 1864. Reported 7 cases sick—1 remittent, 2 intermittent, 3 diarrhoea, 1 bronchitis chronic. The *Massasoit* leaves for Newbern today. Wrote a letter to Paymaster E. Mellach, naval storekeeper, Newbern, regarding express matter.

May 31, 1864. An Army captain (and servant) who has been in the swamps ever since the taking of Plymouth arrived on board this morning; also a civilian who left Plymouth yesterday morning. Both appear to have one story to tell: the ram is ready for action again.

A coal schooner arrived early this morning. Reported 6 cases sick. Weather rather warm. 1.30 P.M. Acting Assistant Surgeon L.H. Kendall and Acting Assistant Paymaster [Jonathan] Chapman of the *Commodore Hull* came on board. I gave the doctor a hernial truss, also ℥ ii of tinct opii. Was a member of a medical board of survey which was held today on board of the U.S.S. *Commodore Hull* to examine and report the condition of Acting 1st Assistant Engineer B[enjamin] F. Bee. The board consisted of Acting Assistant Surgeon Sartori of the *Wyalusing,* Acting Assistant Surgeon Hopkins of the *Tacony,* and Acting Assistant Surgeon Boyer of the *Mattabesett.* We reported him affected with dysenteria chronica, that the disease originated in the line of duty, and we recommended that he be sent North for medical treatment.

The U.S.S. *Seymour* arrived from Roanoke Island today with a mail. I received 2 papers sent me by father, also a notice from Postmaster Dibble, Newbern, saying that a letter was in the post office at that place directed to me upon which 6 cents postage was due. I wrote him a letter enclosing 6 cents in postage stamps. Wonder what the letter contains.

June 2, 1864. The Army steamer *Genl. Berry* arrived today, bringing a mail. I was the recipient of but one letter, and that was

from Alfred D. Moses . . . , dated May 20, in which he informs me
that his brother Edward had died on the 18th of May of typhoid
pneumonia. I was very sorry indeed to hear that my old shipmate
and former commander [of the] barque *Fernandina* had departed
this life and gone to that bourne from whence no traveller returneth. Many a long and happy day we spent together. I ne'er shall
see him more. Poor fellow—peace to his ashes.

I answered Mr. Moses' letter; also sent the protest as regards the
prize *Annie Thompson* to the prize commissioner [East District,
Pennsylvania] at Philadelphia, Commodore Thomas Crabbe, U.S.N.
The nature of said protest is stated in the remarks in this journal
of the 19th of January, 1864. Paymaster Hackett of the *Miami* paid
us a flying visit of a few hours today. He left for Roanoke Island
again in the *Genl. Berry.* Reported 10 cases sick today. All hands
coaling ship this afternoon.

8 P.M. A dark night. Symptoms of a thunderstorm—vivid flashes
of lightning, rolling of thunder heard in the distance. Was called
upon today by the captain of the coal schooner to prescribe for a
sick man. Found said man affected with cholera communis. I
ordered him pil. cath. comp no iii so as to open his bowels more
thoroughly and relieve the engorged liver. 4 P.M. The man feels
quite comfortable.

June 3, 1864. Reported 9 cases sick today—3 fevers, 2 diarrhoeas,
1 hemmorrhoids, 1 subluxation, and 2 bronchitis. 12 M. The Army
transport *Thos. Colyer* arrived. She has a band of music on board.
The musicians played several very popular airs. It is a splendid
thing to drive dull care away. I felt sometimes as though I would
like to "trip on the light fantastic toe" when the band struck up
waltzes, polkas, etc. What the object of this visit is I cannot tell. A
colonel, captain, and lieutenant came on board to see Commodore
Smith.

June 4, 1864. Weather cloudy and rainy. Wrote a letter to Robert
Phillips, Jr., New Castle, Schuylkill Co., Pa., enclosing a *carte de
visite;* also wrote a short note to Mrs. Dr. T. J. Boyer, . . . enclosing
three *cartes de visite,* to be distributed as follows—one to Miss
Carrie, one to Miss Amanda, and one for herself. Reported today 7
cases sick—3 fevers, 2 bronchitis, 1 subluxation, and 1 diarrhoea.
Wrote a long letter to Acting Ensign Christopher Flood U.S.
barque *Fernandina.*   . . . 10.30 P.M. The *Genl. Berry* arrived—no

mail. 12 midnight the *Rockland* arrived—no mail. 1 A.M. Heard the report of an explosion up the Roanoke River. Sounded like torpedoes.

June 5, 1864. Divine service at 10.30 A.M. On account of indisposition I was excused from muster today, having a very violent headache indeed. 7 P.M. I took pil hydrarg. no ii (grs x) so as to relieve the engorged liver.

Grim death, it appears, has been in our midst, for today I understand that one man died on board of the U.S.S. steamer *Tacony* and one man very suddenly at 5 P.M. on board of the U.S. steamer *Seymour.* The *Tacony* has a medical officer; hence the history of the case is known—but the *Seymour* not having any doctor and the man having been apparently healthy yesterday, the diagnosis of said case is doubtful, so that the only way to ascertain the nature and cause of his death is to hold a post-mortem examination upon the corpse. Whether or no that will be done remains yet to be seen. I am willing to perform the duties of an examiner. Thus the old adage, or saying, "In the midst of life we're in death" is well illustrated, or substantiated.

The U.S.S. *Whitehead* left today for Roanoke Island for fresh beef and vegetables. Our paymaster went along. The *Genl. Berry* and *Rockland,* both Army transports, left today again for either Roanoke Island or Newbern. The *Massasoit* remains here.

Reported 6 cases sick today—2 fevers, 1 diarrhoea, 1 dysentery, 1 bronchitis chronic, and 1 bronchitis acute. Surgeon Hopkins of the *Tacony* informs me that he has several cases of scorbutus on hand at present—hence the need of vegetables. I hope the *Mattabesett's* crew will not be unlucky enough to have scurvy in their midst.

June 6, 1864. The dead were buried today at Edenton. It appears that the *Seymour* case died from congestion of the liver—so the surgeon of the *Tacony* reports, who saw the man one hour previous to his death. Reported the following patients: viz., James A. Coleman, lds., 27 Kentucky—dysentery—℞ ol. ricini ℥ i, tinct opii gtts vi; William Bridgett, 2nd-class fireman, 44, England—complains of painful micturation—℞ fluid extract of buchu ʒ i three times a day—also keep his bowels regular; John Mialovinch—dysentery—order him the oleaginous mixture consisting of ol ricini ℥ ii, acaciae, sach alba āā ʒ ii, tinct opii ʒ i, aquae menthae pip f. ℥ iv, M, Sig. Tablespoonful every 2 hours; Michael Flaming—intermittens—

order him the following—℞ quiniae sulphas ℨ i, acaciae pulv grs
xv, mel q.s., ℞, pil. no lx, (50) Sig. One three times a day, or one
every 4 hours; William Smith—remittent fever—convalescent—
order him same pills as Flaming, also ℨ ss. port wine six times a day;
Christian Horn—bronchitis—℞ acaciae pulv., glycyrrh. pulv, sach
alba āā ℨ ss., aquae f ℨ xii, tinct opii f ℨ i, antim. et potas. tart grs ii,
aether spts nitric f ℨ ss., ℞, Sig. Tablespoonful every 4 hours, and
tartar-emetic ointment to chest; Thomas P. Swilling—bronchitis,
chronic—same treatment as Horn.

June 7, 1864. This morning another cargo of contrabands—about
10, male and female, aged from 60 to 2 years—arrived on board.
They escaped from the mainland during the night. The commodore will ship them to either Roanoke Island or Newbern in a day
or two. The contrabands had no news to tell.

Reported same sick as yesterday with the addition of James Car-
son, ord. sea.—chills and fever. Treated them upon general principles. All improving. 10 A.M. general quarters. Exercised the guns
—done some fine shooting. This afternoon we sent up our topmasts
—why and wherefore I cannot tell. It looks as though we intended
to put out to sea. I hope we may, for I am tired of this place as a
station. Would prefer outside blockade duty. Time will show why
we put our topmasts up aloft. Some say we are bound to Fortress
Monroe; others say to Norfolk; whilst some say we merely done it
for pastime. Rather hard work for fun, I think. Am inclined to
think that we intend to leave here.

10.30 P.M. The U.S.S. *Whitehead* arrived from Roanoke Island
with fresh beef and potatoes. Our paymaster returned in her in the
best of humor. Our mail is at Newbern. She reports the *Otsego*,
a double-ender, 974 tons, 10 guns, as being on the swash [narrow
sound or channel lying within a sand bank and the shore] at Hatteras Inlet. She is coming to this sound. Wonder whether she is
our relief. Also reports that a monitor is on her way to this station,
so that everything is lovely. The paymaster brought me quite a
package of honeydew [a kind of tobacco moistened with molasses],
which he purchased at Roanoke Island—cost, $0.07 per paper—so
that I have plenty of the weed at present. The paymaster brought
us some ice. Good boy!

June 8, 1864. At 11.30 A.M. all hands were called to muster to
hear the reading of a congratulatory letter from the Hon. Secretary

of the Navy thanking the officers and crew of the *Mattabesett* for the bravery exhibited during the naval engagement with the Rebel ram *Albemarle* on the 5th of May. Of course we all felt like saying, "Bully for you, Uncle Gideon."   . . .

By George! I feel good. And why? Simply because I came across an obliging chum who had the extreme kindness to give me a dose of the "Oh! be joyful," which was rather a pleasant beverage this warm weather. At 9 P.M. the selfsame individual gratified my palate again. Long may he flourish.

The weather has been rather hot today. Oh, don't I wish I were once more afloat in salt water instead of floating around in this fresh-water pond! I have any amount of fever and diarrhoea patients at present with a sprinkling of dysentery and bronchitis for a change. Thus far I have had no cases of scurvy, although the vessels *Tacony* and *Commodore Hull* have said disease on board. Today at my suggestion the paymaster issued an extra ration of vegetables as a prophylactic. Thus the boys will have tomatoes three times a week. All hands appear to relish the dose. The boys are catching catfish alongside the ship with a hook and line.

The following is a true copy of the congratulatory letter from Hon. Gideon Welles, viz—

Navy Department
May 25, 1864.

Sir:

I have had great satisfaction in receiving and perusing your report as the Senior Officer present, and the reports of the Commanding Officers of the Several vessels that were engaged in the encounter with the rebel iron clad ram "Albemarle" and her tender on the afternoon of the 5th instant in Albemarle Sound.

The Department congratulates all of the officers and men of the U.S. Navy who participated in this remarkable contest between wooden gunboats and a formidable armoured vessel, in which the latter was forced to retreat to prevent Capture; and it particularly thanks you for your vigilant and gallant use of the means placed at your command to thwart the designs of the rebels to regain the control of the Sounds of North Carolina.

Very respy etc. etc.
(Signed)   Gideon Welles
Secretary of the Navy

Captain Melancton Smith U.S. Navy
    Senior Officer
       Sounds of N. Carolina.

Acting Master J. L. Plunkett with an armed crew left the vessel, proceeded ashore, and destroyed a whiskey distillery belonging to the Rebels. They returned on board at 10 P.M. The party deserves great credit.

17

Watchful Waiting

Albemarle Sound, N. C., off mouth Roanoke River, June 9, 1864. At 5 A.M. I was aroused by my steward to see a boy named Jacob Nixon, who was very sick. I had given him a clean matress, pillow, and cot. I also ordered him antimonial and saline mixture, acidulated drinks, wine (sherry), and as a diet soup from the wardroom. Poor fellow—he is rather sick. Hope he may be better in the morning. He has an attack of fever. He at best is a sickly boy.

I reported 6 cases sick in my morning report. Attended to and ordered medicine for 12 patients on board of the U.S.S. *Whitehead.* One of the patients was a severe case of pleuritis. Ate a few cherries today that came from Secesh. The boys had rather a gay time bathing this evening alongside the ship, after which some "tripped on the light fantastic toe" to the tune of a violin played by a shipmate. In short, we have a rather gay crew.

Several refugees arrived on board today. One of them, a Mr. Stevenson, has quite an attack of chills and fever. Ordered him a dose of magnesiae sulphas so as to relieve his alimentary canal.

June 10, 1864. 10.30 A.M. The double-ender *Otsego,* Commander J. P. Bankhead in charge arrived. All hands—officers and all—are in white today. I am sporting white pants and vest. My sick are coming on slowly. Admitted Messrs. Plunkett and Dill today, affected with dysentery and impetigo.

At 4 P.M. I went ashore in the 2nd cutter with an armed crew and landed at the Underhill plantation, there to see a sick child 3 years of age. Found said child affected with bilious remittent. I left calomel, castor oil, quinine, and fever mixture there and told the mother how to use it. Met a doctor there named Doctor Leary, a

Union man; found him to be quite a social sort of fellow. Had a long chat with him. He is a graduate of the University of Pennsylvania, my alma mater. The boys got quite a cargo of cherries. Saw several very fine ladies there. Arrived on board at 7 P.M. Had a pleasant time. The plantation is a splendid one—at least it was in times of peace, from all indications.

Ascertained today that the *Chicopee* was on the swash. Another double-ender—the more the merrier.

June 11, 1864. The *Rockland* arrived today with a mail. I received a box of sherry, a letter from father dated May 30, also the "Med. and Surg. Reporter" for April 16, 23, and 30. Paymaster Mellach arrived on board. Landsman Nunes, whom I sent to the Newbern hospital, has returned on board again. Miss Amanda Corwin of Riverhead, L.I., sent me her *carte de visite;* also cordially invited me to call and see her. Was a member of a board of survey consisting of Surgeons Sartori, Boyer, and Hopkins. We examined and recommended Actg. 1st Asst. Engineer Rodney Nichols of the U.S.S. *Otsego,* affected with bronchitis, to be sent North for treatment. [The patient died at Hillsboro, New Hampshire, eighteen days later.]

June 12, 1864. Divine service at 10.30 A.M. Reported 10 cases sick. Dined on board the *Rockland* today. The *Rockland* left for Roanoke Island at 4 P.M. Messrs. Nichols, Stevenson, and Atchinson left in her. The *Tacony* sent a patient on board today affected with scurvy, or scorbutus. He is to go to the Newbern Naval Hospital. The *Otsego* also sent a hospital patient on board affected with bubo. I shall make their trip as comfortable as possible. Captain [Acting Ensign George W.] Barrett of the *Whitehead* and Captain [Acting Master Francis] Josselyn of the *Commodore Hull* exchanged *cartes de visite* with me—i.e., I gave them one of mine and they promised to send me theirs by mail.

June 13, 1864. At 1 A.M. we got under way and are on our passage to Newbern. 10 A.M. We are aground. Reported 10 cases sick this morning. [Chief] Engineer [Henry H.] Stewart of the *Wyalusing* is a passenger on board.

Today 25 years ago my mother presented my father with another scion of the noble house of Boyer in the shape of a small responsibility y-clept a son, named Samuel P. Boyer. In other words, this is my twenty-fifth birthday. Where will I be 25 years hence? In commemoration of said event I ordered the flowing bowl in the shape of sherry to be circulated freely amongst my messmates. We had a gay, festive, and jolly time. Joy for the time appeared unconfined.

8 P.M. We are still aground.

June 14, 1864. Still hard and fast aground. Would like to see the old *Mattabesett* afloat again. The weather is quite cool. The *Chicopee* appears to be aground also. Reported 11 cases sick, 3 officers and 8 men—4 dysentery, 1 intermittens, 2 bronchitis, 1 dysuria, 1 impetigo, 1 debility, and 1 rheumatism—besides the two hospital cases, scorbutus and bubo.

By the Northern papers of the 11th inst. we ascertain that the standard bearers of the Republican party appear to be Hon. Old Abe Lincoln for President and Hon. Andy Johnson for Vice President—a strong team. . . . Also read of the capture of the U.S.S. *Water Witch* by Rebels in Ossabaw Sound, Ga. . . .

[The *Water Witch,* attacked about three o'clock in the morning of June 3 while at anchor in Ossabaw Sound, fell into the enemy's hands with little resistance, though no formal surrender. Thirteen officers and forty-nine men were taken prisoner. After his release Lieutenant Commander Austin Pendergrast, in command, was court-martialed at Philadelphia, found guilty of "culpable inefficiency in the discharge of duty," and sentenced to a two-year suspension on half pay with loss of rank.]

June 15, 1864. We are once more afloat. Ordered medicine for some sick men of the U.S.S. *Ceres.* Reported 9 cases sick this morning. Wrote a letter to the fleet surgeon, enclosing requisition for medical stores. Received 2 papers today—one from father and one from Mr. Moses. . . .

Off Newbern, N.C., June 16, 1864. Weather rather warm. Recd. letter from sister Beckie dated June 2; answered the same today. Received a letter from Miss Carrie Carlisle . . . dated June 1, in answer to my date May 13.

Reported 5 cases sick today. Sent 2 patients to the Newbern Naval Hospital today: viz., Jacob Nixson, 1st-class boy, 17 years old, born in Germany, affected with adynamia—disease did not originate in line of duty; and Thomas P. Swilling, lds., age 22, born in Georgia, affected with bronchitis chronica, attended with aphonia—disease did not originate in line of duty. I went on shore this morning and remained there until sunset. Had quite a pleasant time. Met quite a number of naval officers.

June 17, 1864. The U.S.S. *Sassacus* left for the North this morning. Took a stroll on shore. Bought 1 hat, bottle of bay rum, mosquito bar, besides several knickknacks. Dined at the Gaston House in company with Messrs. Plunkett, Greenhalgh, and Sackett. Received a letter from Fleet Surgeon J[ohn] L. Fox requesting me to send a list of casualties occurring on board this vessel during the action with the enemy May 5, 1864. I answered same, enclosing required document. Enclosed in a letter to father a copy of the "North Carolina Times" [variously a weekly, a semiweekly, and a daily, published at New Bern 1864-1875 under a succession of names]. Paymaster Mellach gave me one of his *cartes de visite,* and a fine one it is.

June 18, 1864. Was a member of a court of inquiry held today on board this vessel to substantiate a charge against A.A. Surgeon Thos. W. Jamison, U.S.N., by [Acting] Vol. Lieutenant [Francis M.] Green of the U.S.S. *Louisiana.* Upon examination we find said charge substantially correct. [Jamison was dismissed from service August 1, 1864.] Said court consisted of Commander J.C. Febiger, Chief Engineer H.H. Stewart, and A.A. Surgeon S.P. Boyer. Sent my steward on shore today for recreation. Reported 8 cases sick— 2 dysentery, 1 bronchitis, 2 cephalalgia, 1 dysuria, and 1 rheumatism. Recd. a letter from Alfred Moses . . . in answer to my date of June 2. Recd. a letter from the fleet surgeon dated June 13 regarding Benj. F. Bee . . ., who was condemned by a medical board of survey May 31. Answered both letters. Wrote a letter to Miss Carrie Carlisle . . . in answer to hers dated June 1, received June 16. Wrote a letter to the surgeon of the U.S.S. *Wyalusing,* Dr. Sartori, enclosing him a copy of the fleet surgeon's letter. . . . Weather 105° Fahr. in the shade.

June 19, 1864. Divine service at 10.30 A.M., an Army chaplain officiating—at least, a reverend gentleman belonging to the Christian Sanitary Commission.

[Probably an agent of the United States Christian Commission (there was also a United States Sanitary Commission, an important civilian auxiliary that was something of a forerunner of the Red Cross; Dr. Boyer apparently mixed the two), operating under the auspices of the Young Men's Christian Associations "to promote the physical comfort and the spiritual welfare of the brave men of the army and navy . . . wherever they may be found . . . without regard to race, creed, or position." The organization distributed reading matter (particularly Bibles and other religious literature), provided writing equipment and other "comforts," conducted religious meetings, administered private spiritual help, aided the wounded, furnished food and clothing to the destitute, and rendered many other services. Its "delegates" in the field, numbering in 1864 an average of 217, were voluntary workers, receiving no compensation but various privileges such as free transportation over military railways for themselves and their supplies and free transmission of telegraphic dispatches. Bibles and Testaments were donated by the American Bible Society and religious and moral books, periodicals, and newspapers and tracts by various publishers.]

He preached rather a poor sermon—pointed out to us all our bad deeds but forgot to tell us how to get out of the mire. Being rather a young and inexperienced man, of course we have to make allowances.

[Acting Assistant] Paymaster [J. George] Orme [stationed at the naval depot at New Bern], [Acting Assistant] Surgeon [George W.] Wilson [of the *Hetzel*], and [Acting Third Assistant] Engineer [A. D.] Witherell [of the *Hetzel*] dined with us today. After dinner at 5 P.M. Paymaster Meade, Surgeon Wilson, Paymaster Orme, Engineer Witherell, Surgeon Boyer, and Ensign Brown took a stroll on shore. In our rambles we came across an ice-cream saloon and had quite a palatable plate of cream, besides some fine sherry and good cigars. In short, we had quite a pleasant time.

Reported 7 cases sick in my morning report of the sick—1 rheumatismus, 1 dysuria, 1 bronchitis, 1 ophthalmia and 3 dysenteria. . . . .

June 21, 1864. Almost as lazy as yesterday; still I think I will write up a short log. The gay and saucy mess of this ship—i.e., the wardroom mess—at last have a regular organized wine mess, our illustrious, enterprising and efficient paymaster, the jolly sea dog Harry C. Meade, acting as wine caterer. He laid in stores to the amount of a few cool hundred. Thus far I have invested in sherry wine bottles 2, champagne cider 1 bottle, which will last me today, for I have plenty of calls. The paymaster tells me that I am out of debt at last—in other words, that my "dead horse" is worked out [work paid for in advance; term supposedly derived from sailors' celebration of pay resumption by dragging about an effigy of a horse, representing their "fruitless labor," and finally dropping it into the water from the yardarm]. Huzza! Huzza!! Huzza!!! I say. Paid a wash bill of two dollars today. Invested the sum of nine dollars in wine today.

During quarters today a man named Stamp received a bayonet cut across his right cheek two inches in length. His upper eyelid of right eye also was wounded. Said wound penetrated to the bone. I introduced three stitches, applied strips of isinglass plaster, etc. Poor fellow—he was more frightened than hurt.

This day two years ago I entered the service of the United States. . . . . Wonder where I'll be two years hence.

June 22, 1864. The U.S.S. *Chicopee* arrived today. I expect that we will now soon leave for our old station off the mouth of the Roanoke River [the *Mattabesett*, though still in Albemarle Sound, had moved about off Newbern and other places]. Well! Well!! I suppose we will have to meet Mr. Ram once more.

8 P.M. The U.S.S. *Valley City* and the U.S.S. *Ceres* have arrived in port, the former having the latter in tow.

[The *Ceres'* engines were out of order, and the *Valley City* was returning from a joint army and navy expedition up the Pungo River against Confederate guerrillas. Both vessels were repaired at New Bern before resuming duty.]

Nothing of any importance transpired today worthy of note besides the above entries.

June 24, 1864. The weather was very warm today—thermometer 105° Fahr. in shade. Ice water and claret punches were in great demand. My steward took a stroll on shore and remained 3 hours later than his time. Result: he is quarantined as long as the vessel remains in the sounds of North Carolina; in other words, he will not be allowed to go on shore—rather a tough procedure, yet the necessity of the case demands it. Will learn him a lesson for the future. Hope he will benefit by it.

June 25, 1864. The weather was rather hot—thermometer 103° Fahr. in shade. Was ordered in company with Actg. Asst. Surgeons

G.W. Wilson of the U.S.S. *Hetzel* and G[eorge] L. Simpson of the U.S.S. *Chicopee* as a medical board of survey to hold a strict and careful medical survey upon patients affected with chronic diseases who are in the Newbern Naval Hospital. We recommended all the chronic cases to be sent to the Norfolk Naval Hospital, there to be disposed of as the authorities deem proper. I had the honor of being the senior member of the board; therefore I had to do all the writing etc. Was busy nearly all day examining the above cases.

The *Massasoit* arrived with a mail. I received one paper from brother Michael . . . as my share.

The commodore of the sounds, Captain Melancton Smith, has been ordered to his own vessel, the ironclad monitor *Onondaga*, James River, Va. . . . I understand that the captain leaves in the morning. . . . The *Shamrock* is on the swash. She will hereafter be the flagship [her captain, Commander William H. Macomb, assuming command as senior officer].

Pamlico Sound, N.C., June 27, 1864. Left Newbern at 7 A.M. and came to anchor off Roanoke Island at 8 P.M. Thus we are once more in the vicinity of Mr. Ram's headquarters. Wonder if he will show himself again soon. [A reconnoitering party sent up the Roanoke River on June 24 had found that the *Albemarle*, lying at Plymouth, was apparently ready for service again, her smokestack replaced by that of another vessel and her guns mounted.] Rained some today.

Off Roanoke Island, June 28, 1864. Quite a gale prevailing. . . . . Reported 4 cases sick—1 neuralgia, 1 rheumatism, 1 bronchitis, and 1 ophthalmia.

June 29, 1864. Today the commodore, Captain Melancton Smith, left the ship and took passage in the *Rockland* for his vessel, the *Onondaga*, in James River. We cheered ship. All were sorry to see him go. Thus we cease to be the flagship. The U.S.S. *Shamrock* now bears the broad pennant of the flag officer. I understand that we are ordered to the mouth of the Roanoke River again. We leave here tomorrow, I think.

Off mouth Roanoke River, July 1, 1864. 6.50 P.M. We let go our starboard anchor. Thus we are once more in our old station. The report is that the ram intends to pay us a Fourth of July visit. Let her come! The vessels here at present are the *Shamrock* (flagship),

Otsego, Tacony, Mattabesett, and *Wyalusing*—all double-enders. The small steamers *Whitehead* and *Commodore Hull* are the picket boats.

I made out my 2nd quarterly report of sick for 1864. During said quarter I had 546 sick calls, daily average no. of sick 6, daily average cost per man $0.04 29/546, 89 diseases, medical expenses $22.13, besides having an outfit of $600 when I left port. During said quarter 546 cases were admitted—7 of them sent to hospitals, 2 died, and 537 cases discharged to duty.

July 2, 1864. Recd. my medical stores for which I made a requisition upon the fleet surgeon dated June 15. Sent my 2nd quarterly report of sick, 1864, together with copies of bills etc., to the fleet surgeon.

At dusk the whole fleet got under way, heading for the outlet of the sound. We let go our anchor off the mouth of the Perquimans River [navigable by small steamboats for about forty miles]. I understand that the object is to draw the ram out so as to have one glorious fight on the 4th of July.

Weather hot—thermometer 110° Fahr. in shade and 140° Fahr. in sun.

Off mouth Perquimans River, July 3, 1864. Here we are at anchor off the mouth of Perquimans River. Weather as hot as ever. Paymaster, engineer, and myself paid the *Wyalusing* a visit. Dined on board with them. Had a pleasant time.

July 4, 1864. The whole fleet fired a national salute today; ships dressed with flags. The officers of this craft had a jolly time eating and drinking. Too lazy to write notes.

July 5, 1864. A sutler's schooner arrived. Reported having a mail on board. I received a letter from father dated June 22 in answer to my date of the 11th of June. He reports all well and lovely at home. Answered said letter. The Army transport *General Berry* arrived this evening. The Army steamer *Massasoit* blew up the other day at Newbern—boiler bursted, scalding quite a number. Received on board a New York "Herald" of July 2. In it is announced the resignation [June 29, accepted June 30] of Hon. Salmon P. Chase . . . and the appointment [July 1] of Hon. Senator [William P.] Fessenden of Maine [who had been prominent in congressional monetary legislation] as Secretary of the Treasury. Gold is quoted at 225; was as high as 285 at one time [July 1, falling to 230 the next day (following the repeal of the gold bill of June 17, which prohibited purely speculative trading in gold futures and contracting for delivery of gold not possessed at the time), rising to 284 on July 11, and falling after further fluctuation to 187 on September 26. (See pp. 83-84.)]. Awful news.

July 6, 1864. Reported 18 cases sick today—mostly dysentery and fever patients.

July 7, 1864. Took a run to off mouth Roanoke River. Communicated with the U.S. steamers *Commodore Hull* and *Whitehead*. Received on board 12 refugees. Ascertained from them that our torpedo corps had been captured; said corps was in charge of Actg. Master's Mate Baldwin. 2.25 P.M. we arrived off the mouth of the Perquimans River again. Weather hot.

Received a letter today from Alfred Moses . . . dated June 26, in answer to my date of June 19. He enclosed a bill of dues, due the St. Andrew's Lodge, amounting to $2.75. I answered said letter this evening, enclosing $3, to be expended in paying said Masonic dues and the remaining to be expended in whiskey. Mr. Moses appears to have been in a splendid humor when he wrote said letter, judging from the tenor of said epistle.

This evening our caterer, Mr. Plunkett, resigned, and Ensign Brown was elected on the second ballot. Paid a mess bill of $13, having paid $115 ere I left New York, amounting to in all $128 —rather tall. Also paid a wine bill amounting to $21.20; at same time I have a credit of $11.50 in the wine fund.

July 8, 1864. Our old pilot, Mr. Tooker, was transferred to the U.S. flagship *Shamrock*. We were all very sorry to see him leave us. He was a favorite with all hands. Our new pilot's name is [James] Fountain.

July 9, 1864. The *General Berry* has arrived with a mail. I got nary letter. The news are that the *Kearsarge* had sunk the *Alabama* [off Cherbourg, France, Sunday morning, June 19]. Thus ends the pirate's career. All feel happy over the news.

Our worthy master, Jas. L. Plunkett, received a letter from home announcing the birth of a son. Thus he can call himself a man of family. Mr. Plunkett ordered the claret, and all his messmates drank to the health of the young scion. . . .

Another mail arrived this afternoon. We sent a cutter to the flagship for our portion of it. Wonder whether I will be lucky enough to get anything either in the shape of a letter or paper. Think it high time that my friends up North answer my letters. There are no less than a dozen of my letters unanswered. This doing blockade duty is dull and monotonous enough even with plenty of letters, let alone when you receive none or are without any reading matter. I am anxiously awaiting the return of Ensign Brown in the 2nd cutter with the mail. 5.30 P.M. Ensign Brown returned, but I received nary letter. Rather [un] pleasant.

Reported 11 cases sick today, my steward, James Karsner, amongst the number. Poor fellow—he is affected with a slight bilious remittent. I will endeavor to get him on his feet ere long, for I miss his services very much indeed.

July 10, 1864. Divine service at 10.30 A.M. The U.S. *Ceres* arrived from Newbern with a small mail. I recd. a Brooklyn "[Daily] Eagle", July 2, sent me by Dr. Russell D. Adams, formerly my steward. Said paper had the announcement of the commencement of the Long Island Hospital College. Dr. Adams' name was mentioned amongst the list of graduates. May he be successful in his career. I expect to see him enter the service soon as a surgeon.

July 12, 1864. Recd. a mail today. I received the "Medical and Surgical Reporter" for May 8, 15, 21, and 28 today. We are blessed with a cool thundershower. The *Tacony* left for Newbern last evening.

July 14, 1864. A mail boat arrived from Roanoke River bringing a mail and fresh provisions.   . . .

The *Otsego,* having been up the sound off the mouth of the Roanoke River yesterday, returned and reported that the ram had made her appearance at the mouth of the river trying to remove torpedoes, but the *Otsego's* guns caused her to skedaddle again. I should not wonder if she were to come out and show fight again ere long.

Off mouth Roanoke River, July 15, 1864. Here we are once more on our old station, the place where we had a fight with the Rebel ram. We are acting as picket boat. Upon the arrival of the ram, if we cannot keep her in the river, why, then we are to retreat down the sound as far as the Perquimans River, notify the balance of the fleet, when a brisk engagement is expected to come off. We are all sanguine of success.

Reported 11 cases sick—1 remittent, 2 intermittent, 2 bronchitis, 1 diarrhoea, 1 ambustio, 1 abrasio, 1 otalgia, 1 rheumatism, and 1 sore leg. All improving. My steward is somewhat better today.

Upon our arrival here we found the U.S.S. *Ceres* and U.S.S. *Whitehead* acting as picket boats. We relieved the *Ceres*. She goes down the sound to coal ship. 10 P.M. the *Ceres* returned again.

Off mouth Perquimans River, July 16, 1864. We arrived here this morning. The U.S.S. *Chicopee* arrived from Newbern.

Last night some evil-minded person or persons broke the lock off my medical locker and stole therefrom six bottles of whiskey. This morning three persons, named John Patten, lds.; Michael Quinn, q. gunner; and —— Hoey, sea., were found to be intoxicated —evidently the effects of the stolen liquor. All three were confined, double-ironed, in the brig.

We received a mail today. I received a letter from Miss Carrie Carlisle in answer to my date of June 18, postmarked July 4. Also received two papers from father dated July 2.

The surgeon of the *Shamrock* [Acting Assistant Surgeon Philip Hale Barton] came on board today. He appears to be quite a lively *medicus*. This is his first cruise. So far he appears to like the Navy very well. The *Shamrock* took a run in shore and let fly several shots at a schooner supposed to be a blockade runner. Nothing of any account resulted from said firing.

July 17, 1864. Divine service at 10.30 A.M. Weather lovely. Reported 14 sick cases. This appears to be rather a sickly station. My cases are 1 rheumatic, 3 intermittent, 1 ambustio, 1 abrasio, 1 remittent, 1 otalgia, 1 sore leg, 2 bronchitis, 1 sore throat, 1 colica, 1 dysentery. I shall discharge some of the above cases. My steward appears to be improving finely. No signs of my lost medical stores.

July 18, 1864. Received a letter from sister Beckie dated July 7 in answer to my date of June 16. I immediately answered the same, enclosing a two-dollar greenback etc.

Was a member of a medical board of survey, consisting of Actg. Asst. Surgeons Sartori, Boyer, and Barton. We surveyed Actg. 2nd Asst. Engineer J. Madison Case of the U.S.S. *Wyalusing* and recommended that he be sent to the naval hospital, Norfolk, for further treatment. He was affected with tonsilitis. Reported 14 cases sick. My steward is about the same.

July 19, 1864. Rain! Rain!! Rain!!! all day. Received fresh provisions today. It is rumored that we are ordered North. How true the report is I cannot say, but hope it may prove so. My steward still continues rather under the weather—order him tonics etc. A mail arrived today, but I was one of the unfortunate ones. Reported 12 cases sick; will cause some of them to go to duty in the morning —that is, providing the weather is pleasant.

The crew—that is, part of them—have organized themselves into a Glee Club. There are some fine and splendid singers amongst them. Their instruments consist of violin, tamborine, bones, guitar etc. Every evening until 9 o'clock they have a gay time. Some of the boys trip on the light fantastic toe while the music is under way. They all appear to be a jolly set of boys.

July 20, 1864. Still continues to rain. Reported 16 cases sick. My steward is rather slow in gaining strength. Was called as a witness before a court of inquiry consisting of Lieutenants J[ohn] H. Rowland of the *Otsego,* Rufus K. Duer of the *Shamrock,* and A. N. Mitchell of the *Mattabesett* to testify as regards the physical condition of Actg. Master's Mate Chas. Fisher on the 14th instant, said Fisher at that time being on the sick list, at which time he made use of insulting language to one of his messmates. The nature of said affair I will not mention.

One of the messenger boys who has a peculiar propensity of appropriating things belonging to others was today compelled to promenade the deck with a straight-jacket [strait jacket] made of canvas upon which was painted in large letters "Thief." He did not appear to fancy his new uniform. Hope it may prove beneficial.

Had quite a pleasant time today catching catfish with a hook and line. We had them for supper tonight—rather a palatable dish.

July 21, 1864. Received a long and interesting letter from Ensign Flood . . . dated June 25 in answer to my date of June 5. Also found enclosed a note from [Acting Assistant] Surgeon [Stephen B.] Kenney of the *Fernandina.* Wrote a letter to Ensign Flood and one to Dr. Kenney; also wrote an official letter to . . . Kenney . . . enclosing a receipt for medical stores transferred to his steward Feby. 19, 1864, which he is to sign and return to me.

We steamed up the sound toward the mouth of the Roanoke;

arrived there at 2.30 P.M. While there, we received on board about 30 human beings in the form of contrabands, refugees, and recruits. The latter were men that an Army lieutenant had recruited right in the midst of the enemy—rather a ticklish place to open a recruiting office! He reports about 1,200 whites and contrabands concealed in the swamps, waiting for an opportunity to escape. At 6.35 P.M. we arrived back again and let go our port anchor. While at anchor off Edenton, our caterer bought several watermelons, which were served up to the members of the w.r. mess in grand style.

July 22, 1864. The U.S.S. *Wyalusing* left today for Newbern. Hope the officers may have a gay and festive time while there. Reported 8 cases sick today.

8.30 P.M. The crew are having quite a concert tonight under the hurricane deck. The colored portion are on the port side singing camp-meeting hymns, whilst the jolly portion are on the starboard side singing comic, Irish, sentimental, and patriotic songs—quite a contrast. Both parties are trying to make the most noise. . . . .

July 25, 1864. The weather was rather pleasant today. Reported the following cases sick: James H.M. Karsner, my steward, who is suffering from the effects of an attack of remittent fever—order him the following three times a day—℞ quiniae sulphas grs ii, acid sulph aromat gtts viii, aquae f ℥ ss., ℳ; James W. Sullivan, b[oatswain's] mate—intermittent—order him the same medicine as that ordered for my steward; Thos. Lee—ambustio—dress the ulcer with simple cerate; John Moore—bronchitis—order him expectorants; Albert Cornell—catarrhus—order him expectorants; James H. Bunting—abrasio—dress with cerate simplex. Besides the above I have several outdoor patients who, notwithstanding they take medicine, are still able to do duty.

July 26, 1864. A mail boat arrived today. Recd. a letter from Miss A. K. Carlisle . . . dated July 11.

3 P.M. We are anchored off Edenton, or, as I generally called the anchorage, off mouth Roanoke River. I understand that we are to remain here until Saturday next.

Captains [Acting Master Henry H.] Foster and Barrett of the U.S. steamers *Ceres* and *Whitehead* reported to me that they had several sick on board. I shall send them some medicine as soon as an opportunity presents itself.

The last accounts of the ram are that she is still at Plymouth and has no idea of coming out in a hurry. Answered Miss Carlisle's letter.

Off mouth Roanoke River, July 27, 1864. Reported 4 cases sick today. Expended quiniae sulphas ℥ ss, magnesiae sulphas lb i, and pil. cath. comp. no iii for the benefit of the U.S.S. *Ceres'* sick.

Plenty of watermelons, green corn, muskmelons, etc. to be had at Edenton. Our caterer, Ensign Brown, who, by the by, is the prince of all caterers, always manages to keep the wardroom mess well supplied with all the luxuries of the season. Long may he flourish! . . .

July 28, 1864. At 1.30 A.M. the Army steamers *Thomas Colyer* and *Massasoit* arrived loaded with troops. At daybreak they started, joined by the U.S.S. *Whitehead,* on an expedition up the Chowan River. What the object of said expedition is to be remains yet to be seen. Still, whatever the object may be, I hope it may prove successful.

[The expedition, a joint army and navy operation undertaken for the procurement of supplies, was "entirely successful." At Gatesville, North Carolina, the Confederate steamer *Arrow* and ten bales of cotton were captured; at Winton three bales of cotton, one hundred boxes of tobacco, and some bacon were taken and "a quantity of salt" was destroyed; and at Colerain ninety bales of cotton and eighty boxes of tobacco were secured. "A few more expeditions of this sort," wrote Brigadier General I. N. Palmer, headquarters District of North Carolina, New Bern, to Commander Macomb on August 4, "would quite set the Government up in the way of these supplies".[6]]

The weather has an inclination to be of a wet nature. Reported 4 cases sick—viz., my steward—remittent fever, who is convalescent; Albert Cornell—catarrhus, who is improving; Wm. C. Johnson— pleurodynia, who still complains of great pain; Peter Bagley, c[oal] h[eaver], 21, Ireland, who complains of earache (otalgia)—applied behind his ear a blister—syringe out ear, drop glycerine a few drops into ear, introduce a small piece of cotton, and order him tartar emetic gr $\frac{1}{16}$ every 2 hours.

July 29, 1864. Reported the following cases this morning: John C. Robinson, paymaster's clerk—intermittens—℞ pil. cath. comp. no ii; Daniel Doherty, lds., 26, New York—intermittens—took pil.

cath. comp. no iii last night—this morning I ordered him the following—℞ magnesiae sulphas ℥ i, antim. et potas. tart. grs iii, potassae nitras ℨ ii, aquae mentha pip. f ℥ vii, M, Sig. Tablespoonful every two hours; Peter Bagley, c.h.—otalgia—dress blister with cerate simplex—continue the glycerine and tartar emetic; Wm. C. Johnson, c[arpenter's] mate—pleurodynia—continue same plan of treatment; James H.M. Karsner, surgeon's steward—remittens—convalescent—continue the following—℞ quiniae sulphas gr i, acid sulph. aromat gtts viii, aquae f ℥ ss., M, Sig. To be taken every four hours.

At 1 P.M. everyone on board was startled with the cry of "Man overboard!" All immediately rushed to the sides, and in less than no time said party who was overboard was again on deck. He proved to be one Frank Reilly, coal heaver, aged 30, native of Ireland, who while laboring under the effects of suicidal monomania, or, more properly, that branch of insanity termed hypochondriasis, attempted suicide by jumping overboard. When rescued and asked why he done so, he did not appear to have any cause or reason. He talked about imaginary evils. Some of his messmates told me that he acted very strange for the last week or so. I ordered him his hammock, also pil. cath. comp no iii.

At 10 P.M. the *Massasoit, Thomas Colyer,* and *Whitehead* returned from the Chowan River. The *Colyer* had the Rebel screw steamer *Arrow* in tow, also 100 bales of cotton, 100 boxes of tobacco, 2 bbls. of pork, and other commissary stores on board which they captured up the Chowan [see preceding page]. The vessel ascended the river 80 miles. Whilst there, they heard heavy cannonading. No doubt said firing was before Petersburg, Va. [strongly defended city of eighteen thousand on the south bank of the Appomattox River twenty-two miles below Richmond; at the time under siege by General Grant]. They captured two engineers and two contrabands on board of the *Arrow;* her captain, pilot, etc. escaped. The *Arrow* was the only boat that the Rebels had on the Chowan; hence her loss is rather a hard blow for them. The above capturers will have quite a snug pile of prize money due them.

Off mouth Chowan River, July 30, 1864. The U.S.S. *Otsego* arrived this morning. She no doubt comes to relieve us; she brought neither mail or fresh beef. 2 P.M. We are on our way to the fleet off Perquimans River. Arrived there at 4.30 P.M.

Reported the following cases sick: Albert Cornell—catarrhus—continue expectorants; Wm. C. Johnson—pleurodynia—continue same plan of treatment; Peter Bagley—otalgia—continue same plan of treatment; James H.M. Karsner—remittens—order him gentianae ext grs iii three times a day; Daniel Doherty—intermittens—order him quiniae sulphas gr i, acid sulph. aromat gtts viii, aquae f ʒ ss. three times a day; John C. Robinson—fever—order him the mixture that I ordered for Doherty yesterday; Frank Reilly—hypochondriasis—appears more rational this morning—head aches less—bowels still irregular—tongue slightly coated—complains of pain in right side, where he hurt himself yesterday—order him magnesiae sulpha ʒ i, also rub his side with volatile liniment.

Off mouth Perquimans River, July 31, 1864. The U.S.S. *Tacony* and 4 naval tugs arrived today—that is, I saw them today; they, more properly speaking, arrived late last night. The weather was very warm today. Divine service at 10.30 A.M. Reported 9 cases sick today. Robinson, the fever patient, is rather sick today, and Reilly, the attempted suicide, is still continuing in the same condition.

Aug. 1, 1864. Weather rather hot. Reported same cases as yesterday sick. Reilly today managed to get into the fireroom and while there got in behind the starboard blower and enveloped his head with an overcoat (the temperature of the place being about 160° Fahrenheit), evidently with the intention of smothering himself to death. No sooner was he rescued than he was seen trying to get on top of the condenser. When asked his reason for so doing, he answered that they, the firemen and coal heavers, were going to kill him. Poor fellow! I gave him tinct. opii camphorata ʒ ii at 8 o'clock P.M. and put him into his hammock. I will send him to a hospital as soon as I can. I think a change of place and associates will prove beneficial in his case. The rest of my patients are improving slowly.

Paid the caterer of the w.r. mess ten dollars on account of mess bills. Drew twenty dollars from the paymaster on account.

Aug. 2, 1864. We received a mail today. I received a letter from sister Beckie dated July 27 in answer to my letter dated July 18. I answered said letter today. Reilly slept quite well all last night. He eats little or nothing at all to speak of. Shall continue his iron mixture. Mr. Robinson feels somewhat better today; 8 P.M. has a slight fever. The rest of my patients are coming on finely. I reported 13 cases sick this morning. At 8 P.M. Reilly made another attempt to kill himself by rushing on the spar deck and jumping down the fireroom hatchway, and had he not been fortunate enough to land on top of one of the firemen, why he would of killed himself, for he landed head first on said fireman. I therefore had to get him shackled to a ring bolt on the berth deck. He has his hammock etc. to lay on. I also give him tinct. opii camp. 3 ii in aquae f ʒ i so as to cause him to sleep.

Aug. 3, 1864. Today I sent man Reilly to the naval hospital, Newbern. There is no evidence to prove that the disease originated in the line of duty. My steward accompanied him so as to take care of him until he arrives at the hospital. Reported 13 cases sick this morning.

Was the senior member of a medical board of survey held for the purpose of holding a strict and careful survey upon acting Master's Mate Wallace W. Reed, attached to the U.S.S. *Ceres.* Upon examination, we (the board, which consisted of Surgeons Barton, Reynolds, and Boyer) found him affected with remittent fever— duration of disease uncertain—disability originated in the line of duty, our reasons being on account of being exposed to the miasmatic influences while attached to the U.S.S. *Ceres,* doing picket duty in Albemarle Sound. We recommended that he be sent to the naval hospital, Norfolk, for further treatment.

The weather was quite pleasant all day. Paid a wine bill today amounting to one dollar and forty-five cents—rather a small one indeed. The last wine bill amounted to $21.20—quite a contrast. Was busy for one hour today preparing cerate simplex, using wax, adeps, and olive oil. It was rather a warm job.

The *Shamrock* steamed up the sound this afternoon to communicate with the picket boats off mouth of the Roanoke River.

Aug. 4, 1864. Purchased from the paymaster's department three yards of linen, which I intend for sheets and pillowcases. Said linen cost one dollar and thirty-seven and a third cents per yard. My whole bill will amount to four dollars and twelve cents ($4.12)— rather cheap. Reported 6 cases sick today. Weather warm. Invested the sum of three dollars in sutler's stores, consisting of Florida water [a proprietary toilet water], sabins ext[ract?], pomatum and solace. Watermelons are as plenty as June bugs. We have had some splendid ones. Everyone on the ship has as many as he can well stow away.

Aug. 5, 1864. The U.S. steamer *Otsego* left this morning for New-bern. We had quite a shower of rain this morning. Reported 5 cases sick: viz., John C. Robinson—remittens—slight improvement —order him the following—℞ quiniae sulphas grs xvi, acid sulph. aromat f ℨ ss., aquae f ℨ ii, ℳ, Sig. Teaspoonful every 2 hours; David Hall—paronychia—apply lini cataplasm; Richard P. Steel—catarrhus—℞ cough mixture; Peter Bagley—otalgia—syringe out ear with tepid water—introduce glycerine into ear—℞ tartar emetic gr ¹⁄₁₆ every two hours; John W. Patten—intermittent—℞ quiniae sulphas grs ii, acid, sulph. aromat gtts viii, aquae f ℥ i, ℳ, Sig. Take every 4 hours.

The *Cotton Plant*, accompanied by four launches, made her appearance at the mouth of the Roanoke River the other night with the intention of gobbling one of the picket boats, but much to their chagrin the picket boats had their eyes open and saw her approach, upon which a rocket was sent up as a notice to the *Otsego*, which happened to be stationed off Edenton. I suppose the next call will be the ram. All I can say is "Let her come." I think Uncle Sam's webfeet [probably any Navy personnel stationed in the watery sounds region] are ready to give her a warm reception.

5 P.M. the *Pilot Boy*, an Army steamer, arrived. The *Tacony* was shooting at a target with her heavy guns this afternoon. Her shooting, or firing, was not as good as the firing done by the *Mattabesett*.

Aug. 6, 1864. The *Pilot Boy*, having been up the sound, reports that the ram was at the mouth of the Roanoke River. What her intentions are remains yet to be seen. A mail arrived this morning, and my portion consisted of four papers—the Reading "Journal" [probably the *Berks and Schuylkill Journal*, a weekly published at Reading from 1816 to 1910], the "Gazette" [the Reading *Gazette and Democrat*, a weekly, 1840-1878; known its first eight years as the Reading Gazette], the "Daily Reporter" [unidentified], and the Philadelphia "Daily Age" [published as the *Daily Age* 1863-1866, as the *Age* 1866-1874, and as the *Illustrated New Age* 1874-1875]. Father sent me the first two papers, and brother Michael was kind enough to forward to my address the two latter. Slight thunderstorms. Reported six cases sick this morning, all appearing to be improving. 1 P.M. reported J. W. Sullivan sick—chills.

We steamed up the sound toward the mouth of the Roanoke River, the *Tacony* taking the lead, the *Shamrock* next, and the

Mattabesett brought up the rear. We heard that the ram was out. At 1.35 P.M. we anchored off Bluff Point, within ten miles of the mouth of the Roanoke River.

Off Bluff Point, Aug. 7, 1864. General muster at 10 A.M. Roll called; Articles of War read. 10.30 divine service. Weather hot— thermometer in shade 105° Fahr., in sun 130°. Reported 9 cases sick. Wrote a letter to M. P. Boyer. . . . 5 P.M. Commenced to rain. Heavy thundershowers. The executive officer of the *Chicopee,* Lieutenant [Edward A.] Walker, took lunch with us today. Messrs. Walker and Mitchell (of our ship) used to be college mates at Annapolis Naval School.

The *Tacony* lies at anchor off mouth Roanoke River. The *Shamrock, Chicopee,* and *Mattabesett* and two tugs are at anchor at Bluff Point.

Aug. 8, 1864. Weather quite warm. Reported 8 cases sick today: viz., Patrick King, c.h.—burn—dress with chalk cerate; R. P. Steel —catarrhus— ℞ expectorants; David Hall—paronychia—lanced and applied lini cataplasm; William Rogers—diarrhoea— ℞ camphor mixture; James W. Sullivan—chills— ℞ pil. cath. comp. no iii; Moses Williams, lds.—vulnus contusum— ℞ lini cataplasm; A. F. Dill—sore arm—apply resin cerate; John C. Robinson—remittens —continue tonics etc.

9 P.M. The U.S.S. *Wyalusing* arrived, and another vessel looking like a double-ender is coming up the sound. Wonder whether she is our relief. Hope she may so prove to be. Time will tell.

From late papers received tonight we ascertain that Grant undermined part of Petersburg and sent part of said town up in the air.

[A heavy mine planted under one of the most important Confederate works at Petersburg, Virginia, was exploded early in the morning of July 30, blowing up a six-gun fort with its equipage and two hundred men and leaving a huge crater. In the costly furious combat that followed, the Federals were repulsed.]

The Rebels have destroyed the greater part of Chambersburg, Pa., by applying the torch.

[Stirred by vandalism committed during the Lynchburg campaign by the Federals under General Hunter, a Confederate mounted brigade of three thousand crossed the Potomac on July 29 and advanced on Chambersburg.

The inhabitants, refusing to pay the $500,000 in currency or $100,000 in gold that was demanded, hurried their money and valuables into hiding. The next day the town was set afire; about two-thirds of the community, or two hundred and fifty houses, was burned. A state commission subsequently fixed the losses at more than a million and a half dollars.]

Rather a tough affair, but such is the fate of war! The effects of civil war are desolation and ruin, poverty and distress etc.—so says an old adage; and it is not far from the truth. Oh, for the good old times of peace and plenty!

Aug. 9, 1864. My steward returned on board today. He feels quite comfortable. Reilly arrived safely to the hospital. Recd. a letter from father dated July 17. Said letter had been missent to Port Royal—hence the delay in reaching me. I received said letter today.

5.30 P.M. Acting as a picket boat off mouth of the Roanoke River. We relieved the *Tacony*. At present there are 6 double-enders in this sound—viz., *Shamrock, Chicopee, Wyalusing, Otsego, Mattabesett,* and *Tacony*—rather a good-sized fleet. Reported 8 cases sick today. The U.S.S. *Ceres* has a surgeon's steward at large on board. He arrived today. Hope he may have a pleasant time and very few sick.

Off mouth Roanoke River, Aug. 10, 1864. This morning at 2 o'clock I was roused out to see a patient. It appears that Ensign Dill was taken sick at that time with an attack of cholera communis —severe vomiting, purging, and griping. I ordered mustard cataplasm to stomach and anodynes internally. Today he takes slippery-elm tea as a demulcent to soothe the irritated condition of his alimentary canal. My case of vulnus contusum (Moses Williams) is in rather a sad plight. His wound, which was caused by the teeth of a brother contraband, has taken on rather a malignant action. I cauterized it well with argenti nitras, after which I applied a lini cataplasm. The rest of my patients are quite comfortable. The weather is rather warm today. 10 P.M. The tug arrived and anchored on our starboard beam.

Aug. 11, 1864. Weather quite pleasant. Patients coming on finely. Expended 1 bottle ol. ricini, alum 3 vi, pil. cath. comp no xii, and some volatile liniment for the benefit of the sick of the U.S.S. *Ceres*. The *Ceres* has gone to Edenton for vegetables etc. She returned with melons etc. Recd. a mail today. I recd. the "Medical and

Surgical Reporter" for June 4, 11, and 18; also a *carte de visite* of Mrs. Chas. Hallett.   . . .

Aug. 12, 1864. Weather rather warm. Two white women with six children, all refugees, arrived on board today. They feel as happy as bugs in a rug. Expended tinct opii ℥ i, ol terebinthinae ℥ vi, and alum lb. ¼ for the benefit of the medical department of the U.S.S. *Ceres.* Reported 8 cases sick today—all improving except Mr. Robinson, my case of remittent fever, who has rather a high fever today. I ordered him the following: ℞ potassae nitras ℨ ii, antim. et potas. tart. gr i, pulv acaciae ℨ ii, ext glycyrrh. ℨ ii, aquae anisi. f ℥ iii ss, aquae destilate f ℥ iii ss., ℳ, Sig. Tablespoonful every two hours as a diaphoretic—allow him acidulated drinks and soup as a diet.

18

Interim Duty

Albemarle Sound, N. C., off mouth Roanoke River, Aug. 13, 1864. The U.S.S. *Wyalusing* arrived to relieve us. Chief Engineer [H. H.] Stewart and [Acting Assistant] Paymaster [A. J.] Pritcher [Pritchard] came on board to see us. Both are well and hearty. They say that we are ordered to Norfolk, Va., there to receive two 11-inch guns, when we are to return again and fight the ram. Rather good news!

[Since the charges of powder used in the encounter with the *Albemarle* on May 5 (thirteen pounds in the nine-inch gun and ten in the hundred-pound rifle) were believed to have been too light to be effective, the new guns were fitted to be fired with thirty pounds of powder and solid shot— and even they, believed Rear Admiral Lee, should be fired while the ship was touching the ram. The *Chicopee* also was to receive replacements.]

The latest news from Mobile, Ala., are that the Rebels sunk the monitor *Tecumseh* and that we in return captured two Rebel ironclads, sunk one, passed the forts, and captured Admiral Buchanan of the Rebel Navy. Bully news for us! Huzza!

[Mobile, lying behind its natural water barrier, was one of two major Southern ports not yet under Federal control. The double entrance to Mobile Bay was guarded by formidable Forts Morgan, Gaines, and Powell and Admiral Franklin Buchanan's naval force, composed of the powerful steam ironclad ram *Tennessee* and three consorts (the *Gaines,* the *Morgan,* and the *Selma*—two built at Mobile and the third at Selma), besides a few miscellaneous gunboats and small craft, all supplemented by carefully planted torpedoes. Outside, Admiral Farragut, afraid to attack with his fourteen frail wooden ships alone, awaited urgently requested re-enforcement. On the morning of August 5 his entire fleet, now including the monitors *Manhattan, Winnebago, Chickasaw,* and *Tecumseh,* moved in for action. The *Tecumseh* struck a torpedo in the channel and sank almost immediately, carrying down most of her officers and crew. In the course of battle the Confederate *Selma* was captured and the *Gaines* so badly crippled that she was run ashore and burned; the *Morgan* escaped, creeping that night along the shore to Mobile. The *Tennessee* made a gallant attempt to carry on the fight unassisted. Unable to withstand the concentrated punishment, however, she surrendered without having succeeded in ramming a single ship. Admiral Buchanan (one of his legs shattered) and the rest of the wounded of both fleets were taken to Pensacola for hospital care. That night Fort Powell was evacuated and blown up by the Confederates, and within two days Fort Gaines, closed in between Farragut and a cooperating land force, had submitted. With the fall of Fort Morgan, strongest of the three defenses, the work of effectively bottling up Mobile was completed.]

1.15 P.M., off Bluff Point. We are at anchor once more in vicinity of flagship. The *Wyalusing* remains on picket duty. The yeoman of this ship painted me an oil painting of the *Mattabesett,* for which I paid him the sum of ten dollars. Rather tall; nevertheless, it is quite a relic. I should be sorry to part with the same. Received a mail, and as usual I was lucky enough to receive nothing. "Phanzy my pheelinks." The weather is rather warm. Reported 7 cases sick —all improving more or less.

Was told by good and reliable authority that the *Mattabesett* was ordered North and that we were to sail in the morning. Destination not mentioned. Wonder whether it will be Baltimore, Norfolk, Philadelphia, or New York. Would prefer either of the two latter ports. Time will tell. Suffice it therefore to know that we are ordered out of this confounded hot Sound. I am sick and tired of this station; don't fancy the locality at all. Would prefer doing blockade duty in salt water and kill time by capturing prizes. Oh, for a rich prize so as to relieve the consumptive condition of our ports moniaes [porte-monnaies].

Off Roanoke Island, Aug. 14, 1864. Arrived here at 10 A.M. Transferring shot and shell to an ordinance schooner [the *Charles S. Carstairs,* chartered in February, 1862, for use as an ordnance store vessel]. Actg. Master's Mate Isaac Peirce of this ship has been ordered to the command of the ordinance schooner—quite a gay command. We are on our way to Hampton Roads, Va. to report for instructions as to where to go to be fitted for and receive the new guns. Reported 8 cases sick.

Pamlico Sound, N. C., within sight of Hatteras Inlet, Aug. 14, 1864. 8 P.M. At last we are out of Albemarle Sound and at anchor in Pamlico Sound. We intend to get under way again in the morning. Everyone on board in good humor. Homeward bound at last. We have four hospital men on board, ordered to naval hospital, Norfolk—all sent from the U.S.S. *Chicopee.* Reported 8 cases sick.

August 15, 1864. 8 A.M., still at anchor in Pamlico Sound. It appears that the water is too low to proceed any further at present. Reported 11 cases sick—rather a large list, considering time and station. Shall endeavor to reduce it in the morning. All hands overhauling the rigging fore and aft. The vessels at anchor in Hatteras Inlet are within sight. The weather is rather warm today; still the salt-water atmosphere makes it rather pleasant. We would prefer being over the swash and on the broad Atlantic, steaming under 4 bells toward Fortress Monroe. Some say that we will go to Norfolk; others will have it that we intend to go to that place and from there proceed to New York. Would prefer the latter place.

Aug. 16, 1864. We made a desperate attempt to get over the swash and failed beautifully. Yes, like the "thirty thousand Frenchmen who marched up the hill and then marched down again," we were compelled to return in vicinity of our morning anchorage.[7] During our attempt we came in contact with a schooner and carried away her forestays and anchored her port anchor, besides other trifling damages. Altogether the whole affair was a grand fizzle. Pilot says we will get over in the morning. Weather rather changeable all day. Reported 9 cases sick.

Aug. 20, 1864. At last we are on the swash hard and fast. We expect to get over the confounded concern as soon as the tide raises. Reported 6 cases sick. Weather rather warm. Mess stores rather low.

Off Fort Clark [taken by the Federals in August, 1861], *Hatteras Inlet, N.C., Aug. 20, 1864.* Huzza! Huzza!! Huzza!!! We're afloat once more—over the swash at last. We intend to coal ship tonight and tomorrow leave for Hampton Roads. All hands are jubilant and in the best of humor.

At Sea, off Hatteras, N. C., Aug. 21, 1864. At 1.05 P.M. we got under way and made tracks for Hampton Roads. 2 P.M. we are outside of Hatteras Inlet and going it 12 knots. Huzza for Hampton Roads! Reported 8 cases sick: viz., 1 remittens, 1 orchitis, 2 diarrhoea, 1 catarrhus, 1 paronychia, 1 vulnus contusum, and 1 rheumatismus chronica.

Hampton Roads, Va., off Fortress Monroe, Aug. 22, 1864. Arrived here this morning. Wrote a letter to father announcing our arrival. The U.S.S. *Eutaw* (double-ender) left this morning for Norfolk. The weather is quite pleasant. Reported 7 cases sick. Took a run in town and had a gay and happy time. Dined at the Hygea Hotel.

Aug. 23, 1864. Hampton Roads 8 A.M.; Chesapeake Bay 5 P.M. Paymaster paid me one hundred and fifty dollars on account. Today I sent per Adams Express Company one hundred dollars to B. Frank Boyer . . . requesting him to place it in bank to my account.

Reported 7 cases sick today. Some of the officers who had been on shore all last night returned on board this morning rather the worse for their carousal last night. They had rather a jolly time last night, from all accounts.

At 1 P.M. we got under way and are now, 5 P.M., steaming up the Chesapeake Bay en route for Washington, D.C. We received our orders this morning at 11 A.M. Everyone is in fine humor. Thus we are going to Washington to see Uncle Abe and Old Gideon, for we belong to "Gideon's band."

Washington, D.C., Navy Yard, Aug. 24, 1864. We arrived here today. Wrote a letter to father announcing our arrival. Paid a mess bill of $22.25. Paymaster advanced me $50 on account.

Aug. 26, 1864. Recd. the following letters today: one from Surgeon Kenney . . . dated Aug. 10 in answer to my date of July 21; one from sister Beckie dated August 15; one from Ensign C. Flood . . . dated Aug. 12, enclosing a photograph of Mr. Townsend; also two papers that father sent me. Took a stroll about town. Had a gay and festive time in the city in the evening. Became acquainted with any amount of naval and marine officers.

Potomac River, Aug. 27, 1864. After transferring the battery, powder, and shot, we left the Washington Navy Yard and are on our way to Baltimore, Md., where we are to be repaired etc. [Second Assistant] Engineer [George W.] Magee [attached to the Bureau of Engineering], U.S.N., accompanies us to Baltimore. He is Engineer Hawkins' guest.

Washington is a perfect hotbed of iniquity.

Baltimore, Md., Sept. 29, 1864. [Dr. Boyer made no entries in his diary during the month his ship was being repaired in Baltimore.] Today we leave this place for Washington, D.C. We arrived at this station on the 28th day of August. During said period I had quite a gay and festive time. Paid the Reading people a visit. Enjoyed myself hugely. In short, all us officers had a good time. Made several conquests in the art of love.

This morning I had quite a large number of sick. Several cases were parties affected with "lady's fever"—i.e., cases of venereal. Poor fellows—rather a tough road to travel for a few minutes' enjoyment. But all right, my covey; such are the fortunes of war and love.   . . . .

Washington, D.C., Oct. 1, 1864. We arrived at this station last evening. We are to remain here until the 8th, when we are to go to sea—where I cannot say.

Made out my 3rd quarterly report of sick. During said quarter I had 552 sick entries; sent one man to the hospital and discharged one. Weather rather cool. Very few items of interest to note down in my log.

Oct. 2, 1864. Articles of War read by captain this morning. My steward went on shore yesterday and has not as yet returned. Where can he be? Has he deserted? Hope not; time will tell. Wrote a letter to Miss Sue Yeager . . . to Mrs. Beckie P. Cutler . . . Weather rather cool. Reported 9 cases sick.   . . . .

Oct. 8, 1864. We left Washington today en route for Fortress Monroe, Va. [Immediately after her arrival early in the morning of October 11 with nine of twenty launches and cutters requested for army use, the *Mattabesett* was sent up the James River, the vessels for the military in tow.]

James River, Oct. 11, 1864. We are on our way to City Point, Va. [at the juncture of the Appomattox and James Rivers, ten miles from Petersburg; under Federal occupation since May 5, 1864]. The scenery on this river is truly rural. Whilst at Piny Point [Piney-point, Maryland, a post hamlet on the east side of the Potomac River, fourteen miles from its mouth] we purchased oysters. Ate right hearty, all hands fore and aft, and ere long the doctor had quite a lively time ordering medicines etc. Today some of them are quite sick. Reported 15 cases sick. . . . .

Hampton Roads, Va., Oct. 14, 1864. Had a stroll on shore. Saw and had a long talk with Fleet Surgeon J.L. Fox. He paid the vessel a visit this afternoon. He is quite a jolly old sea dog—a perfect gentleman. At 7 P.M. we left for Beaufort, N.C.
[Now headquarters of the North Atlantic Blockading Squadron, Rear Admiral Lee (replaced by Rear Admiral David D. Porter on October 12) having been instructed in late July to transfer his base to that point and "visit Hampton Roads only when the public emergency requires it, giving your principal attention to the blockade, which has latterly become very inefficient."[8]]

At Sea, Oct. 15, 1864. We are at anchor off Cape Lookout [North Carolina]. Weather has been rather pleasant all day. Reported 14 cases sick.

Beaufort Harbor, N. C., Oct. 16, 1894. We arrived at this anchorage this morning. The following vessels are at anchor here. *Quaker City, Keystone State, Niphon Calypso, Arletta,* and several smaller gunboats the names of which I do not remember, besides any amount of schooners. Dr. Whitehead [Acting Assistant Surgeon Ira C. Whitehead] of the *Quaker City* came on board and informed me that my services were needed on board the U.S.S. *Keystone State* as a member of a medical board of survey; Doctors Whitehead, Rice [Assistant Surgeon John McD. Rice of the *Eutaw*], and Boyer comprised said board. We ordered the patient to be sent to the Norfolk Naval Hospital. We had rather a pleasant time. Paymaster Meade and myself dined on board of the *Quaker City*. In the evening Paymaster Ely [Acting Assistant Paymaster Griswold L. Ely of the storeship *Release,* stationed at Beaufort] and Captain Marshall—the former of the Navy and the latter of the Army—paid us a visit. We spent rather a pleasant evening together drinking claret, eating olives, and chewing tobacco; in short, we had a jolly time. Wrote a letter to father this evening. The weather was rather pleasant. Reported 14 sick.

Oct. 17, 1864. Took a stroll on the beach and attempted to catch fish; had a pleasant tramp but caught no fish. Reported 10 cases sick. Weather pleasant. The men are busy coaling ship. In the evening Dr. Emery [Acting Assistant Surgeon Alfred E. Emery], [Acting Assistant] Paymaster [J. S.] Stimson, and [Acting] Master [Laust E.] Degn of the U.S.S. *Keystone State* paid us a visit. They are perfect gentlemen and all are rich, having made fortunes capturing blockade runners etc.

Oct. 20, 1864. The U.S.S. *Maratanza* arrived today. Dined with Capt. Davis of the U.S. revenue cutter *Forward* today and had a very pleasant time. Capt. Davis is a lieutenant commander. [According to Treasury Department personnel records Alfred B. Davis of the U.S. Revenue Cutter Service was commissioned as a captain on July 11, 1864.]

Oct. 21, 1864. The U.S.S. *Mount Vernon* arrived today from off Wilmington [still accessible to blockade runners]. Her surgeon is Dr. Berrett [Acting Assistant Surgeon William H. Berrett]. I had the pleasure of meeting him today on a board of medical survey. The survey was held on board the U.S.S. *Shokokon* [persistently spelled *Shockokon* by the diarist] in the case of George Godfrey, lds., 23, Miss. The surgeon's steward in charge, Wm. Brophy, called for the survey. The board consisted of [Acting Assistant] Surgeon [John W.] Hamilton of the *Maratanza,* Surgeon Berrett of the *Mount Vernon,* and Surgeon Boyer of the *Mattabesett.* We reported as follows:

In obedience to your order of this date we have held careful survey on George Godfrey of the U.S.S. *Shokokon,* rated landsman, born in Mississippi, aged 23 years, shipped at Rock Island, Illinois, and we respectfully report: We find him affected with hemeralopia [nyctalopia] (night blindness). The duration of his disability will probably be temporary. We recommend that he be retained on board the *Shokokon.*

Very Respectfully,
—— Hamilton, A.A. Surgeon
—— Boyer, A.A. Surgeon
—— Berrett, A.A. Surgeon

To Commander Benjamin Moore Dove, U.S.N.
Commanding U.S. Naval Station, Beaufort, N.C.

I hardly think that the surgeon's steward in charge of the U.S.S. *Shokokon* will like, or fancy, the above report; nevertheless, it was our only remedy.

Oct. 23, 1864. The U.S.S. *Tristram Shandy* arrived today. Her surgeon's steward in charge came on board and requested my presence on board to see a man who had hurt his shoulder. I went on board and examined him. I found that he had merely bruised himself and not injured himself severely. I recommended liniments to be rubbed in smartly. I also saw a case of remittens. Recommended tonics etc. Captain Devens [Acting Volunteer Lieutenant Edward F. Devens] of said vessel also was unwell. I ordered a cataplasm of mustard $\frac{1}{3}$, flaxseed $\frac{2}{3}$ to be applied to his abdomen and solution of sulphate of morphia internally. I shall in the morning order him a cathartic. He is suffering from the effects of a bilious colic.   . . .

Oct. 24, 1864. Paid a visit to Captain Devens of the *Tristram Shandy*. Found him somewhat better this morning. I ordered him pil. cath. comp. no. iii and told him to continue the poultice to his abdomen.

The blockade runner *Hope* of Wilmington, N.C., an English-built vessel flying the English flag, arrived today. She was captured by one of our tugs [the *Eolus*]. Rather a valuable prize. At the request of Capt. Dove, senior officer present, I paid the *Hope* a visit and ordered medicine for three of the men. Whilst on board I made the acquaintance of Captain Blake and Mr. Holden, the supercargo of the *Hope*. Had champagne, claret, brandy, oranges, figs, and some good cigars; in short, I enjoyed myself. Shall call on board again in the morning. Ordered some medicine —jalapa grs xx, calomel grs x—for a contraband on board the *Arletta*.

4 P.M. Went on board the *Tristram Shandy* and saw Capt. Devens. Was compelled to give him an injection, the pills not operating. I remained on board until 6 P.M., at which time he had had a fine passage. He appears to suffer considerable gastric pains. Since he has had a passage, I at his request ordered him an anodyne consisting of opii tinct zingiberis tinct, chloroform, and water. Promised to call and see him in the morning.

There appears to be eight new cases of yellow fever on shore at Beaufort. The captain therefore has stopped our going on

shore—a very wise precaution. I reported the following cases sick
this morning: viz., Wm. H. Herring, gunner—syphilis; Samuel E.
Tuthill, ord. sea.—syphilis; John Lewis, lds.—syphilis; Chas.
Holmes, lds.—phthisis; Joseph C. Smith, lds.—pneumonia; Robert
Harley, quartermaster—rheumatis; James H. Bunting, ord. sea.—
intermittens; William Sherlock, fireman—intermittens; Peter
Thompson, ord. sea.—abrasio; James Burns, fireman—gonorrhoea;
Jeremiah O'Sullivan, coal heaver—ulcus. All of these patients are
in a fair way of recovery. At present I am kept rather busy—plenty
of medical duties to perform and no steward to assist me. I would
have no objection to see the *Mattabesett* out at sea cruising, for
then we might accidentally catch a prize. "All work and no prize
money makes Jack a lazy dog."

Oct. 25, 1864. This morning I found Capt. Devens . . . in quite a
pleasant condition. I therefore ordered him cornstarch, tapioca,
etc. as a diet. Took lunch with his clerk at the captain's table
and had several drinks with his executive officer, Mr. Wood [Act-
ing Ensign Benjamin Wood], who is a perfect gentleman. I must
say that all on board treated me as perfect gentlemen should;
they all appeared to appreciate my services and thanked me very
kindly for what I had done. I also paid the *Hope* another visit
and had the satisfaction of hearing that all the sick were better
and in a fair way of recovery. Whilst on board I had plenty to
eat and drink; in short, I enjoyed myself hugely.

Today the men practiced target shooting with small arms, and
Mr. Mitchell, our executive officer, reports that they done some
fine firing. I am pleased to hear it, for ere long the boys will have
to show their bravery in battle. The weather has been quite
stormy all day. . . . My sick on board are coming on finely.

Oct. 26, 1864. The U.S.S. *Pequot* arrived today, and the U.S.S.
Tristram Shandy and prize steamer *Hope* left this anchorage.

Oct. 28, 1864. Several large steamers in the offing. Two arrived
yesterday. Ensign Brown is at Beaufort after the mail. He has returned. I received nary letter.

Oct. 29, 1864. The U.S.S. *Nansemond,* U.S.S. *Britannia,* U.S.S.
Keystone State [in the harbor when the *Mattabesett* came in on
the 16th], and U.S.S. *Alabama* have arrived. At 4 P.M. Captain
Dove . . . sent his gig for me and requested me to examine Captain

James H. Porter, acting ensign, commanding U.S.S. *Nansemond,* as regards his physical qualifications to perform the duties of an acting master in the U.S. Navy. I found him every way (physically) qualified and as such reported him, after which Captain Porter gave me his gig to proceed on board the *Nansemond* and see the executive officer, Mr. Henderson [Acting Ensign James B. Henderson, who had been acting master's mate on the *Fernandina*], an old shipmate of mine. I found him well and in good humor. Spent quite a pleasant time while on board. The paymaster, chief engineer, Engineer Sackett, the pilot, Master's Mate Fisher, and the doctor (myself) went a fishing in the dingy this afternoon. We had a gay time and caught several fine fish.

The U.S.S. *Osceola,* a double-ender, arrived today.

Oct. 30, 1864. Paymaster Meade, Master Plunkett, Ensign Brown, and myself paid the paymaster, doctor, and first lieutenant of the *Osceola* a visit. Dined with them, after which we all adjourned on board the *Mattabesett* and had a festive time. The *Osceola* left at 5 P.M. for sea. . . . .

Nov. 1, 1864. I have had quite a busy time today. Have been the senior surgeon of two surveys—one in the case of Commander A[ndrew] J. Drake, U.S.N., commanding U.S.S. *Iosco,* affected with adynamia. Recommended him to be sent North for further treatment. The other case was John Dillon, quartermaster on board the U.S.S. *Shokokon,* affected with inguinal hernia. Recommended him to be sent to the naval hospital, Norfolk, Virginia, for treatment. The board consisted of [Charles] Sturdevant of the *Lilian,* . . . [Kirk H.] Bancroft of the *Iosco,* and . . . Boyer of the *Mattabesett* [all acting assistant surgeons]. The same board also paid Beaufort a visit. The nature of our visit need not be mentioned; therefore suffice it to say that we had rather a gay time. Had the pleasure of meeting Captain Devens of the *Tristram Shandy.* He was in splendid humor; took several drinks with me in my room. Lieutenant [Charles L.] Franklin [executive officer] of the *Iosco* also paid us a visit. He likewise examined my room; also tested the contents of my locker.

Nov. 3, 1864. Quite a batch of gunboats have arrived. The *Osceola* had quite a chase yesterday after a prize but did not catch her [probably a white side-wheel steamer (believed to be a privateer) sighted on October 31 steering toward Wilmington and pursued nearly ten hours, only to be lost in a fog bank]. Some of the rest were more successful, for two fine prizes arrived here today [probably the British steamer *Annie,* captured by the *Wilderness* and the *Niphon* the evening of October 31 off New Inlet, North Carolina, while trying to run the blockade with a cargo of about five hundred bales of cotton, thirty tons of tobacco, and a quantity of turpentine, and the British steamer *Lucy,* captured by the *Santiago de Cuba* the morning of November 2 fourteen hours from Wilmington bound to Nassau, New Providence, with over four hundred bales of cotton and twenty-five tons of tobacco].

Madame Rumor says that we are to go on the blockade and try our hand. Hope we may, for I have an idea that we will be successful. There is a report that the Rebel ram *Albemarle* (the ugly customer that we saw and felt on the 5th of May last) had been blowed up and that Plymouth, N.C., was in the possession of Federal troops. Good news; hope the report may be true. Lieutenant Cushing of the Navy did the work. Long may he live.

[On the dark, rainy night of October 27th the daring twenty-one-year-old Lieutenant William B. Cushing, his plans and preparations for the "important and perilous undertaking" carefully made, slipped up the Roanoke River in a steam picket launch with fourteen officers and men to blow up the *Albemarle,* still lying about eight miles from the mouth of the river. Under severe enemy fire he exploded a torpedo under the ram, which soon sank. His launch completely disabled, the men had to jump overboard. Two were drowned and eleven taken prisoner, only Lieutenant Cushing and one other escaping. Lieutenant Cushing and his command were subsequently given a vote of thanks by Congress for their skill and gallantry.

[In order to obstruct the passage of Federal ships to Plymouth, the Confederates sank two schooners in the river on either side of a wrecked vessel, the *Southfield.* Commander Macomb's fleet, attempting the capture of the town, turned back and ascended the Middle River, entering the Roanoke above Plymouth and approaching from the side opposite that originally contemplated. The capture was made on October 31.[9]]

Received an official letter from Fleet Surgeon Jno. L. Fox dated Oct. 22 relating to quarterly report of sick for 3rd quarter, 1864. I answered said letter, stating that I had sent my report direct to the Bureau of Medicine and Surgery . . . on the 1st of Oct.

while we were at the Washington Navy Yard. I hope the letter will satisfy Surgeon Fox.

Had quite a pleasant time this afternoon on board the *Iosco*. Received a small package today from Beaufort, N.C. All my messmates are having the benefit of said package.

Nov. 7, 1864. Today I was a member of a medical board of survey held upon the following vessels: viz., U.S.S. *Kansas* and U.S.S. *Wm. Badger.* The patient on board the *Kansas* was a 2nd-class fireman named John T. Hodges, affected with chronic headache. We recommended that he be retained on board the *Kansas* and undergo a more heroic plan of treatment. The one on board the *Wm. Badger* was a 1st-class boy named Mitchell, affected with adynamia, caused by an attack of measles some time ago. We recommended that he be transferred to the Norfolk Naval Hospital for further treatment and that the disease originated in the line of duty. The board consisted of Acting Assistant Surgeon[s] [Max G.] Raefle of the U.S.S. *Fort Donelson,* . . . Boyer of the U.S.S. *Mattabesett,* and Tuttle of the U.S.S. *Pequot* [Robert C. Tuttle, listed in the *Navy Register* as being stationed on the *Governor Buckingham;* possibly transferred to the *Pequot*]. In the evening the chief engineer and surgeon of the U.S.S. *Nyack* called on board . . . to see us. We had rather a lively time of it.

The U.S.S. *Pawtuxet* arrived today. She is, like ourself, a double-ender. The *Osceola* and *Iosco* left today for the Wilmington blockade.

Nov. 8, 1864. Today I requested a medical survey on Charles Holmes—phthisis, and Joseph Smith—pneumonia. The request was granted, and the following [acting assistant] surgeons comprised the medical board of survey, viz., [Henry] Johnson of the *Pawtuxet,* Sturdevant of the *Lilian* and Tuttle of the *Pequot.* Upon examination they found the former affected with phthisis, the latter with pneumonia; the duration of their disease doubtful; that the disease did not originate in line of duty. Recommended that they be discharged from the U.S. naval service. After the survey I of course done all I could to make the time pass away pleasantly. I had my locker well stocked with liquor etc.

Several gunboats arrived today. Some of our vessels had a chance of firing several shots at the pirate *Tallehassa* [*Tallahassee*].

[On November 5-6 the privateer, returning to Wilmington after a brief cruise (the second in her depredatory role), was pursued by the *Sassacus* for twenty-six hours, only to be lost sight of steering for the eastern bar; the next day the *Montgomery,* the *Lilian,* the *Quaker City,* and the *Osceola* took up the chase but were outstripped in a running battle as she scurried into port.[10]]

Nov. 9, 1864. Visited the following vessels today and had rather a good old time: U.S.S. *Lilian,* U.S.S. *Pawtuxet,* and U.S.S. *Wm. Badger.* The *Pawtuxet, Nyack, Montgomery, Fort Donelson,* and *Lilian* went to sea today.

Recd. . . . the "Medical and Surgical Reporter," no. 400, 1, 2. Wrote a letter to Dr. S. W. Butler, editor and proprietor . . ., enclosing $5 for another year's subscription.

The *Newbern* [spelled the same way in the Navy *Register* but *New Berne* in the official navy records] is reported as at anchor outside.

Nov. 10, 1864. I had the pleasure of receiving the following mail: viz., a letter from sister Beckie dated Oct. 13, one from Mr. Chas. Hallett . . . dated Oct. 10, one from Alonzo H. Boyer . . ., the "Raftsman's Journal," . . . Aug. 24, which Miss Carlisle sent me, and . . . the "Medical and Surgical Reporter," no. 404 and 5. I answered Alonzo H. Boyer's letter today. Wrote a letter to Fleet Surgeon John L. Fox announcing the discharge from the United States naval service of Chas. Holmes, lds.—phthisis, and Joseph C. Smith, lds.—pneumonia, in accordance with general Order no. 28, date October 29, 1864, giving the commander of a vessel the right to discharge all patients unfit for service, their diseases not originating in the line of duty. Was busy part of the day in dissecting and stuffing a toadfish for our gunner, Wm. H. Herring.

Nov. 11, 1864. Today I was the senior member of a board of survey to survey the following medical cases on board the U.S.S. *Aries:* Mathew O'Brien, lds., 21—anchylosis; Richard Martin, ord. sea., 24—pneumonia, Jno. Hughes, lds., 20—hypotrophic cardia; I. F. Brown, 1. c. fire. [first-class fireman], 31—bronchitis chronica; H. S. Stevenson, capt. hold—syph. second. The survey was called by Dr. Fowler [Acting Assistant Surgeon Arch. C. Fowler]. The board consisted of Drs. Boyer, Jones [Acting Assistant Surgeon Daniel W. Jones] of the *A.D. Vance,* and Gregory [Acting Assistant Surgeon Justus E. Gregory] of the U.S.S. *Chippewa.* O'Brien, Martin, Hughes, and Brown were recommended to be discharged from the U.S. naval service, and Stevenson was recommended to be retained on board the ship for further treatment. The same board also held a survey on Alden Carpenter, fireman, on board of the U.S.S. *Pequot,* and upon examination they found him affected with bronchitis chronica and recommended that he be discharged from the U.S. naval service.

Nov. 12, 1864. Today I was the senior surgeon of a medical board of survey held on Maurice Wagg, acting master's mate, of the U.S.S. *Tristram Shandy,* affected with adynamia. We recommended that he be transferred to the Norfolk Naval Hospital for further treatment.

Nov. 14, 1864. Today I was the senior surgeon of a medical board of survey consisting of Surgeons Boyer, Tuttle, and Greene [Acting Assistant Surgeon R. H. Greene of the *Seneca,* which had been on cruising duty off Wilmington and had left New Inlet, disabled, two days before in tow of the *Alabama*]. The board condemned the following parties of the *Keystone State:* Edward Brogan, c. h.—rheumatism acuta—to Norfolk Naval Hosp.; John Devereaux, lds.—epilepsy—discharged from service; John Frisbrie, lds.—syph. secondary—discharged from service. Expended six dollars for wine fund. Advanced the sum of five dollars to Jos. C. Smith, lds. . . .

Nov. 18, 1864. Were I to enumerate, as I have heretofore done whilst on other stations, all the vessels that arrive and leave this anchorage daily, why, I should be compelled to be busy writing all the time, for they number by tens—nay, hundreds; consequently I merely note down items that might hereafter prove of some interest. I even do not note down my sick, having only one or two cases of interest on hand—and they come under the head of venereal. We are all anxiously awaiting the arrival of orders of some kind, for we do not fancy this being at anchor all the time. The most work I do now is doing duty as a member of medical surveys. I understand that 3 surveys are to be held tomorrow— two cases on board the *Alabama* and one on board of the *Shokokon*—and that I am to be a member of the board holding said surveys. . . .

Nov. 20, 1864. Was a member of a medical board of survey, consisting of Surgeons Whitehead, Hamilton, and Boyer, in the case of Michael Doyle, actg. 3rd asst. engineer, of the U.S.S. *Shokokon.* We found him affected with scrotal hernia and recommended that he be transferred to the Norfolk Naval Hospital for further action.

Actg. Asst. Surg. Benj. Hammell [appointed November 1, 1864] has been ordered to the *Shokokon.* He formerly was a college chum of mine; is a good boy.

Nov. 21, 1864. Wrote a letter to Charles Underkofer.   . . .
Recd. a letter today, in answer to my date Nov. 8th, from S. W. Butler,   . . . "Medical and Surgical Reporter," . . . informing me that he would accept the enclosed five dollars as full pay for the past and future to Jany. 1, 1866, and would send me the back numbers that I mentioned— . . . in short, all the numbers from Oct. 14 to 1st Jany., 1866—so I am all right as regards receiving said medical journal.

Surgeon Sturdevant of the U.S.S. *Lilian* (Capt. [Thomas A.] Harris, actg. vol. lieut., in command) came on board to see me and requested my presence in a consultation regarding some of his cases—one in particular, and that a case of paraphimosis of a boy of about 11 years of age. I done so and gave him the full benefit of my knowledge of medicine etc. I had the pleasure of satisfying his mind etc.

The weather has been rather wet all day. Reported 4 cases sick: viz., bubo, adenitis, vul. contus., contusio. Rather a fine pair of neighborly cases. Bubo is an inflammation of the lymphatic glands of the groin; so is adenitis, only the former case is a case of syphilis, and the latter case a case of injury. Vul. contus. is a contused wound, and contusio is merely a contusion or bruise without breaking the skin. Rather a queer coincidence. One of our master's mates, named Smith, came to see me tonight and complained of a chronic diarrhoea. I ordered him a blue pill so as to affect his liver. Tomorrow I shall order him the oleaginous mixture.

Nov. 22, 1864. Wrote rather a long letter to Jerome L. Boyer. . . . Said gentleman is a cousin of mine and quite an intelligent young man. The weather has been quite cold all day. This evening we had a slight snowstorm. Reported six cases sick today. Mr. Smith, my case of diarrhoea, is taking the following mixture today: ℞ creta praep., catechu pulv. āā ℨ i, acaciae pulv., sach. alba āā ℥ ss., ol. caryophylli gtt. v., aqua f. ℥ v, ℳ, Sig. Table-spoonful every two hours. The rest are coming on finely.

Today I received the following numbers of the "Medical and Surgical Reporter": 399, 401, 402, 404, and 405. Paymaster Meade's brother Bob left today for New York.

Nov. 23, 1864. Was a member of a medical board of survey, con-sisting of Surgeons Hamilton, Boyer, and Eddy [Acting Assistant Surgeon George S. Eddy, stationed on the *Gettysburg*], held in the cases of George Word, lds.—inguinal hernia, and Adam Powell, lds.—phthisis, of the U.S.S. *Gettysburg.* We recommended that they be transferred to the Norfolk Naval Hospital for further action. . . . .

Nov. 28, 1864. Was the senior member of a medical board of survey held on the following cases: viz., Walter S. Land, lds., 34, Va., *Yantic,* Camp Chase, Ill.—diarrhoea ch.; Wm. Butler, lds., Tenn., 23, *Yantic,* Camp Chase, Ill.—phthisis; and Jas. Moore, lds., Phila., 27, *Yantic,* Phila.—chronic rheumatismus. . . . Diseases did not originate in line of duty. All recommended to be dis-charged from U.S. naval service. The board consisted of [Assistant] Surgeon [Isaac] Poole, U.S.S. *Kansas;* [Acting Assistant] Surgeon H. R. Watts [listed in squadron data as stationed on the *Pequot* but in the Navy *Register* to January, 1865, as on the *Hunchback,* whose personnel list included no surgeon], U.S.S. *Mackinaw;* and Surgeon Boyer, U.S.S. *Mattabesett.*

Dec. 1, 1864. . . . The captain has received sailing orders [dated November 28, to proceed to the sounds of North Carolina to relieve a double-ender there in need of repairs]. We leave this place in the morning.

None on sick list.

19

End of the Blockade

Off Fort Clark, Hatteras Inlet, N. C., Dec. 3, 1864. We are once more on our way to the sounds of North Carolina. Little did I think when we left Albemarle Sound sometime in August last that we would be compelled to do duty again at this place, and when we will leave the sounds remains yet to be seen. We left Beaufort Harbor, N. C., early this morning and anchored off Fort Clark at 4 P.M. Our destination is Plymouth, N. C. . . . the place of the ram fight May 5th, 1864. Since we left the sounds, the fleet have destroyed the ram *Albemarle* and regained possession of Plymouth. We all expect to spend the winter at Plymouth. I am afraid that I will have a large sick list during the spring months if we remain doing duty off Plymouth long. At present I have but one man on the list—one Thomas Howie, cox[swain], . . . affected with colica.

Dec. 4, 1864. Weather rather stormy. Took a stroll on shore. Entered Fort Clark. Mounts 18 guns, heavy calibre. Nothing of any account transpired up to time of writing—viz., 4 P.M. Wrote a letter to father. Reported two cases sick—viz., Thos. Howie, cox.—colica, and Henry Harris, fire.—catarrhus. Wrote a letter to J. B. Henderson, actg. ensign, U.S.S. *Nansemond*, Beaufort, N. C.

Dec. 6, 1864. Made an attempt to cross the swash and had the satisfaction of running aground. 7 P.M., still hard and fast aground. Reported one man sick.

Pamlico Sound, N. C., Dec. 7, 1864. Weather rainy. . . . The U.S.S. *Tacony* (double-ender) arrived at Hatteras Inlet today. Her destination is Beaufort, N. C., and off Wilmington, N. C. Came inside to avoid the storm prevailing outside. Captain Truxtun [Lieutenant Commander William T. Truxtun] and Chief Engineer Dukehart paid us a visit.

Dec. 10, 1864. Off the swash once more and on our way to the sounds. Reported 4 cases sick. The *"Matty"* at 7 P.M. aground, in vicinity of marshes within sight of Roanoke Island.

On the 7th inst. the following was sent to the captain:

We, the undersigned wardroom officers, being desirous of enjoying the fragrant weed y-clept tobacco, and the weather not permitting us to smoke on deck with any comfort, would most respectfully request permission to smoke in the wardroom of this ship.

(James L. Plunkett, A. Master
(Henry C. Meade, A.A. Payr.
(Samuel P. Boyer, A.A. Surg.
Signed   (John T. Hawkins, 2nd Asst. Eng.
(A. F. Dill, A. Ensign
(F. H. Brown, A. Ensign
(J. Greenhalgh, A. Ensign

To Commander J. C. Febiger, U.S.N.
Commanding U.S.S. *Mattabesett*

The captain sent word back that we could not smoke in the wardroom; so of course we don't smoke here.

Croatan Sound, N. C., Dec. 11, 1864. Still hard and fast in the mud. Wrote a letter to father today. Weather rather dirty—rainy and foggy. Reported the following cases sick in my morning report: Thos. McIntyre, lds.—adenitis—apply tinct iodine and lini cataplasm—℞ tinct ferri chloridi gtts vii three times a day; Henry Harris, fireman—herpes zoster—keep bowels open and apply tinct iodine; Robt. Harley, quartermaster—rheumatism—order him potassae nitras grs v three times a day; Thomas Hyron, lds.—catarrhus—℞ magnesia sulphas ℥ i, calomel grs vi; Uriah Hartman, marine—cephalalgia—bowels opened last night by means of a cathartic—apply two small blisters, one behind each ear—internally sherry wine ℥ i three times a day, also flaxseed tea.

Dec. 13, 1864. Weather cold—thermometer 27° Fahr. at times and 50° Fahr. at other times. The other day the *Otsego* and two tugboats were blown up by torpedoes about 12 miles above Plymouth. No one hurt on board the *Otsego*, and only a few on the tugboats.

[The *Otsego* was sunk by submerged Confederate torpedoes in the Roanoke River just below Jamesville in the evening of December 9, the first day of a joint military and naval expedition to capture Rainbow Bluff, North Carolina. The only injuries sustained were a few slight bruises and scratches and one minor leg wound. The next morning the tug *Bazely* was blown up, two men being killed. The river was so full of torpedoes that it had to be dragged with small boats before the larger vessels, which could go only about five miles a day, could proceed. The *Shamrock,* flagship, was left behind because she could not go "stern-foremost."]

The *Mattabesett* is still hard and fast aground. On account of having no steam, we (the officers) have rather cold quarters to live in at present. I only hope that we may get off the bar so that we can steam up again and have warm quarters. Report 6 cases sick: viz., McIntyre, Harris, Hartman, Harley, McLaughlin (boil), Lamon (sore leg); and discharged to duty Hyron.

Dec. 16, 1864. Still hard and fast aground. Weather rather cold. Whilst looking over old docs. today, I came across the following rules and regulations of the Newbern shebang: viz.,

NAVY CLUB
Rules and Regulations

1st Each member shall pay an entrance fee of two dollars and pay the sum of five dollars monthly, in advance, the money to be expended in fitting up the clubhouse and purchasing the necessary furniture.

2nd No person not belonging to the navy shall become a member of this club without a unanimous vote, and no person in the naval service without a two-thirds vote of all the members.

3rd The president shall be elected by unanimous vote and shall have whole and sole control over all money, property, stores, etc. that may be in possession of the club, subject to the disposal of two-thirds of the members, and shall hold office for 3 months, to be elected on the last Saturday of the fiscal year.

4th Any member wishing liquor shall fill up a card with his name, description of liquor, and date. All liquor accounts shall be settled promptly at the expiration of the month.

5th Any member who shall not promptly settle his accounts, or be guilty of ungentlemanly or unofficerlike conduct, shall by a vote of two-thirds of all the members be expelled.

6th The billiard table shall be for the exclusive use of members, and there shall be a tax of ten cents for each single and twenty cents for each double game.

7th No liquors shall be taken out of the clubhouse, nor shall any be sold to a person not a member.

8th In consequence of existing squadron regulations, the clubhouse shall be opened at 9 A.M. and closed at sunset, unless by special vote of two-thirds of the members on the preceding day.

9th No candidate for admission shall be voted unless he make application in writing or through the president, and it shall be the duty of the president to notify all officers newly arriving in port of the existence of this club.

10th The president is authorized to make such rules and select such servants as he shall deem proper for the harmony and comfort of the club.

11th None but wardroom officers shall be eligible to become members.

A mail arrived today, and I was unfortunate enough to receive a paper and nary letter. Where are all my friends? Wrote a letter to Hon. S. J. W. Tabor, Fourth Auditor, Treasury Department, Washington, D.C., regarding the prize sloop *Anna [Annie] Thompson* and cargo, captured Jan. 16, 1864, by the *Fernandina*. . . . .

Off Plymouth, N. C., Dec. 24, 1864. We arrived here this morning [with five barrels of 20-pounder charges for the *Shamrock* and immediately began coaling before going on guard duty]. The *Shamrock* (flagship) stationed here. The *Wyalusing, Chicopee,* and other boats are up the river. This place looks rather hard; nearly every building is more or less marked by our shots. Saw the remains of the ram *Albemarle* as we passed up. She is pretty well used up. Our station is above the town guarding a road. It is rumored that the Rebels are a going to make an attack on the place with 30,000 men.

[Confederate General Robert F. Hoke was rumored to be advancing on Plymouth by the Columbia Road; some said that he was already between Tarboro and Jamesville and that General A. P. Hill's division was at Rainbow Bluff. Colonel Jones Frankle, commanding a Union land force at Plymouth, while believing such stories to be based on the fact that about eight thousand Confederates had left Weldon, North Carolina, a few days before, probably for Wilmington (though two deserters from Wilmington boarding the *Shamrock* December 18 had reported three regiments as having left Weldon on the sixteenth "to reinforce Hamilton and Rainbow Bluff"), had requested naval vigilance.[11]]

If they come, why, we will have warm work.

Taking all in all, this is a pretty fair place to be at. Turkeys etc. are plenty. We expect to live cheap hereafter; heretofore our bills were high. Wrote a letter to father enclosing twenty dollars.

Christmas, Dec. 25, 1864. Turkeys appeared to be plenty all day. Nothing unusual transpired today.

Dec. 26, 1864. Two men, named John Bogus, sea., and Carrol Emery, lds., deserted at 5 o'clock this morning. Acting Master J. L. Plunkett with an armed boat's crew sent in search of them. Hope they may catch them. Have returned. No traces of the runaways. . . .

Dec. 28, 1864. Ensign Dill with an armed boat's crew started up the river for the dingy in which Emery and Bogus escaped the other night. He returned at 3 P.M. dingy in tow, also having two Rebel deserters with him.

Dec. 29, 1864. The rest of the fleet have arrived from up the river today. . . .

Dec. 30, 1864. Was senior member of a medical board of survey, consisting of Surgeons Boyer, Barton, and Holman [Acting Assistant Surgeon Samuel Holman, stationed on the *Wyalusing*], held in the case of John Lewis, lds., attached to U.S.S. *Mattabesett,* and report as follows: disease—phthisis; duration—indefinite; origin— not in line of duty; recommendation—that he be discharged from the U.S. naval service. I also was senior member of a board, consisting of Surgeons Boyer, Barton, and Simpson, held in the case of Actg. 3rd Asst. Engineer Levi Lord of picket boat no. 1 and report: disease—rheumatism, chronic; duration—doubtful; origin —in line of duty, from exposure on board Lieut. Cushing's torpedo boat; recommendation—that he be transferred to Norfolk Naval Hospital for further action.
[Lord's name does not appear in an official list of the fifteen officers and men who took part in the destruction of the *Albemarle;* the only person who escaped besides Lieutenant Cushing was Ordinary Seaman Edward J. Houghton of the *Chicopee.* Lord was one of the several officers of the *Otsego* commended for their "zeal and gallantry" in the capture of Plymouth on October 31.[12]]

Dec. 31, 1864. Wrote a letter to Surg. Chas. Eversfield [stationed at the navy yard at New York; listed in the Navy *Register* to January 1, 1865, as furloughed], New York, in relation to a surgeon's steward.

Jan. 2, 1865. The greater part of our crew left today for home (times expired), and we got quite an invoice of new men. Dr. Simpson sent me two sick men to treat. . . . .

Jan. 4, 1865. Wrote a letter to B. Frank Boyer . . ., enclosing check for one hundred dollars. Paid mess bill of $20. Paymaster advanced me $154 on account—check for $100 and cash $54 and some odd cents. Took the caterership of the wardroom mess on the first of the month, and today I made the first assessment, taxing each member twenty dollars to commence with. Made out my 4th quarterly report of sick for 1864 and duplicate, together with vouchers for medical stores, annual return (form C) of medicine, instruments, stores, etc., all of which I sent to Fleet Surgeon Jno. L. Fox.

Jan. 6, 1865. This morning Acting Master J. L. Plunkett with an armed crew left the ship for John Johnston's plantation [possibly belonging to a "Mr. Johnston" who was a partner of C. C. Poole in a supply store at Coanjock (Coinjock) Bridge, below Plymouth, kept by permission of the Federal military] after some poultry for the crew. Whilst Mr. Plunkett was going through the underbrush on shore, the hammer of his rifle happened to be caught by a branch, thereby causing the hammer to explode the cap and discharging the contents of said rifle through his right foot. I immediately, as soon as he was brought on board, attended to his case. 8 P.M. he feels quite comfortable.

Jan. 7, 1865. Recd. letter from Beckie, date Nov. 24, 1864. Answered it today. Mr. Plunkett feels quite comfortable. Made out the following request today:

[That a medical survey be held to determine the disposition of Acting Master James L. Plunkett, suffering from vulnus sclopeticum (gunshot wound). A board, consisting of Assistant Surgeons Boyer, Barton, and Holman recommended that Plunkett be transferred to the Norfolk Naval Hospital for further treatment, and that he be accompanied by a medical officer. The board also recommended that, since the temporary naval hospital at Newbern had been abandoned since the epidemic of yellow fever "last fall" (571 cases and 278 deaths among the troops stationed at that place), a temporary naval hospital be set up at Plymouth.[13]]

Jan. 10, 1865. Acting Master Plunkett left today for the Norfolk Naval Hospital for further treatment. [Acting Assistant] Surgeon

[George C.] Raynolds [unattached since his ship, the *Otsego,* was blown up by torpedo on December 9] accompanies him as medical officer. He has my best wishes.

Jan. 13, 1865. Received the following order today: . . . "You will proceed on shore at this place [Plymouth] to assist A. A. Surg. Barton of this vessel the *Shamrock* in the treatment of James Reid, affected with erysipelas. . . . W. H. Macomb, Commander, Cmdg. Dist. Sounds, N[orth] A[tlantic] S[quadron]." Of course I went on shore and aided in the treatment of the above case and shall continue so to do until my services are no longer required.

Jan. 20, 1865. The erysipelas patient on shore is quite comfortable. Reported 24 cases sick this morning, consisting of coughs, chills, rheumatism, boils, and felons. Received a letter from father dated Jan. 8 last night and answered it same day.

An expedition started up the Chowan [Roanoke] River for the purpose of destroying the Rebel ram at Halifax [probably the unfinished gunboat *Halifax,* later captured "in the stocks"]. Hope it may prove successful.

Jan. 21, 1865. The U.S.S. *Shamrock* left for Newbern, N. C. There being rumors afloat that the Rebels intend to attack Newbern, . . . the *Shamrock* went to help hold the place.

[Rear Admiral Porter had ordered Commander Macomb on January 19 to move all the heavy vessels he could spare from Plymouth down to New Bern. Macomb feared an attack in his absence on Plymouth instead "while we are so shorthanded there."]

I received a letter from Surgeon Barton transferring James Reid, erysipelas patient on shore, to me to treat. I shall go on shore in the morning and see the man. Lieut. Campbell [Acting Lieutenant Daniel A. Campbell, who had been relieved of brief command of the *Monticello* (off Wilmington) in late December, 1864, by Lieutenant Cushing] and Ensign Chapman [Acting Ensign John H. Chapman, commander of launch number five in the expedition up the Roanoke River] arrived on board.

Jan. 22, 1865. I went on shore and found the [erysipelas] patient rather weak and nervous. I ordered him the following: ℞ quiniae sulphas gr i, tinct ferri chloridi gtts x, aquae f ʒ i, ℳ. To be taken every 2 hours during daytime, and at night tinct. opii gtts xv if he is restless. Also allow him sherry wine ʒ i occasionally. For sore mouth and throat allow him potassae chloras grs xii, aqua f ʒ i. Use as a gargle and swallow a teaspoonful occasionally; and if he feels like eating, allow him tapioca, tea, and coffee. I will not apply tinct iodine, for the doctor has done so yesterday (I mean Dr. Barton). At times he feels and talks quite rational.

Jan. 23, 1865. Saw Reid today. Shall continue same plan of treatment. I think I can safely assert that he is in a fair way to recover. Hope he may, for he appears to be a splendid seaman. Ordered medicine for Major Fuller [Major Nehemiah P. Fuller of the Second Massachusetts Heavy Artillery, four companies of which under Colonel Frankle were stationed at Plymouth], Mr. Miller [unidentified], and a married lady today, the first having had chills, the second laboring under the effects of misplaced confidence, and the third party laboring under general debility. Workmen are working on the *Albemarle* preparing to raise her. Hope ere long to have the pleasure of seeing her afloat and flying the Stars and Stripes. Reported 22 cases sick. Recd. a letter from B. Frank Boyer . . . dated Jan. 12, in answer to my date Jan. 4, acknowledging receipt of $100. I answered said letter today. Received a small tract, title "A Visit from St. Nicholas" [by Clement C. Moore; published in New York, 1865, by Hurd and Houghton], also the following note, all in one envelope: For your own amusement—signed Jessie; postmarked Baltimore, Md., Dec. 24, 1864. I wrote quite a letter to the donor, Miss Jessie Henderson, 75 Broadway, Baltimore, Md. She is one of Eve's fairest daughters. . . .

Jan. 25, 1865. Whilst attending to my sick list, I received notice that I was to go on shore and attend to a man belonging to the Army that had broken his clavicle, or collar bone. I immediately went ashore and applied . . . a wedge-shaped pad in left axilla (the left collar bone being broken), a hoop-shaped pad in right axilla, and a sling to left elbow. In short, I made use of Fox's apparatus; at least I tried to follow his style of procedure. The object in all those cases of fracture is to place the shoulder upwards, backwards, and inward. I have no doubt but what Surgeon Denny of the Army [Assistant Surgeon James H. Denny, Second Massachusetts Heavy Artillery, temporarily away on duty] will be satisfied with my mode of procedure. Besides the above I attended to 4 or 5 other Army patients. At present I have my hands full—plenty of patients all around. My services are in great demand.

Wrote a letter to Dr. S. W. Butler, editor "Medical and Surgical Reporter," . . . enclosing $4.20 for one year's subscription for said journal, to be sent to . . . Dr. John M. Battin, U.S.N., U.S.S. *Valley City*, Plymouth, N.C. . . . .

Feby. 2, 1865. Surg. Denny of the Army has arrived and has been wounded in left thigh. I at present am attending to his patients on shore. Recd. a letter from Surgeon Chas. Eversfield, N. York, in answer to my date Dec. 31, '64.

Feby. 3, 1865. Surg. Denny is improving. Attended to his morning sick call of patients. Had quite a busy time of it—two cases of hernia, fracture, and a host of chills and catarrhus patients. My patient Jas. Reid is improving slowly—continue tonic plan of treatment.

Feby. 5, 1865. Lieut. Stewart, U.S. Army, luxated his right wrist today. I immediately reduced said dislocation, after which I applied an anterior-posterior splint and roller. The Army hospital practice is doing well. My patient Reid is improving slowly. I have any amount of private practice. Surg. Denny is doing right well. . . .

Feby. 17, 1865. Today John McGovern, lds., 22, Ireland, affected with rheumatic abscess of left thigh, died after an illness of one month and 14 days.

Feby. 18, 1865. John McGovern was buried today in one of the graveyards attached to one of the churches on shore, Lieut. Mitchell acting as chaplain. The U.S.S. *Shamrock* arrived today. Wrote a letter to Hon. S. E. Ancona . . . for a copy of the report of the Secretary of the Navy for 1864.

March 29, 1865. The Army left on an expedition; consequently I took charge of the Army hospital. Had 64 cases to treat.

Pamlico Sound, N.C., May 19, 1865. Returned on board again, having been to Norfolk, Va., undergoing an examination for actg. passed asst. surgeon, U.S.N. The ship is homeward bound—i.e., New York. The *Wyalusing, Tacony, Agawam, Commodore Hull, Shokokon, Hunchback*, and *Lockwood* all have gone home. [The

Agawam had actually been transferred to Hampton Roads, where she was later designated senior officer's vessel.] The *Shamrock, Massasoit,* and *Iosco* remain in the Sound.

Brooklyn Navy Yard, New York. May 31, 1865, the U.S.S. *Mattabesett* went out of commission, and I left New York for home June 2.

[It is interesting to note that Dr. Boyer made no mention of the end of the war. One senses in reading the manuscript that the diary was playing out by the beginning of the year 1865. By the end of the first week of February lapses began to appear. No entries were made between the 6th and the 17th, none between the 18th of February and March 29, and none between March 29 and May 19. The diarist's preoccupation first with his duties as medical officer in charge of the army hospital at Plymouth and then with his examination at Norfolk for promotion could in part explain the silence during the last period, but certainly not wholly. Could it be that the navy personnel felt that it had completed its task before the fighting on land had come to a decision? Notes after May 19 were jotted down hurriedly and somewhat carelessly in pencil.]

PART FOUR

POSTWAR SERVICE: THE U. S. SUPPLY STEAMER *NEWBERN*

20

Duty on a Coastal Supply Vessel

Brooklyn Navy Yard, New York, June 6, 1865. Reported for duty as an acting passed assistant surgeon [one of twelve listed in the Navy *Register* to January 1, 1866; ranking with lieutenants] on board of the United States supply steamer *Newbern.*

At Sea, June 19, 1865. Passed Admiral Dahlgren in his flagship, the *Pawnee,* today.

[Rear Admiral Dahlgren was on his way North, having just relinquished command of the South Atlantic Squadron. His own flagship (the *Philadelphia*) not being seaworthy, he had shifted his flag to the *Pawnee,* detached from the squadron in need of extensive repairs. "And so," he wrote in his diary, "ends a command of two years of one of the largest fleets ever assembled under American colors—as many as 96 at one time."]

We are on our route to Port Royal, Key West and New Orleans.

Port Royal, S. C., June 22, 1865. Discharged some cargo at this place. All well.

Key West, Fla., June 27, 1865. Coaling ship, discharging stores, etc. for the vessels of the West Gulf Squadron. Met a large number of naval officers. Had a glorious time.

Navy Yard, Pensacola, Fla., July 2, 1865. Had a glorious time whilst anchored here. Took a ride on horseback and enjoyed myself hugely.   . . . .

Key West, Fla. [by way of Mobile Bay, New Orleans, and back to Pensacola]. July 18, arrived here; commenced to coal ship. H. B. M.'s Consul [A. G.] Butterfield [vice-consul from Great Britain to the Confederate States at Key West 1864-1865] will take passage with us to New York. July 20, left Key West.

Charleston, S. C. July 22, arrived at Charleston. Took a stroll on shore at night. Found the greater part of the city in ruins. Truly the ways of the transgressor are hard. July 23, paid Fort Sumter a visit—one mass of brickwork and iron.   . . . Slept on shore tonight at the Charleston Hotel. Good beds and a splendid table; bill cheap. July 25, left for New York. Have 40 patients in hand—some rather sick.

New York. July 28, arrived here. July 29, wrote to the 4th auditor regarding prize money. Aug. 1, paid a visit to Riverhead, Long Island. Had a pleasant time there until the 3rd inst. in the company of Miss [Maria K.] Corwin. Aug. 3, took a run down home. Had a pleasant time until Aug. 10. Aug. 26, left New York for the South.   . . .

Key West, Fla., Sept. 2, 1865 [by way of Port Royal]. Arrived here today. Raining very hard. Weather rather cooler than what it was last trip. Wrote a letter to Miss Corwin and one to father.

Sept. 4, 1865. Coaling ship. Took 100 contrabands, more or less, on board as passengers for Apalachicola and Pensacola, Fla. Left for Apalachicola at 5 P.M.

Off Bay of Apalachicola, Sept. 7, 1865. Arrived here last night. This morning supplied the *Mahaska* with fresh beef and ice. Transferred the greater part of the darkies to the U.S.S. *Mahaska.* 11 A.M. Up anchor and off for Pensacola. I might here state that while at Key West I purchased 500 cigars (Havanas) for $50 per thousand, worth $100. They are a pleasant-flavored cigar, a regular luxury for those who are fond of the fragrant weed y-clept tobacco.

Pensacola Bay and Navy Yard, Sept. 8, 1865. Arrived here this morning. Supplied various vessels. Found all hands from the senior officer, [Commander James F.] Armstrong [on retired list, in temporary command of the navy yard at Pensacola], down to the dirtiest boy drunk as lords.

Gulf of Mexico, Sept. 9, 1865. Left Pensacola this morning for New Orleans.   . . . Sept. 14, [left] New Orleans at 4.40 P.M. for Pensacola, Fla.   . . .

Pensacola, Fla., Sept. 16, 1865. Arrived here today. Had a severe case of epilepsy to treat last night. Today he is better. He was a fireman named Daughterman.

Sept. 19, 1865. Left Pensacola at 4.45 P.M. for Key West. Daughterman had another attack of epilepsy at 6 A.M.

Key West, Fla., Sept. 22, 1865. Arrived here this morning. Coaled ship today. Blowing a stiff breeze. Raining nearly all the time. Wrote a letter to father. Sept. 24, at 10.10 A.M. we left Key West bound for Port Royal, S. C. . . .

Portsmouth Navy Yard, Va., Oct. 2, 1865. Arrived here this morning [by way of Port Royal, S. C., bound for New York]. Our object in coming here is to coal ship. Saw Mr. Brown and Mr. Wymen about some money that the latter owes me. Mr. Brown promised to investigate said affair and let me know about it per letter in a day or two. Sent in my quarterly report of sick for 3rd quarter, 1865; also wrote to the 4th auditor about some prize money and back pay. Weather rather warm. 3 P.M. Having finished coaling ship, we are now once more homeward bound.

Navy Yard, New York. Oct. 3, 1865. Arrived in New York. Oct. 5, leave of absence for seven days granted unto me. Took a run home to Reading, Pa. Had a gay and festive time. Oct. 13, arrived in New York again.

Riverhead, Long Island. Oct. 14, 1865. Took a run up to Riverhead, Long Island, to pay Miss Corwin a visit. Found her awaiting my arrival at the depot. Found Mr. and Mrs. Corwin, Hannibal, and Wallace all in good health and best of spirits. My lady love, Miss Tute, was delighted to see me. Spent a happy evening in her company. Rained all night.

Oct. 15, 1865. Rain! Rain!! Rain!!! Was compelled to remain in the house all day. Had no serious objection, simply because I had one of Eve's fairest daughters for a companion, the heads of the family enjoying themselves taking naps whilst us youngsters were having a nice time all to ourselves. At 3 P.M. p[oppe]d q[uestio]n.

Shelter Island [at the east end of Long Island], *Oct. 16, 1865.* Miss Corwin and myself, on a visit to Chas. Hallett, Esq., and wife, arrived here at 12 M. Found them enjoying excellent health. Both pleased to see Tute and myself. Tute and myself had rather gay times out in the woods hunting wild grapes, lounging, etc. Oct. 17th, left Shelter Island for Riverhead. . . . Oct. 18, left Riverhead for New York. Arrived there at 10 A.M. . . .

Navy Yard, New York, Oct. 20, 1865. Wrote a letter to Tute, enclosing photo of mine; also sent her per mail 1 dozen medium eagle naval buttons for dress. Oct. 21. Left for the South. 2 P.M. Ship sprung a leak. 2.30 P.M. All O.K. again and under way, passing all and every ship ahead of us that had half an hour the start. All in good spirits. Our former chief engineer, Mr. Maples [Acting First Assistant Engineer Isaac Maples], detached, and Acting 1st Asst. Engineer [Thomas] Dobbs takes his place. Wrote a letter to father ere we started South.

At Sea, Oct. 22, 1865. Today I detected a small hemorrhoid, external to the sphincter ani. This is the first time that I ever was affected with piles. Cause of said hemorrhoid—too free living and undue exercise whilst on shore. I applied cold water quite freely. Oct. 23. No apparent change in size of hemorrhoid. Continue cold-water application. Made one application of tannic-acid ointment. Took internally potassii bitartras 3 i. Don't fancy piles very much. Will be pleased to get rid of Mr. Hemorrhoid. Ship rolling, tossing, pitching, rocking, and knocking about considerably, making it anything but agreeable to be on board. The beauties of life on the ocean wave not quite as pleasant as the author of "Life on the Ocean Wave" would seem to wish to portray in his song.

Oct. 24, 1865. Out at sea in the midst of an awful storm. Every timber groaning, the winds howling. Every nail has its peculiar shriek. Ship having a rough time with the elements. All hands out of humor. Captain says he never saw such a storm before. Feel as though I would like to flog the man that wrote "Life on the Ocean Wave." Think him considerable of a humbug. His ideas were fallacious. Don't wish to see many such storms. Will feel better when the storm is over.

Port Royal, S. C., Oct. 25, 1865. Thanks to the Almighty, our staunch timbers, and brave captain, we have weathered the storm. Once more we are at anchor in a good and quiet harbor. The storm has passed on. Wrote to father.

At Sea, Oct. 26, 1865. Left Port Royal last evening at 5 P.M. Weather pleasant; everything is lovely and the goose hangs high. Sold a box of cigars to Dr. [William J.] Simon [assistant surgeon on board the *New Hampshire,* flagship of the Atlantic Squadron] for six dollars and fifty cents. Hemorrhoids feel better. Am taking the following: ℞ potassae bitart., sulphur lot. āā 3 ss, M̶. Sig. To be taken three times a day in a wineglass of sherry wine. 2 P.M. discovered a wreck in the distance—i.e., piece of a wreck with 4 men upon it. 2.30 P.M. picked them up. Found them to be one American, two Englishmen, and 1 Frenchman, surviving men of the ship *Mersey*, Liverpool. They had been without anything to eat and drink ever since Monday last.

The officers and crew consisted of 14 men. The captain died last night. The balance of them were drowned or killed. As soon as they arrived on board, I administered to them some whiskey and small doses of bread and water and coffee; the paymaster issued to them a complete suit of clothing. Their only food consisted of seaweed and shoes. The Frenchman tried to cut a vein so as to let his comrades suck his blood; he has quite a deep cut in his left arm. They were picked up in latitude 29°07′ north, longitude 80°27′ west, Cape Canaveral [Florida], bearing south by west 40 miles off. The ship had been loaded with mahogany. Poor fellows—how thankful they felt when we picked them up! They saw two steamers and one ship pass them. Had some idea of drawing lots to see who was to die to save his comrades.

Off coast Florida, Oct. 27, 1865. Picked up at 9 A.M. the topgallant yard ship marked *John Mayo*. 9.30 A.M. spoke ship *Margaret* of New Orleans, loaded with cotton, in distress. She was under the colors of Prussia. Took her in tow. We intend to tow her to Key West, Fla. She suffered severely from the storm of Monday and Tuesday—another victim. This makes two parties that we have saved from destruction. Truly the *Newbern* is acting the part of a good Samaritan.

My patients—i.e., *Mersey* men—are doing right well. This morning I told them that they might eat anything except salt junk. One of them, the American, named Charles G. Clayton, had quite a high fever. Ordered him magnesae sulphas ʒ ss to open his bowels; allow him plenty of cold water to drink. The rest of the boys feel quite smart, only a little sore—effects of salt water.

The skipper (captain) of the *Margaret* sent us on board some brandy and claret. The brandy fair quality (so said my messmates who drank it; I, not using distilled liquors, cannot say); the claret was a superfine quality, having tasted it myself.

During the day we saw quite a number of persons on the beach. Whether shipwrecked or no we could not say; still they were at a place where we could not succor them. They have an opportunity of going into the interior.

Another ship wrecked and high and dry on the beach. She went ashore last Monday. Named *John Wesley*, from New Orleans to Liverpool, loaded with cotton; master, Patten. Took seven men from her, the captain, mates, and steward preferring to remain by the ship. Five miles to the southward of the *John Wesley* lies another wreck, the barque *J. M. Howard*. The captain of the *John Wesley* says that to his knowledge there are quite a number of wrecks between this place and Key West.

Key West, Fla., Oct. 28, 1865. Arrived here today at 2 P.M. Passed today quite a number of wrecks. Wrote letter to Miss Tute Corwin, also one to father. Weather lovely. Oct. 29. Weather warm. Was compelled to make my appearance today all in white. Took a delightful drive around the island. Gathered quite a number of different seaweeds.

Oct. 31, 1865. Put in our claim for salvage as regards the Prussian barque *Margaret*, which we rescued and towed to Key West on the 28th. Mr. Maloney, our lawyer, says that our claim is good, also that we will get large salvage. Bully for us! I hope we may, for I would like to raise the wind. Won't I feel quite elated when I pocket the stamps [paper money, so referred to probably because of the use of stamps as currency in the early days of the war]. Wrote a letter to father, informing him of my good health etc. Reported 2 cases sick—one case of icterus (jaundice) and one case of contusio (bruised finger). Both are coming on finely. Went to a circus tonight.

Nov. 1, 1865. Wrote letter to H. A. Summons, Reading, Pa. Had a gay and festive time in the ward room tonight; singing, dancing, and sparring was the programme. Cognac and claret flowed as freely as oil; cigars had to suffer some. Nov. 2. 5.30 P.M. Left Key West for Tampa Bay. Left barque *Margaret* safe and secure in the harbor of Key West.

Off Tampa Bay, Fla., Nov. 4, 1865. At anchor, and rather a tough-looking anchorage. We are to supply the U.S.S. *Sagamore*, after which we will cut stick for Apalachicola Bay, Fla.

Tampa Bay, Fla., Nov. 4, 1865. At anchor in the bay. Weather cloudy and every indication of a storm. Are supplying the *Sagamore*. Expect to leave as soon as we have supplied her. There don't appear to be any inducement to keep us at this place any longer than what we can help. I want to go on as soon as possible so as to return to Key West ere many days, for I expect letters from home and some important ones from Miss Tute. 12.20 M. Raining. 5 P.M. Got under way and left for Apalachicola Bay. . . .

Off Apalachicola Bay, Nov. 6, 1865. At anchor awaiting the arrival of the U.S.S. *Mahaska.* Still at anchor here 12 M. 2 P.M. Got under way, and are en route for Pensacola. Did not supply the *Mahaska* for the simple reason that she did not make her appearance.

Pensacola Navy Yard, Fla., Nov. 7, 1865. Arrived here this morning. Wrote a letter to father. None to report sick of ship's company. Nov. 10. 10.40 A.M. Left Pensacola for New Orleans.

Quarantine, Mississippi River, Nov. 11, 1865. Arrived here at 11.20 A.M. Doctor boarded us. I informed him that all was O.K. We passed on again for New Orleans.

New Orleans, La., Nov. 11, 1865. Arrived here at 7 P.M. Wrote to father, announcing our arrival. Nov. 12. Paid F. H. Brown, chief officer of the *Palmyra*, Capt. Sinclair, a visit. Had a splendid time. Dined with him. Took a stroll around town. Saw the elephant some [gained worldly experience, probably at some cost]. Mr. Brown used to be an acting ensign in the service and as such was a shipmate and messmate of mine on the U.S.S. *Mattabesett.* . . . Nov. 16. Commence taking on cargo. We have some of the Rebel ram *Tennessee's* guns on board, which are to be taken to the commanding officer of the New York Navy Yard.

At Sea, Nov. 21, 1865. Left New Orleans for Pensacola at 6 A.M. today. Wrote letter to father on the 19th. 4 P.M. Crossed the bar of the Mississippi; once more at sea. Expect to be at Pensacola in the morning.

Pensacola, Fla., Nov. 22, 1865. Arrived here this morning at 10 A.M. In the evening the minstrels from the U.S.S. *Potomac* came on board and performed for us. All the officers in the harbor were on board. Capt. Renshaw of the late Confederate Navy, who is a going North with us (for his pardon), was quite lively. He sang "Columbia, the Gem of the Ocean" and the "Gunpowder Treason and Plot" [a ballad about the Gunpowder Plot in England in November, 1605, frequently sung by early Americans, particularly in New England, on "Pope Day", or "Guy Fawkes Day"]. It appeared rather strange to hear him sing a Yankee song after having handed down the Stars and Stripes when the Rebels took the Pensacola Navy Yard. The old captain damns the Rebels; says that he "was a damn fool" for leaving the service. "Yes!" says he. "I must say that I kicked my —— out of the service." Thus we have another one of the victims of the so-called Southern Confederacy.

[The Pensacola Navy Yard was surrendered without a struggle at one-thirty in the afternoon of January 12, 1861, to a commission appointed by the governor of Florida, backed by an armed regiment. The order to strike the flag was passed from the commandant, Captain James Armstrong, through the executive officer, Captain Ebenezer Farrand, to the senior lieutenant, Francis B. Renshaw. The colors were hauled down not by Lieutenant Renshaw personally but by a seaman, William Conway, under his direction. After remaining a prisoner on parole for a few days, Lieutenant Renshaw resigned his commission of twenty years' standing in the United States Navy and, in his own words, "tendered my services to the sovereign State of Florida, with whose destiny, whether it be right or adverse, I am fully identified."]

Key West, Fla., Nov. 25, 1865. At 11.30 A.M. arrived here this morning, [having left Pensacola on November 23]. Received two letters, one from father dated Nov. 6 and one from Tute dated Oct. 23, also two papers which Miss Tute sent me. Answered both letters today. Like a ninny, I gave my letters to an officer on the *Marigold,* expecting that a mail would leave by her for New York *via* Havana, and after she left, I found that it was all nonsense; so of course they will get my letters sometime by Christmas next instead of in 5 or 6 days.

Nov. 27, 1865. Today the salvage claim regarding the Prussian barque *Margaret* was decided, and on account of something being left undone on our part or else our claim was not pushed, we have only decreed unto us the small, insignificant sum of seven thousand dollars ($7,000), when everyone said that we ought of had at least $75,000. So much for Key West justice. Hereafter I hope all foreign crafts may be lost, for all I have to say. The idea of us saving property to the amount fo $200,000 and only receiving the small sum of $7,000 for our trouble! Madam Rumor says that the money is to be paid in the morning. Hope so, for however little the sum may be, I am anxious to pocket my share of the stamps.

Nov. 28, 1865. Today the salvage money was paid, and my small portion was two hundred dollars. Rather a small pile—still it is better than nothing; I don't object to pocketing it. At 11.25 A.M. we left Key West for Port Royal, S. C., with a very large cargo of naval stores (in fact, I am afraid that we are too heavy-laden for comfort and benefit), also quite a large number of passengers, consisting of naval officers going North on leave etc. and merchant captains who have lost their ships during the late gale. We have had a lively euchre party tonight in the wardroom.

Port Royal, S. C., Nov. 30, 1865. Arrived here this evening. Understand that we are to take on board some sick sailors and marines for the Brooklyn Naval Hospital.

Off Wilmington, N. C., Dec. 3, 1865 [by way of Charleston]. Arrived here this morning. We are to comunicate with the *Lenapee.* Whether she is at Fort Fisher or at Wilmington remains yet to be seen. The captain went on shore in his gig to ascertain.

At Sea, Dec. 4, 1865. At 10 A.M. left from off Wilmington, N.C., and on our way to New York. Took sick men on board from the *Lenapee* for the hospital. Dec. 5. The weather is quite boisterous. We are pitching and tossing some. Very cloudy and raining at times.

New York, Dec. 7, 1865. Arrived in New York. Dec. 9, took a run down to Riverhead, Long Island; had a pleasant time whilst there. Dec. 10, dined with Mr. Hallett. Dec. 12, left Riverhead and arrived in New York at 3 P.M. Dec. 13, left New York for Reading, Pa. Enjoyed myself hugely until Friday, when I left for New York. Dec. 16, received a letter from Miss Corwin, the contents of which did not please me, she being inclined to listen to and believe the yarns of others ere she would mine. Hence today I sent her her letters, photo, and ring, requesting mine in return. At same time I wrote a letter to her brother Hannibal, explaining why and wherefore I would not call on him again. I might here state that whilst I was at Reading, I sent per express to Miss Corwin a handsome album, value $15, also some fancy photos, value $8, also a splendid double-barrelled shotgun to her brother Hannibal. I expect an answer to mine of today ere long, in which I enclosed all her letters. I am afraid that this love affair of mine is all up in a spout. Well! she was the only girl I ever did truly love and the last, for I don't think I can ever love a girl the same as I loved her.

Wrote to Hon. S[tephen] J. W. Tabor, 4th Auditor, Treasury Department, Washington, D.C., regarding some prize money due me from prizes captured by the U.S.S. *Mattabesett* whilst in the sounds of North Carolina. Wrote letter to A. F. Dill, Woonsocket, Rhode Island, regarding some money due me.

Navy Yard, New York, Dec. 19, 1865. Received a letter today from Miss Tute, enclosing her photo again, which I had sent her on the 16th, asking my forgiveness etc. and hoping that we continue being on the same terms that we were on ere I received her letter dated Dec. 15. Of course I had no objections. On the contrary, I sat down and answered her letter, asking forgiveness on my part, and acknowledged that I was rather hasty and was willing to consider the engagement good. Today I sent her a Spanish shellwork box per express, also subscribed in her name for Frank Leslie's "Lady's Magazine" for 1866. Sent her the receipt. Also sent her a copy of Frank Leslie's miscellany [probably a collection of "Frank Leslie's Unrivalled Publications" advertised in *Frank Leslie's Illustrated Newspaper,* various combinations being from time to time offered on club terms], "Illustrated [News]paper," "Phunny Phellow" [a comic magazine published in New York by Ross and Tousey, and Street and Smith, from 1859 to around 1876; leading cartoonist—Thomas Nast], and "Comic Monthly" [published in New York from 1859 to around 1881; leading artists—Frank H. T. Bellow and Frank Beard].   . . . .

At Sea, Dec. 23, 1865. Weather lovely—quite a contrast with the state of the weather yesterday, when Old Boreas was out in all his glory. Today Old Sol has favored us with his presence. Reported 2 cases sick.

Dec. 24, 1865. We are in the midst of an awful storm, worse by far than the gale of Oct. 24. Were unable to eat a regular meal today. Were compelled to take luncheon.

Christmas, Dec. 25, 1865. Last night was a rather rough and stormy one. Everyone thought that the old *Newbern* was a case at last. Don't wish to spend another such a day or night; would prefer pleasant weather by far. This is not a very merry Christmas for us. Ship rolling rather too much for comfort.

December 26, 1865. Last night Old Boreas was in all his glory. The Storm King was in the midst of a carousal. Everything looked rather blue; all hands felt rather ticklish. Today we are in the midst of a fog. Truly, verily indeed, we are having a streak of ill luck. . . .

Key West, Fla., Dec. 31, 1865 [by way of Port Royal]. At 11 A.M. we arrived at this anchorage. The weather splendid. Everyone dressed in white—quite a contrast to the style of goods or wearing apparel up North. This evening Paymasters Lyon and Clark [Assistant Paymaster George A. Lyon, of the *Potomac*, and, probably, Acting Assistant Paymaster Frank Clark, ordered to the *J. C. Kuhn*, temporarily in the Gulf Squadron], Engineer Dobbs, [Acting] Ensign [Milton] Webster [of the *Newbern*], and myself attended divine service in the Episcopal church of this place. The church rather a large one—will seat one thousand persons. Seats very comfortable. Ten chandeliers, four globe lights to each one, and twenty smaller lights lit up the church. The chandeliers all dressed with boxwood evergreen branches. The ceiling and sides also beautifully decorated with boxwood branches. In short, the whole church looked green and cozy.

Besides all that, Lieutenant General Winfield Scott, the "Old War Horse," accompanied by a lieutenant, formed one of the congregation. The "Old Warrior" looks aged and is rather feeble—and well he might, for he is eighty odd years of age [he died on May 29, 1866, at West Point, just before his eightieth birthday]. God bless him! May he live many a long and happy day to come. The text is to be found in "The First Epistle General of John," chap. II, verse 17: "And the world passeth away, and the lust thereof: but he that doeth the will of God abideth for ever." The sermon was not bad. Did not fancy the parson's style of delivery.

Jan. 1, 1866. Weather hot. Wearing white pantaloons today. Wrote letter to father. Reported 2 cases sick—one case of neuralgia and one of gonorrhoea. 8 P.M. Lovely evening. All the officers except myself ashore drinking eggnog etc., making New Year's calls, all in a glorious condition, whilst I am all alone on board reading. Not drinking rum or smoking tobacco, consequently I cannot enjoy myself amidst a party that are killing time per means of rum and tobacco. Yes! I am determined to lead the life of a teetotaller hereafter.

12 midnight Paymasters Clark and Lyon returned on board drunk as lords. Are in the best of humor, Lyon singing "Hard

times coming knocking at the door" ["By'n bye hard times come a-knockin' at the door," from Stephen Collins Foster's *My Old Kentucky Home*], awaking up all hands. I was compelled to turn out several times to quiet Lyon. Truly the old maxim "Liquor in, wit out" is a truism [probably from "Where the drink goes in, there the wit goes out"—*Jacula Prudentum*, a collection of proverbs by George Herbert, early seventeenth-century English poet]. The cabin crowd all "sound on the goose" [meaning "true to the slavery cause" in Kansas during the antislavery crusade; perhaps here used in some other sense]. The citizens of Key West appear to enjoy themselves today. Parties, sociables, and balls appear to be the order of the day. The colored portion of the community are having a "fancy-dress ball."

Jan. 2, 1866. Poor boys that were drunk last night are feeling rather sore this morning. Head feels as though twenty rolling mills were in full blast within their cranium. Muscles feel sore as though they had been pounded with stones. Every joint aches them; parched tongues; thirsty as fishes; acid and iced drinks in great demand. "Truly the way of the transgressors is hard." "They that dance must pay the fiddler." " 'Tis pleasant to get drunk but an awful job to get sober"—so says Lyon. Today he is on the "swell-head stool of repentance"; says he does not intend to get drunk again. Hope not, for I do not like to see a man make a fool of himself.

Jan. 3, 1866. Weather hot. White clothing in great demand. Finished coaling ship today. Commenced taking in a cargo of lumber, which we are to take to Pensacola. Gave unto Surgeon [George or Lewis] Taylor of the Army two vaccine virus so as to vaccinate the troops at this place, smallpox having made its appearance in the midst of the soldiers. Also purchased a small quantity of coral for brothers Frank's and Mike's family. 7 P.M. Raining quite smartly. A stiff northeaster springing up. Blowing big guns.   . . .

Jan. 5, 1866. Gen. Scott's surgeon called on me regarding the old general's health etc.   . . . .

Pensacola, Fla., Jan. 8, 1866. Arrived here at 4.30 P.M. Stiff breeze blowing outside at 8 P.M.   . . . .

At Sea, Jan. 20, 1866. Left Pensacola at 3 P.M., on our way to Tampa Bay, Fla., with stores on board for the U.S.S. *Sagamore.* We have the tug *Rose* in tow. 5.30 P.M. The tug signalized that she was leaking badly. We are compelled to turn about, or around, and return to Pensacola. 6 P.M. On our way to Pensacola.

Pensacola Bay, Fla., Jan. 21, 1866. Arrived here this morning with the tug. We left again at 9 A.M. for Tampa Bay. Hope we may have better luck this time.

Tampa Bay, Fla., Jan. 22, 1866. 5.30 P.M. came to anchor in Tampa Bay. Jan. 23. The paymaster, chief engineer, and executive officer with a boat's crew started early this morning in the 3rd cutter for Tampa, there to communicate with the U.S.S. *Sagamore*. The captain has been very sick yesterday and today with neuralgia. Feels slightly better today. Jan. 24. At 9 A.M. the *Sagamore* arrived from Tampa. 1 P.M. We got under way and started for the outside. . . . We expect to be outside in the Gulf ere long. Weather lovely. The paymaster and party returned on board this morning. They all had a pleasant time. The captain feels quite comfortable again.

Gulf of Mexico, Jan. 25, 1866. Actg. 3rd Asst. Engineer R[obert] E. Murray had himself relieved of the sum of three hundred and ten dollars sometime during the night. The steerage steward, by the name of Whitney, is suspected and at present is in double irons. This is the second time during the last three months that Murray has been robbed. Thus he has lost in all $530. Hope the thief may be detected. If Whitney is guilty, punish him severely; if innocent, why, let him off. The weather has been lovely all day.

Key West, Fla., Jan. 26, 1866. Arrived here this morning. Weather lovely. Coaling ship. Wrote letter to father, also one to Miss Corwin. Jan. 27. Coaling ship and taking in stores. 2 P.M. Washing down decks. 3.30 P.M. Mail on board. 5.10 P.M. Left Key West for New York. Weather rather hot today. Citizens of Key West wearing white and light clothing. . . . .

New York Bay, Feby. 1, 1866. At 9.12 P.M. we let go our anchor in the bay. It took us 5 days, 4 hours, and 7 minutes to travel the distance from Key West to New York. Feby. 4. Today I called upon Miss Corwin at the residence of her cousin, Charles Corwin, No. 122 Nassau St., Brooklyn, N.Y. Remained with her until 9.30 P.M., when we parted, after having exchanged letters and rings, the best of friends. Thus our engagement is broken off. Miss Corwin has my best wishes. I promised to write her occasionally, also to call on her whenever I am at leisure. . . . .

Navy Yard, New York, Feby. 16, 1866. Last week I took a run down home. Had a pleasant time. Discharging cargo. We are to sail South on the 20th. Feby. 21. . . . During our stay in New York I have had a very pleasant time. Spent most of my evenings in company with Miss Corwin. I bid her an affectionate adieu last night. 11 A.M. Left for the South.

Off Beaufort Harbor, N. C., Feby. 24, 1866. We are at anchor off the harbor of Beaufort, N. C., in the midst of a fog, awaiting to communicate with the *Lenapee* and *Agawam.* Wrote a letter to [Passed Assistant] Surg. [Wm. K.] Van Reypen of the *Lenapee,* informing him that I had some medical stores on board for distribution, and sent it to him per Mr. Trathen [Acting Ensign Charles Trathen of the *Newbern*]. Also wrote to father, announcing our safe arrival here. Mr. Trathen returned at 1 P.M. and reports that no medicines are needed on board the vessel. 3 P.M. We are under way once more, off for Port Royal.

Port Royal, S. C., Feby. 26, 1866. Arrived here at 8 A.M. . . . Wrote note to Dr. Nelson [Surgeon H. C. Nelson] U.S.S. *New Hampshire,* informing him of the fact that there were medical stores on board the *Newbern* for distribution. He answered by saying that he was well supplied with medicines at present. Recd. letter from father dated Jan. 7. 12.30 P.M. Left Port Royal for Key West.

Key West, Fla., March 1, 1866. Arrived at this anchorage this morning. Weather lovely. The *Muscoota, Sagamore,* and *Chocura* at anchor here. Signalized to the vessels that medical stores could be had by applying to the surgeon of the *Newbern.* Mar. 2. At 5.30 P.M. we left Key West for Pensacola. Weather pleasant. Looks rough in the Gulf. . . . .

Pensacola Navy Yard, Fla., March 5, 1866. Arrived here this morning. Recd. letter from Miss Corwin . . . Dec. 26, '65, which I enclosed with an answer and returned to her today. Being as I had returned all her other *love* letters, our future letters will be mere *friendly* ones. March 7. Weather pleasant. Still discharging cargo. Furnished supplies to the naval hospital [and to the] *Potomac* and *Yucca* thus far.

March 9, 1866. Commenced loading ship with cargo of guns, ammunition, etc. The captain and Mr. Murray left for New Orleans, La., at 5.30 P.M., to be gone for one week. March 11. Weather windy. All hands to quarters for general inspection at 10 A.M. Messrs. Trathen and Dobbs inspecting ship. . . . March 12. Furnished medical stores to the *Maria A. Wood* and the *Potomac.* The U.S. supply steamer *South Carolina* arrived today from New Orleans, heavy-laden with stores. March 17. St. Patrick's Day. Our Irish boys are "wearing the green." Boys busy loading ship with shot and shell. Weather quite cool. *South Carolina* still at anchor here. March 18. At 5.40 P.M. the admiral [Commodore Joseph Lanman, commanding the Atlantic Squadron] arrived in his flagship, the *Estrella,* and came to anchor astern of us. March 19. Issued medical stores to the surgeon of the *Estrella.* The U.S. supply steamer *South Carolina* left this anchorage. Commenced to rain at 3 P.M. March 20. Was a member of a medical board of survey held on some hospital patients (19), which we condemned, and I am to take charge of them going north. Weather rainy. The *Chocura* arrived from Key West. . . . March 22. The captain and Mr. Murray arrived on board, having been to New Orleans. Received on board for transportation north to the Brooklyn Naval Hospital eighteen patients from the Pensacola Naval Hospital. Weather lovely.

Gulf of Mexico, March 24, 1866. We left Pensacola Navy Yard this morning for Key West. Weather lovely. Issued to the medical officer of the *Cowslip* measure glass 4 oz., no. 1. 8 P.M. We are afloat once more in the Gulf of Mexico. Weather has been beautiful all day. Sea as smooth as glass. . . . .

Key West, Fla., March 27, 1866. Arrived here this morning. Recd. letter from father, enclosing a *carte de visite* of sister Beckie, dated March 6, 1866. . . . Citizens wearing white.

At Sea, March 30, 1866. Left Key West this morning. 12 o'clock meridian at sea, off coast of Florida. 10 P.M. eclipse of moon. At 9.30 P.M. I acknowledged the power of Old Neptune for the first time since I have entered the U.S. Navy—that is, I had to vomit quite freely, the rolling, pitching, and tossing of the ship causing me to become seasick. March 31. Ten sail in sight. Weather lovely. Paymaster paid me one hundred and thirty-two dollars and twenty cents—money due me up to April, 1866. Judge Boynton, a passenger, is quite seasick.

Port Royal, S. C., April 1, 1866. All Fools' Day, and all afloat. All hands to muster today at 10.30 A.M. Captain Holley [Acting Master Robert Y. Holley, commanding the *Newbern*] read Articles of War. At 4.05 P.M. we arrived in the harbor of Port Royal, S.C. The flagship *New Hampshire* and a double-ender are at anchor here. We are compelled to anchor here for the night. Some officers of the *New Hampshire* came on board in the evening. 10.30 P.M. furnished medical stores to the U.S.S. *Tacony.* . . . .

New York Harbor, off Battery, April 5, 1866. We arrived here this morning. . . . April 9. Arrived on board again today, having been up to Riverhead, L.I., on a visit to Miss Corwin. . . . .

New York Navy Yard, April 13, 1866. Arrived on board today at 4 P.M., having been to Reading on visit. Arrived home on Wednesday evening at 6 P.M. Left home this morning at 10 A.M. Whilst home I had my diplomas and some large lithographic paintings framed and hung up in my room. Also ordered some "Medical and Surgical Reporters"—vols. 11, 12 13—to be bound. Sister Lizzie [sister-in-law, Elizabeth Clouser Boyer, wife of Benjamin Franklin Boyer] made me a present of a beautiful wrapper, or dressing gown, whilst home. April 14. . . . Paymaster [Edward H.] Cushing and Engineer Murray under treatment for intermittent fever. . . . April 17. Purchased Hodge's "Great System of Obstetrics" [probably Hugh L. Hodge, *The Principles and Practice of Obstetrics* (Philadelphia: Blanchard and Lea, 1864; second edition, 1866)] and West's "Diseases of Infancy and Childhood" [Charles West, *Lectures on the Diseases of Infancy and Childhood* (Philadelphia: Lea and Blanchard, 1850, and other editions]. Also invested the sum of $16.50 in silverware—table and teaspoons, fork, knife, and napkin ring. April 21. At 1.30 P.M. we left the Navy Yard for Port Royal, S. C. . . .

Port Royal, S. C., April 28, 1866. Arrived here this morning [after a rough passage and many delays off Hatteras]. Commenced to coal ship. Weather rather warm. . . . May 4. Received on board today from the U.S.S. *Lenapee* three sick men for transportation north—one named Francis Clark, sea.—compound fracture right leg—doing well; John McManus, lds.—diarrhoea chronic—rather debilitated; and William Jackson, lds.—enuresis—doing so so. May 5. Left Port Royal harbor at 3.14 P.M. for New York. Was member of a medical board of survey held upon the U.S.S. *New Hampshire*. Recd. two sick men on board for the Brooklyn Naval Hospital from the *New Hampshire*.

New York Harbor, off Ellis Island, May 9, 1866. Arrived here this morning from Port Royal. . . .

Navy Yard, New York, May 11, 1866. Purchased some underclothing and half hose today: viz., three pairs drawers, $1.75 per pair—$5.25; three undershirts, $2.50—$7.50; 1 doz. half hose— $6. . . . I also purchased three black neckties for $1.55, thus spending in all $20.30. . . . Sent in a requisition for medical stores today to the chief of Bureau of Med. and Surg.

May 12, 1866. 2nd Asst. Engineer C[harles] J. McConnell [on special duty at Philadelphia] paid me a visit today. Had a pleasant time. . . . Purchased pair shoes for $8, velvet mat $5. . . .   May 17. Received a letter from 4th auditor, Treasury Department, authorizing the paymaster to pay me the difference of sea pay between an actg. asst. surg. and an actg. passed asst. surg. from May 19th to 31st, of May, 1865, inclusive, amounting to $8.90, which Cushing refused to pay. Yesterday I received my requisition from the chief of Bureau Med. and Surg., signed and approved. Medicines received from the laboratory. . . . .

At Sea, May 22, 1866. At 4 P.M. we left for Port Royal. Today I was made a present of a black-and-tan terrier slut—name, Gypsy. May 23. Weather pleasant. Capt. Holley prohibits the playing of cards on board hereafter. . . . .

At Sea, May 29, 1866. Left Port Royal this morning, having the U.S.S. *New Hampshire*, a frigate, in tow, the double-enders U.S.S. *Agawam* and *Tacony* (flagship) accompanying us. We are on our way to Norfolk, Va. When outside the bar of Port Royal, the *New Hampshire* fired a salute of 13 guns, saluting Commander Lanman. Weather pleasant.

Hampton Roads, Va., June 2, 1866. Arrived here this morning with the *New Hampshire*. Left again at 11.30 A.M. for New York. Added a few words to Miss C's letter, also that of father's dated May 26, and then sent them on shore.

New York Harbor, off Battery, June 3, 1866. At 7 P.M. we came to anchor off the Battery, opposite Ellis Island. Wrote to father, Michael, Frank, and David. June 4. Purchased a pocket case of instruments at Geo. Triman's and Co., 63 Chatham Street, New York, for $25, also some silver sutures for $0.50. Had my seal ring lettered with a B. Expense—$1.25.

Reading, Pa., June 13, 1866. My birthday. Mother gave me a dinner in honor of the event. All her children dined with her, also some relatives. Had a pleasant time. Was the happy recipient of several valuable presents. Brothers Frank and Mike presented me the pocket case I bought the 4th for $25. . . .

Navy Yard, New York, June 18, 1866. Left Riverhead [where he had gone on the 16th] at 7 A.M. Arrived on board ship at 11.30 A.M. I might here mention that a few days ago I sent per mail to Miss Amanda Corwin Wilkie Collins' novel "Armadale" [London: Smith, Elder and Company, 1866; and New York: Harpers, 1866], also at same time to her brother Hannibal two colored lithographs, the *Newbern* and *Mattabesett.* . . . .

Reading, Pa., June 30, 1866. On a visit home.   . . . Had a pleasant time.

New York Navy Yard, July 4, 1866. Remained on board all day. Had no desire to go on shore.   . . . July 7. Weather hot—thermometer 95° Fahr. in my room, 98° in the shade, and 118° in the sun—warmest day we have experienced for some time. Received medical stores for distribution in Atlantic and Gulf Squadrons. Received a hypodermic syringe per express from brother Jefferson as a birthday present. I sent to his address per Adams Express Hodge's "Obstetrics" as a birthday present. . . .

July 21, 1866. Left New York for the South. Received letter from Miss Corwin.   . . .

Off Beaufort, N. C., July 24, 1866. Supplied the U.S.S. *Yantic* with medicines.

Off Wilmington, N. C., July 25, 1866.   . . . Mr. Dickerson, the coast pilot, being sick with an attack of cholera communis, I arose at 4 A.M. to attend to him. 9 A.M. He is asleep after receiving quite a large dose of opium.

At Sea, July 29, 1866. We left Charleston, S. C., this morning for Port Royal. We had the engine repaired whilst here. On the 27th I sent to Miss Corwin a Charleston paper in which was noticed our arrival. Mr. Dickerson feels quite smart again. Arrived in Port Royal in the afternoon and left a few hours afterwards. Supplied the *Tacony* with medicines. . . .

Key West, Fla., Aug. 2, 1866. Arrived here this morning. Commenced to coal ship. Bo't 500 cigars (Havana) in one lot and 200 cigars in another lot. Weather hot. Supplied the *Paul Jones* with medicines.

At Sea, Aug. 3, 1866. Left Key West at 6 P.M. and stood up the coast some distance in order to ascertain whether or no there was a ship on fire and in distress. The people at Key West reported a smoke out at sea. 7.30 No signs of a ship on fire; therefore we went about and are heading for the Dry Tortugas.

Aug. 4, 1866. At anchor off Fort Jefferson, Dry Tortugas ["Gibraltar of America" and "Key to the Gulf," serving during the Civil War period not only as a powerful defense outpost but as a military prison as well]. Landed 4 prisoners, who are doomed for life here for murdering U.S. soldiers at Charleston, S.C. 1 P.M. left for Pensacola.

Off Pensacola, Fla., Aug. 6, 1866. At anchor. . . . Aug. 7. Supplied the *Estrella* with medical stores; then we left for the Pensacola Navy Yard. Wrote a letter to Miss Corwin asking her again to renew our engagement by asking her to be my wife. . . .

Pensacola Navy Yard, Fla., Aug. 8, 1866. Supplied *Potomac* with medicines. . . . Aug. 9. Supplied naval hospital and the *Yucca* with stores. Wrote to Michael P. B. Aug. 14. Member medical board of survey at Pensacola Naval Hospital 10 A.M. Condemned 1 officer and 4 men—all going north with us. Aug. 15. *Mahaska* left for the Rio Grande. Aug. 16. U.S.S. *Chocura* arrived. Sick men for North arrived on board. Aug. 18. Supplied *Chocura* with medical stores.

Aug. 20, 1866. Recd. two sick men from *Chocura* for a northern hospital. U.S.S. *Muscoota* arrived and signalized 10 men sick with fever and the surgeon, J. W. Boyden, dead [Assistant Surgeon J. Wesley Boyden]. Dr. Boyden died of the fever. Madam Rumor has it that it is yellow fever.

[According to then Lieutenant Commander Alfred T. Mahan, stationed on the stricken vessel, "near a hundred men, half the ship's company, were down with fever." While "not malignant," the epidemic had resulted in three deaths, including the only doctor on board. The *Muscoota* was taken out of commission the following month. Mahan and Boyer were subsequently to be shipmates on the *Iroquois* in the Asiatic Fleet.[1]]

Aug. 21. Capt. Holley sick with dengue. ℞ pil. co no iii at 6 P.M. Aug. 22. Volunteered as medical officer of the *Muscoota*. Had an interview with Commodore [John A.] Winslow, commanding Gulf Squadron, regarding my volunteering. Commodore said he would think over it. ℞ quiniae et ferri citras grs v ter die for Capt. Holley.

U.S.S. Muscoota, *Aug. 23, 1866.* My services were accepted. Dr. A[lexander] Mackenzie, a. a. surgeon [stationed at the naval hospital at Pensacola], relieves me, and I arrived on board at 12 o'clock. 94 cases of remittent fever, severe type, simulating yellow jack. Busy all day attending sick. Left Pensacola at 5 P.M., *Newbern* towing us.

Gulf of Mexico, Aug. 24, 1866. [On board U.S.S. *Muscoota*.] Issued to all hands fore and aft, sick and well, whiskey ℥ ii, quinine gr i, morning and evening. Cleaning ship. Changed clothing of the sick and had them all washed, for they were filthy. Tapioca, chicken, and beef broth as a diet. Aug. 25. Rain all day. 69 on list, all doing well. Continue same treatment. Aug. 26. Arrived at Key West at 6 P.M. Health officer says we have yellow fever—hence won't let us remain here. Wants to quarantine us. Don't see it. Off for Portsmouth, N. H. 61 on list—29 taking medicine, rest whiskey etc.

Atlantic Ocean, Aug. 27, 1866. 50 on list; 11 return to duty. All doing well. Aug. 28, 43 on list; one new case. Stormy all night. Aug. 29, 35 on list. Washing the clothing of the sick. Weather lovely. Aug. 30, 30 cases; one new case. All doing well. Aug. 31, 29 cases. Lovely night. Sept. 1, 27 cases of fever. Gong 7.30 A.M. Sick coming on finely. Sept. 2, served out the last whiskey ration. 20 cases on list. Foggy all day and night.

Quarantine, Portsmouth Harbor. Sept. 3, 3.30 P.M., arrived here. . . . Weather cold and damp. 18 cases—13 cases fever and 5 all sorts. Sept. 4, old health officer came on board and ordered us into quarantine. Yellow flag at foremast head [beakhead, a small plat-

form at the fore part of the upper deck]. Wrote to father, . . .
Payr. Cushing, and Miss C—. Sept. 5, weather cloudy. Sutlers
supplying us with grub. 9.30 A.M. prayer; 6.30 P.M. prayer. . . .
6 cases. Sept. 6, all coming on finely. . . . Sept. 8, recd. official
document from chief of Bureau of Med. and Surg. . . . thanking
me for my services on board this vessel. Prayer 9.30 A.M. and 6 P.M.
Sept. 9, general inspection 9.30 A.M. Weather stormy. Prayer 6 P.M.
No fever cases. Sept. 10, airing bedding, all hands. Recd. letter
from Miss C—. . . . 6 P.M. prayer. Recd. official letter of thanks
from Secretary of the Navy. Sept. 11, received orders to rejoin the
Newbern ere the 20th. Health officer will leave me go on the 13th.
Engineer Snyder [Second Assistant Engineer Henry Snyder] presented me with a meerschaum cigar holder. Sept. 12, recd. letters
from father and Michael with enclosures. Prayer 6.30 P.M. H[ealth]
o[fficer] examined ship etc. for first time. Sept. 13, left ship for
New York. Paid mess bill, $9.25.

New York, Sept. 14. Arrived here at 7 A.M. Reported to [Rear]
Admiral [Charles H.] Bell [commandant, navy yard]. Left for
Reading at 12 M. Arrived home 6 P.M. Sept. 15, took Essie Snag
out to dinner. Had pleasant time. Presented my adopted sister,
Beckie Henry, with two silver butter knives—value, $7.50—as a
wedding gift. Sept. 16, called on Hon. S. E. Ancona. . . . Brother
David at home with mother. Sept. 17, left for New York. *Newbern*
not here. Paid $2.75 for tobacco and $3.50 for photographs.

U.S.S. Newbern, Navy Yard, New York. Sept. 18, reported for
duty again. Sept. 19, recd. letter from Miss C—. Drew $27.74
mileage. Purchased French work for $7.80. Sept. 20, transferred
John A. Hearn, lds., to hospital—fracture. Sept. 21, . . . wrote to
father and Booth; sent telegram to Booth to come as my steward. . . . Sept. 22, wrote to Hon. S. E. Ancona, enclosing photo.
Recd. letters from Drs. Mackenzie and Tryon. Recd. med. stores
for distribution. Sept. 23, wrote to Miss C—. Sept. 24, paid mess
bill, $43. Called on some ladies. Sept. 27, left for the South. Sept.
28, 29, and 30, in the midst of an awful gale.

Port Royal, S. C., Oct. 1, 1866. Arrived at Port Royal. Discharging cargo. Made out my 3rd quarterly report of sick and sent to
the Bureau of Medicine and Surgery. U.S.S. *Memphis* arrived and
left for New York.

At Sea, Oct. 4, 1866. Picked up 5 men on a raft 56 miles off from land, the surviving men of a crew of 15 belonging to the English ship *Ambrosine,* from Plymouth, loaded with timber. Had been in the water 12 hours. Poor fellows—they looked rather hard. Give them each a tumbler full of port wine. The paymaster gave them each a suit of flannel. I gave Capt. Owens pil. cath co. no iii three hours after he came on board, he being in high fever; also bathed the whole party with fresh water. They felt thankful for their deliverance.

[Here the diary ends. It began again only after the lapse of more than a year—when the surgeon was ordered to the Orient. The young doctor reached Yokohama at a critical period in Japan's history—the Meiji Restoration, which marked the beginning of that nation's transformation from a feudal hermit kingdom to a modern power. From early April, 1868, until late October, 1869, he wandered with the Asiatic Squadron around the islands of Japan and sailed as well into ports of China, Formosa, and the Philippines. He not only watched over "his covey"—the sailors he sought to protect from the strange new hazards they met—but wrote with relish of his visits to shrines and temples, to teeming cities with fascinating and unfamiliar people and customs, to the castle of a great Prince to treat him medically, and even to villages and fields in an East that at the time was little known in the West (see *Naval Surgeon: Revolt in Japan, 1868-1869,* Bloomington: Indiana University Press, 1963). Dr. Boyer died in early 1870, only a few months after his return to the United States.]

Notes

THE SETTING AND THE DIARY

1. One-half of the net proceeds from the sale of prizes was by law set aside for the naval pension fund; the remainder was distributed in the form of bounty to personnel aboard captor vessels, although lack of Congressional appropriation for this purpose resulted in frequent delays in settlement.

PART ONE   THE DOCTOR JOINS THE NAVY

1. Surgeon James M. Greene, retired, stationed at the Philadelphia Navy Yard; Surgeon Joseph Wilson, Jr., whose last cruise had expired in November, 1861, ordered to the *Michigan*, on lake duty; Surgeon Henry O. Mayo, whose last cruise had expired in February, 1862, ordered to the *Powhatan*, being made ready to join the South Atlantic Blockading Squadron; and Surgeon Edward Shippen, whose last cruise had expired in March, 1862, ordered to a receiving ship at New York.

Identification of naval officer personnel, included in the text whenever feasible, is for the most part taken from the annual *Register of the Commissioned, Warrant, and Volunteer Officers of the Navy of the United States* (Washington: Government Printing Office), hereafter referred to as *Navy Register*.

2. The Naval Home and Hospital, at Gray's Ferry Avenue and Bainbridge Street, was established in 1826, the main building (a three-story marble structure) being erected five years later. During the Civil War the institution overflowed with wounded, sick and retired naval officers and sailors; in 1863 nearly a thousand patients were admitted to the hospital department, in comparison with the 179 admitted in 1860, and there was a "great want of additional accommodations." In March, 1864, Congress appropriated $75,000 for extension of the facilities, but "enormous prices" made it inexpedient to start the project at the time.

See Frank H. Taylor, *Philadelphia in the Civil War, 1861-1865* (Published by the city, 1913), p. 206, and *Report of the Secretary of the Navy,* Dec. 5, 1864 (Washington: Government Printing Office, 1864), p. 1181.

3. "Acting" officers were volunteers appointed for temporary duty. Rank of medical personnel, extended in 1847 to include pursers (later paymasters), was purely relative, entailing "no authority to exercise military command and no additional right to quarters." Despite a wartime increase that gave assistant surgeons the relative rank of master, passed assistant surgeons that of lieutenant, surgeons of less than five years' standing that of lieutenant commander, surgeons of between five and fifteen years' standing that of commander, and surgeons of more than fifteen years' standing that of captain, staff officers felt that line officers were determined to degrade the Medical Corps. See *The Principles of Naval Staff Rank; and Its History in the United States Navy, for Over Half a Century.* By a Surgeon in the U.S. Navy, 1869.

PART TWO   SOUTH ATLANTIC BLOCKADING SQUADRON:
THE U.S. BARQUE *Fernandina*

1. Charleston, "principal focus of the contraband trade with Europe," was very difficult to blockade. Obstruction of the main channel leading into the harbor by the sinking of sixteen old vessels (mostly whalers) in December, 1861, and a similar enterprise involving about twenty vessels sunk in Maffitt's Channel a month later had been only temporarily effective. Despite earnest efforts on the part of the squadron, blockade running was frequent, especially under cover of fog or darkness. On April 3, 1862, the Senate Committee on Naval Affairs inquired as to possible laxity. See *Official Records of the Union and Confederate Navies in the War of the Rebellion,* published under the direction of the Secretary of the Navy (Washington: Government Printing Office, 2 ser., 30 vols., 1894-1922), I:12: 416-424, 551, 552, 691, 720; I:13: 186. Hereafter cited as *O.R.* (Navies).

2. See *O.R.* (Navies), I: 12: 741-742; I: 13: 3-4.

3. See *Georgia, A Guide to Its Towns and Countryside,* compiled and written by workers of the Writers' program of the Works Projects Administration in the State of Georgia (Athens: University of Georgia Press, 1940), p. 280; Margaret Davis Cate, *Our Todays and Yesterdays, A Story of Brunswick and the Coastal Islands* (rev. ed.; Brunswick, Georgia: Glover Brothers, 1930), p. 38; and

Burnette Vanstory, *Georgia's Land of the Golden Isles* (Athens: University of Georgia Press, 1956).

4. Third Rhode Island Artillery. Captain Shaw, officer in charge of Company D of this regiment, led a detachment in an assault on Battery Wagner on Morris Island, S. C., in July, 1863, and was among those subsequently cited for their "gallantry, zeal, and coolness during the attack." In January, 1864, he was mustered out and recommissioned major, Fourteenth Rhode Island Heavy Artillery, U.S. Colored Troops. See *The War of the Rebellion: A Compilation of the Official Records of the Union and Confederate Armies,* prepared under the direction of the Secretary of War (Washington: Government Printing Office, 4 ser., 70 vols. in 128, 1880-1901), I:XIV: 388, 390; I:XXVIII, Pt. i:22, 213, 215; I:LIII:14. These records are hereafter cited as *O.R.* (Armies). See also Thomas H. S. Hamersly, compiler and editor, *Complete Regular Army Register of the United States: for One Hundred Years (1779 to 1879)* (Washington: T.H.S. Hamersly, 1880), p. 752.

5. A popular two-act "domestic drama" by Richard John Raymond, first produced about 1832 at the Cobourg Theatre in London as "The Farmer's Daughter of the Severn Side; or, Mr. and Mrs. Toodles." After an initial American appearance at Baltimore as "The Broken Heart; or, The Farmer's Daughter," it was presented in October, 1848, at Burton's Theatre in New York as "The Toodles." Usually given in conjunction with one or two other pieces, it was a favorite offering of various companies, including that of the "voluble and comic" John Sleeper Clarke (a brother-in-law of Edwin Booth), whose depiction of the drunken Timothy Toodle at the Winter Garden was highly praised in the early sixties. Season after season in one or another playhouse "the immortal Toodles" made up a part of the entertainment relished by "lovers of wholesome, if somewhat rough and uncouth local skits." The play was well adapted to amateur as well as to professional production. See George C. D. Odell, *Annals of the New York Stage* (14 vols.; New York: Columbia University Press, 1927-1945), VII, 48, 320-321, 480, 554, 637; and *A Catalog of Books Represented by Library of Congress Printed Cards* (167 vols.; Ann Arbor: Edwards Brothers, 1942-1946), 123: 360.

6. A number of songs alluded to by Dr. Boyer were unpublished. "Paddy's Wedding," for instance, which is included in a collection of Irish airs and songs made by William Forde, musician of Cork,

"in or about the period from 1840 to 1850," was published for the first time in 1909. P. W. Joyce, *Old Irish Folk Music and Songs* (London: Longmans, Green, 1909), p. 289.

7. *O.R.* (Navies), I:12:321, 382, 392-393; I:13:200; and I:14:346.

8. Mabel L. Webber, compiler, "The Early Generations of the Seabrook Family," in *The South Carolina Historical and Genealogical Magazine,* XVII (Jan., 1916), 23; *Palmetto Place Names,* compiled by workers of the Writers' Program of the Works Projects Administration in the State of South Carolina (Columbia: sponsored and published by the South Carolina Education Association, 1941), p. 125; Samuel Gaillard Stoney, *Plantations of the Carolina Low Country* (Charleston: Carolina Art Association, 1938), p. 60; and A. S. Salley, State Historian, Historical Commission of South Carolina, to W. Hampton Logan, Aug. 13, 1948, courtesy of Margaret Davis Cate.

9. See *O.R.* (Navies), I:13:506; *O.R.* (Armies), I:XIV:375; and island literature, especially *A Guide Book of St. Simons Island, Georgia* (published by St. Simons Island Women's Club, 1951).

10. See Samuel P. Bates, *History of Pennsylvania Volunteers, 1861-1865,* prepared in compliance with acts of the legislature (3 vols.; Harrisburg: B. Singerly, state printer, 1870), 3:411-413, 450, and *O.R.* (Armies), I:XIV:390.

11. Major Otis F. R. Waite, *New Hampshire in the Great Rebellion, Containing the Histories of the Several New Hampshire Regiments, and Biographical Notices of Many of the Prominent Actors in the Civil War of 1861-65* (Claremont, N.H.: Tracy, Chase and Company, 1870), pp. 169-195.

12. See *O.R.* (Armies), I:XIV:667, and James G. Randall, *The Civil War and Reconstruction* (New York: D. C. Heath, 1937), p. 658.

13. See *O.R.* (Armies), I:XIV:375; III:II:152, and *O.R.* (Navies), I:13:145.

14. See Sarah Forbes Hughes, ed., *Letters and Recollections of John Murray Forbes* (2 vols.; Boston: Houghton Mifflin, 1900), I, 300-301.

15. See *O.R.* (Armies), I:XIV:1, 189-192, 195-198, 374-378, 429; II:IV:916, and *Appleton's Annual Cyclopaedia* (1863), III, 426.

16. See *O.R.* (Armies), I:XIV:189-191; I:XLVII, Pt. ii:187; I:XLXII, Pt. iii:630, and *Official Army Register,* VIII: 310. Also *Appleton's Annual Cyclopaedia* (1862), II, 756-757.

17. *O.R.* (Navies), I:12:592, and *O.R.* (Armies), I:XLIX, Pt. 1:344; IV:I:627, 789. The island is delightfully pictured in Cate, *Our Todays and Yesterdays,* pp. 45-48, 269, and in Burnette Vanstory, *Georgia's Land of the Golden Isles,* pp. 156-162.

18. See Cate, *Our Todays and Yesterdays,* pp. 81-83, and Vanstory, *Georgia's Land of the Golden Isles,* pp. 113, 154.

19. *Our Todays and Yesterdays* and *Georgia's Land of the Golden Isles* contain the best descriptions of the lives and times of these distinguished families.

20. *O.R.* (Navies), I:14:150.

21. Cate, *Our Todays and Yesterdays,* pp. 131-132, Vanstory, *Georgia's Land of the Golden Isles,* pp. 121-128, and *Dictionary of American Biography* (22 vols.; New York: Scribner, 1928-1944), IV, 468-469.

22. *O.R.* (Navies), I:12:336-339; *Palmetto Place Names,* p. 12; and *Beaufort and the Sea Islands* (in American Guide series), prepared by the Federal Writers' Project, Works Progress Administration, South Carolina (Savannah, Ga.: sponsored and published by the Clover Club, 1938), p. 8.

23. See George W. Dalzell, *The Flight from the Flag* (Chapel Hill: University of North Carolina Press, 1940), pp. 143-145, and *O.R.* (Navies), I:19:582.

24. *O.R.* (Navies), I:13:655.

25. The term generally applied to volumes in the Collection (or Library) of British and American Authors, begun in 1841 by the printing and publishing house of Christian Bernhard, Frieherr von Tauchnitz, who started his firm at Leipzig in 1837.

26. See *O.R.* (Navies), I:13:496-497, 517-518, 524, 540-541, 551-553.

27. See Vanstory, *Georgia's Land of the Golden Isles,* pp. 116-121.

28. *O.R.* (Navies), I:13:659, 740.

29. Appointed December 19, 1862; probably stationed on the *Wamsutta* when recommissioned on February 2, 1863, after having been out of service for repair, to replace Acting Assistant Surgeon Samuel F. Quimby. His name is not included in the alumni register of University of Pennsylvania men who served in the Civil War.

30. *O.R.* (Navies), I:8:422-437.

31. *Ibid.,* I:13:193, 342, 627-628, 705-706, and Dalzell, *The Flight from the Flag,* pp. 64-71.

32. Carl Epping, vice consul from the Netherlands at Savannah in 1861, carried on a prosperous export business in ship timber and

lumber for German markets, spending the bulk of his time in Savannah, Darien, and New York. Opposed to the rebellion of the Southern states, he put his property in charge of servants at the beginning of the war and fled to New York and thence to Europe. According to a claim subsequently filed by him, "his lady," and a third person, this property was between 1862 and 1866 "taken in . . . various ways and at different times . . . seized by the United States Army and Navy and appropriated to their uses, the Confederate army not daring to seize and appropriate property belonging to an official representing a foreign power in their midst." As soon as peace was restored, the firm was reopened and "foreign trade with Germany for foreign gold" re-established. Epping asked Congress for compensation for the alleged damage, which included the loss of flats, winches, boats, rope, anchors, and chain valued at $30,000; a choice lot of naval stores valued at $2,400; 800,000 feet of superior pitch-pine timber for spars, masts, and other purposes as well as 120,000 feet of lumber for the German market, valued at $15,000; 770,000 feet of prepared timber for the German market, valued at $11,000; furniture, bedding, and provisions in a two-story house near Darien, together with cattle on the place, valued at $4,000; two first-class carriage horses, carriage, two mules, wagon, harness, and so forth, valued at $2,500; rental of two-story dwelling, outhouses, and grounds near Darien occupied by Federal troops and officers from June, 1865, to April, 1866, valued at $900; new office building with furniture, iron safe, books, and valuable papers, together with fences and outbuildings, appropriated by General Sherman, valued at $7,500; dwelling, wharf, warehouse, and office in Brunswick, valued at $3,500; and frame dwelling at Marietta, Georgia, with its contents and fences, valued at $6,000. Both in the House and the Senate the Committee on Claims reported adversely to Epping's memorial on the grounds of insufficient proof. H.R. Misc. Doc. 11 (ordered to be printed Dec. 11, 1872), 42nd Cong., 3rd sess.; Sen. Rept. 598 (ordered to be printed May 12, 1880), 46th Cong., 2nd sess.

33. Small photographic portrait mounted on a card, introduced in Paris in 1858 and in the United States about two years later; originally intended merely as a visiting card but extended so widely in use as to give the collodion process in photography a great impetus.

34. *O.R.* (Navies), I:13:390, 423, 737-738, 766, 787; I:14:3-8,

30-31; and *Diary of Gideon Welles* (3 vols.; Boston: Houghton Mifflin, 1911), I, 217, 236-237.

35. Farragut was commander of the West Coast Squadron, surveillant of the lower Mississippi until July 15, 1863, when he turned command of the river north of New Orleans (captured in April, 1862) over to Acting Rear Admiral David D. Porter, commander of the Western Flotilla above Vicksburg, so that he might give "more particular attention to the outside work, blockading, etc." The report was, of course, only one of the rumors that floated often over the blockade.

36. One who practices petty deceit or sham, particularly in cheating the public under the guise of legitimate business deals; origin of term, perhaps connected with the word "funk," an obsolete meaning of which is offensive smell or smoke, attributed to New York City, Peter Funk being described at length in the novel, *The Perils of Pearl Street.*

37. *O.R.* (Navies), I:14:227.

38. The surgeon felt very strongly about the mosquitoes, but this passage may have been copied from one of the newspapers he so avidly read.

39. See *O.R.* (Armies), I:XIV:226, 463, 317-319, 466-467, and I:XXVIII:10-13.

40. *O.R.* (Navies), I:14:249, 262-266, 290-291, 710-711.

41. *Ibid.,* I:14:305.

42. The only Pennsylvania troops listed in the official table of troops in the Department of the South dated June 30, 1863, as being stationed on St. Helena Island are nine companies of the Seventy-sixth Regiment, under Colonel De Witt C. Strawbridge. The Forty-seventh Regiment had been stationed at Beaufort, South Carolina, the previous October, but at the time of writing it was at Key West and Tortugas, Florida, from which district it was removed in February, 1864. *O.R.* (Armies), I:XIV:388, 435; I:XXVI, Pt. i:532, 708; I:XXVIII, Pt. ii:9; I:XXV, Pt. i:486.

43. No Captain Pocotaligo is listed in either *O.R.* (Armies) or the *Official Army Register.* The "soger" may have been referring to the town of Pocotaligo, Beaufort County, South Carolina. One colored regiment, the Fifty-fourth Massachusetts, was stationed on St. Helena Island and another, the Third South Carolina (five companies), on Hilton Head. *O.R.* (Armies), I:XXVIII, Pt. ii:9.

44. *O.R.* (Navies), I:14:275-277.

45. Sources consulted contain no mention of a St. Luke's Church in Beaufort. The diarist may have meant St. Helena's, one of the early parish churches, built in 1724 for a congregation organized twelve years previously. During the Civil War St. Helena's was greatly damaged; for a time it was used as a hospital, tombstones from the graveyard being taken up and pressed into service as operating tables. It was probably not, however, "the oldest Episcopal church in 'Dixie,' " although the original structure of the mother church of the colony, St. Philip's at Charleston (built in 1682), had been replaced and most of the original parish churches and chapels of ease (small plantation churches) were no longer in existence. *Beaufort and the Sea Islands*, p. 27, and *South Carolina: A Guide to the Palmetto State* (in American Guide series), sponsored by Burnett R. Maybank, Governor of South Carolina (New York: Oxford University Press, 1941), pp. 141, 174, and 298.

46. *O.R.* (Navies), I:2:322-346, 655-656; II:1:249.

47. The schooner *Major E. Willis* of Charleston, sent North for adjudication immediately after her capture April 19, 1863, may have been sold without delay and entered under British registry as the *Arrow*. The only British schooner *Arrow* mentioned in the official war records, however, was a sixty-ton vessel captured February 25, 1862, off Fernandina, Florida. *O.R.* (Navies), I:12: 562-563; I:14:147-148.

48. See *Diary of Gideon Welles*, I, 268, 273, 307-312, and *O.R.* (Navies), I:13:353-354; I:14:230, 240, 295, 311, 319-323, 359-360, 380-381.

49. The lines quoted are a parody on Fitz-Greene Halleck's "Marco Bozzaris," a poem describing the death of the brave Greek chieftain of that name, who "fell in a night attack upon the Turkish camp at Laspi, the site of the ancient Plataea, August 20, 1823, and expired in the moment of victory." See *The Poetical Writings of Fitz-Greene Halleck . . . ,* ed. by James Grant Wilson (New York: D. Appleton and Company, 1869), pp. 13-17 and 369, note 1. Major General Henry Wager Halleck, called by the soldiers "Old Brains," was at the time military adviser to President Lincoln, with the title General-in-chief.

50. General Gillmore was directing the Federal army's participation in the joint military and naval operations against Fort Sumter, at the time under steady bombardment; General Beauregard ("Old Beau") was commander of the Confederate forces at Charleston.

51. *O.R.* (Navies), I:14:401, 414-415, 444.

52. A plantation song written by John Washington Smith, a minstrel, and first sung in 1849; a very popular number among minstrels of the time.

53. The Christy referred to was probably George Christy, one of the "giants of burnt cork" of the time, known for his acting, dancing, and playing of the bones, although it could have been Edwin P. Christy, originator of the popular Christy minstrels, whose greatest fame as a performer was in singing ballads, especially Stephen Collins Foster's songs, or Charles Christy, another actor and vocalist in the field of minstrelsy. The Morris was probably one of the Morris brothers (Lon and Billy), who "began to entertain the intellectuals" in Boston in 1857, or else Charles Morris, another brother, who was with the troupe for a time but later had his own company. Sanford was the Sanford of the "giants of burnt cork," or Sam S. Sanford, "one of the most famous minstrels of his day, and a pioneer in the business," who built the first minstrel theater in Philadelphia in 1853 and after its destruction played at the Eleventh Street Opera House from 1855 to 1862. Mulligan could not be identified. The juba was a breakdown danced to the accompaniment of clapping, patting of knees and thighs, stamping, and singing; it was especially noted as danced by "Master Juba," colored dancer in "White's Serenaders," who either took his name from the dance or gave his name to it.

54. Sunbury, home of two signers of the Declaration of Independence, had been in the late colonial period a rival of Savannah in coastal trade. It suffered greatly during the Revolution, however, an increase in accessibility of Savannah through road improvement and of Darien through bridge construction, loss of the county seat, two disastrous hurricanes, and the ravages of epidemic disease hurried its decline. By the middle of the nineteenth century the town was "an extinct metropolis." Bank Jones is unidentified, and the only Laurel View found is a plantation on the Midway River owned by United States Senator John Elliott, who died in 1827.

55. *O.R.* (Navies), I:15:256-257, 269.

56. Krenson and Hawks, a firm engaged in ship construction and repair; senior partner, Frederick Krenson. Krenson advertised in the Savannah *Daily Morning News* in 1858 and 1859. The partnership was first advertised in January, 1861 (dissolved in August, 1868). Information from Georgia Historical Society, courtesy of Margaret Davis Cate.

PART THREE   NORTH ATLANTIC BLOCKADING SQUADRON:
THE U.S. *Mattabesett*

1. *O.R.* (Navies), I:9:658, 684, 686, 762-763; I:18:142; II:1:259; and *Appleton's Annual Cyclopaedia* (1864), IV, 63.

2. Under Federal occupation since its capture by General A. E. Burnside in March, 1862, the town had escaped much of the destruction that many other places had suffered. The Gaston House was a hotel on South Front Street, not far from the Neuse—later called the Chattawka, the Indians' name for their prewhite settlement. The Governor's Mansion, a part of Tryon Palace (on George Street), was designed by John Hawks and erected in 1767-1770 by Governor William Tryon as combination capitol and governor's residence; it was regarded by some as "the most beautiful building in the Colonial Americas." The main structure was destroyed by fire in 1798, but the whole has been restored and turned into a state park. Here in Newbern was held the first provincial convention in defiance of the British on the eve of the Revolution.

3. See Richard C. Holcomb, *A Century with Norfolk Naval Hospital* (Portsmouth, Va.: Printcraft Publishing Co., 1930), pp. 123, 288-297, and *O.R.* (Navies), I:9:416.

4. *O.R.* (Navies), I:9:733-748, 763; see also Daniel Ammen, *The Atlantic Coast* (New York: Scribner, 1885), p. 209.

5. Then sing as Martin Luther sang:
"Who loves not wine, woman, and song,
He is a fool his whole life long!"
—William Makepeace Thackeray, "The Adventures of Philip. A Credo." Stanza 1.

6. *O.R.* (Navies), I:10:320-321.

7. A reference to the nursery rhyme (first printed in 1642):
The King of France went up the hill
With twenty thousand men;
The King of France came down the hill,
And ne'er went up again.

8. *O.R.* (Navies), I:9:199; I:10:307, 567.

9. *Ibid.*, I:10:610-624; I:11:11-27.

10. See *ibid.*, I:3:137-185, 324-337, 701-795, 836, and Dalzell, *The Flight from the Flag*, pp. 182-189, 193-196. See also Ammen, *The Atlantic Coast.*

11. *O.R.* (Navies), I:11:160, 166-171, 697.

12. *Ibid.*, I:10:623; I:11:18.

13. Actually the New Bern Hospital did not discharge its last patients until 1865, and there had previously been a naval hospital at Plymouth.

PART FOUR   POSTWAR SERVICE: THE U.S. SUPPLY
STEAMER *Newbern*

1. See A. T. Mahan, *From Sail to Steam* (New York: Harper & Bros., 1907), pp. 193-194.

Index